GEORGE BUSH AND THE GUARDIANSHIP
PRESIDENCY

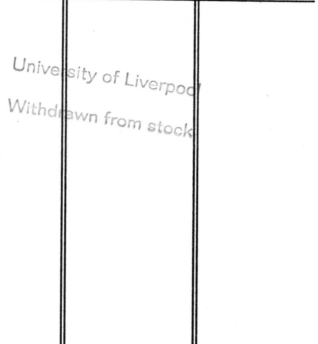

George Bush and the Guardianship Presidency

David Mervin
Reader in Politics
University of Warwick

Published in Great Britain by

MACMILLAN PRESS LTD

Houndmills, Basingstoke, Hampshire RG21 6XS and London
Companies and representatives throughout the world

A catalogue record for this book is available from the British Library.

ISBN 0–333–61354–6 hardcover
ISBN 0–333–73865–9 paperback

Published in the United States of America by

ST. MARTIN'S PRESS, INC.,

Scholarly and Reference Division,
175 Fifth Avenue, New York, N.Y. 10010

ISBN 0–312–12961–0 clothbound
ISBN 0–312–21199–6 paperback

Library of Congress has cataloged the hardcover edition as follows
Mervin, David.
George Bush and the guardianship presidency / David Mervin.
p.   cm.
Includes bibliographical references (p.) and index.
ISBN 0–312–12961–0 (cloth)
1. United States—Politics and government—1989–1993.   2. Bush,
George, 1924–   I. Title.
E881.M47 1996
973.928'092—dc20   95–53273
                                                         CIP

First edition 1996
Reprinted (with alterations) 1998

This book is printed on paper suitable for recycling and made from fully managed and
sustained forest sources.

10   9   8   7   6   5   4   3   2   1
07   06   05   04   03   02   01   00   99   98

Printed and bound in Great Britain by
Antony Rowe Ltd, Chippenham, Wiltshire

To Alice

Contents

Preface to the 1998 Reprint

At the conference on the Bush presidency held at Hofstra University in April 1997, doubt was cast on my contention that the physician's maxim of 'Do no harm' was central to an understanding of Bush's approach to governance (see pp. 34, 78 and 158). I should, perhaps, have supported my assertion more fully in the original hardback edition of this book, for the evidence is substantial. C. Boyden Gray, Counsel to the President, and one of those closest to George Bush, told me in an interview, 'President Bush's view about this is . . . the very first thing you do – and if you can't do this you ought not to be in government at all – is do no harm. It's sort of a first rule of a doctor, it's also the first rule of a public official. First, do no harm.' President Bush himself, in a speech in North Carolina on 15 November 1991, said 'Let me tell you what we won't do. The first rule of economic policy puts me in mind to (*sic*) the Hippocratic Oath: Do no harm.' Similarly, on 9 March 1992, the President, in speaking about welfare dependency, said 'The government's first duty is like that of the physician: Do no harm.'

DAVID MERVIN

Preface

This book is not, in any sense, a biography of George Bush; it is rather a narrowly focused study of his presidency. Considerations of relevance and the relatively few words available precluded dealing with many matters that others might find of interest in Bush's incumbency. For instance, my coverage of foreign policy issues is somewhat limited in scope and there is nothing here on Bush's alleged role in the Iran-Contra affair. Similarly, one of the great dramas of the period, Clarence Thomas's nomination to the US Supreme Court, receives only cursory mention.

My purposes in writing this book have been threefold. First, to scrutinize Bush's presidency on his own terms, to attempt, in other words, to understand how he saw his office and what he sought to achieve. Second, to consider how far Bush succeeded in meeting the monumental challenges that all presidents face in seeking to impose their priorities on what Richard Neustadt aptly characterizes as 'that maze of personalities and institutions and individuals called the government of the United States'. My third purpose has been to use the Bush example as a vehicle for a modest contribution to the study of the presidency in a more general sense.

Like other authors, I have had a lot of help. I am most grateful to the British Academy for their award of a research grant. I am indebted also to the University of Warwick for both additional financial assistance and the study leave necessary for the conduct of the research for this book.

Interviews with senior White House staff constitute the core of the research for this study. Not all my requests for interviews were successful, but most were and those that agreed to talk to me are listed on pages xiii–xiv. The kindness and cooperation I uniformly received from these people was extraordinary. They spoke frankly and at length about their experiences at the highest levels of the Bush Administration and, in so doing, contributed much to my understanding. In some cases they agreed to be interviewed more than once and others kindly met my convenience by coming to my hotel for the interviews.

Almost all of these conversations were taped and, in each case, they were conducted 'on background'. Accordingly, I agreed that I would not quote any interviewee in an identifiable way without checking with them first. This process led to some useful clarifications. It also caused me to remove one throwaway line while, in a handful of instances, sensitive comments have been made anonymous. It must be emphasized, however, that responsibility for the interpretation placed on these interviews rests with me alone.

The tapes and transcripts of these interviews are, at present, held by the Bush Presidential Materials Project, 701 University Drive East, Suite 300, College Station, Texas 77840–1899. These items are to be placed in the future Bush Presidential Library and are available to scholars under the conditions indicated in the previous paragraph.

This research also included conversations with a number of other authoritative sources including Louis Fisher of the Congressional Research Service; Jeff Eisenach of the Progress and Freedom Foundation; Terry Eastland of the Ethics and Public Policy Center; Charles Cooper, Assistant Attorney General in the Reagan Administration and Peter Liebold from the staff of Senator John Danforth of Missouri. I am most grateful for the additional help generously provided by these individuals.

My heartfelt thanks are also due to my friend of many years' standing, K. Larry Storrs of the Foreign Affairs Division of the Congressional Research Service at the Library of Congress. The hospitality, help and intellectual stimulation provided by Larry Storrs and his wife EJ made my visits to Washington infinitely more enjoyable and profitable than they would otherwise have been.

In developing my ideas on the Bush presidency I have had the benefit of advice and assistance from many quarters. These include my students at Warwick as well as a variety of friends and colleagues on both sides of the Atlantic. In particular, I was privileged to have the help of two distinguished American students of the presidency – Professor James Pfiffner of George Mason University and Professor Bert Rockman of the University of Pittsburgh. The former plied me with source material while also making most helpful comments on a number of chapters. Bert Rockman, meanwhile, read and commended on the entire manuscript. I am most grateful for all this generosity although, of course, the responsibility for any errors of fact or interpretation is entirely mine.

My appreciation is also due to Hayley Gilder, Secretary of the Department of Politics and International Studies, University of Warwick, for her skilful rendering of interview tapes into transcripts. Finally, and most important of all, I must thank my wife, Dr Kathleen McConnell Mervin, for all that she has contributed in so many different ways.

DAVID MERVIN

List of Interviewees

This research included interviews with the following:

Paul Bateman – Deputy Assistant to the President for Management and Director of the Office of Administration. Interview 15 November 1993.

David Q. Bates – Assistant to the President and Secretary to the Cabinet. Interview 17 November 1993.

Phillip D. Brady – Assistant to the President and Staff Secretary. Interview 15 November 1993.

Nicholas E. Calio – Assistant to the President for Legislative Affairs. Interview 19 November 1993.

Andrew H. Card, Jr. – Assistant to the President and Deputy to the Chief of Staff; subsequently Secretary of Transportation. Interview 15 November 1993.

James W. Cicconi – Assistant to the President and Deputy to the Chief of Staff (Staff Secretary). Interview 8 November 1993.

David F. Demarest, Jr. – Assistant to the President for Communications. Interview 12 November 1993.

C. Boyden Gray – Counsel to the President. Interviews 10 November 1993 and 21 March 1994.

Richard Haass – Special Assistant to the President for National Security Affairs. Interview 24 March 1994.

Edith E. Holiday – Assistant to the President and Secretary to the Cabinet. Interview 17 November 1993.

Constance Horner – Assistant to the President and Director of Presidential Personnel. Interview 10 November 1993.

Ronald C. Kaufman – Deputy Assistant to the President for Presidential Personnel and subsequently Deputy Assistant to the President for Political Affairs. Interview 19 November 1993.

John G. Keller, Jr. – Deputy Assistant to the President and Director of Presidential Advance. Interview 18 November 1993.

Bobbie G. Kilberg – Deputy Assistant to the President for Public Liaison. Interviews 19 November 1993 and 30 March 1994.

Charles E.M. Kolb – Deputy Assistant to the President for Domestic Policy. Interviews 12 November 1993 and 29 March 1994.

William Kristol – Chief of Staff to the Vice President. Interview 23 March 1994.

C. Gregg Petersmeyer – Assistant to the President and Director, Office of National Service. Interview 16 November 1993.

James P. Pinkerton – Deputy Assistant to the President for Policy Planning. Interview 8 November 1993.

Roger B. Porter – Assistant to the President for Economic and Domestic Policy. Interview 23 November 1993.

Edward M. Rogers, Jr. – Deputy Assistant to the President and Executive Assistant to the Chief of Staff. Interview 3 November 1993.

Gen. Brent Scowcroft, USAF (Ret.) – Assistant to the President for National Security Affairs. Interview 28 March 1994.

Katherine Super – Deputy Assistant to the President for Appointments and Scheduling. Interview 16 November 1993.

Gail Wilensky – Deputy Assistant to the President for Policy Development. Interview 14 November 1993.

Clayton Yeutter – Secretary of Agriculture, Chairman of the Republican National Committee and, finally, Counselor to the President for Domestic Policy. Interview 22 March 1994.

Introduction

George Bush, it is widely believed, was a failure in the White House. For some, his inability to gain re-election to a second term is sufficient evidence in itself of a less than successful presidency. Critics can also point to the shortage of significant legislation passed in Bush's name; his failure to address effectively a variety of domestic problems and the anaemic state of the economy at the conclusion of his four years in office. Even George Bush's ostensibly greatest triumph, victory in the Gulf War, has been subjected to savage criticism.[1] However, the calculation of success or failure in the White House is less straightforward than it sometimes seems.

The first thing to be said is that if Bush was a failure in office he hardly stands alone. Remarkably few presidents can be counted as successes, largely because the United States is an extraordinarily difficult country to govern. Governance is not easy anywhere, but the problems in America are especially formidable. They include an anti-authority, anti-leadership political culture; a Constitution that makes for a centrifugal rather than a centripetal distribution of power; an independent judiciary and an awesomely powerful legislative branch. The latter may well be controlled by the opposition, but even when it is not it is a chronically decentralized, individualistic and undisciplined body, full of members close to their constituents, beholden to interest groups, and generally unresponsive to the demands of party loyalty.

Elsewhere in the world, parties facilitate coherence and direction in a political system; they provide means whereby leaders can gain the agreement, the cooperation, or at least the acquiescence, of other leaders in that system. In the US, by contrast, parties are incapable of adequately fulfilling such functions. In the late twentieth century they lack the patronage resources they once commanded, they are largely bereft of serious programmatic commitments and are denied control of the processes whereby candidates are nominated. Parties have relatively little to offer presidents as they struggle to come to grips with the problems of governance.

1

A vast, amorphous federal bureaucracy presents another major area of difficulty for presidents attempting to impose their priorities on the policy-making machinery. The bureaucracy participates in both the formulation and the implementation of policy; however, it is a body led by political appointees whose loyalty to the White House may be questionable and staffed by career civil servants who often have their own agendas and are far less amenable to central direction than many of their counterparts elsewhere in the world.

Since the 1960s at least the media have provided further obstacles to the exercise of presidential power. Presidents now conduct public business and much of their private lives under the constant surveillance of television cameras. News broadcasts have supplanted parties, political meetings and peer group discussions as sources of voting cues for the electorate and television news executives have assumed agenda setting functions. Meanwhile journalists, from both the print and the electronic media, armed with First Amendment freedoms and energized by investigative zeal, have, in recent years, made governance even more difficult than it was in the past.

In addition to the constants mentioned above every chief executive must deal with a unique set of circumstantial variables. Even allowing for the weakness of American political parties a president with comfortable majorities in Congress stands a better chance of achieving his agenda than if the legislature is controlled by the opposition. Similarly, some presidents are elected with large popular vote totals while others fail to win even a majority of the votes cast, a variable that will affect the chances of success or failure in the White House. Furthermore, the combination of opportunities and constraints facing any given president will be dependent on the ethos of the time with president-led governmental action much more acceptable to the American people in some periods than in others.

These are some of the reasons for the modest levels of achievement of those who occupy the White House. They help to account for the fact, noted by John Kennedy, that while the president 'is rightly described as a man of extraordinary powers . . . he must wield those powers under extraordinary limitations . . . Every president must endure a gap between what he

would like and what is possible.'[2] Any appraisals of presidents
need to incorporate such considerations while, as far as possible,
excluding the personal political preferences of the analyst.

The scholarly verdicts on the Bush presidency are not yet
in, but it is difficult to believe that they will be favourable; he
is most unlikely to perform well in any future presidential
'greatness' poll. While there are ample reasons for criticizing
Bush's stewardship, some of which will be explored in this
book, it should also be recognized that his conservative, non-
activist, guardian approach doomed him from the start to an
unsympathetic hearing in the academic community.

THE POLITICS OF ACADEME

There is plenty of hard evidence to support the allegation,
often made by Republican politicians, that most academics in
the relevant fields are liberals and/or Democrats.[3] For instance
a fairly recent poll of the American professoriate found that
88 per cent of 'public affairs' faculty identified themselves as
liberals while 12 per cent claimed to be 'middle of the road'
and, remarkably, 0 per cent opted for the conservative label.
In humanities departments, including history, 76 per cent were
liberals, 9 per cent middle of the road and 15 per cent conservatives. Social science faculty, embracing, of course, political
scientists, broke down as 72 per cent liberals, 14 per cent middle
of the road and 14 per cent conservatives.[4] More specifically,
a 1989 poll of members of the Presidency Research Group of
the American Political Science Association found that 63.6 per
cent identified as Democrats, 19.5 per cent as Republicans
and 16 per cent as Independents. Of this same group of presidency specialists, 67.5 per cent voted for Walter Mondale in
1984 as against 23.9 per cent who cast their ballots for Ronald
Reagan.[5]

These disparities in the academic community would, of
course, be less important if we could be confident that scholars
did not allow their personal ideological and partisan preferences to enter into their evaluations of presidents. Reason to
doubt whether such restraint is in fact exercised was suggested
by another poll among members of the APSA in 1984. This
showed first that 76 per cent of American politics specialists

were Democrats, but, more interestingly, also revealed that 96 per cent of those who identified as Democrats rated Ronald Reagan's 'overall performance in office' as only fair or poor, whereas 4 per cent adjudged it excellent or good. By contrast, of the Republican identifiers 71 per cent found Reagan's performance to be excellent or good, while 29 per cent deemed it to be poor or fair.[6] It is surely reasonable to conclude that such starkly different collective impressions are likely to have been driven by ideological and partisan considerations.

Historians it would seem are no less culpable in such matters. In the late 1980s, Robert K. Murray and Tim H. Blessing conducted a poll among American historians designed to incorporate President Reagan into earlier presidential 'greatness' rankings. At the end of this rather elaborate exercise involving 481 respondents out of 750 who were sent a detailed questionnaire, Reagan was ranked 28th out of 37 who have served in the White House. Out of six categories (Great, Near Great, Above Average, Below Average and Failure) Reagan was placed in the Below Average group between Zachary Taylor and John Tyler. According to this tabulation Reagan was inferior to chief executives such as Chester Arthur, Benjamin Harrison and William Howard Taft. Furthermore, leaving aside the rather special case of Richard Nixon, Reagan was effectively deemed to be the worst President of the United States in six decades.[7]

This is all rather odd for, irrespective of the merits of his policies and any doubts as to the quality of his intellect, Reagan appears to have been more successful than most modern presidents in imposing his priorities on the political system. His mastery of the process, in other words, despite some unfulfilled ambitions and a few serious set-backs, was, relatively speaking, quite impressive.[8] Murray and Blessing chose not to ask those polled either their political affiliation or what they took into account in making their evaluations, but, as I have argued elsewhere, further examination of their poll data suggests that those polled freely indulged their hostility to Reagan's policies in their evaluations of his presidency.[9]

It is also the case that much of the literature on the presidency is shot through with values and assumptions that lead inevitably to negative evaluations of Republican presidents.

Two figures dominate that literature – Franklin Roosevelt and Richard Neustadt. Most historians and political scientists have consistently and enthusiastically applauded Roosevelt's attempts to live up to Woodrow Wilson's maxim that a president 'should be as big a man as he can'. They have admired FDR's determination to make the presidency 'pre-eminently a place of moral leadership'; they have delighted in his vigorous expansion of the role of the federal government, applauded his commitment to social and economic reform and been impressed by his exceptional talents as a war leader. Roosevelt, according to William Leuchtenburg, enjoys demi-god status among historians and has cast a long shadow over his successors. 'From 1945 to the present, historians have unfailingly ranked him with Washington and Lincoln, and the men who succeeded him found one question inescapable: How did they measure up to FDR.'[10]

Among the political scientists there has been no more avid Roosevelt admirer than Richard Neustadt, the author of perhaps the most influential book on the presidency ever written. The status of *Presidential Power* as a classic work is undeniable – it has contributed much to our understanding of the politics of the presidency, yet it needs to be understood that it is a book heavily laden with liberal Democratic values. Throughout, Franklin Roosevelt's style of presidential leadership is presented as *the* model to which all who enter the White House should aspire, whereas President Eisenhower is portrayed almost as a figure of fun, a pathetic 'Roosevelt in reverse'.[11]

No doubt Neustadt's influence helps to account for Eisenhower's poor showing in early presidential greatness polls and it is worth noting that his ranking improved considerably when revisionists demonstrated that he was not really the indolent, passive chief executive of legend.[12] In other words, this later research showed that Eisenhower, in truth, had a sophisticated understanding of how power was exercised and led skilfully, if quietly, from behind the scenes, – he was not, after all, so totally removed from the Roosevelt model as everyone had thought. Nevertheless, Eisenhower is unlikely to climb the presidential rating tables very much higher given his conservative views and the liberal preferences of those making the evaluations.

THE ACTIVIST PRESUMPTION

Even if it is not a sufficient condition, for a modern president to enjoy the approbation of the scholarly community it seems that it is obligatory for him to be a chief executive in the liberal Democratic tradition best exemplified by FDR; a tradition which extends back to Woodrow Wilson and embraces Harry Truman, John Kennedy, Lyndon Johnson and, to some extent, Bill Clinton. For such presidents:

> 'government' appears as a vast reservoir of power which inspires them to dream of what use might be made of it. They have favourite projects, of various dimensions, which they sincerely believe are for the benefit of mankind, and to capture this source of power, if necessary to increase it, and to use it for imposing their favourite projects upon their fellows is what they understand as the adventure of governing men . . . the art of politics is to inflame and direct desire.[13]

This vision, shared by most students of the presidency, demands that chief executives be activists; success in the White House requires presidents who are architects of change; they are obliged to be doers and reformers. As Richard Rose has said, 'presidential scholars show a strong bias towards . . . activism', while Murray and Blessing observe that 'activeness' was an essential ingredient of presidential success for the historians they polled.[14] Similarly, Charles O. Jones in outlining 'the dominant perspective' used in evaluating the American political system notes that 'the good president, by this perspective, is one who makes government work, one who has a program and uses his resources to get it enacted. The good president is an activist; he sets the agenda.'[15]

Activism cannot sensibly be an end in itself. Not all legislation is conducive to the public good; some may arouse expectations that cannot be met and some would, no doubt, be better left off the statute book altogether. In discussing the merits of the veto, Alexander Hamilton alluded to conservatives, those who 'consider every institution calculated to restrain the excess of lawmaking, and to keep things in the same state in which they happen to be at any given period as much more likely to do good than harm.[16] In the same tradition, John C.

Calhoun said: 'There is often in the affairs of government more efficiency and wisdom in non action than in action.'[17] More recently, the conservative commentator Terry Eastland has suggested the liberal Democratic shibboleth 'Let's get the country moving again' is widely accepted in the United States today whereas 'it is considered impolite to ask exactly *where* . . . Presidents are expected to try to get it moving regardless of the facts of the situation ostensibly calling for movement or the government's competence to perform whatever is to be done or its authority to do so in the first place.'[18] As scholars rather than partisans, we are obliged to accept the legitimacy of a conservative tradition that embraces figures such as Calhoun, Calvin Coolidge, Eisenhower and Bush.

Activism is, of course, not restricted to liberal Democrats. Some Republican presidents nurture similar ambitions. They have come into office dissatisfied with the status quo and bent on bringing about change. Richard Nixon, for example, said: 'Seeking office by itself is not a worthwhile goal. What separates the men from the boys in politics is that the boys seek office to be somebody and the men seek office to *do* something . . . All the great leaders I have known have had goals greater than themselves. They sought high office not to be great but to do great things.'[19] In office, Nixon pursued a reform agenda, but was hardly an advocate of fundamental change. Ronald Reagan, by contrast, despite the impressions he sometimes conveyed of passivity, was, at heart, a radical conservative who aspired to bring about fundamental change, to reverse the thrust of the New Deal and its successor, the Great Society.

In evaluating Republican presidents like Nixon and Reagan it is not unreasonable to apply the same sort of criteria that might be used in measuring the success of similarly activist Democratic incumbents. Leaving aside any personal policy preferences we may entertain, and taking due account of the circumstantial variables appertaining during their time in office, we can legitimately ask of any such president: How far did they succeed in mastering the policy process to fulfil their ambitions for change? How many bills were passed into law in their name? How significant were those bills? Did they represent no more than minimal change, or did they really make a difference? Presidential success, it is assumed, can be calculated by some sort of 'scorecard'.[20]

GUARDIANSHIP

The problem with such 'scoreboard' calculations is that they include a presumption in favour of activism. They assume the desirability of change, whereas some presidents have no such aspirations; they 'come into office with a felt belief that success means holding the line against change in one way or another.'[21] Eisenhower and Bush clearly fall into this category. They were conservatives in the traditional sense of being largely content with things as they were. Such presidents are moreover, sceptical about what can be achieved by passing laws. Thus in an era when liberal Democrats were clamouring for the passage of laws as solutions to that most troubled of domestic problems, civil rights, Eisenhower took a different view. He was convinced that racial attitudes would not be altered by legislation: 'I do not believe that prejudices, even palpably unjustified prejudices will succumb to compulsion.'[22] George Bush, in campaigning for the Senate a few years later, similarly expressed his opposition to civil rights laws: 'I believe that the solution to this grave problem lies in the hearts and goodwill of all people and that sweeping federal legislation like the Civil Rights Act can never succeed.'[23]

Bush, like Eisenhower before him, was to become a guardian president. He was a conservator rather than an advocate of change. He sought to limit rather than to extend the reach of government and poured scorn on the social engineering of liberal Democratic presidents.[24] For the guardian governing is 'a specific and limited activity, namely the provision and custody of general rules of conduct, which are understood, not as plans for imposing substantive activities, but as instruments enabling people to pursue the activities of their own choice with the minimum frustration'.[25] Such thinking lay behind Bush's enthusiasm for free trade and deregulation and his reluctance to manage the economy. In domestic policy generally, he was guided by the physician's maxim of 'do no harm' and went out of his way to lower popular expectations of what could be accomplished by governmental action. In international affairs too, Bush as a guardian president was inclined to be cautious, anxious not to arouse hopes that could not be fulfilled while holding himself in readiness to deal with crises as they arose.

Guardian presidents like Bush do not present themselves to the electorate as expansive, omniscient leaders with solutions at hand to all manner of problems. It could be said of his administration as it was of Eisenhower's, that it was 'committed to conserving rather than creating, guarding rather than building.'[26] Presidents of this ilk harbour no grand schemes for reordering the world, and rather than embarking on crusades they are content to be reactive leaders, dealing with problems as they arise on a case-by-case basis. Such chief executives are likely to be short on charisma and flamboyance, to be disinclined to resort to rhetorical appeals and to specialize in working quietly behind the scenes. Such low-key notions of presidential leadership have little appeal to many scholars. Most academics are not taken by the implicit, or explicit, satisfaction with the status quo that such views appear to represent. Presidents, they believe should be dynamic, expansive leaders, alert to problems of injustice and deprivation and ready to harness the power of government for the public good. As far as possible, in other words, presidents should adopt Franklin Delano Roosevelt as their model.

EVALUATING PRESIDENTS ON THEIR OWN TERMS

The starting place for this study of George Bush's presidency is that he, like all presidents, is entitled to be judged on his own terms rather than on those favoured by his opponents, whether in the real world or in academe. As Richard Rose said in alluding to the hostility of scholars to President Reagan's policy objectives, he could reasonably 'ask political scientists to confine their judgement to how well he handled the political process'.[27] My scrutiny of Bush's incumbency will accordingly deal mainly with matters of process. That is to say, I am not at all concerned here with the desirability or wisdom of this president's policies with regard to the economy, abortion, civil rights, international affairs or anything else. My interest is rather in his competence, or effectiveness as a leader, on his capacity for statecraft, defined by Bert Rockman as his ability to 'steer the political system towards outcomes in accordance with [his] goals'.[28]

In studying any president, the legitimate questions to be asked include: What were his goals and how successful was he in overcoming the limitations on his powers to accomplish those objectives? What style of executive leadership did he adopt? How did he organize the White House? What techniques of management did he use and how well did he use them? How far did he succeed in getting the American people to follow where he chose to lead? What success did he enjoy in gaining the cooperation of Congress given the balance of party strength in the legislature? Was he able to bring the bureaucracy to order and to impose his priorities on the federal judiciary? Why was he more or less successful in fulfilling his agenda than other incumbents; how far was he the victim or the beneficiary of forces beyond his control?

These are the sort of questions that will be addressed in this book. What was Bush trying to achieve and how did he, in the words of John Kennedy cited earlier, seek to narrow, 'the gap between what he would like and what is possible'? In recent decades presidents have sought to escape these difficulties by drawing policy-making more and more into the White House and relying increasingly on their personal staff to help them fulfil their agendas. Unlike other appointees, White House staffers are men and women who have no other constituency but the president himself; they are hired and fired by him and are expected to devote all their energies to helping him achieve his goals. In contrast to cabinet and sub-cabinet members and senior bureaucrats, personal staff derive their authority from the president alone, and are much less likely to be torn by conflicting loyalties.

The president's personal aides, those who serve in the White House Office, have what John Hart identifies as three functions: coordination, gatekeeping and promotion.[29] Coordination is concerned with ensuring that policy-making and budgeting across the administration conforms with the president's wishes, gatekeeping refers to controlling access to the chief executive who would otherwise be swamped by a multitude of demands, while promotion involves the creation and maintenance of public support for him and his aims.

The White House Office of today has a staff of between three and four hundred.[30] There were 380 in the Bush White House and between 80 and 90 of these, at any one time, were senior or commissioned staff.[31] The most important members of this group were the 'staffers', the Assistants and Deputy Assistants to the President characterized by one of their number as people:

> who enjoyed truly remarkable power and discretion . . . who would sift through options papers long before a short list made its way into the Oval Office. They are the presidential gatekeepers who often determine whom he sees, where he'll speak and what he'll say; whether his cabinet will meet with him and when; what the topics will include; and what his major and minor foreign and domestic policy initiatives will entail.[32]

In the research for this book, I focused on this relatively small group of staff members at the heart of the Bush presidency. I interviewed approximately a third of those who served in these positions between 1989 and 1993, including 14 out of the 22 who, as Assistants to the President, were his most intimate advisers. Excluding the Office of the First Lady, there are 23 units within the White House Office. I interviewed senior staff from 14 of these units plus the Vice President's Chief of Staff. These interviews provided me with an invaluable set of windows through which I could view and better understand this presidency.

Rather than imposing any preconceptions on Bush's incumbency, I have endeavoured to scrutinize it from a White House perspective, giving voice, where possible, to some of those who worked closely with George Bush – men and women who were personal friends of the President, who admired him, who shared his views and were dedicated to doing what they could to fulfil his agenda.

Chapter 1 is devoted to some discussion of Bush's personality, his view of the world, his life experience, his political career prior to becoming President and his 'guardian' conceptions of presidential power. In the chapter that follows, I have outlined the strategies of leadership deployed by George Bush. As a preliminary to that discussion, I compare Reagan's 'outsider' mentality with Bush's 'insider' inclinations. I then discuss the emphasis in Bush's appointments policy on personal rather than ideological loyalty. Subsequent sections cover Bush's relations with Congress, his inadequacy in using his office as a bully pulpit, his relations with the press and his lack of ease before television cameras.

The organization of the presidency under Bush is the subject of Chapter 3. While most cabinet members were long-standing personal friends of the President, the Cabinet collectively met infrequently and usually only for mundane purposes. In common with other recent administrations major decisions under Bush were made in the executive mansion, by the President advised by senior White House staff. The legislative liaison and communications offices of the White House Office receive particular attention in this chapter; the tenure of John Sununu as Chief of Staff and that of his successor, Samuel Skinner, are also dealt with.

Chapter 4 begins by returning to the matter of statecraft; that which I argued earlier is the legitimate subject of atten-tion for political scientists. What was on Bush's agenda and how far he succeeded in meeting his objectives are the ques-tions at issue here. In discussing Bush's domestic policy achievements his staff repeatedly drew my attention to the Clean Air Act of 1990 and the Americans with Disabilities Act of the same year; for some of his staff, as for the President himself, his Points of Light programme was a major domestic policy initiative. These three accomplishments are the focus of discussion in this chapter.

As I suggested above 'scorecard' evaluations of presidents are inappropriate in the case of guardian presidents and this is pursued further in Chapter 5. *Congressional Quarterly* presidential success scores provide relevant evidence for assessing the performance of activist reforming presidents, but they are far less relevant in the case of conservative guardian presidents like Bush. Furthermore, preventing undesirable legislation from passing is central to the purpose of such pres-idents and the veto for them is an invaluable weapon. Bush's unusual degree of success in wielding the veto is not reflected in his low CQ scores. Such calculations also ignore the value of signing statements as a means of undermining the force of legislation, another stratagem available to guardian presi-dents that are covered in this chapter.

The failure of Congress in 1990 to pass a budget deal worked out between the administration and congressional leaders was a humiliating rebuff for Bush and a defining event for his presidency; this is the subject of Chapter 6. It begins with a consideration of the background to Bush's 'no new taxes' pledge and touches on the crucial role of Richard Darman, the Director of the Office of Management and Budget. While partly a result of the inherent tendencies towards ungovernability in the political system, the budget débâcle of 1990 also placed Bush's leadership in a poor light; demonstrating his lack of interest in domestic policy, as well as inadequacies in his organization of the White House and in his use of the bully pulpit.

Chapter 7 commences with a discussion of how foreign and national security matters were handled in the Bush administration and continues with a section on Central America. The United States troubled relationship with Nicaragua had bedevilled the executive branch's dealings with Congress in the Reagan years; James Baker, Bush's first Secretary of State, manoeuvred skilfully in 1989 to neutralize this source of contention between the President and Congress. Relations with Panama proved troublesome in that same year, but General Noriega soon provided an opportunity for swift and decisive military action that met with widespread approval within the United States. The second part of this chapter deals briefly with Bush's reactions to the momentous events taking place in Eastern Europe and the Soviet Union leading to the end of the Cold War.

If the budget crisis of 1990 provided one defining event for the Bush presidency the war in the Persian Gulf, the subject of Chapter 8, provided another. The former proved to be a leadership disaster, whereas the latter showed the President in an infinitely more favourable light. This is particularly the case if the analysis is concentrated primarily, as it is here, on the period between August 1990 and February 1991. Arguably, this crisis showed Bush at his best to set against the ineptitude of his leadership during the budget débâcle.

My final chapter allows me to pull together some conclusions while also touching on a number of important issues that could not be covered in any depth in the context of a relatively short study. Amongst these will be Bush's efforts to influence the federal judiciary, including his nomination of Clarence Thomas to the US Supreme Court. Consideration will also be given to the vagaries of Bush's civil rights policies, his handling of the abortion issue and the causes of his failure to gain re-election in 1992.

My interviews allowed me to draw on the experience and opinions of some of those at the very centre of the decision-making process. The insights provided by these key figures are important to an understanding of the Bush presidency, but, in my early chapters particularly, it may appear that I have presented this material somewhat uncritically. It seemed to me, however, that this was necessary in the interests of arriving ultimately at a suitably balanced appraisal that considered Bush on his own terms. Later parts of the book, most notably Chapters 6 and 9, are more critical.

1 The Making of a Guardian President

Presidents are entitled to be considered on their own terms rather than those of their political adversaries. It is necessary therefore to begin by recognizing that George Bush was a conservative and, as such, held views at odds with those that generally prevail in the academic community. When he was Vice President, Bush told the Ripon Society: 'I am a conservative. I voted along conservative lines when I was in Congress. I took conservative positions before assuming this job. I take conservative positions now.'[1] Some on the right of the Republican Party have questioned Bush's claim to the conservative label, but there is little doubt that he is a conservative in the broad sense of that term. He is, to use Michael Oakeshott's terminology, of a conservative 'disposition', tending to favour the status quo, to abjure crusades, to be deeply sceptical of innovation and to see the role of government in minimalist terms.[2]

Throughout his political career Bush rejected the liberal reformist nostrums associated with Franklin Roosevelt and his would-be emulators. In his autobiography Bush, in reflecting on his political philosophy in the 1950s, which by then 'had long been settled' said: 'I supported much of Harry Truman's foreign policy in the late 1940s. But I didn't like what he and the Democratic Party stood for in the way of big, centralized government – the attitude that "Washington knows best" and the policies and programs it produced. I considered myself a conservative Republican.'[3]

That early commitment to conservatism can be seen as arising from the influences Bush was exposed to during his youth, combined with his early experience in living and working in the very different environment provided by the oil fields of Texas. His beginnings were marked by wealth and privilege; born in Massachusetts, he was the second son of an investment banker who later became a United States Senator. His childhood was spent in Greenwich, Connecticut, in a house with three maids and a chauffeur to take him and his elder brother to preparatory school. After secondary education at an elite private school – Phillips Academy, known as Andover – Bush served with distinction as a bomber pilot during the Second World War, flying 58 combat missions and being awarded a Distinguished Flying Cross.[4] When the war ended Bush completed his education at Yale, another elite bastion; he majored in economics, earned a Phi Beta Kappa key and played a lot of sport.[5]

By his own admission, Bush evinced little interest in politics in the early years of his life. Nevertheless during this formative period he began to acquire values and attitudes that would later become politically relevant.[6] The dominant ethos was clearly one of conservatism tempered with the norms of *noblesse oblige*, and through the combined influences of family, church and school the young Bush absorbed the shibboleths of what one who shared the experience has characterized as an 'Eastern establishment creed'; this included maxims such as 'The meek shall inherit the earth.' 'Gentlemen don't ask people to vote for them,' 'Real men don't boast.' 'It's more blessed to give than to receive,' 'Public service is the purpose for entering politics.'[7]

George Bush's father, by all accounts a major influence on his thinking, personified this creed. Despite long hours as a businessman he devoted much of his time to voluntary and community work and impressed upon his children the obligation of the well born and privileged to enter public service. According to Bush himself, 'Our father had a powerful impact on the way we came to look at the world. Dad taught us about duty and service.'[8] Confirmation that the future President followed his father's teaching in such matters was offered later by Barbara Bush: 'Some people are motivated by money, some people by power and some people by public service. I put George in the latter category. He had no great ambitions to make a lot of money. I don't think you'd ever put George down as power mad. It's just public service.'[9]

After a long career in business, Prescott Bush became a candidate for the United States Senate at the age of 55, a decision which George Bush found not at all surprising, 'because I knew what motivated him. He'd made his mark in the business world. Now he felt he had a debt to pay.'[10] In the Senate, the elder Bush proved to be a congenial, dignified and diffident member of an institution that at that time was noted for its club-like atmosphere.[11] Close to Eisenhower, Prescott Bush was a moderate conservative with little interest in disturbing the status quo; he favoured civil rights and was troubled by Joe McCarthy's rampaging, but while 'he was respected widely and believed in principles, [he] left no substantive footprints.'[12]

The early influences on George Bush, in other words, were those of the Eastern establishment, of a patrician caste reared on hierarchical and elitist assumptions, largely content with things as they were and where any doubts that might arise from the existence of inequality and other societal ills could be assuaged by public service.[13] An emphasis on duty and service is consistent with that lack of vision that Bush was so often charged with. It involves no lust for change, but requires individuals to give something back in return for the advantages that have been bestowed upon them. They are obliged to serve, to offer their talents, their skills, and even their lives if necessary, to their country. As one of the most astute of Bush observers, David Hoffman, put it: 'Bush's vision of the country reflects the impact of a privileged childhood in which he was drilled with the importance of "giving back" to society some of the good fortune he inherited.'[14]

The conservatism that Bush grew up with was moderate, non-confrontational and relatively non-ideological, marked by civility, compassion and community. However, more than two decades of life and politics in Texas were to expose him to conservatism of a rather different stripe. After graduation from Yale in 1948 he and his wife set off for west Texas where he began work as a trainee in the oil industry. Two years later he struck out on his own and with a partner formed an independent oil company that traded in leases and royalties. These moves were less adventurous than they might seem. The trainee position was in a subsidiary of a company headed by 'a close family friend, [a] surrogate uncle and father confessor to all the Bush children.'[15] Furthermore, when Bush formed his own company, crucial investment support came from his uncle and from clients of his father's firm.[16] For all that, Bush was now subject to the intense anxieties of a high-risk, relentlessly competitive business where fortunes could be won and lost overnight. While cushioned from the dire financial losses facing others his business activities were certainly not without risk. 'No one really knows how much oil is underneath what land; mineral leases are complicated, and there's a lively market in them: Deciding where to drill, what equipment to use, whom to hire, how far to keep going – these are tricky judgments on which a lot of money is riding.'[17]

By declining in 1948 the readily available option of remaining in the cosy, structured environment of his youth and heading for Texas, Bush came under the influence of a different conservative tradition. He was brought into contact with the individualistic political culture of the Southwest where the role models were not the well born and the well connected but those who had made vast fortunes from inauspicious beginnings, a region where largely untrammelled capitalism was king and taxes, bureaucrats and all forms of government were despised. This was a part of the country where a neopopulist brand of conservatism flourished; it was harsher than its Eastern counterpart, more materialistic, marked by 'new money' rather than 'old money', less moderate and less compassionate and not tempered by genteel norms of duty and service.[18] After a decade in west Texas Bush moved eastwards and settled in Houston, eventually making it his political base. Houston is a town which 'conveys a sense of rugged individualism and laissez-faire; however diverse now, much of it remains very conservative. Can there, for example, be another major city anywhere that has no zoning? "Private property is sacred here," a local political figure explains. "People feel they should be free to do whatever they want with it." '[19]

This was the sort of conservatism that had Barry Goldwater as its standard bearer when Bush first ran for public office, and came into its own in 1980 with the election of Ronald Reagan to the White House. As will become clear when we examine his presidency, Bush remained primarily a product of his upbringing, but there is little doubt that his experience in Texas left a mark. When he sought election to the US Senate in 1964 Bush enthusiastically embraced Goldwater's agenda; he denounced the pending Civil Rights Act, attacked Martin Luther King, opposed Medicare and foreign aid and demanded that the United States leave the United Nations if the People's Republic of China was admitted. [20] Bush later disowned some of these views on the grounds that they were forced upon him by electoral considerations. Nevertheless his world view was, in part, shaped by the Texas phase of his career, adding influences that arguably contributed to some of the ambiguities in his thinking that were later to cause him difficulties.

THE MANNER OF THE MAN

Ingratiation, the ability to render oneself agreeable and like-able to others, is a major resource in a polity marked by an absence of ideology, insubstantial parties and an intense frag-mentation of power.[21] Presidents like Franklin Roosevelt and Ronald Reagan exploited to the full their great capacity to be ingratiating – using it to develop productive relations with the press, with legislators and with the public at large.[22] When Reagan was in office, public opinion polls showed that many of those who disapproved of his policies nevertheless found him to be a likeable man.[23]

Despite poll rankings sometimes far in excess of anything Reagan achieved, Bush was never publicly liked in the same way. Particularly towards the end, Bush was seen in many quarters as a rather cold-blooded and uncaring patrician, out of touch with the needs and discontents of ordinary people. Senior members of Bush's staff argued that such negative percep-tions of him and the invidious comparisons with his predecessor arose, in large part, from television induced distortions of reality. As the consummate television politician Reagan had managed to project an image of warmth and charm that obscured the reality of a rather cold and remote figure who had diffi-culty in remembering the names of members of his own Cabinet and was personally close to no one other than his wife.

According, to Bush's senior aides he is a far more admirable human being than media images conveyed while he was in office. We are assured that he was, in fact, a man of great warmth, kindness and sensitivity, who lacked pretension, was elaborately considerate as an employer and obsessively loyal to his friends. Thus James Cicconi, Staff Secretary and Deputy Chief of Staff, spoke with feeling of Bush's 'endearing qualities':

. . . a man who really didn't take himself too seriously, who was one of the most personable and kind people. Generous to a fault, really concerned with individuals and their problems. He took a very personal interest in everybody that worked in the building and how they were doing and how they were treated.[24]

Testimony to the unusual kindness and decency of the President and the First Lady was provided by John Keller, Director of Presidential Advance, who said '[They] are two of the most honorable, kind, honest people you would ever meet in your life.' When pressed Keller went on to say that while Bush might have some limitations as a leader, 'as a human being and a person I can't come up with any negatives for somebody like him, I just can't.'[25] Gregg Petersmeyer, Assistant to the President for National Service and a longstanding Bush protégé, spoke of his talent for dealing with people on a 'retail' basis in contrast to Reagan's undeniable strength in 'wholesale' politics: 'George Bush is the most admirable man that one will ever see in that office on a one to one basis. He has got a tremendous soft and warm heart. He hurts for people; feels for people.'[26]

Gail Wilensky, Deputy Assistant to the President for Policy Development, saw a difference between the public and the private man. The President was an 'incredibly nice man . . . a wonderful human being, unpretentious, funny. The woodenness that he sometimes portrayed in a crowd, speaking, is absolutely the opposite of what you see and feel when you meet the man . . . [he] just exudes personal warmth.'[27]

Contrary to the impressions of some of his critics Bush's intimates stressed his modesty and humility. Peggy Noonan referred to 'his diffidence and his determination. None of the great-man manner, self-deprecating, modest.'[28] One of those closest to him, C. Boyden Gray, Counsel to the President, suggested that Bush was given less credit than he deserved for his achievements while in the White House because of an inbred unwillingness to boast: 'He did all this, but because he was brought up by his mother never to talk about himself you know it just never came across.'[29]

Andrew Card who served in the White House as Deputy Chief of Staff and then in the Cabinet as Secretary of Transportation, said simply of Bush: 'He is a humble man.'[30] This view is endorsed by David Demarest, Assistant to the President for Communications, who, in illustrating the point, refers to his experience in going over speeches with the President while travelling on Air Force One: 'He would sometimes apologize for making changes in his speech . . . he cared about a researcher, or a speech writer not having their feelings hurt. He would say things like, "now don't tell him I really didn't like this, but I really don't like this page . . . I know they put a lot of effort into it." '[31]

That George Bush is personally a decent, civilized, even likeable human being seems beyond dispute.[32] These qualities allowed him to ingratiate himself with those with whom he came into contact and to make friends of them wherever possible. By assiduously cultivating personal relations throughout his career by telephone calls, thank you notes and Christmas cards Bush created a political resource of some consequence.[33] The value of that resource will become apparent in subsequent chapters when appointments, legislative relations and foreign policy are under consideration.

For Bush personal relationships were always far more important than political ideas. Some of the most devout Bush loyalists have remarked on his extravagant lack of interest in ideas. The President's eldest son, George W. Bush, told James Pinkerton who as Deputy Assistant to the President for Policy Planning, was responsible for injecting some ideas into the Bush White House: 'The problem with my old man is that he thinks you can solve problems one at a time, with good character, good judgment, a good team, and all that stuff. Jebby [his brother] and I understand that you need ideas, principles – based on belief.'[34]

Gregg Petersmeyer, almost as close to Bush as to be a surrogate son, commented very similarly. As he saw it the President worked very hard in dealing with individual decisions as they came down the conveyor belt towards him, but he was disinclined to step back and say:

'What is it of all these things on the conveyor belt that I think is the most important to define and project?' . . . he's not contemplative. He doesn't sit back and say there really are three things I care about. He's a man of action. He'd much prefer to go play tennis or write a note to somebody. . . . [He's not] interested in ideas for ideas' sake. I think he's interested in the application of ideas and people and leadership to certain situations.'[35]

Bush's lack of interest in ideas touches on a charge that was to haunt him throughout his presidency, his perceived lack of 'vision.' Unlike Reagan he was not driven by any desire to change the world, he was broadly satisfied with things as they were and saw no need for a blueprint or a master plan of reform. Leadership demanded honour, integrity, a sense of public service and experience. There was no 'need for an overarching vision. Rather, he believes he possesses the right training and the intuitive sense to make correct decisions as problems come his way. He is the embodiment of pragmatism: self confident about his ability to find solutions without holding to a master blueprint.'[36]

When asked late in his presidency why Americans should re-elect him Bush gave an answer that had little to do with ideas or issues: 'I've tried to serve with a sense of decency. I think people look at that. I think we have tried to look at family values. We try to live them. We talk about my caring, and I do. And I think those things come through . . . I think [the American people] say, Hey, these times have been rough, but the President's doing his best, and I disagree with him on this or that, but he's a good man.' As Richard Brookhiser noted, Reagan confronted by the same question would have mentioned two issues: 'cut taxes, fight the evil empire', and Clinton would have referred to a multitude of issues, whereas Bush 'ultimately answers it with himself'.[37] If we are to consider Bush on his own terms, however, his answer makes sense. It was a logical response for a president who saw no need for change and on numerous occasions vaunted American society and the political system. Such circumstances required not visionaries, but honourable, decent and experienced leaders, qualities which Bush could claim to possess.

RELEVANT EXPERIENCE ?

In campaigning for the presidency George Bush made much of his curriculum vitae, exuberantly proclaiming on occasion, 'Ready from day one to be a great president.'[38] On the face of it, Bush certainly did appear to be far better qualified for service in the White House than some recent incumbents. Jimmy Carter, for instance, had undeniably been a man of high intelligence, but his prior experience as Governor of Georgia, a relatively small state with a part-time legislature overwhelmingly controlled by the Democrats, was less than suitable preparation for the rigours of executive leadership in Washington. Furthermore, Carter's campaign as an outsider, fiercely critical of Congress and its procedures, ensured that his relationship with the legislature would be a difficult one.

President Reagan also campaigned as an outsider in 1980. He had gone into politics after a long career in the entertainment industry and this was followed by two terms as the governor of one of the largest and most important states. However, Reagan's knowledge in the principal area of responsibility for a chief executive of that era – foreign affairs – was derisively inadequate. In contrast to his two predecessors, Bush entered the White House with what one source referred to as 'the best vitae in American public life' while another went so far as to say that he had 'the best résumé [and] the best experience' of any modern president.[39]

When Bush sought the presidency in 1988 he undoubtedly had behind him a long and varied record in national politics. He had made his electoral debut 24 years before when he unsuccessfully sought a seat in the United States Senate; he was elected to the United States House of Representatives in 1966 and served for two terms. After another abortive attempt to reach the Senate he was appointed, by President Nixon at the end of 1970, to the position of US Ambassador to the United Nations. At the beginning of 1973 Bush became Chairman of the Republican National Committee. Briefly considered in 1974 as a possible nominee to be Gerald Ford's Vice President, George Bush instead became head of the US Public Liaison Office in the People's Republic of China. In 1976 President Ford appointed him Director of the Central Intelligence Agency where he served for slightly less than a year. After losing the contest for the Republican nomination to the presidency in 1980 to Ronald Reagan, Bush was chosen by the latter as his running mate and served as Vice President from 1981 until 1989.

Closer scrutiny of Bush's record in public life prior to 1989 however, raises questions about just how well qualified he was for the presidency. Service in the national legislature is undeniably a useful experience for a future chief legislator, but Bush's congressional career was relatively short and came to an end 18 years before he entered the White House. Whilst in Congress he compiled a conservative voting record while being careful to maintain cordial relations with his oppponents. He was neither confrontational nor controversial, quickly slipping into the congenial, deferential and cooperative mode required by the norms of the institution.[40] 'Above all, he was a pragmatist more attuned to the interpersonal dynamics of politics than devoted to ideology.'[41]

It is reasonable to assume that Bush's four years in Congress gave him some understanding of the convoluted mechanisms whereby that body conducts its business; it will also have helped him later to comprehend better the motivations of legislators. Nevertheless most of those who had served with him in the House had left by the time he became President; his service had been too brief for him to acquire a position of real influence and being of a conservative disposition he had been disinclined to put together a consequential legislative record.[42]

As United States Ambassador to the United Nations Bush began to acquire the foreign policy expertise that was to become one of his greatest strengths. It was, however, a modest beginning, based more on establishing potentially useful personal relationships with fellow diplomats than on any real participation in the making of American foreign policy. Whilst Bush was at the UN, Henry Kissinger, the National Security Adviser, blocked direct access to President Nixon in the foreign policy area and the Ambassador suffered humiliation on the key issue that came to the fore during his tour of duty – the controversy over the seating of communist China.[43]

Unaware of the secret diplomacy then being conducted with China by Nixon, Kissinger and Secretary of State William Rogers, Bush worked hard in an unsuccessful effort to ensure that Taiwan at least retained a seat in the General Assembly on the admission of the People's Republic. This had been US policy previously and Bush beavered away innocent of the fact that the hope of seating Taiwan had been abandoned months previously by those really responsible for the making of foreign policy in the Nixon Administration.[44]

George Bush's foreign policy role was not noticeably greater during the Ford Administration. When he became head of the United States liaison operation in Beijing it was made clear to him that his duties were very limited. Henry Kissinger 'explained that Bush was to be little more than a listening scout for the US. He was not there to implement policy Initiatives would be handled by Washington, meaning Kissinger himself.'[45] In a biography heavily favourable to Bush his China period is referred to as a 'sabbatical' and as an 'exotic interlude'; his presence in Beijing was 'insignificant. He was playing in Kissinger's sandbox. Bush did the backslapping and tailwagging as a mere public relations man while Kissinger came and went on his high-level, substantive dealings with the Chinese power wielders.'[46]

As Ford's Director of the Central Intelligence Agency, Bush won plaudits for helping to restore the morale of an institution that had recently been battered with severe criticism. He energetically courted the media and repeatedly testified on Capitol Hill, but his work at the Agency was almost entirely concerned with public relations and image-making rather than matters of substance. And even at the CIA the ever-present Henry Kissinger continued to prevent Bush from becoming more involved in policy matters by denying him access to intelligence material of the highest classification coming into the State Department.[47]

Two terms as Reagan's Vice President provided the most impressive entry on Bush's résumé when he ran for the presidency in 1988. Much has been made of the insignificance of the vice presidency in the past. Franklin Roosevelt's first Vice President, John Nance Garner, famously declared the office to be 'not worth a bucket of warm spit'.[48] In similar vein Thomas Marshall, who held the position under Woodrow Wilson, observed that the vice president 'is like a man in a cataleptic state: he cannot speak; he cannot move; he suffers no pain; and yet he is perfectly conscious of everything that is going on about him.'[49] In the modern era Lyndon Johnson was bitterly frustrated as Kennedy's Vice President; Hubert Humphrey suffered similarly in the Johnson White House and Spiro Agnew had difficulty in even getting to see President Nixon and was used primarily as a political hatchet man.[50]

In recent decades it would seem that vice presidents have fared rather better; they have been given offices in the White House, have acquired sizeable personal staffs and been asked to take on important responsibilities.[51] Thus Bush assumed the chairmanship of a number of presidential task forces designed to coordinate the implementation of policies extending across several agencies. One of these, the Task Force on Regulatory Relief, gave Bush a role of some significance in furthering deregulation, a central plank of Reagan's economic policy. Bush also chaired the South Florida Task Force, concerned with combating the drug trade and was appointed chairman of the Terrorism Task Force.[52]

In addition, President Reagan made considerable use of his Vice President for foreign policy purposes. By the spring of 1987 Bush, in his capacity as Vice President, had travelled to no less than 73 countries; in many cases these visits were for funerals or other ceremonial purposes, but more than a few had a substantive purpose.[53] It is claimed, for instance, that Bush played an important part in persuading European governments to accept Pershing and cruise missiles, an essential preliminary for one of President Reagan's principal foreign policy achievements, the INF treaty.[54] It is also the case that George Bush met with the President on a weekly basis and in 1985 Reagan went so far as to say: 'I don't think there's ever been a vice president that has been as much involved at the highest level in our policy-making and our decisions than George, or that has been a better vice president than he has. He's been the best.'[55]

It is evident that vice presidents now enjoy much higher profiles than before and regularly accept major assignments. Nevertheless there is ample reason to question the value of service as vice president as preparation for the presidency. Despite the changes of recent years, vice presidents are still destined to remain presidential acolytes and errand boys. Abject loyalty to the President is an essential requirement of the job; those who take it on, in other words, are obliged to sacrifice their independence and self-respect. If they should be foolish enough to display a mind of their own, to dissent from the president's policies, either openly or though leaks, they will quickly find themselves isolated, denied influence in the making of decisions and in grave danger of losing their claim to the succession. Arthur Schlesinger Jnr, who favours abolition of the office, has remarked with his usual pungency: 'Under most Presidents, the Vice Presidency is much less a making than a maiming experience' leading not to 'education but emasculation'; a position that constantly demands 'sedulous loyalty, deference, self-effacement and self-abasement'.[56]

Few vice presidents have met these requirements more meticulously than George Bush. When selected as Reagan's running mate, despite having, among other things, assailed Reaganomics as 'voodoo' economics in the primaries, Bush immediately told his staff: 'We're now a wholly owned subsidiary and we're going to behave like one.'[57] Subsequently, those who attended meetings at the highest level in the Reagan White House reported that the Vice President hardly ever expressed an opinion and was always elaborately deferential to the President.[58] Bush, however, remained unrepentant, shrugging off gibes that he was a 'lapdog' or that he had 'placed his manhood in a blind trust,' insisting that 'in our family loyalty is not a character flaw.'[59]

Bush's resolute unwillingness to be seen as in any way less than completely loyal to President Reagan was reinforced by his delicate relationship with conservatives in his party. Right-wing Republicans had long doubted his conservative credentials and his presidential ambitions demanded that he should be careful not to alienate a vital element of the coalition required for his election in 1988. In the long run, however, Bush's obsessive unwillingness to put any light between himself and Ronald Reagan had seriously adverse consequences. It contributed to what were ultimately profoundly damaging perceptions of him as a political 'wimp', as a man lacking in beliefs and convictions.

The indignities that are heaped upon vice presidents make service in that office, in some ways, an unsatisfactory preparation for the desperately difficult problems of leadership that presidents must grapple with. Nevertheless, Bush's eight years in the post had some value given the importance that foreign policy assumed during his presidency. His overseas missions on Reagan's behalf had improved his understanding of the issues and his meetings with world leaders facilitated the personal diplomacy that, a few years later, was to become a hallmark of his own conduct of foreign policy.

Overall, however, Bush's pre-presidential political experience was of limited relevance. He had held a range of national offices, but none of them were in the fullest sense leadership positions. In each case he was not a principal decision-maker, policy-making was not his responsibility, he was, at best, a number two carrying out the mandates of others. None of this had prepared him for the monumental challenges that every president faces; he had no real experience of wrestling with Congress, the bureaucracy, interest groups and public opinion in order to fulfil an agenda. He came to the presidency, according to David Hoffman, 'having prepared extensively in the sense of watching and absorbing, but also with scant experience in actually wielding great power, in pushing others to reach his goals, in mastering the fine art of political leadership.'[60] To put it another way, George Bush's training in statecraft was far less sufficient than he and others suggested.[61]

A GUARDIAN IN THE WHITE HOUSE

As I indicated at the beginning, those who become presidents are entitled to be considered in the light of how they see their role and how successful they are in achieving their goals. One problem with this line of analysis in the case of George Bush lies in the widespread suspicion that he did not really have goals; many, even within his own party, have accused him of having no clear sense of where he wanted to lead the country, of being without convictions or beliefs, of wanting office not to achieve lofty purposes, but merely for the 'honor of it all'.[62] Shortly before Bush was elected President, George Will, an influential conservative critic, wrote:

> Sure he has a purpose: he wants to be president. But he seems to want that only because it is the next rung up, and climbing the ladder of public life is his life. This is an old axiom: Some people seek office to be something; others seek office to do something. Bush is one of the former. In this, the contrast with Ronald Reagan is complete.[63]

While not without some validity this indictment requires further consideration. The comparison with Ronald Reagan is, for instance, somewhat invidious. A clear-cut, pre-conceived, radical agenda was, without doubt, one of Reagan's strengths yet, in that regard, he was unusual. Presidents typically take up office without a clear sense of what they intend to do. Even great achievers like Franklin Roosevelt could be said to have lacked 'vision', to have become president without a master plan or blueprint. As Theodore Lowi argues, 'no one knew Roosevelt's specific positions and plans until after he became president in 1933,' and much the same could be said of Kennedy, Nixon, Carter and Clinton.[64] Critics in the media and on the right of his party like Will constantly berated Bush for his failure to work to a 'roadmap' in the way that Reagan had done ignoring the fact that his non-ideological, case-by-case, reactive, problem-solving style was more attuned to the American political tradition.

Comments by George Bush in 1988 provide some understanding of how he saw his role and what he hoped to achieve in office. Unlike Reagan in 1981 he had no desire to lead a crusade. 'We don't need to remake society,' he said as his campaign got under way. 'We don't need radical new directions.'[65] This not only reflected Bush's cautious conservative instincts, it was also appropriate for a candidate who had been a loyal Vice President and now sought to ride into office on the back of a popular incumbent widely perceived to have been largely successful in office.

In his speech accepting his party's nomination at the Republican convention Bush spelled out his responsibility to build on the foundations laid by Reagan, saying: 'I am your candidate because the most important work of my life is to complete the mission we started in 1980. And how, and how do we complete it? We build on it.' Bush went on to glory in the successes of Reaganomics before recognizing that: 'Things aren't perfect in this country. There are people who haven't tasted the fruits of the expansion . . . farmers . . . urban children . . . the homeless.' But the key to the solution of these problems lay in economic growth which would be secured 'by maintaining our commitment to free and fair trade, by keeping government spending down, and by keeping taxes down.'

The latter crucial article of the Reaganite faith was enshrined in the famous pledge 'Read my lips: No new taxes,' while other goals specified by candidate Bush included '30 in 8' – thirty million jobs in eight years, 'first-rate' schools for every American child, a 'drug-free America', laws designed to ensure that the 'disabled are included in the mainstream', and environmental legislation. In foreign policy he would continue with the present administration's policy of 'peace through strength' coupled with further work towards disarmament.

Having indicated his determination to carry the Reagan revolution forward Bush added an emphasis of his own, deploring the recent emergence of materialism, complaining of greed, graft, corruption and self-centredness and declaring 'I want a kinder and gentler nation', a theme that he took up again at his inauguration, asking:

> Have we changed as a nation even in our time? Are we enthralled with material things, less appreciative of the nobility of work and sacrifice? My friends, we are not the sum of our possessions. They are not the measure of our lives. In our hearts we know what matters. We cannot hope only to leave our children a bigger car, a bigger bank account. We must hope to give them a sense of what it means to be a loyal friend, a loving parent, a citizen who leaves his home, his neighborhood, and town better than he found it.

In line with these echoes from his upbringing, the new President also used his inaugural address to reiterate his belief that many social problems were best taken care of, not by the expenditure of public money, but by voluntary service – sentiments that gave rise to the establishment of the Points of Light Movement, a development much derided elsewhere, but, for Bush, a particularly important part of his programme.[66]

It is evidently not the case that Bush had no agenda. He saw no need for fundamental change and inclined to the view prevalent in the Eisenhower administration 'that the less the government did, the more the people would progress and prosper.'[67] Nevertheless, Bush did have goals and, as we have seen, in accepting the nomination he advanced a number of specific proposals designed to consolidate the achievements of the previous administration while also smoothing off some of the rougher edges.[68] It was not a programme likely to meet with the approval of his political opponents and even within the Bush Administration there were those who found it thin, insubstantial and insufficiently activist.[69] William Kristol, the Vice President's Chief of Staff, confirmed that there was a group within the White House including himself, Dan Quayle and Jack Kemp, Secretary for Housing and Urban Development, that chafed under Bush's passivity and advocated 'an activist, conservative agenda, à la Reagan, or, in some respects, more à la Thatcher.'[70]

Bush's approach to the presidency can be contrasted with some of the alternatives. Liberal Democrats, among whom most political scientists are to be found, have required presidents to be activists, innovators and reformers. They have been expected to take up office armed with creative ideas and legislative proposals designed to relieve American society of its many ailments. Presidents, it is assumed, cannot sit on the sidelines while so many citizens suffer from inequality, poverty, illiteracy, drug abuse, disease and other forms of distress.

Vigorous leadership from the White House to deal with these and other problems has been an imperative for liberal Democrats. They have encouraged presidents not to be too finicky about the Constitution, an instrument, as they see it, that needs to be interpreted creatively, stretched, if necessary, to accommodate desirable extensions of the reach of government, for the power of government in the right hands could be a potent force for good. It followed that the president's principal role was that of chief legislator, for by formulating and passing laws governments could provide the muscle and the money required to improve the conditions of life for the American people. The number of bills passed in the name of the president was a crucial measure of his success in office. Presidents, in short, should be like FDR or Lyndon Johnson, they should, above all else, be activists and innovators in the White House.[71]

Conservatives, on the other hand, tend to despise big government and remain sceptical as to what can be achieved by passing laws. This has not, however, prevented some Republican presidents from becoming innovators or advocates of substantial change. Theodore Roosevelt provides a good example and Richard Nixon can be similarly categorized. The latter's heroes were 'Teddy Roosevelt . . . a man of action who could think and Woodrow Wilson . . . a man of thought who could act.'[72] As we saw in the previous chapter, Nixon distinguished between 'men' and 'boys' in the White House. The latter sought office for the sake of it while the former wanted to make use of the power they acquired.[73] As President, Nixon was one of the 'men'; he was innovative in international affairs and an activist in domestic policy, vigorous in pursuit of a full agenda including major items such as welfare reform, government reorganization, the introduction of a 'new' federalism and the establishment of the Environmental Protection Agency.

In domestic policy, Ronald Reagan was even more of an innovator than Nixon had been. He came into office profoundly dissatisfied with the status quo and bent on funda-mental change. Notwithstanding a notoriously disengaged operating style, Reagan was not content to leave things largely as they were. Unlike say Eisenhower and Ford, he was not prepared broadly to accept the assumptions of the New Deal and the Great Society. By comparison Reagan had high ambitions; he embarked on a frontal assault against, what he saw as, a high taxation, big spending, big government system. Reagan, in other words, was attempting to alter the terms of the political debate and was, in that sense, an innovator.

George Bush lacked both the opportunity and the inclina-tion to be an innovator and proved instead to be a guardian in the White House. By definition guardians, who guard, protect or preserve, are largely satisfied with the status quo, even though they may recognize a need for marginal change. This was Bush's position in 1988. At the Republican conven-tion he argued that, in general, all was well in America, even if there were a few imperfections in need of attention. Three years later Bush still persisted with this line of argument vaunting the 'greatness' of America's 'free enterprise system [that] lets one person's fortune become everyone's gain,' and going on to say 'no system of development has nurtured virtue as completely and rigorously as ours, and we've become the most egalitarian system in history and one of the most harmonious.' Such problems as there were, could be largely left to the 'common decency' of the American people, in other words philanthropic effort and volunteer activity. [74] This satis-faction with the existing state of things extended to the political system; Bush retained an unwavering faith in American political institutions, asserting: 'I believe in the integrity of the process. I believe our institutions can still work.'[75]

Guardian presidents are unlikely to be flamboyant, charismatic leaders. They are disinclined to be visionaries and they do not come armed with an ideology, or a master plan. Leadership for them is not about crusading, nor is it about working to a blueprint, it is about problem-solving on a case-by-case basis. As Bush began his campaign for the presidency he said: 'I am a practical man. I like what's real. I'm not much for the airy and the abstract. I like what works. I am not a mystic, and I do not yearn to lead a crusade.'[76] At his inauguration the President contrasted his approach with that of other, more ambitious, leaders when he said: 'Some see leadership as high drama, and the sound of trumpets calling. And sometimes it is that. But I see history as a book with many pages – and each day we fill a page with acts of hopefulness and meaning.' [77] This was to see executive leadership, as other guardian presidents have done, as a quiet, low-key, largely behind-the-scenes activity with an emphasis on prudence and caution.[78]

This is not likely to satisfy Bush's many critics who demand to know why he wanted to be president in the first place if he had no plan and no ambitions to change the world. Was this not proof that he just wanted to be president for the sake of it? This is to misunderstand how a guardian president sees his role. He takes the view that the United States needs at the helm, not a visionary or an ideologue, but a qualified and competent leader able to deal with problems and crises as they occur. As Ed Rogers, a senior member of the White House staff, saw it, Bush's ambition to be president arose from the conviction that he was especially well qualified to meet the demands of the office. He believed, 'I will effectively handle whatever comes my way, I will handle it better than anyone else . . . I am the best equipped person through experience, temperament, beliefs, philosphy and upbringing. I am the best person to handle the challenges that are presented by the presidency.'[79]

The guardian president is also deeply sceptical of the power of government to correct the ills of society, a view which Bush has consistently held. When he ran for the Senate in 1964 he cast doubt on the pending Civil Rights bill, arguing, like Eisenhower, that progress in race relations would only come about through moral suasion: 'I believe that the solution to this grave problem lies in the hearts and goodwill of all people and that sweeping federal legislation like the Civil Rights Act can never fully succeed.'[80] Nearly three decades later Bush's doubts as to the possible gains from government action remained, he was a president, 'grounded in the belief that government has only limited power, to fix the economy, revive the cities, change the cycle of poverty or radically attack social ills.'[81]

Guardian presidents such as Bush do not share the dreams of hyperactive chief executives like Lyndon Johnson, with their infinite faith in what government can accomplish given the will and the right sort of leadership. After Johnson's election in his own right, the first session of the 89th Congress saw the passage of 84 out of 87 major measures proposed by the President and, before he left office, there were close to 500 social programmes in place providing 'for everything from flood control to birth control to rat control' and much else besides.[82]

None of this impressed Bush who was to condemn Johnson's Great Society for its failure to eradicate social problems, for being a 'crusade [that] backfired'.[83] He wrote off such schemes in his inaugural address. 'The old solution, the old way, was to think that public money alone could end [social] problems. But we have learned that that is not so.' Rather than throwing money at the ills of society it was necessary to draw on 'the goodness and the courage of the American people', to engage the talents of the elderly and the energy of the young in community service, to return to timeless notions of 'duty, sacrifice, commitment, and a patriotism that finds its expression in taking part and pitching in.'[84]

Guardians not only question the positive value of government action, but are concerned that such action, far from improving the situation, may make matters worse. In defence of that position Bush took to invoking the Hippocratic Oath, saying on one occasion in reference to urban problems: 'The government's first duty is like that of the physician:Do no harm.'[85] That same caution was to be found in Bush's approach to foreign policy. He told Brent Scowcroft, his Assistant for

National Security, shortly after taking office: 'I want to do some-thing important [in foreign policy], but I want to proceed prudently. I don't want to do anything dumb.'[86]

In 1990, Bush was criticized for his cautious reaction to the efforts of the Baltic states in trying to break free from the Soviet Union, and responded: 'I don't want to do something that would inadvertently set back the progress that has been made in Eastern Europe.' The President went on to express his concern about the possibility of backlash by elements hostile to Gorbachev if the US went too far in its support of the Baltics. He continued: 'I love the old expression of Yogi Berra's. You say, "What happened to the Mets, Yogi?" He said, "Well, we made the wrong mistakes." I expect in this job I'll make plenty of mistakes, but I don't want to make the wrong mistakes.'[87]

The crisis for the Bush presidency brought about by the slide of the American economy into recession provoked simi-larly circumspect responses. In October 1991, the President resisted advice that the economy should be stimulated by a tax cut saying: 'What I don't want to do is to make the situa-tion worse.' Later in a speech in Rome Bush said: 'You notice when tax cuts were proposed, long term interest rates shot through the roof. I have a responsibility to see that I don't make proposals that will set back the economy.'[88] Once again Bush had shown that 'Do no harm' was the leitmotif of his Administration. Unlike Kennedy, Johnson, Nixon or Clinton, Bush disdained intervention in the economy. apparently believing that given time the recession would correct itself, the business cycle would turn again. Bobbie Kilberg, Deputy Assistant to the President for Public Liaison reported Bush as saying, 'massive intervention does not make sense, but this economy is going through changes which are fairly funda-mental, it has got to restructure itself.'[89]

Other sources have drawn attention to the President's tendency to talk about the economy in weather terms, alluding to the recession as a 'thunderstorm' and as a 'hurricane' in the devastation that it caused. According to one who heard these remarks they were 'a sign of the true Bush on the economy . . . There is nothing a president can do about it but take cover and live through it and wait for the sunshine.'[90] Such views were, of course, anathema to liberal activists and to some in

Bush's own party, but the President believed, according to his Staff Secretary 'that:

> . . . recessions happen; that they are the result of business cycles. That government action can perhaps help to even them out to some degree – maybe take out the lowest of the low. But, by and large, these are business cycles that do change in time. And the thing we need to do is to keep consistent economic policies that foster a good climate for business so that the economy can come back.[91]

As a guardian in the White House Bush also believed that he had a responsibility to prevent others in government from doing harm and it was in that spirit that he wielded the veto regularly and, as we shall see, successfully. In addition, Bush assumed the role of guardian to the Constitution, believing that since Vietnam and Watergate, Congress and the media had become excessively assertive at the expense of the presidency.[92] This had been most notably the case in the realm of foreign policy where, as will become clear in later chapters, Bush consistently and aggressively fought to preserve presidential prerogatives.

Yet if Bush battled tenaciously in defence of his constitutional position in foreign policy, his apparent passivity in domestic affairs was to become a source of recrimination central to his defeat in 1992. His Democratic critics castigated him for his laissez-faire attitude towards the economy and interpreted his disdain for grandiose schemes of social reform as the insensitive responses of a patrician, personally untouched and unmoved by the concerns of ordinary people. His political enemies in the media and Congress denounced him as a do nothing president prepared to sit on his hands in the face of recession and deep-rooted social problems.

Even within his own party, Bush's inaction in domestic policy provoked intense criticism. Right-wing Republicans were no less opposed to big government than the President, but that did not, in their view, justify making the presidency a centre of inaction in domestic policy. In 1991, Jack Kemp, Secretary for Housing and Urban Development in Bush's Cabinet, obliquely criticized the President when he said: 'The White House is the epicenter of national policy. There are problems of poverty and despair and economic decline in many people's neighborhoods which the president has both a moral and political obligation to address.'[93] Like others on the right of the Republican Party, Kemp believed there were conservative answers to pressing urban problems such as welfare dependency, unemployment, drug abuse, education and crime, but, as his comment implied, translation of those ideas into goverment policy required real leadership from the White House.[94]

As we have seen, conservative Republicans also lambasted Bush for not being more like Ronald Reagan. For not having a vision of where he wanted to take the country, for lacking a blueprint, or master plan, for appearing to have so few settled beliefs, or convictions, for being so irredeemably pragmatic. In this analysis however, I am not concerned with the wisdom or otherwise of George Bush's policy preferences. I am examining his incumbency in the light of how he saw his role, what he was trying to achieve, and the methods he used in attempting to reach those goals. The latter will be considered in the next chapter.

2 Strategies of Leadership

Guardian presidents have only limited agendas. Sceptical of what can be achieved by governmental action they are inclined to be passive rather than activist in office. Nevertheless, like all presidents, they are engaged in a constant struggle to impose their preferences and priorities on the notoriously intractable American political system. In grappling with these daunting problems different presidents deploy varying strategies and techniques and the purpose of this chapter is to review George Bush's utilization of some of these approaches. Accordingly, I will touch on his appointments policy, his legislative relations, his reluctance to make use of the bully pulpit, his relationship with the press and his lack of comfort with television. First, however, it will be useful to compare and contrast the fundamentals of Bush's style of presidential leadership with those of his predecessor.

AN INSIDER IN THE WHITE HOUSE

Reagan was, of course, a conviction politician with an ideological edge to his conservatism. He arrived in Washington, moreover, as a quintessential outsider, as a chief executive who, despite a veneer of charm and geniality, regarded bureaucrats and legislators as the enemy, as political adversaries to be overcome using whatever means were necessary.

For Reagan and his senior advisers, gaining control of the federal government demanded a hard-headed approach to appointments; if career bureaucrats were to be brought into line they had to be supervised and directed by carefully selected presidential appointees. To obtain one of these positions it was not enough to be an enthusiatic campaign worker, a competent administrator, or a good Republican; most important of all, appointees had to be fully committed to the ideas and progammes that Ronald Reagan had advocated in campaigning for the presidency.[1]

Congress meanwhile was best regarded as a hotbed of ruthless opponents, unremittingly hostile to all that Reagan hoped to achieve. For a few years the Senate under Republican control was reasonably responsive to the popular will, but 'the House [was] a different matter, with recent incumbent reelection rates of 98 percent or better [and Democratic control] ever since 1954. The lower chamber, part of the permanent government syndrome, frequently combined with other elements of the establishment in attempting to thwart the Reagan program.'[2] To overcome such resistance Reagan had no inhibitions about going over the heads of members of Congress to appeal to their constituents. During the epic struggle over the budget in 1981 Reagan's exceptional communications skills were complemented by his staff launching grassroots lobbying blitzes in selected congressional constituencies, where voters and key campaign contributors were induced to pressurize pivotal legislators.[3]

The Reaganites, it is clear, were more than willing to play hard-ball with Congress and the President's mastery of television was a major resource in that regard. Moreover, not only was Reagan an effortless performer before television cameras, he was also content to devote most of his efforts to being the front man of his administration. That is to say, provided that the broad principles he stood for were being respected, he was pleased to leave to his staff the details of policy formulation and implementation while he concentrated on promotion and salesmanship.

It was Reagan's ideology and his outsider status that lay behind his confrontational style and his demands for fundamental change. Bush had no interest in changing the world and came from a totally different background. He sought the presidency out of a conviction that he was especially well qualified to address problems as they arose; he had been brought up to revere public service and had himself held a range of government jobs. At the beginning of his 1988 campaign, he said:

> I do not hate government. I'm proud of my long experience in government. I've met some of the best people in the world doing the people's business in the Congress and in the agencies. A government that serves the people effectively and economically, and that remembers the people are its master, is a good and needed thing.[4]

Similarly, shortly after taking office, Bush spoke to an audience of high-ranking career civil servants in the federal government. The President told these senior Washington bureaucrats: 'You are one of the most important groups I will ever speak to. What we really have in common is that each of us is here to serve the American people. Each of is here because of a belief in public service as the highest and noblest calling.'[5] These were sentiments wholly unpalatable to good Reaganites who despised bureaucrats and all they stood for and took very seriously their leader's maxim: 'Government is not the solution to our problem; government is the problem.' For Bush, by contrast, those who worked in government were not enemies, they were people he knew, who shared his values and his commitment to public service – they were people he could do business with.

APPOINTMENTS

While Bush respected career officials in the federal government in a way that Reagan did not, he nevertheless understood how important the appointment process was as a principal means whereby presidents gain control of the executive branch. In the modern age, 'The personnel resources at the president's disposal are considerable: 600 top-level cabinet and White House appointments, 700 non-career Senior Executive Service (SES) appointments, and 1,700 Schedule C appointments, along with many other honorary and commission appointments.'[6] Bush recognized that he would need good loyalists, not only in the White House and his Cabinet, but also throughout the federal bureaucracy to monitor and lead government departments.

As James Pfiffner has observed: 'The major criterion for all new Presidents in their appointments is loyalty, but loyalty comes in many guises: partisan, personal, ideological.'[7] Party loyalty is, at best, a weak reed in the American context, and ideology, while highly relevant in the case of Reagan, could hardly serve for a distinctly non-ideological president like Bush. The single most important criterion for appointment in the Bush administration was, at the outset at least, longstanding personal loyalty to George Bush. No one better personified this quality than Chase Untermeyer, the first Assistant for Presidential Personnel. He had been associated with Bush since his student days; first as a campaign worker when Bush ran for Congress in the 1960s, and then as an intern on Congressman Bush's staff. After serving in the Texas House of Representatives 1977–81, Untermeyer became Vice President Bush's Executive Assistant. He was then Assistant Secretary to the Navy in Reagan's second term, before, in early 1988, being appointed by the Republican National Committee to prepare for the transition to a possible Bush presidency. After the 1988 election, Untermeyer took charge of personnel recruitment for the incoming administration.

In staffing his Administration Bush was able to draw on the many personal relationships he had developed over the years. According to Constance Horner, Untermeyer's eventual successor, the President 'knew probably more Americans than any other human being has ever known, and he knew them with a kind of conscious attention . . . He spent time cultivating thousands of personal relations.'[8] For years Bush and his wife meticulously attended to friends and colleagues, carefully keeping in touch with those they had met in Texas, at the UN, in Washington and abroad; these relationships were kept alive by thank you notes, telephone calls and a Christmas card list that, according to one source, was 30,000 strong by 1986.[9] By drawing people into his circle in this way and holding them there, Bush put together a valuable leadership resource. Fiercely loyal himself, he could expect that loyalty to be reciprocated and, in the right circumstances, it could be a substitute for party or ideology.

As the Bush administration began to take shape the *New York Times* reported one anonymous friend of the President as saying: 'Loyalty is his ideology, his vision.' The article went on: 'Republicans agree that if ideology was the the most important quality in the Reagan appointments, the loyalty factor shaped the Bush team. Mr Bush has stocked his Administration with old friends from similar affluent Ivy League backgrounds . . . [he] prefers to appoint people he knows and with whom he is comfortable.'[10]

In explaining why the Bush White House was so relatively harmonious at the beginning, at least, Untermeyer said that people were appointed who came from the same background

as the President, sharing 'a basic consensus that what matters
is public service, plain and straight dealing, and the essential
issues that propel American life, such as family, military
service, and hard work in the private sector . . . Many of them
have worked on Bush campaigns going back to Texas days or
the late 1970s. They are a part of the President, if you will.'[11]
This comment refers to White House staff, but given the size
of the President's circle of friends it was possible also to place
large numbers of them among the rank and file political
appointees in government agencies. Some cabinet secretaries
particularly close to the President like James Baker, Nicholas
Brady and Robert Mosbacher could be allowed largely to
select their own subordinates, but tighter control was needed
in other departments.[12]

One of those responsible for such matters, Ronald Kaufman,
Deputy Assistant to the President for Presidential Personnel,
saw his responsibility as follows. In selecting 140 or so
political appointees for, say, the Department of Health
and Human Services, he was obliged to ensure that those
appointed would move the army of bureaucrats in that
department in the right direction. 'It is very important that
people the President trusts and knows best, who understand
best where [he] wants to move his country philosophically
and policy wise, get those jobs . . . Just because a guy's got
a great résumé it doesn't necessarily mean he can motivate
that army [in] the direction that the President wants him
to.'[13] Despite Kaufman's references to philosophy and
policy it is clear that, at the beginning, personal loyalty to
George Bush was the dominant criterion for appointment
in contrast to the ideological loyalty demanded of those
who sought posts in the Reagan Administration. 'The
Reagan folk had opinions; they were more concerned
with things like abortion [and] deep philosophical questions
. . . That was their litmus test. My litmus test was more of
[personal] loyalty.'[14]

By his own admission fanatically loyal to Bush himself,
Kaufman stressed the vital importance of personnel to the
process of governing and spoke of lecturing Senate Republicans
on the need for state and regional appointees unreservedly
loyal to the President. According to Kaufman, the venerable
Republican Senator Strom Thurmond welcomed him to a lunch

by saying: 'Ron, thanks for coming, we are here to discuss our appointments for regional jobs.' Kaufman responded, 'With all due respect they are not your regional appointments, they are George Bush's appointments. Let me just tell you . . . these are George Bush's important foot soldiers, to make sure he gets re-elected by carrying through his policies in the region.'[15]

In making appointments at the beginning the Bush Administration was also at pains to recruit more women. Furthermore, as part of his effort to differentiate himself from Reagan, the new president was anxious to appoint from ethnic minorities and laid stress on the need for ethical soundness among appointees.[16]

It is interesting to note, however, that later in his administration Bush appeared to have second thoughts about his appointments policy, downplaying his emphasis on personal loyalty and replacing it with a concern for policy orientation. Untermeyer eventually left the White House to be replaced by Constance Horner and Kaufman moved sideways to become Deputy Assistant to the President for Political Affairs. Horner, a Reagan Democrat, assumed responsibility for appointments in 1991, believing that she had been selected by Bush to change course:

> I think he wanted me to introduce a policy orientation to a greater extent than had been [the case] at the beginning of his administration. I had a reputation as being a heavily policy orientated conservative and I think I was selected because going into an election year the President believed that he was vulnerable for lack of policy rigor in his appointments. I think he was occasionally distressed to discover that some issue he had a history of being committed to was not being well served through some of his appointments.[17]

Ultimately, it seems, as the 1992 election approached, Bush and his advisers came around to the view that personal loyalty was not enough in making appointments. They had become increasingly aware of the disaffection of the far right of the Republican Party, a development that eventually culminated in Patrick Buchanan's challenge for the nomination.

LEGISLATIVE RELATIONS

The success or failure of a president, however limited his agenda, is greatly dependent on his relationship with Congress. Despite Reagan's laid-back, wisecracking geniality in meetings with congressional leaders, his Administration had adopted an aggressively confrontational approach. By comparison Bush's objective situation and his instincts were quite different. He had neither the desire, nor a mandate, for radical change; both Houses of the legislature were under Democratic control and he entered the White House as a former congressman and Washington insider who gloried in having more friends in public life than anyone else.

As he took up the reins of office, Bush went out of his way to give the impression that he wanted a more civilized and less confrontational relationship with Congress – one that stressed conciliation, compromise and bipartisanship. At his inaugural ceremony the President made gestures designed to prepare the ground for executive–legislative harmony. He effusively hailed Dan Rostenkowski, the Chairman of the mighty House Ways and Means Committee, with a 'Hi Danny' and ostentatiously greeted other long-serving Democratic friends such as Senator Daniel Inouye of Hawaii and Representative Jack Brooks of Texas.[18] And then, during his address, the President turned to the Democratic leadership and said:

> To my friends – and yes, I do mean friends – in the loyal opposition – and yes, I mean loyal – I put out my hand. I'm putting out my hand to you, Mr Speaker. I'm putting out my hand to you Mr Majority Leader . . . The American people want action. They didn't send us here to bicker. They asked us to rise above the merely partisan.

Once again Bush used words that Ronald Reagan would never have uttered, but he evidently was hoping to overcome the problems of divided government by adopting a 'kinder, gentler' style of legislative leadership.

In furtherance of this strategy Bush, as usual, drew on personal relationships, allegiances that 'have always been much more important to Bush than political ideas, policy preferences

or any abstract intellectual concern'.[19] Arising from his own
service in the institution, he already numbered senior members
of Congress among his friends and he now worked to supple-
ment and strengthen these links. Members of Congress,
accompanied by a few carefully selected constituents, were
invited to the White House; some legislators were given
guided tours of the family quarters by the President himself
who also took to appearing regularly on Capitol Hill to socialize
with old friends, playing racquetball with Representative Sonny
Montgomery and lunching with Representative John
Hammerschmidt.[20] The potential benefits to be obtained from
such activity were spelled out by one congressman. 'He builds
personal bridges, and that makes the margin of consideration
for him broader,' said Representative Charles (Chip) Pashayan
Jr, Republican of California. 'It's harder for someone who has
some personal affinity with George Bush to deny him when
he makes a request.'[21]

The determination of Bush, at the beginning of his presidency, to work with rather than to go to war with Congress
was evident from an exchange in December 1988 between the
President-elect and Wayne Valis. The latter had been responsible for liaison with business groups in the Reagan
Administration and, in that role, had played a large part in
generating the telephone blitz that had made possible Reagan's
dazzling triumphs in 1981 in getting Congress to agree tax
and budget cuts.[22] Now flanked by some 'trade association
heavies' Valis explained the value of mobilizing business
interests at the grass roots as a way of applying pressure on
individual members of Congress only to have Bush respond:
'We are not going to do it that way Wayne.'[23] Reflecting on
this incident later Valis said: 'We were stopped in our tracks.
It was unilateral disarmament in the face of George Mitchell
and company'.[24]

The beginning of a new era in legislative relations was
announced by Bobbie Kilberg, Deputy Assistant to the President
for Public Liaison. 'This is a very different White House,' she
remembered telling a gathering of business executives. 'George
Bush does not believe in confrontation. He believes in the art
of the possible, he believes in conciliation, he believes in
consensus and he believes in civility. He would not be comfortable with a public liaison office mounting massive grassroots

campaigns.' Other presidents had used threats and reprisals against members of the legislature, whereas Bush 'does not like the thought of going over the heads of his friends in the Congress.'[25]

It was not just strong-arm tactics that Bush objected to, as Kilberg was to find out in an incident involving one of the President's closest friends in Congress, Representative 'Sonny' Montgomery, Democrat of Mississippi, who joined the House in 1966 when Bush himself was first elected to that body. An abiding memory for Kilberg from her time in the White House is of being upbraided by a testy President for having the temerity to encourage interest group representatives to telephone Montgomery. The President surrounded by agents moving down a corridor in the White House stopped on seeing Kilberg and said, 'Come here. Did you have a whole bunch of [people] call up Sonny Montgomery?' 'Well yes, I did.' 'Why did you do that?' 'Well we need that vote sir.' Bush responded: 'He's a friend of mine. Don't you do that [again] without asking me.' Later, as Kilberg noted, the President shed such inhibitions; eventually 'he began to clearly see that you just had to beat members of the Congress over the head,' but for the moment he adamantly refused to make use of what had been one of Reagan's most potent weapons.[26]

The contrast between Reagan the outsider and Bush the insider was neatly drawn by William Kristol '[Bush] really was a creature of Washington and didn't like the idea of populist pressure on Congress or on the executive branch. Reagan was the opposite. '[He] always understood himself to be, whatever the self-deception and whatever the limitations, basically a populist spokesman for the people against the establishment'.[27]

We must be careful, however, not to make too much of Bush's conciliatory approach to Congress, for there were occasions when he was prepared to play hard-ball with legislators. As will be made clear later, Bush under the influence of his tough-minded Counsel, C. Boyden Gray, made repeated use both of signing statements and vetoes to shape public policy and to defend his prerogatives against congressional encroachment.[28]

THE BULLY PULPIT

Another strength of the Reagan Administration had been the President's ability to deliver speeches that caught the attention of the media and the nation and pressured Congress into cooperation. Bush, by contrast, was always disinclined to use his office as a bully pulpit. As will become apparent in subsequent chapters, this was a major flaw for, in the modern age, skill at 'going public' has become an essential requirement of presidential leadership, indispensable not only to campaigning, but to governance.[29] Bush's reluctance to mount the bully pulpit was a matter of aptitude and inclination. Even the sturdiest of Bush loyalists readily concede that he lacked the exceptional talent for communication possessed by his predecessor. 'Reagan could go to the American public with his own great personal communication skills and really make the Congress squirm, often forcing them into altering their positions. Bush didn't have that ability.'[30]

For Reagan, moreover, making telling speeches was a priority, whereas Bush saw his role in a different light. He insisted on being a 'hands-on' chief executive rather than a salesman, or a mere mouthpiece for his administration. C. Boyden Gray argued that Bush could deliver effective speeches, but chose not to expend effort in that way. 'He could on occasion give a good speech . . . like the acceptance speech in 1988, the acceptance speech of 1984 as Vice President . . . He has the capacity to do it . . . [but] for one reason or another he didn't want to do it.' [31] Gregg Petersmeyer believed that the President took the view that 'He wasn't supposed to be making speeches . . . he was supposed to be making decisions.'[32] According to another senior aide Bush had 'a visceral antipathy to public communication . . . he thought poorly of it, he thought it was cheap.'[33] James Cicconi explained that the President tended 'to distrust the power of rhetoric'. On occasion, such as the crisis created by the invasion of Kuwait, he could be articulate and compelling, but, in general, he took the view that 'leadership consists of doing the right things, making the correct decisions, making the tough calls and being willing to be held accountable to those standards.'[34]

Some Bush loyalists contend that he was less effective than Reagan as a communicator because of his greater awareness of the complexity of issues. Reagan's simplistic stances made for good sound bites and could be readily comprehended by the public, whereas Bush's recognition of the many variables was detrimental to good speechmaking and conveyed a wishy-washy image of a man without convictions.[35]

One staff member commented on Reagan's propensity to see political questions in black and white terms, while Bush 'saw the grey, saw the complexity of issues.'[36] Similarly, Kilberg suggested that Bush took the view that it was necessary to:

> . . . lower the rhetoric . . . [while] recognizing the complexity of life today in the domestic arena . . . [Some people] saw things in black and white; [they] thought everything was going to hell in a hand basket and wanted simple solutions to complex problems. [They] wanted people to rhetorically tell them what they wanted to hear and make them feel better. George Bush wasn't going to do that; that was pandering of the sort that he did not believe in.[37]

For conservatives particularly, deregulation was one of the great issues during the Reagan-Bush years and Clayton Yeutter agreed that Bush's more sophisticated position led to communication problems. Like others on the right of his party Reagan favoured deregulation almost without qualification, whereas Bush's position was more complicated. While generally enthusiastic about deregulation, he accepted that: 'there are times when regulation is appropriate.' This 'was a very sound rational reasonable position, but sometimes . . . [such] positions get you into trouble . . . [suggesting a] weak . . . ambivalent . . . or nebulous position.'[38] The fact that Bush had to deal with issues that were less clear-cut than they had been during Reagan's time was conceded by the conservative William Kristol: 'To apply some of these conservative principles to areas like health care and welfare or whatever is more complicated than simply cutting taxes or building SDI. Managing the break up of the Soviet empire, in some respects, is more complicated.'[39]

By 1992 the onset of recession had become the most pressing issue in domestic politics and David Demarest, head of the White House communications operation, gave some insights into the President's agonizing over how that issue should be addressed. Bush apparently believed that the state of the economy faced him with two choices. On the one hand he could engage in 'a lot of empathetic rhetoric', stressing his concern for those who were suffering from economic distress and leaving aside the fact that the economy, despite its present difficulties, was fundamentally sound. Suitably 'empathetic' speeches were compiled, but Bush worried that if he spoke in those terms people would conclude 'that the President thinks that things are really bad' and the effect of this would be 'to drive this economy further into the ground.' On the other hand, if he gave upbeat speeches emphasizing the underlying strength of the economy this would only seem to confirm the claims of the press and the pundits that the President was out of touch. Given these two choices Bush went 'right down the middle. He said: 'I know there are people out of work, I know that people are hurting, I know that there are a lot of families out there that are struggling to make ends meet, but I also know that this economy is not as bad as people are portraying it.' As Demarest pointed out this was 'a muddled message from a communicator . . . and therefore doesn't get through.'[40]

As a communications specialist Demarest also provided an interesting riposte to those on the right of Bush's party who have pilloried the President for his failure to use his office as a bully pulpit. 'Speeches get coverage when they do one of two things,' Demarest noted, 'when they attack or . . . if you announce a new program.' However, 'a new program means new dollars. You are in a budget deficit [and] you are not going to be announcing many new dollar items.' Furthermore, conservatives, in particular, 'wouldn't have wanted us to announce new spending programs. What they wanted us to do was to attack Congress, over and over and over again.' The problem with that strategy was that 'George Bush doesn't believe that gets you where you want to go.' He takes the view that given the low regard in which 'the American people hold politicians these days that will just come across as more noise; as people not being able to solve anything in Washington.'[41]

Finally, it can be said in defence of Bush's failure to make use of the bully pulpit that the circumstances under which he held office were not conducive to the use of rhetoric. Great oratory may be appropriate for presidents who see themselves as agents of change, but that was not Bush's mission. 'We are entering,' Peggy Noonan said, 'an anti-rhetorical age.

There seems to be a rhythm to such things. FDR's great oratory was followed by that of the more prosaic Truman.'[42]Like the latter, Bush came into office with a mandate in domestic affairs to maintain the course set by his predecessor; similarly, on the international scene, it fell to him to preside over a fraught period of change – arguably in neither arena was tub-thumping rhetoric called for.

THE FOURTH ESTATE

If a president is to fulfil his objectives a good relationship with the various forms of media is crucial. Those who work in the print and electronic media influence public opinion by their selection of news and their criticisms of those in government. They also play a major role in setting the public policy agenda. Presidents constantly at odds with the media will face grave difficulty in governing, as many have discovered. Ronald Reagan's innate friendliness, his self-deprecating humour and his easy charm initially served him well in his dealings with journalists. However, he later became increasingly inaccessible to the press. Relatively few press conferences were held and those that did take place were elaborately stage-managed and rather stilted affairs. Otherwise members of the White House press corps found that they were largely restricted to shouting questions at a hearing-impaired President as he made his way to and from a loudly clattering helicopter.

George Bush came into office intent on creating a healthier relationship with the press. As he had done with Congress, he held out the hand of friendship to journalists seeking to draw them into a mutually beneficial relationship with him. The President informed his press secretary Marlin Fitzwater that 'he wanted to get to know a lot of reporters on a personal level, he would like to have a more informal relationship with them.'[43]

In pursuit of this strategy Bush met with journalists far more frequently than 'the Great Communicator' had ever done. In the first year of his presidency he appeared at 32 press conferences as against the 47 that Reagan held over a period of eight years.[44] The new President also met constantly with journalists on an impromptu basis, inviting them to dinner in the White House and watching movies with them.[45] In other words, Bush began his presidency by carefully courting the media, with Fitzwater frankly explaining: 'George Bush recognizes the press's need to get information and its value to him as a leader of the country. You tell the press what you are doing and you tell them why and you hope to do it in such a way that they understand and support'.[46] It is evident that by making himself accessible, drawing journalists into his network of personal relationships and speaking frankly to them, Bush hoped in the early days of his presidency to neutralize potential media hostility and to enhance thereby his governing capability.

At the beginning, Bush's attempts to get the press on his side appeared to pay off; his 'relations with the White House press corps were good.'[47] In the long run however, his strategy proved to be much less successful, with several of his most senior staff ultimately complaining bitterly about his treatment at the hands of the press. When asked in 1993 whether the press had been more antagonistic to Bush than other presidents John Keller said, 'Oh God yes, God yes. I mean, it was so blatant at some points during the [1992] campaign.'[48] C. Boyden Gray, one of those closest to the President, said simply: 'The press, they are adversaries, they are the enemy, so I guess you have to expect them to [act like] the enemy.'[49] David Demarest was more measured, but thought that the press was always harder on Republicans than Democrats.[50] The media were 'extremely harsh on Bush' according to Gail Wilensky, who added that press hostility 'was much worse than for Reagan' mainly because he was suspected of selling out to the right.[51]

GOVERNING WITHOUT TELEVISION

Since the 1950s the place of television in American politics has assumed gargantuan proportions. It has become the primary vehicle of political communication, monopolizing elections, supplanting parties and driving newspapers to the wall. Television executives nowadays are able to assume agenda setting functions and, in the right hands, as Ronald Reagan demonstrated, television can be an awesomely potent instrument of government. George Bush's attempt to govern without television, or at least to downsize its role, has been given less attention than it deserves. The possibility that such an attempt would be made was aired by Peggy Noonan: 'Some president is going to put TV in its place. Someday a smart man or woman will come in and say I don't exist to feed that thing. Get it back in its cage. I have a country to govern. It will be an interesting presidency. (It may be Bush's.)'[52]

After years of complaining of being manipulated by Reagan's image-makers, television reporters in early 1989 discovered that the new administration had a different approach. There was to be no equivalent of Michael Deaver to take charge of Bush's image; there would not be a theme of the week and presidential trips would not be tailored to meet the requirements of nightly television news broadcasts. Lesley Stahl of CBS News recalled that the Reagan White House was obsessive about 'making the evening news. They set their clock by Dan Rather's schedule', whereas the Bush staff had different priorities: 'This White House doesn't care if the President gets on the evening news or not.'[53] This was confirmed six months later by research done by the Center for Media and Public Affairs. In monitoring the television network coverage of the first 100 days of three presidents it was established that there were 336 items about Bush, 790 about Reagan and 906 about Carter.[54]

In part these differences reflect the contrasting agendas that Carter, Reagan and Bush brought to the White House. The first two were outsiders challenging the old regime; they stood for change, for confrontation and conflict, all of which made them eminently newsworthy. Bush's emphasis on continuity, conciliation and compromise on the other hand, did not make for riveting television news items. Beyond that Bush was never able to conceal his distaste for image-making, for packaging, for the public relations aspects of a president's role. His final legislative liaison chief, Nick Calio, spoke of Bush's unwillingness to 'communicate through sound bites or by creating perception. He had a specific aversion to that.'[55]

Bush's resistance to all forms of handling and lack of amenability to direction for image purposes was noted by his Director of Advance John Keller, who observed that if Ronald Reagan was told 'to walk straight and walk left, he would walk straight and walk left, [but] George Bush wouldn't do that. He would not take instruction that literally.' Advance staff who had worked for Reagan would throw out ideas and would have to be diplomatically told, 'That's a great idea but this guy's not Ronald Reagan. He won't do that, you can't tell him to do that. He will look at you like you have got something growing out of your head.' In Keller's view Bush's disdain for image-making was a mark of his integrity; he resisted packaging out of 'not wanting to lie to the American people, not wanting to mislead them . . . he was almost too honest for his own good to be a president, or to be a politician in these times.'[56] On the other hand, while Bush may have been averse to packaging for governing purposes, he showed no such reluctance when campaigning for office in 1988.[57]

The lack of enthusiam for image-making was also a matter of Bush's style. As we have seen, unlike his predecessor, he believed that his primary function was governing rather than salesmanship. As one distinguished Bush watcher, David Hoffman, put it, the President 'views the communications part of his job with more than a little suspicion. It does not seem to him a natural way to advance his goals, which he would rather push with private diplomacy and politicking. He devotes himself to personal relationships and is uncomfortable with the impersonal nature of the mass media.'[58]

It was presumably the President's lack of comfort with television that accounts for the relatively few occasions when he gave prime time addresses to the nation. By late November 1981 Reagan had given seven such addresses while Bush gave only two during the comparable period. One devout Bush loyalist, Bobbie Kilberg, conceded that delivering speeches from the Oval Office for the benefit of television was not his forte: 'He couldn't talk to a box.' He was far better talking off the cuff in situations where he could make eye contact with his audience. Under these conditions he was, according to Kilberg among others, very impressive, whether talking one on one, to an audience of two thousand in an auditorium, or at an informal press conference: 'He could communicate. He was extraordinary in sessions in the Roosevelt Room around the table.' In contrast to his predecessor, 'he could discuss any issue in depth, answering the secondary and tertiary questions, in addition to the primary question, and knowing precisely what he was talking about.'[59]

The difficulties posed by television for Bush went beyond his discomfort with the camera when making speeches. Relatively few Americans would see much of those speeches anyway and their perceptions of the President were heavily dependent on the images he conveyed as he went about his duties, as all modern presidents do, under the constant surveillance of television cameras. Even walking across the White House lawn to a waiting helicopter is a source of images, either favourable or unfavourable. Such occasions were effort-lessly handled by an instinctive, highly trained and experienced performer like Reagan, but Bush was a different matter, lacking the instinct and the training. This was highlighted by Richard Ben Cramer, with some literary licence, in comparing the two men when Bush was Vice President:

> You watch Reagan do something public, anything, like walk across the lawn to his chopper: every movement is perfect. There he goes . . . with his big western walk, shoulders back, hands swinging easy at his sides, the grin raised to perfect angle, then one hand aloft in a long wave . . . and every instant is a perfect picture. It doesn't even matter if they're screaming questions at him. At any one millisecond, as the shutter clicks, the President is perfect: relaxed, balanced, smiling, smooth.
>
> Now watch Bush make for his chopper: hey, he knows that agent! – not part of his detail, but he met him on the last trip to Houston, got a kid who wants to go to West Point, wrote a letter for him. So Bush twists around and waves to the agent – lets him know he's seen him, bends his head back to Bar to tell her, that's Keith, the *agent* remember? 'MR VICE PRESIDENT? MR VICE PRESIDENT?' a photographer is yelling, and it's Fred, the *Life* guy, who was on the trip to Cleveland last week, so while he's talking to Bar, and pointing to the agent, he makes a face to Fred, to let him know he doesn't have to shout. He *knows* him see. Fred's a friend! And there's Steely waiting at the chopper stairs, Jack Steel! Known him for – God! Twenty-five years? And so he's got to goose Steely, let him know he's glad to see him, and he's making a face at Bar about the way the

photographers are shouting, and he twists around to see if the agent has seen him, oughta ask him, but the engine's so loud, and the wind's whipping his hair in his face, which he's screwing up to yell, as he pauses – gotta ask him – trying to balance, crouching in the engine wind, one foot up on the stairs: 'Hey! How's your *son*? . . . YOUR SON? . . .' And at any one moment, as the shutter clicks, Bush looks like a dork.[60]

The inability of Bush to cope with the various demands of television was partly a matter of personality. From his birth he appears to have been bereft of histrionic talent; his sister 'affirms that George has never been an actor in any sense. He plays it straight whatever it is. What you see is what you get.'[61] Others close to Bush have confirmed that he is a rather transparent man, singularly lacking in the guile and the art of dissembling so necessary in both the theatre and politics. His father was a singer of note, but none of that talent surfaced in his second son, who lacked both the ability to project himself and the sense of timing that singing requires.[62]

There were other personality characteristics that placed Bush at a disadvantage on television. As Duffy and Goodgame suggest he was too frenetic and too 'hot' for a medium best suited to cool relaxed performers in the mould of John Kennedy and Ronald Reagan. And while Bush's wondrously fractured syntax may have been charming and unexceptional in private conversation it did nothing to enhance his image on television.[63]

We may reasonably assume that the inadequacies of George Bush when confronted with a television camera were also related to his upbringing. Given the chronic weakness of party in the United States, electoral politics requires candidates willing to sell themselves to the voters as individuals. To use a distinctively American word, those who seek public office are obliged to grandstand, defined in Webster's as 'to act or conduct oneself with a view to impressing onlookers.' However, Bush had been brought up in a household where such behaviour was unacceptable. His mother, according to his wife Barbara, an even more important influence on the future President than his father, taught her children that any form of braggadocio was to be avoided. Dorothy Bush continued with such admonitions even when her children were mature adults, rebuking her son for referring to his war record in a campaign speech.[64] In his autobiography Bush describes an incident where his mother chastised him after reading news reports of his speeches: 'You're talking about yourself too much George.' He explained that the voters were entitled to hear about his qualifications leading his mother to concede reluctantly, 'Well I understand that, but try to restrain yourself.'[65] It seems that by temperament and upbringing, George Bush lacked the exhibitionist tendencies that American politics requires in the television age.

Furthermore, his guardian style of presidential leadership did not make for good television pictures. As we have seen, that style involves a low-key, non-flamboyant approach to leadership which emphasizes behind-the-scenes, problem-solving, rather than high-flown rhetoric. Rhetorical flourishes and guardianship do not sit well together whereas rhetoric or 'leadership as high drama and the sound of trumpets calling' delights media moguls as Reagan and his image-makers knew only too well. Guardians and conservatives moreover are reluctant to inflate public expectations; they are constantly on guard against any tendency to delude the people into thinking that government can do more than is really feasible. Bush's aides took the view that the overexposure of their man on television was likely to give just such an impression. 'It's not honest,' said Fitzwater the White House press secretary. 'The president of the United States cannot solve every problem from warts to AIDS.'[66]

CONCLUSIONS

The strategies of leadership deployed by George Bush were, quite obviously, far removed from those used by Ronald Reagan. Reagan stood outside the system, denouncing its inadequacies and aggressively demanding fundamental change. Such an approach could hardly be expected from Bush given his establishment roots, his contentment, broadly speaking, with things as they were and his long record of service in a range of public offices. Rather than villifying the bureaucracy, castigating the national legislature or striving to manipulate the media, Bush held out his hand, hoping to circumvent such obstacles through personal relationships. This president, furthermore, had neither the aptitude nor the inclination to use his office as a bully pulpit. He declined, in other words, to make use of a strategy that all modern presidents with activist ambitions have deemed essential. Similarly, Bush had a powerful aversion to all forms of image-making and strove to govern without television. The question of how far these strategies were either well-conceived or successful in their application will be addressed more fully elsewhere in this book.

3 Organizing the Presidency

It is self-evident that the presidency is a collective rather than an individual institution. Media pundits and academic commentators may use terminology such as 'the age of Roosevelt', 'the Johnson years' and 'the Reagan era', but these are simplistic labels concealing the truth that every modern president is utterly dependent on a large White House staff. A suitably skilled and effective staff is essential if a president is to stand any chance of carrying his 'choices through that maze of personalities and institutions called the government of the United States'.[1]

In wrestling with the acute problems of governance in the United States presidents not only have staff, they are also given the opportunity to place political appointees into leadership positions in the executive branch. However, the loyalty of such appointees to the president and his agenda is by no means guaranteed. From Cabinet members on down, political appointees are subject to conflicting pressures. They are brought within the ambit of career civil servants, they are influenced by pressure groups and they may be intimidated by congressional committees. Political appointees, in other words, cannot be relied upon to do the president's bidding. While appointed by him they are not answerable to him alone and there is always a danger that they will 'go native' in the department to which they are assigned.[2]

Presidential staff, while not immune to the possibility of divided loyalties, are less vulnerable to external pressures and are, accordingly, less likely to pursue agendas other than the president's. On the other hand, the fact that virtually all presidential staff are hired and fired at the discretion of the chief executive alone has consequences for democracy. Holding those who make policy acccountable to the people is one of the hallmarks of a democratic polity, whereas the proximity of White House staff to the president and his dependence on them creates a situation where vast power may reside in the hands of non-elected officials.

These concerns were brought into sharp relief by the Watergate crisis when the American public became aware of the marginalization of Richard Nixon's Cabinet and the major roles assumed by presidential aides such as H.R. Haldeman and John Ehrlichman, senior White House staff who, by definition, were subject neither to election nor to Senate confirmation, and were answerable only to the President.

THE CABINET

The election of Jimmy Carter in 1976 was partly attributable to Watergate and at the beginning of his term the new President insisted, with typical hyperbole, that 'there will never be an instance while I am President when the members of the White House staff dominate or act in a superior position to the members of our Cabinet.'[3] As John Hart has shown, however, Carter failed to live up to his promise, with the Cabinet in his Administration proving to be no less prone to domination by White House staff than it had been in previous presidencies.[4]

The relegation of the Cabinet to a secondary role in policy-making has long been a feature of the American national government. Franklin Roosevelt made scant use of his Cabinet and the same can be said of Truman, Kennedy and Johnson. Eisenhower's formalistic approach to governance led him to make more use of Cabinet meetings, yet even he did not come remotely close to the cabinet government model associated with parliamentary systems. Whilst Cabinet meetings were held regularly, Eisenhower was not disposed to place the Cabinet at the forefront of policy-making; it 'served more as a sounding board than as a policy-considering body.'[5] The possibility of making a reality of cabinet government was floated during the Reagan transition, but when faced with the realities of government his Administration proved to be 'one of the most staff directed and centralized presidencies of the modern era.'[6] Under Reagan the full Cabinet met rarely and delegated extensively to a system of cabinet councils while the really important policy decisions were taken within the White House.

George Bush's long experience in government may account for his showing little inclination to overstate the possibilities

of cabinet government when running for the presidency in
1988.[7] During his Administration meetings of the Cabinet
took place 'about once every four to six weeks' and these
were, according to David Bates, the first Cabinet Secretary,
briefing sessions rather than policy-making exercises.[8] This was
confirmed by Bates' successor Edie Holiday: 'For the most
part [Cabinet meetings] were opportunities for information
exchange and not working policy development meetings. They
were opportunities for the President to hear what was on the
mind of the Cabinet . . . and for the Cabinet to share key
issues that they were working on.' At times of crisis, such as
the budget imbroglio of 1990 and the Gulf War, Cabinet
meetings assumed a somewhat greater importance. Thus
during the War, 'there were still information exchange meetings, but it was a time of war and so there was a very active
and aggressive interest on the President's part in having
members of his Cabinet understand what [the Administration]
was trying to do and what was happening [while also providing
them] with an opportunity for input.'[9] Vice President Quayle
describes Bush Cabinet meetings as 'stilted, boring affairs.
Instead of creative ferment and the clash of ideas, there were
droning reports – Carla Hills would give one about trade, and
then Baker would give one, and Darman another, and so on.
The truth is, Cabinet meetings are an anachronism.'[10]

Following the precedent set by the previous administration
cabinet councils for domestic policy were established parallel
to the statutorily required National Security Council. An
Economic Policy Council was set up, chaired in the President's
absence by the Secretary of the Treasury, while the Attorney
General became chairman of the Domestic Policy Council.
These councils facilitated 'broad inter-agency policy-making'
with the Domestic Policy Council, for instance, providing a
forum for the development of a drugs strategy, an issue of
concern not only to the Office of National Drug Control
Policy, but also to the Department of Health and Human
Services, the Department of Justice, the Treasury and the
State Department. The Clean Air Act, one of Bush's most
important legislative accomplishments, went through the
Domestic Policy Council, and the Economic Policy Council
'resolved all trade matters and trade policy decisions for recommendation to the President.'[11]

While these cabinet councils were undoubtedly valuable arenas for the consideration of complicated policy detail, there is little reason to suppose that the really momentous issues of policy were dealt with at that level. One observer noted that the Bush White House regularly bypassed 'the cabinet council system in resolving key issues', while another, Burt Solomon, reported that a senior Bush aide had said that 'the most important issues are "rarely" entrusted to Cabinet councils.'[12]

It is clear that the workings of the Bush Administration, like almost all others, were far removed from cabinet government; Cabinet meetings were infrequent and were usually used for briefing and information exchange purposes. Cabinet councils played a part, but did not make the decisions on the major policy questions. Nevertheless, there is a sense in which George Bush can be said to have 'made more effective use of his Cabinet than had most of his recent predecessors.'[13] While the Cabinet as a collectivity may have meant little, some individual members in the early months were believed to carry weight to an unusual degree.[14]

In May 1989 concern among senior presidential staff at Cabinet members announcing major decisions without informing the White House began appearing in the press. One such incident was the announcement by Veteran Affairs Secretary, Edward Derwinski, that his department would not be appealing against a federal judge's ruling on Agent Orange, the controversial defoliant used in Vietnam. Without consulting the President, Derwinski thereby reversed a decade of government policy on the issue. In a newspaper article discussing this affair an Administration official was quoted as remarking that the White House was 'reactive to its own Cabinet members. Bush's own style is kind of reactive not to lay down priorities for these guys. The President wants leadership to come from the Cabinet. He regards White House staff as facilitating information, not really shaping policy. So he's letting the Cabinet do their own thing.' Major players in the Cabinet were identified as James Baker, Secretary of State; Jack Kemp, Secretary of Housing and Urban Development; Defense Secretary, Richard Cheney; Secretary of Commerce, Robert Mosbacher; and Transportation Secretary, Samuel Skinner. Nicholas Brady, Secretary of the Treasury, was characterized as 'unassertive' but his close friendship with the President 'provides him with special access.'[15]

David Hoffman and Ann Devroy of the *Washington Post* wrote in a similar vein a few months later, observing 'For now, Bush is not inclined to impose discipline on his brood, associates say. Particularly in domestic policy, Cabinet members say they feel Bush has given them wide latitude, as long as they do not stray from his overall goals.'[16] The 'For now' at the beginning of this quotation was particularly apt for by 1990, power, in domestic policy, was shifting sharply away from the Cabinet and becoming narrowly concentrated in the hands of the most senior of senior White House staff, most notably John Sununu, the Chief of Staff, and Richard Darman, the Director of the Office of Management and Budget. It was inevitable that such movement would occur as Stephen Hess explained a few months into the Bush Presidency: 'Whatever power Bush's Cabinet wields now is the most it is likely to get. For during any Administration's course, White House impatience with bureaucratic inertia and Secretaries' tendency to reflect their agencies outlook ensures that power will "drift" into the White House. At best, Bush has only slowed the inevitable.'[17]

The extent to which this shift occurred was, however, limited somewhat by George Bush's leadership style. As we have seen, an essential feature of Bush's approach to leadership was his emphasis on personal relationships and his Cabinet was made up almost entirely of people whom the President knew well personally – it was indeed 'A Gathering of Friends.'[18] Senior members of the Cabinet included longstanding and close friends such as James Baker, Nicholas Brady and Robert Mosbacher. Others had served alongside Bush in previous administrations. Carla Hills, who became US Trade Representative, had been Secretary of Housing and Urban Development in the Ford Administration. Richard Thornburgh, the Attorney General, was first appointed to the post by President Reagan. Similarly, William Webster had been Director of the FBI and Director of the Central Intelligence Agency in the Reagan Administration before reappointment to the latter position by Bush. Elizabeth Dole, the Secretary of Labor, had been a senior member of Reagan's White House staff before becoming his Secretary of Transportation. Bush's first Secretary of Agriculture, Clayton Yeutter, had served in the Nixon and Ford Administrations and had been a Cabinet officer as US Trade Representative during Reagan's second term. Richard Darman had been an Assistant to President Reagan and then Deputy Secretary at the Department of the Treasury. Richard Cheney, Secretary of Defense, had been Ford's Chief of Staff. Edward Derwinski held junior office in the Reagan Administration and had been in the US House of Representatives when Bush was a congressman.

Given the close personal ties between Bush and his Cabinet and his method of operating there was little chance of his allowing White House staff to wall him off from cabinet secretaries in the way that H.R. Haldeman and Donald Regan had done with regard to Richard Nixon and Ronald Reagan. This was, after all, the man who almost made a fetish of keeping in touch with friends and acquaintances; as one of his senior staff remarked, 'Bush saw everybody he wanted to see. He was not an isolatable [*sic*] figure.'[19] Edie Holiday, who became Cabinet Secretary in June 1990, explained in some detail the mechanisms whereby Bush maintained contact with members of his Cabinet. Ms Holiday and her staff acted as a two-way conduit between Bush and the executive agencies. They looked after the President's interests by keeping abreast of initiatives and 'big surprises' emanating from government departments while also acting as an advocate for Cabinet officers in the White House. The latter need arose 'when their policies were being discussed or heard, or if they wanted to come and see the President.' Alternatively, 'if they thought something was happening against their wishes', it was the Cabinet Secretary's duty to say, 'no you can't do this without talking to Secretary X because he or she has a very real interest in this issue . . . [We were] eyes and ears for the Cabinet in the White House and eyes and ears for the President in the Cabinet.'[20]

As in all administrations Cabinet members from time to time felt cut off from the President and became convinced 'that some decision had been made where the President had been misled or had not heard their side of the story.' Nevertheless, Ms Holiday insisted, 'our President was accessible to any Cabinet member on any issue within a certain time . . . there were times when he couldn't get to a Cabinet member because of pressing business, but we maintained channels of communication.' There was nothing to prevent a Cabinet officer from 'picking up the phone and calling the President, or the President picking up the phone and calling the Cabinet members . . . [this was done] quite frequently; the President encouraged that.' It was also possible for Cabinet members to send written communications to the President on Fridays with the understanding that they would be transmitted directly to him rather than being filtered through the White House staffing process. In short, according to his Cabinet Secretary, President Bush 'worked very hard to maintain separate channels of communication with his Cabinet'.[21]

For all that, as will become apparent later, there is little question but that Cabinet members took second place to White House staff principals when major policy decisions were being made, most notably in domestic policy. Such tendencies may cause alarm among academic purists, but they were eminently justifiable according to Andrew Card who served both in the White House and the Cabinet – for the first three years of the Bush Administration he was Deputy Chief of Staff and then became Secretary of Transportation. Card had no doubt that it was:

> . . . up to the White House to give direction to Cabinet agencies. There were Cabinet members who were not able to pursue their own agenda, but it wasn't their job to pursue their own agenda, it was to pursue President Bush's agenda . . . The White House role in directing the Cabinet is entirely appropriate; the Cabinet is not a management structure, it is a body designed to discuss policy priorities and then manage the bureaucracy.[22]

Vigorous support for Card's position was provided by James Pinkerton, Deputy Assistant to the President for Policy Planning, an 'ideas man' or the closest in the Bush White House to an intellectual in residence. Pinkerton was scornful of anything like cabinet government for the United States. Cabinet members, he insisted:

> . . . are the slaves of their own constituencies . . . They are seemingly incapable of producing any policy that doesn't reflect the institutional bias of their department. So to talk about cabinet government means you are talking about the

education department doing what the education lobby wants it to do; the same with agriculture and so on down the list. That's not leadership, that's some sort of academic senate . . . where everybody gasses away and nothing happens.

Pulling major decisions into the White House was essential in Pinkerton's view; he also thought the problem of account-ability could be taken care of by getting rid of the president at the next election if his White House dominated adminis-tration should be found wanting.[23]

THE WHITE HOUSE OFFICE

According to the *US Government Manual*:

> The White House Office serves the President in the perfor-mance of the many activities incident to his immediate office. The staff of the President facilitates and maintains communication with the Congress, the individual members of Congress, the heads of executive agencies, the press and other information media, and the general public. The various Assistants to the President are personal aides and assist the President in such matters as he may direct.[24]

The White House Office is the 'command centre' of the modern presidency; it exists to advance the president's agenda and it is here where major policies are formulated.[25] In the latter regard, Nicholas Calio and James Cicconi echoed the sentiments expressed above by Andrew Card and James Pinkerton. For example, Calio indicated that while policy on relatively minor matters might be formulated at the depart-mental level the really important decisions were made in the White House. 'Policy making on marine mammals might go on at the Commerce Department . . . but policy making on tax and budget matters is generally pulled within the White House. The Treasury Department has a major role and the Office of Management and Budget does, but the work center and the point of entry is generally at the White House.'[26]

James Cicconi saw the dominance of White House staff in the policy-making process as an inevitable outcome of the emer-gence of the modern presidency: 'It was part of the evolution of the presidency into an institution which the American people looked to more, [asking it] to provide leadership in a variety of areas that were traditionally left more to cabinet departments . . . There is no doubt that there is a lot of involvement and even a degree of interference by policy people in the White House with what the agencies do.' This could be justified, Cicconi argued, on three grounds: first, 'there was a tendency for agencies to become the captives of the bureaucracy;' second, 'for any major initiative to succeed the involvement of the President and the White House was vitally important,' and third, 'virtually all major policy initiatives these days had inter-agency ramifications [whereas this was not] necessarily true 20 or 30 years ago.'[27]

As these and other witnesses have confirmed cabinet government in the United States is unworkable and presidents are greatly dependent on the assistance provided by their closest aides. 'It is the White House staff on whom modern presidents rely to coordinate the development of their important policies, to control the flow of sensitive information, to keep a close watch on Cabinet responses and to manage crisis actions.'[28] In broad outlines the nature of the White House staff operation remains the same from one presidency to another, but differences of emphasis and structure occur reflecting the contrasting personalities and leadership styles of different chief executives.

There were 23 units in the Bush White House Office ranging from the Office of the Chief of Staff to the Office of the First Lady. [29] The research for this book was based on interviews with a number of those responsible for these various operations. Included amongst these were the offices of the Chief of Staff, the Staff Secretary, National Security Affairs, the President's Counsel, Communications, Public Liaison, Legislative Affairs, Management and Administration, Economic and Domestic policy, National Service, Advance, Appointments and Scheduling, Political Affairs, the Cabinet Secretary and Presidential Personnel. The functions of several of these units have already been touched upon and this will occur again in subsequent chapters. For instance, it will become apparent later that the President's Counsel was an especially significant office in the Bush White House. The Office of National Service was particularly important to Bush and its functions are discussed in Chapter 4. Brent Scowcroft, the Assistant for

National Security Affairs, was, unquestionably, a major player in the Bush White House and his role is discussed in Chapters 7 and 8. In the present chapter I will focus initially on Bush's first Chief of Staff before some further consideration of legislative liaison. I will also discuss Communications and Public Liaison and conclude with the tenure of Samuel Skinner as Bush's second Chief of Staff.

CHIEF OF STAFF I – JOHN SUNUNU

John Sununu, Bush's Chief of Staff for the first three years of his presidency, has been heavily criticized by both journalists and academics. According to *The Economist*: 'Mr Sununu's time as George Bush's tyrannical chief of staff was . . . disastrous,' while Bert Rockman, a senior presidential scholar, when asked to compare Sununu with predecessors in the post said:'I think he is one of the worst. He is clumsy as hell and has no political instinct or sense. He is tied to the fringe of the Republican Party and has kept Bush focused on that fringe while the economy and other issues have brought the president into trouble with the electorate.'[30]

In some respects Sununu was an unlikely candidate for the Chief of Staff position. Bush tended to surround himself with people much like himself, whereas Sununu was clearly not in that category. A Lebanese-Greek American, born in Cuba, and a former professor of engineering, Sununu had made his political reputation as an abrasive Governor of New Hampshire. The link with Bush dated back to the 1988 primary season when the Vice President was beaten into third place in the Iowa caucuses and looked likely to lose in New Hampshire. In desperation, Bush turned to Sununu who commanded an effective state organization and was able to provide the advice and direction needed for Bush to win the New Hampshire primary convincingly. As a reward for these efforts, crucial to Bush's elevation to the White House, Sununu was appointed Chief of Staff.[31]

Some support for the generally negative perceptions of Sununu's tenure in the post has been provided by middle level staff. Kristin Taylor, Director of Media Relations, was bemused by the Chief of Staff's use of obscene language, his apparently constant state of rage and his gratuitous alienation of presidential friend and foe alike. As she saw it, in the end, 'what was originally conceived to be the perfect political balance – the good cop/bad cop dynamic duo of George Bush and John Sununu – actually turned out to be much too much bad, not quite enough of the good.'[32] Charles Kolb, who from March 1990 was Deputy Assistant to the President for Domestic Policy, remarks on Sununu's intolerance of opposition from any quarter, whether in the White House itself, the media or Congress. The Chief of Staff had a 'penchant for belittling those who disagreed with him' and his domineering style stood as an obstacle to policy innovation. 'People kept their mouths shut to avoid being yelled at.' John Keller avoided Sununu wherever possible, declining to expose himself to being screamed at: 'Sununu was a great screamer. He'd have these tantrums that were just ludicrous.'[33]

Some of Sununu's more senior White House colleagues took a more charitable view of his conduct. C. Boyden Gray, the President's Counsel and close friend, was a major figure in the White House and something of a Sununu rival who clashed with him on occasion. Nevertheless, Gray was adamant, 'I had a very good relationship with Sununu. You always got into arguments with him because he was an intellect of the highest order. He knew what he thought and he knew what he was doing and when you got into arguments with him they were fierce . . . but he never bore any grudges and if he got mad or impatient with your point of view it would last for 30 seconds and then be gone.'[34]

Andrew Card, the Deputy Chief of Staff, was an old hand who had served in the Reagan White House and observed several chiefs of staff in action. In his view Sununu was 'outstanding' in the role, second only to James Baker. He combined high intelligence with good political sense, brought necessary discipline to the White House and the Cabinet while complementing the President's management style. 'He was extremely valuable in forming a constructive relationship with Congress on the Clean Air Act and the Americans with Disabilities Act, two of the premier issues in the Bush Administration.' Sununu's command of the detail of legislation was exceptional and he 'was very tough in driving policy from concept to reality'. It was only when his personal problems intruded that his value to the President was lost.[35]

The perspective of one of those principally responsible for legislative liaison was provided by Nicholas Calio. Personally, he got on 'extremely well' with Sununu and was impressed by his accessibility to people like himself. Calio acknowledged that the Chief of Staff's abrasive style sometimes made for difficulties in congressional relations, but added,: 'When he got involved in an issue he would come up [to Capitol Hill] and deal with the members and talk to the members and do what had to be done. Overall he had a productive relationship with Congress.'[36]

The first Staff Secretary, James Cicconi, was full of praise for Sununu's leadership in the early part of the Bush presidency. During that period the White House was a 'fairly collegial place [which] functioned pretty well. A smooth running staff operation was put in place and the President's major priorities from the campaign were dealt with.' The Chief of Staff could be abrasive, but he also had a sense of humour and was endearingly unpretentious. All this seemed to change however, with the abortive budget agreement of 1990. From then on Sununu and his collaborator in the budget negotiations, Richard Darman, the Director of OMB, became excessively 'defensive and critical of others. This criticism was aired openly, particularly by Darman, and as a result senior staff meetings became rather awkward affairs'.[37]

A number of those who observed Sununu at close range obviously do not altogether confirm the intensely negative impressions of his stewardship that have appeared in the press and the academic literature. While by no means uncritical, these witnesses recognize that there were advantages to the Chief of Staff's modus operandi and see that some of the charges made against him are less than fully sustainable.

One of the complaints against Sununu was that he made himself a gatekeeper in the Bush White House comparable to Donald Regan, Reagan's second Chief of Staff, who came close to controlling all forms of access to the President.[38] There was, however, little chance of this happening to the same extent given Bush's hands-on approach and his emphasis on personal relationships. As I noted earlier, it was not easy to isolate Bush; it was an essential part of his nature to keep channels open and active and he communicated with whoever he chose, whenever he was inclined to do so.[39] Nevertheless by 1990 complaints began surfacing in the press from Republican leaders about the President becoming 'too isolated and too dependent on his chief of staff'.[40]

The conservative Republican, Representative Vin Weber of Minnesota, had remarked on this tendency earlier in the year. He argued that Sununu 'really does dominate the decision-making process at the White House totally.' In what is obviously a reference to the pre-Regan, Reagan White House, Weber said that in the previous administration:

> You'd ask, 'how do I influence the decision on this issue?' and it would be 'you need Jim Baker,' and on issue X, it would be 'see if you can get his friend Ed Meese to talk to the President," or on something else, it would be, "enlist Cap Weinberger." When you ask how to influence decision-making in the Bush White House, it's always the same answer: Sununu.'[41]

Weber was concerned with decision-making rather than access and presumably he had domestic policy particularly in mind. The dominance of Sununu in that arena was made possible by the President's well known lack of interest in domestic matters. There was never any chance of Bush being isolated and allowing anyone else to take control of the making of foreign and national security policy, whereas his conservative, guardian posture with regard to domestic affairs created a vacuum that Sununu, and his ally Darman, moved to fill.

As Bush himself recognized, his style of leadership required a hard-nosed chief of staff.[42] If the President was to be conciliatory and accommodating towards powerful adversaries such as Congress, the media and interest groups, he needed someone to run the White House who would be tough, uncompromising and even brutal on occasion. A head man was wanted who would bring order to a large staff and would ensure that decisions were made. This person would give direction to the Administration and would fulfil the vital function of making certain that White House officials and Cabinet members were working for the fulfilment of the President's agenda rather than some other order of priorities.

It made good tactical sense for Bush to appoint someone like Sununu to head his staff for, as Andrew Card saw, he complemented the President's more genteel, kinder, gentler approach.[43] It made it possible for Bush to make agreeable statesmanlike noises on key issues, confident that whatever he said would be offset by his belligerent Chief of Staff. One press commentator compared Bush and Sununu to a wrestling team where one played off against the other: 'Gentleman George and Snarlin' Sununu. Bush may call himself the "environmental President" and the "education President," but he has Sununu to make sure this rhetoric stays relatively cheap.'[44]

Sununu was also valuable to Bush as a 'lightning rod', in that he deflected odium for unpopular decisions that would otherwise fall on the President and undermine his standing with the public.[45] It is also particularly useful for conservative, guardian presidents such as Eisenhower and Bush, instinctively sceptical of what can be achieved by passing laws or spending public money, to have on their staff prominent naysayers, senior aides who can help them in resisting populist pressures – Sherman Adams performed that function for Eisenhower and Sununu recognized that he was expected to do much the same for Bush: 'I know it means I'm going to be perceived as the guy who has to say no, and the president as the guy who . . . might say yes. There hasn't been any planning in the roles; it's just something I understood when I took the job – that end of the stick would be mine.'[46]

Another role assumed by Sununu was that of the link between the Administration and conservative Republicans. Those on the right of the party had longstanding doubts about the President's conservative credentials and for a while at least Sununu appeared to provide some reassurance to an essential element of the coalition that had elected Bush. As a devout Catholic he was in a position to help keep the President in line on abortion and he was also influential on scientific and technological matters. Some of Sununu's colleagues doubted the strength of his conservative convictions beyond his abhorrence of abortion, but in any case his credibility with the right was eventually to be badly eroded by the 1990 budget deal.[47]

The ultimate *raison d'être* of a president's chief of staff is to assist the chief executive in the infinitely problematical endeavour of fulfilling his agenda and there is plenty of evidence that Sununu took that responsibility very seriously indeed. Strenuously denying that he did anything that did not meet with the President's approval the Chief of Staff said:

> There is a fundamental premise that everyone in this city minimizes and that is I'm no freelancer. I meet with the president dozens of times during the day . . . [he] knows I'm following his agenda. What other people may look at is the result not being what they would have liked [but] the aspect of our relationship that is critical is that I know enough about the president to do exactly what he wants done. Exactly what he wants done.[48]

Confirmation of Sununu's unstinting devotion to Bush's objectives was offered by Ed Rogers, his Executive Assistant. He observed that Sununu is a man who approaches nothing half heartedly; he becomes 'totally consumed and absorbed' by what he becomes involved with. Accordingly, in the White House, he became 'a true Bush believer, a Bush zealot . . . we used to say around the White House, if Bush had a runny nose, Sununu had double pneumonia. If Bush kind of grimaced and didn't want to see somebody, Sununu would make them an enemy and make them an enemy for the rest of his life!'[49] Similarly James Pinkerton believed the Chief of Staff was obsessively dedicated to the cause of serving Bush and willing to use for that purpose his 'own self as the battering ram against all comers'.[50]

The Chief of Staff not only rigorously pursued the President's agenda, he also ran the White House in a manner that faithfully reflected the reactive, non-ideological, guardianship style of the President. As one former staffer commented: 'This is a White House consumed with day-to-day tactics, much like the president is. At the morning staff meetings, all you heard is what's up, what's going on, what do we have to react to today. It's not how do we want to approach the next week, the next several weeks.'[51] The absence of a grand plan, or of weekly sub-themes in the manner of the Reagan White House, was, of course, consistent with the President's preferences. At one stage Rogers complained to the Chief of Staff about the Administration's lack of an overall strategy – dealing with everything on an ad hoc basis, he said, 'is killing us.' Sununu was clearly unmoved. 'Look, you want a strategy, my strategy is to maintain maximum flexibility so that I can take advantage of opportunities as they arise.'[52] This was, of course, the very essence of the style adopted by George Bush.

As we have seen, Sununu's aggressive, abrasive style had value as a counter to the President's more congenial posture. Some of those close to Bush doubted whether his kid glove approach in dealing with a deeply partisan Congress was appropriate.[53] Arguably, a legislature firmly under the control of the opposition warranted grim resolution and tough talking from the Chief of Staff. Moreover, interest groups and the media are enormously potent forces in American politics that need to be vigorously resisted if the chief executive is to keep control of the policy process. Having said that, Sununu undoubtedly overplayed his hand on innumerable occasions, arrogantly and sometimes brutally laying into friend and foe in a manner often damaging to the cause he was so dedicated to, the advancement of the President's agenda.

Notwithstanding Calio's defence discussed above and the problems of divided government, there is little doubt that Sununu's extravagant belligerence towards Congress was often a serious liability. Every president has to work with Congress and there is little to be gained from treating the legislature with undiluted contempt. Democratic Senator Timothy Wirth of Colorado was offended by the Chief of Staff's 'condescending attitude' towards many of those on Capitol Hill. 'He has no respect for the intellectual capacity of any of us. He comes up here with that kind of attitude, and our attitude is, who elected you? He in no way acknowledges that there are smart people in Congress too.'[54]

During the 1990 budget negotiations with congressional leaders, Sununu and his ally Richard Darman outraged legislators by their boorishness and studied rudeness. Finally, the very senior Democratic Senator Robert Byrd of West Virginia could stand it no longer and said:

> I have had 30 years in the US Senate, and I have participated in many such summits and I have never in my life observed such outrageous conduct as that displayed by the representatives of the President of the United States. Your conduct is arrogant. It is rude. It is intolerant. I know the President of the United States. I respect him, and I know

that if he knew of your outrageous conduct in these meetings that he would not tolerate it.[55]

Byrd, like Wirth, was a Democrat, but Sununu was hardly
any less savage in his dealings with leading Republicans in
Congress. In the early months of the Bush Administration it
was reported in the press that Sununu had taken exception
to comments made by Representative Robert Michel of Illinois,
the House Republican leader and had 'dressed Mr Michel
down in terms that many in the House found insulting.'[56]
Representative Mickey Edwards of Oklahoma, the Chairman
of the House Republican Policy Committee found himself in
a telephone shouting match with the Chief of Staff over presidential prerogatives in foreign policy. Edwards reported that
Sununu had hung up on him three times as he tried to enlighten
him on the contents of the bill in question.[57] After the
infamous 1990 budget deal was made public Republican
Senator Trent Lott of Mississippi made some critical comments
on television; when the Chief of Staff was asked to react to
Lott's remarks he said: 'Senator Lott has become an insignificant figure in this process.' Subsequently, Lott made clear his
anger at the calculated insult while drawing attention to the
foolishness of Sununu's behaviour given his position as the
spokesman for a minority president. 'I'm going to be here for
sure for four years and two months and maybe longer. There
are only 45 Republicans over here, and one day they are
going to need my vote.' When asked about the possibility of
reconciliation Lott said: 'He is going to have to crawl over
here and beg for it . . . He just stuck the wrong pig.'[58]

The leaders of powerful interest groups normally regarded
as the natural allies of Republican presidents were also not
immune to humiliating tongue lashings from President Bush's
principal aide. Richard Lesher, the President of the US
Chambers of Commerce, aroused Sununu's wrath by having
the temerity to support Senator Daniel Moynihan's proposal
to cut the payroll tax for Social Security. Contacting Lesher
by phone, Sununu indicated his displeasure by announcing
'I'm going to chain-saw your balls off.'[59] Similarly, in 1991,
Bobbie Kilberg made arrangements for a White House meeting
with leaders of the American Medical Association to discuss
the highly sensitive health care issue. Sununu believed the

AMA had purposely misled the White House about its position and then made public statements detrimental to the Administration's stance. At the meeting the Chief of Staff's behaviour was so abusive and insulting as to cause consternation among his own staff. More importantly, it provoked bitter resentment in the AMA delegation, and as a result, Kilberg recalled, 'for months they wouldn't work publicly with any of us.' The AMA leaders also speedily made sure that this unseemly verbal brawl received maximum publicity. 'It was all over the tabloids in five minutes. They left and went out to the steps where the press were waiting and proceeded to say that Sununu had insulted them and that they were leaving.'[60]

As Bush's Chief of Staff, John Sununu was not the unmitigated disaster often suggested, but he was, at best, a mixed blessing. The President needed a tough-minded zealot in the White House to complement his own more decorous style. The good cop/bad cop routine had its uses, as did the Sununu link with the right. Sununu clearly did possess considerable administrative skill; with him at the helm the White House did function reasonably efficiently – decisions were made and the President's agenda, such as it was, was broadly implemented. Nevertheless, for all the Chief of Staff's famous intellect and hard-headedness, he could also be remarkably naive.

One of the keenest and closest observers of Sununu, Ed Rogers, commented on his inability to understand the lasting damage caused by his abrasive behaviour. He seemed to think 'that he could insult somebody and humiliate them at 2 o'clock, share a friendly encounter with them at 4 and everything would be OK.' As we have seen, this may have worked with some equally formidable figures such a C.Boyden Gray, but it was ill-advised as a general strategy. Rogers also found it strange that, unlike most people, Sununu was prone to be much harsher in his treatment of total strangers than he was in dealing with those close to him. 'A freshman congressman would come in, or someone he'd never met before representing the AMA or whatever and he would soak them, really chewing them out from the time they set foot in the office . . . strangers didn't get that sort of deferential, formal, listening, smiling and nodding that goes on here in Washington.'

Another of Rogers' shrewd observations may help to explain

the enigma of John Sununu – an exceptionally intelligent and able politician who seemed unable to grasp how counter productive gratuitous insults and crass behaviour could be. 'Sununu felt no pain,' Rogers explained. 'Pain is a helpful mechanism in that it lets you know that you are involved in behaviour that is bad for you. You put your hand on the stove and it burns you and you know you should move your hand, or else your hand will be consumed by fire . . . He felt no pain and you have to, to some degree, to be a good chief of staff.'[61] This is to suggest that Sununu lacked basic sensitivity: that he was insensitive to the outrage and resentment that he gener- ated and oblivious to the harm that it could do to him and the man that he served. In the early part of Bush's presidency this mattered less, but when the going got rough in 1991 with the onset of recession and the steep decline in the President's popularity, the adverse consequences of Sununu's behaviour became more apparent. It was now, with the 1992 election rapidly bearing down on him, that the President needed allies. He needed the support of the sort of people in Congress, the media and the interest groups that Sununu so delighted in offending. It was George Bush's increasing awareness of this, plus the concerns about Sununu abusing his public office for private purposes, that led finally to his departure from the White House.[62]

After the Chief of Staff, Assistants to the President are the principal members of his staff and it is not without significance that the Bush Administration began with 13 assistants compared with the 22 in the last year of Reagan's presidency and 20 in the first year of Clinton's. As an unambitious, conservative, guardian president with a limited agenda, an aversion to image- making and a distaste for florid speech- making, Bush had less need of an extensive staff. In particular, it is not surprising that the legislative liaison and communications operations in his White House were smaller and less highly regarded than they had been in the Reagan years.

LEGISLATIVE LIAISON

Frederick McClure, Bush's first Assistant for Legislative Affairs, was a low-profile, former Senate aide with a substantially smaller, less-well paid and inexperienced staff when compared to Reagan's.[63] Furthermore, it became clear at an early stage that legislative liaison was firmly under the control of John Sununu, the Chief of Staff, who assumed the chairmanship of a legislative strategy group within the White House.[64]

Members of Congress soon became convinced that McClure was 'out of the loop', that he was not privy to decision-making at the highest level and that he was not invested with the authority to speak on the President's behalf.[65] The weakness of the congressional relations section of the White House Office became glaringly apparent during the abortive and very damaging struggle to secure the nomination of former Senator John Tower of Texas as Secretary of Defense. The rejection of the Tower nomination on the floor of the Senate by a vote of 47–53 was only the ninth such rejection of a Cabinet nominee and the first since 1959.[66]

Evidence of the subordination of legislative liaison to the Chief of Staff (and on this occasion to the Director of the Office of Management and Budget) was provided during the budget crisis of 1990. Nicholas Calio, at that point Deputy Assistant to the President for Legislative Affairs in the House, had a special responsibility for tax issues. However, the first he knew of the President's crucial abandonment of his 'no new taxes' pledge was when he was faxed a copy of the five-line statement already released by Marlin Fitzwater, the Press Secretary. As Calio ruefully observed, Bush's reneging on his most important election promise caused uproar among House Republicans and drastically 'undermined party unity'. The lack of any forewarning to legislative liaison staff made their job immeasurably more difficult. 'We had no time to warn anybody on the Hill. [An essential requirement in] legislative affairs because it can ease whatever kind of obstacles are created later.'[67]

Staff responsible for maintaining good congressional relations might have also regretted the statement that Sununu made on 9 November 1990 to a group of conservatives. Rather than conceding that the budget deal was a disaster for the Administration the Chief of Staff claimed that it was a triumph that provided for restrictions on future spending and would, therefore, act as a restraint on those who lusted after big government. As Sununu saw it, the President would now be able to use his veto more, focusing on 'preventing things from taking place. Let me suggest the following,' he went on. 'There's not another single piece of legislation that needs to be passed in the next two years for this president. In fact, if Congress wants to come together, adjourn, and leave it's all right with us. We don't need them.'[68]

At first sight this was a distinctly imprudent statement, demoralizing to legislative liaison staff and gifting valuable ammunition to the President's political enemies. Indeed, in the coming months, the liberal media and Democratic spokesmen repeatedly seized on Sununu's remark as evidence of the Administration's barren and callous approach to the recession and other problems. It should be remembered, however, that Sununu spoke for a guardian president; for a chief executive who had no time for the activist, reforming model so beloved of liberal Democrats and political scientists. As we saw in Chapter 1, Bush had always doubted the efficacy of government action as a means for curing social ills and regularly invoked the physician's maxim of 'do no harm' as a first rule for public policy-makers.[69]

Nicholas Calio, who eventually replaced McClure as Bush's overall chief of legislative liaison, understood and agreed with the President's reasoning:

> There were many things, in our view, that Congress involved itself in, that government involved itself in, that really [they] shouldn't – micro-managing markets, micro-managing foreign policy. And a lot of the stuff Congress did wasn't any good. Our job was to stop things getting done; it was more defensive than offensive . . . Congress is constantly casting around for legislation on all sorts of issues; it doesn't always help, it doesn't always make things better, in many cases it makes things worse.[70]

Calio's guardian president boss could hardly have expressed his position more clearly himself.

David Demarest, Assistant to the President for Communications, put a slightly different gloss on Sununu's infamous remark. In indicating that it would be just fine with the Administration if Congress left immediately and passed no legislation for the next two years Sununu was, according to Demarest, saying:

The answers to America's problems are not in Congress . . . the answers are in the communities, the answers are in the states, the answers are in your own backyard. When you ask John Q. Public what is going to rebuild his neighborhood, or what's going to get drugs out of his school, they are going to say the family, the schools, their teachers, their ministers, their churches. Congress is going to be about fiftieth on the list.[71]

As Demarest saw all too clearly, Sununu's statement had disastrous political consequences and it undoubtedly contributed to Bush's defeat in 1992; nevertheless it did coincide with the President's world view and his conservative, guardian notions of governance. It is important to bear this in mind if we are to consider Bush's presidency on his own terms rather than those of his political adversaries.

COMMUNICATIONS

Demarest, on his appointment as Director of Communications in the Bush White House, was surprised to discover how wide his responsibilites would be and how few staff he would have to aid him in meeting those obligations. Unusually, he had no longstanding connection with Bush prior to his service as Communications Director, or principal 'spin doctor', in the 1988 campaign. Demarest's White House responsibilities were to be much wider; he was now placed in charge of speech-writing, public liaison and integovernmental affairs. Public liaison staff facilitate two-way relationships betwen the president and interest groups and make possible the building of coalitions in support of his policies. The intergovernmental affairs office, on the other hand, is responsible for communication between the chief executive and state and local governments.[72] In the previous Administration, there had been separate Assistants to the President for public liaison and intergovernmental affairs. Furthermore, 'while Ronald Reagan had roughly 60 or so people to fulfil these functions, I would have 25 to do all that, and that took me by surprise.'[73]

Critics of the Bush presidency have made much of the downsizing of the communications operation that had existed during the Reagan years and have been much taken by allegations that speech-writers were less well paid and were denied White House Mess privileges.[74] A different perspective on these matters is offered by Demarest. The fact that he had wider responsibilities and fewer staff led the press to assume that the President 'wasn't interested in speeches and wasn't interested in the kind of grassroots efforts in building coalitions that Ronald Reagan was interested in. I don't think that in reality it meant that at all.' It was simply the case that the new regime wanted to create new structures within the White House and as 'mine was one of the biggest staffs to start with it got a disproportionate hit in terms of trying to staff these other functions.'

As to the claims about pay and mess privileges for speech-writers, seen by some as deeply symptomatic of a devaluing of such activity, Demarest pungently remarked: 'It was a crock, it was an absolute crock.' Far from not being allowed to employ speech writers at more than $40 000, as Podhoretz claimed, he had hired speech-writers at $60 000 and the matter of mess privileges was without significance. To eat in the White House Mess it was necessary to hold a commission, that is to say to be either an Assistant to the President, a Deputy Assistant to the President or a Special Assistant to the President. Some Reagan speech-writers had held commissions, but it was decided that this would not happen in the Bush White House. 'Because they didn't get commissions they didn't get Mess privileges, but I never took this as any kind of targeting at the speech-writers, of devaluing their function and ironically, none of the people that became speech-writers for Bush ever had a commission.'[75]

PUBLIC LIAISON

The Office of Public Liaison had been an essential element in the Reagan White House. By carefully cultivating the leaders of a myriad of sympathetic interest groups, those who worked in public liaison were able to mobilize support in the country on behalf of the President's policies.[76] As Bobbie Kilberg made clear, George Bush was deeply sceptical of public liaison activity for two reasons. First, as noted in the previous chapter, as a former member of Congress himself, he had a fastidious aversion to going over the heads of legislators. Second, he believed that the office had become altogether too big under Reagan:

> . . . with some staff members promoting their own agendas and becoming captives of their constituencies; representing the interests of those constituencies to the White House rather than the interests of the White House to the constituencies. Bush realized that it had to be a two-way street, but he felt that an imbalance had occurred in the later Reagan years. What the President wanted was a very lean, small shop that focussed on his priorities and that was an integral part of the communications apparatus reporting directly to the Assistant to the President for Communications.

Bush was determined to avoid a recurrence of what had happened in the Reagan White House, where public liaison had been 'a free standing operation headed by an Assistant to the President and viewed as a separate office representing all those pesky interest groups that were going to make life difficult for [the Administration].'[77]

It was also the case that, whereas under Reagan public liaison was dedicated to maintaining fruitful relationships between the White House and conservative activists, the early Bush years were different.[78] Much to the chagrin of right-wing observers, public liaison now worked to build bridges with all sorts of interest groups, even those who were not natural Republican allies:'We opened the doors to meetings with all sorts of people on child care, on welfare reform, on campaign finance reform . . . and we just got lambasted by the right wing.' Later in Bush's term, the spirit of accommodation was less apparent: 'Everybody kind of pulled up the gate a little bit and we could no longer get the President's time for groups that were not supportive.'[79]

Reflecting the President's reservations about public liaison, Sununu placed it under the communications umbrella and made provision for it to be led not by an Assistant to the President, but by two Deputies, Kilberg and Sichan Siv. In the Reagan years there had been a paid staff of close to 60 whereas under Bush that would be reduced to between 11 and 16.[80] While broadly agreeing with the President's scepticism about public liaison, Kilberg conceded that 'we were much too small, we were hampered . . . we had no support staff whatsoever and we had to rely on interns . . . you just cannot operate in an optimum manner with that small a staff.'[81]

A number of presidential aides remarked to this author on the inadequacies of communication in general in the Bush White House and there has been some tendency to lay the blame at the door of staff responsible for this function.[82] However, this may be less than fair. To take one example, the great communications débâcle of the Bush presidency arose from the budget deal of 1990 between the White House and congressional leaders. This definitive event in the history of the Bush Administration will be considered in more detail in Chapter 6 but for the moment it should be noted that it is hardly appropriate to blame communications staff for this catastrophe.

During the negotiations that led to this ill-starred deal, Demarest, the Director of Communications, was completely excluded from the inner circle of policy-makers and he and his staff had no forewarning of the agreement struck with congressional leaders, including the explosively controversial reversal of the President's electoral pledge of 'no new taxes'. Moreover communications staff were not told in advance that the President, in a televised address to the nation, would ask Americans to contact legislators to urge them to support the deal.[83] Public liaison staff, in other words, were given no opportunity to prepare the ground for the appeal by the President, which, not surprisingly, backfired miserably.

The inadequacies of the communications 'shop' in the Bush White House are surely best explained by the personality and leadership style of the President himself. Even if the press and right-wing commentators got some of the details wrong it seems that George Bush's lack of interest in speech-making was the key factor in the undoubted downgrading of speech-writing. As Peggy Noonan said about speech-writers after she had left the Bush entourage: 'They're intrinsically important, but are they important in terms of the political pecking order? They're just above the people who clean up after Millie (the President's dog).'[84]

The very fact that Bush and his closest advisers allowed the Assistant responsible for communications to be totally excluded from the budget negotiations in 1990 surely says much about the low priority accorded his function. The contrast with the standing of someone like Michael Deaver on Reagan's staff is revealing. One of the most experienced and senior figures in the Bush White House, Clayton Yeutter, in reflecting on the Administration's difficulties in getting its message across, commented ruefully: 'I sometimes wonder whether the greatest communications genius in the world could have made that happen.'[85]

CHIEF OF STAFF II – SAMUEL SKINNER

Anyone who doubts whether there were any advantages of consequence to Sununu's style of managing the White House would be well advised to speak with senior staff who also served under his successor. Such witnesses provided me with a picture of an organization descending into chaos after Sununu's replacement by Samuel Skinner. By no means was this entirely attributable to the new Chief of Staff. Indeed, part of the blame rests with Sununu for he left behind a demoralized and faction-ridden staff. His brutal style coupled with his determination to concentrate decision-making in domestic policy in his own hands had contributed much to the demoralization. And the collapse of collegiality in the Bush Administration dated from the 1990 budget deal, for which Sununu bore a large share of the responsibility.

Skinner had been Bush's campaign manager in Illinois in 1988 and had then been appointed to the Cabinet as Secretary for Transportation. Regarded as one of the better Bush appointments, Skinner became Chief of Staff at the end of 1991.[86] The timing of his arrival could hardly have been worse with the White House in considerable disarray. Apart from the difficulties arising from Sununu's tenure, the President's standing in the polls was in steep decline and his former Attorney General, Richard Thornburgh, had recently been well beaten in a crucial US Senate election in Pennsylvania. To add to these difficulties the recession was deepening and Patrick Buchanan was preparing to challenge the President for the Republican nomination.

These circumstances would have tested the most talented of

administrators, but, within a short time, Skinner was seen to be well out of his depth. He introduced some restructuring of the White House and made it more inclusive, but the effect seems to have been to add to the weakness of an already foundering Administration. Senior staff spoke of innumerable, interminable meetings 'where nothing ever got decided and nobody tracked what happened in one meeting as opposed to another meeting and where there were no implementation procedures.'[87] Preparations for the 1992 State of the Union message degenerated into what Kilberg described as a 'circus . . . where there was nobody in charge. Under Sununu we would have had things running like clockwork, and decisions would have been made and actions would have been implemented.'[88] Further evidence of the confusion under Skinner was provided by John Keller. 'There was no leadership, it was management by committee; you couldn't get a decision out. There were different meetings being scheduled at different times of the day. There were different participants but on the same topic; different answers would come out of them and you wouldn't know which one to trust.'[89]

Another staff member recognized that it could be said in Skinner's defence that, unlike Sununu, he was concerned to run the White House by consensual methods:

> Sam tried very hard to seek a way to find consensus and as a result a lot of times decisions were delayed and we found ourselves in meetings upon meetings when Sununu would have said 'do it'. It was a very different style of management. [Both] were trying to serve the President to the best of their ability, but were just very different in style.[90]

One of the most senior members of Bush's entourage was severely critical of Skinner as an administrator.'Sam just doesn't have administrative skills . . . he would either have a decision on his desk forever and just not make it, or he would swing to the other extreme and make a capricious decision in fifteen seconds . . . you can't do that and sustain the credibility of the place and [maintain] the respect of the people that work there.' Consequently, Skinner's standing in the White House was quickly undermined: 'He undercut himself with his own shortcomings.'[91]

How is the Skinner appointment to be explained? It should

be said first that he was a fervent Bush loyalist who had served the President in the 1988 campaign and had been something of a presidential troubleshooter as Secretary of Transporation. Moreover, in the latter role, Skinner was believed to have been a particularly good administrator. In addition, Skinner had strengths that his predecessor lacked. A contest-winning salesman with IBM early in his career, he was a notably outgoing and friendly man with 'an ability to get on with almost anyone, including Democrats'.[92] There was little chance of Skinner abusing senior members of Congress in public, or of launching gratuitous, verbal assaults on interest group leaders.

Unlike Sununu, Skinner was not impervious to pain, with one source describing him as 'very, very sensitive to criticism.'[93] Indeed in several respects the one chief of staff was the obverse of the other. 'Sununu certainly had his shortcomings. He was an autocratic chief of staff and that's not the ideal personality for the job. He had fundamentally sound management and administrative skills [but lacked] human relations skill. Sam Skinner was the opposite, he had great human relations skills, everybody loved Sam, but he had horrible management skills.'[94] It may be that the ideal chief of staff would be a combination of Skinner and Sununu, and James Baker, who replaced Skinner in the summer of 1992, came close to filling the bill, but his appointment came too late to save Bush from electoral defeat.

4 A Guardian's Agenda

By definition guardians have only limited agendas. As conservators they are largely content with things as they are. They are not driven by the reformist zeal that characterizes other presidents and they are deeply sceptical as to what can be achieved by governmental action. As Stephen Hess said of Eisenhower: 'His aspirations as president were limited to two overriding objectives: peace abroad and a balanced budget at home. In keeping with those aspirations, his view of the presidential role was circumscribed.'[1] George Bush's ambitions were similarly modest.

In campaigning for the presidency in 1988 he revealed no grand vision of how the world should be remade. Unlike fellow Republicans such as Goldwater and Reagan he did not see himself as any sort of crusader; he offered himself to the voters not as an architect of fundamental change, but as a leader dedicated to broadly preserving the status quo, as a candidate who would be a guardian president. The previous administration had moved the country in new directions and that movement needed to be consolidated and built upon. Some modifications and adjustments were needed, a case could be made for modest incremental change, but nothing more than that.

From the beginning Bush made no apology for being a reactive leader, believing that he was especially well qualified to deal with problems as they arose. Early in his presidency it was reported that his decision-making was characterized by 'a case-by-case approach that is centered on the details and circumstances immediately at hand and less on ideology or concern about consistency . . . [he] is confident that if he makes enough of what he calls the "right decisions," his actions will cumulatively move the country in the right direction.'[2]

Grandiose schemes of social engineering like the New Deal and the Great Society held little appeal for Bush: 'I have no great love for the imaginings of the social planners.'[3] Politicians needed to guard against arousing undue expectations, and the value of legislation as a vehicle of reform was, in any case,

86

doubtful. Many of the objectives of would-be reformers were best met by private rather than public action; by charities and voluntary work rather than by governments.

Contrary to the liberal Democratic craving for expanding the role of government, Bush was dedicated to shrinking the size of government wherever possible, to ensuring 'that government intrudes as little as possible in the lives of the people.'[4] And, as a conservative Republican, he was particularly averse to government interference in the economy. He saw it as his responsibility to 'set the economy free' by keeping taxes low, diminishing the burden of regulation, reducing public expenditure and promoting free trade.

Governance for a president like Bush was a low-key, low-profile affair with little room for ideology or flamboyant rhetoric. Leadership was best effected through conciliation, compromise and behind-the-scenes negotiation rather than by noisy confrontation. The first rule for those responsible for the making of public policy was 'do no harm' and chief executives had a duty to restrain Congress in this regard. They needed to act as a bar to undesirable legislation, using the veto, or the threat of its use, to modify bills, or to keep them from the statute book altogether. Finally, for a guardian president no part of his job is more important than the conduct of American foreign policy. This is his principal preoccupation and it is here that his skills as a crisis manager are likely to be most severely tested.

Bush not only saw himself as a guardian in the White House, he also faced notably unpromising circumstantial variables, making a nonsense of simple comparisons between his achievements in office and those of other incumbents. FDR, for example, became president during a period of domestic emergency and enjoyed the support of vast majorities in Congress. Similarly, Johnson's much admired performance as chief legislator in the early years of his presidency was made possible by massive congressional support and the mood of the country engendered by the Kennedy assassination. Reagan, in 1981, could reasonably claim a mandate for change and for six years had the advantage of a Republican controlled Senate.

There was no emergency and no clamour for change in January 1989. Both the public opinion polls and the 1988 election results were rightly interpreted by Bush as signifying a desire among the American people for continuity rather than anything more than marginal change. As George C. Edwards commented at the time: 'I don't see any great demands in the country for policy change. The period is just not one for great change.'[5] Shortly before he entered the White House Bush himself specifically eschewed any desire to embark on a dramatic 'first hundred days' in the time-honoured manner of FDR. Bush said: 'I've been a part of this administration and it isn't like there is a need for radical change.' He acknowledged that action would be required to deal with the deficit, but beyond that he planned to build on the 'tremendous successes' of the Reagan years. 'That's at least the approach that I'm going to bring to the job . . . People understood that when they were voting. They weren't looking for a radical shift.'[6]

Even if Bush had not been a guardian president and had entertained activist ambitions the line-up of party strength in the House and the Senate after the 1988 elections would have made the fulfilment of any such agenda most unlikely. With large Democratic majorities against him in both houses Bush's standing *vis à vis* Congress as he took up office was the weakest of any president elected in the twentieth century, an unenviable distinction which had previously belonged to Richard Nixon. In 1969 there were 58 Democrats and 42 Republicans in the Senate, compared to 55 Democrats and 45 Republicans twenty years later. However, in the House in 1969, Nixon could claim the support of 192 Republicans whereas Bush, in 1989, had to work with 175 Republicans as against 260 Democrats.[7]

These are some of the factors that need to be kept in mind in evaluating the Bush presidency. We need to understand how he saw his role rather than measuring him against yardsticks provided by his political opponents. He had neither the desire for, nor a mandate for, fundamental change and was content to be a reactive rather than a visionary leader. Instead of an activist or an expansionist in the manner of liberal Democratic and even some Republican presidents Bush was a minimalist seeking to limit the reach of government. Nowhere was this more the case than in economic policy where, as he saw it, government meddling could be harmful to the self-correcting mechanisms of a free market economy. It was incumbent on presidents to engage in defensive activity designed to prevent the passage of legislation harmful to the national interest and the management of foreign policy was their paramount. These are the conditions under which Bush assumed the presidency and they provide the terms on which he is entitled to be judged.

A LIMITED AGENDA

In assessing the effectiveness, or capacity for statecraft, of any president the crucial question is what policies did he espouse and how far did he succeed in imposing them on the political system? In the case of a guardian president this may seem to present difficulties in that, by definition, such chief executives take up office unencumbered by ambitious policy programmes. Nevertheless, limited though it was in scope, George Bush could not avoid having an agenda of some sort when he ran for the presidency in 1988. A quandary for a guardian is that he doesn't want to do very much, but can hardly afford to say so. The voters are bound to ask what he intends to do if elected and will be unimpressed by purely negative answers. In campaigning Bush often spoke as if his experience and qualifications were alone sufficient to merit his election, but the realities of electoral politics required that he also offer some specifics.

In accepting the Republican nomination Bush said: 'I'm a man who sees life in terms of missions – missions defined and missions completed.' He went on to outline the elements of a programme before concluding: 'This is my mission. And I will complete it.' Necessarily Bush's 'mission' did not include major change; his principal purpose would be securing and building on the gains of the Reagan era. 'The most important work of my life is to complete the mission we started in 1980. And how, and how do we complete it? We build on it.' The previous administration had restored the strength of the American economy and 'with the right leadership it will remain strong.' Economic success was dependent on growth and this would continue provided the United States maintained its 'commitment to free and fair trade [and] by keeping government spending down and by keeping taxes down.' From this flowed Bush's ill-fated pledge of 'no new taxes'.

He also undertook to create 30 million jobs in eight years, to improve the educational system and to work for a drug-free America. In addition, disabled people were to be brought into the mainstream and environmental concerns were to be accorded a high priority. While distancing himself from Reagan's fiercely anti-government rhetoric Bush emphasized in his acceptance speech the need to keep government in its proper place and stressed the virtues of voluntary organizations, 'a brilliant diversity spread like stars, like a thousand points of light in a broad and peaceful sky'.

As Bush saw it, reviving the innate strength of the American economy had been one of President Reagan's most significant achievements, a development paralleled by a necessary strengthening of the nation's defences which had, in turn, brought great gains in international affairs. Bush undertook to continue with this policy of 'peace through strength', tempered by further cuts in strategic and conventional forces. Another high priority would be efforts to accomplish a total ban on chemical and biological weapons. At the Convention Bush also made the first of a number of appeals for a 'kinder and gentler nation' in which harmony and tolerance prevailed and where the evils of materialism and corruption were eradicated. In the same spirit Bush in his inaugural address invoked the timeless ideals of 'duty, sacrifice, commitment, and a patriotism that finds expression in taking part and pitching in'. Bush was then not entirely without an agenda. In his acceptance speech and elsewhere he did lay out a broad outline of what he hoped to achieve, a limited programme which can be used for evaluative purposes.[8]

Some years ago, James MacGregor Burns noted that since Franklin Roosevelt, 'the classic test for greatness in the White House has been the chief executive's capacity to lead Congress.'[9] Clearly for a guardian president, imposing himself on the legislature is somewhat less crucial than for dedicated activists like Roosevelt and Johnson et al., but for all that the effectiveness of any president is greatly dependent on his ability to get Congress to conform to his wishes.

In this regard the Bush administration began in a most unpromising fashion with the defeat in the Senate of the President's first nomination for Secretary of Defense John Tower. This rejection of a Cabinet nominee was only the ninth

in the history of the United States and the first since 1959.[10]
Furthermore, no president had ever before been denied a
Cabinet choice in his first term. This humiliating setback at
the outset of Bush's presidency had ominous implications for
his leadership. As one magazine noted, 'A primal command-
ment for new Presidents, particularly those faced with a
Congress controlled by the opposition party: Thou shalt avoid
early defeats. The opening days are the time when Congress
and the public – and foreign leaders – are sizing up the new
man. The perceptions they form early are likely to color their
view of the President throughout his term.'[11]

On its face the selection of Tower had seemed to be a sound
choice. A good relationship with Congress is essential for any
Secretary of Defense and Tower had for 24 years (1961–1985)
been a member of the Senate himself; Congress moreover, is
notorious for treating its 'own' kindly. It is also valuable for
presidents to place in key Cabinet positions appointees whose
loyalty can be relied upon and Tower had ben a close political ally of George Bush for a quarter of a century.

In explanation of this disastrous reverse commentators
focused on the inexperience and tactical errors of John Sununu,
the Chief of Staff, Frederick McClure, the chief lobbyist, and
those who worked for them. As an exercise in legislative
liaison the effort to get Tower confirmed was unimpressive.
The crucial vote in the Armed Services Committee took place
when the President and his Chief of Staff were in Japan, vote
counting proved unreliable and the administration managed
to offend deeply the most important congressional player of
all in the nomination process, Senator Sam Nunn of Georgia,
the chairman of the Committee.

The President's staff failed to appreciate how damaging
allegations of womanizing, conflict of interest problems and
excessive drinking were to Tower's case. Ultimately, the latter
charge proved to be the most telling with Nunn announcing:
'I cannot in good conscience vote to put an individual at the
top of the chain of command when his history of excessive
drinking is such that he would not be selected to command a
missile wing, a SAC (Strategic Air Command) bomber squadron
or a Trident missile submarine.'[12] On 23 Febuary 1989 the
Tower nomination was rejected by the Committee in a straight
party line vote of 11–9, a decision that was confirmed by the

full Senate on 6 March by a vote of 53–47. Senator Dole, the Minority Leader, and other Republicans, excoriated the Democrats who voted solidly against the nomination, for partisanship, whereas the President adopted a more moderate tone, regretting the 'groundless rumors' that lay behind the rejection, while adding: 'Now, however, we owe it to the American people to come together and to move forward.'[13]

This comment was more in line with the conciliatory sentiments that Bush had expressed at his inauguration and a few weeks later the advantages in such an approach were seen in the agreement struck with Congress over aid to the Contras. This agreement, discussed further in Chapter 7, was the result of quiet, painstaking negotiation behind the scenes, and represented a notable triumph for the White House to set against the Tower fiasco.

As we have seen, guardian presidents are not disposed to be activists in the White House. It is not in their nature to proliferate legislative initiatives, a stance which, unfortunately for them, runs counter to the 'dominant perspective' of American politics. That which says that a good president, 'is one who makes government work, one who has a program and uses his resources to get it enacted. The good president is an activist: he sets the agenda.'[14] Presidents are expected, moreover, to get away to a fast start, to 'hit the ground running', to emulate, as best they can, the spectacular success of Franklin Roosevelt in his first 'hundred days'.

At the end of the first hundred days of the Bush presidency, White House staff went out of their way to downplay the significance of such benchmarks. And yet given the 'dominant perspective' they felt obliged to brief newsmen on the President's achievements so far. As one senior aide put it, 'while we do not acknowledge the significance of the first 100 days we acknowledge that everybody is going to write 100 day stories.'[15] In conducting such briefings there was little to point to that had actually been completed other than the Nicaragua accord and a budget agreement negotiated with the legislature in a similar spirit of conciliation and compromise, but widely criticized as being largely meaningless.[16] Initiatives that the Administration were said to have in train included a plan to rescue savings and loan institutions and legislation to deal with third world debt, child care, education and ethics in government.

The slimness of Bush's legislative record in the early months of his Administration was charitably received, even in the liberal press, but media comment became far more severe later in 1989.[17] Newspapers were now inclined to make much of the analysis of congressional rolls calls by the *Congressional Quarterly* showing that Bush won only 63 per cent of the votes on which he took an unambiguous position in 1989, the lowest figure for any elected first-year president since CQ began compiling such figures.[18]

A notably trenchant attack against 'The Can't Do Government' was launched by *Time* magazine highlighting the various pressing problems both at home and abroad that were not receiving attention, and holding the President, in particular, responsible for this state of affairs. In a response wholly fitting for the press spokesman of a guardian president Marlin Fitzwater retorted: 'You liberal writers are just like the Democrats in Congress. You think Government isn't doing anything unless it's taxing and spending and creating new bureaucracies.' For their part the writers of the article concluded with the alternative, and much more fashionable view of what a president's role should be:

> The conservative complaint that only liberal elitists think that Washington must actually *do* something is self-evidently silly. Of course the government must do something. That is why it exists: to act in ways that improve the lives of its citizens and their security in the world. The list of missed opportunities and ignored challenges is already much too long. The sooner Government sets about doing its job again, the better.[19]

Not all the challenges went unanswered however and in 1990 Congress approved a sweeping environmental reform bill as well as legislation to provide relief for disabled Americans. Bush himself and members of his staff have invariably cited these two enactments when asked to identify the principal, domestic policy achievements of his presidency.[20]

THE 1990 CLEAN AIR ACT AMENDMENTS

For some years before Bush became President Congress had been wrestling with the clean air issue. This was a problem desperately difficult to solve given the divisions and conflicts of interest across the country in such matters and the vagaries of a regime of separated powers, weak parties, potent pressure groups and legislators tied closely to their constituents. Environmentalist members of the House and Senate were convinced that existing laws needed to be strengthened, but they were opposed by others worried about the costs of any such changes to business and consumers and the consequences for employment. 'Few argued against the value of clean air, but the potential price in lost jobs and increased costs to industry and consumers left Congress intractably divided for a decade.'[21]

Those in Congress who pressed for change were concerned by the failure of the Environmental Protection Agency to fulfil the promises of the Clean Air Act of 1970, particularly during the eight years of the Reagan Administration. Any attempts to move forward on clean air during the Reagan era faced resistance from the White House and from formidable congressional barons, men such as Representative John Dingell of Michigan, Chairman of the Energy Committee and resolutely opposed to the passage of bills harmful to the automobile industry. Similarly, Senator Robert Byrd of West Virginia, the leader of the Senate Democrats, used his control over scheduling to thwart acid rain proposals that he believed would damage the sulphur coal mining industry in his state. In short, with regard to the clean air issue, there was a log-jam on Capitol Hill, an impasse unlikely to be broken without leadership from the White House, which, rather surprisingly, Bush was to provide.

In accepting his party's nomination Bush endeavoured to distance himself from Reagan on the environment issue saying specifically, 'we must clean the air.' In some respects Bush was an unlikely champion of the environmental cause. As Reagan's chairman of the Task Force on Regulatory Relief he had been the Administration's point man for deregulation, a role which found him enthusiastically endorsing various EPA authored changes in regulations designed to dilute the effects of earlier clean air legislation.[22] Nevertheless, Bush, in June 1989, honoured his campaign commitment by presenting to Congress a clean air proposal, an initiative applauded by one not usually sympathetic source, as follows: 'Mr Bush, simply by joining the debate in a serious way, has moved the middle ground. The question seems no longer to be whether there will be the new law that circumstances require, but how soon and what kind.'[23]

The debate sparked off by the Administration's proposal was taken up in the Senate by the Environment and Public Works Committee which, in late 1989, reported out a bill far stronger than either the President's bill, or a corresponding measure under consideration in the House. The Senate Committee bill, like other versions including that finally signed into law, had four main sections. One of these involved tightening the controls on emissions from motor vehicles; a second was concerned with urban smog; a third dealt with toxic air pollutants and a fourth was aimed at acid rain.

The heavy costs implied by the Senate bill, estimated at $42 billion by the EPA, antagonized both industry and the White House with the President threatening to veto any measure with a cost more than 10 per cent higher than the $19 billion price tag put on his bill. Subsequently, a month of negotiations behind closed doors by representatives from the Senate and the Administration produced a compromise measure behind which Senate leaders and representatives of the White House were able to unite. It was reported by Roger Porter, Assistant to the President for Economic and Domestic Policy and Bush's chief negotiator on the clean air bill, that 'The President is extremely pleased with this agreement.'[24]

Progress on clean air in the Senate was greatly helped by the replacement of Robert Byrd as Democratic leader by the environmentalist Senator George Mitchell of Maine who battled to fend off amendments that would have destroyed the deal worked out with the White House. Byrd, however, while no longer leader, was Chairman of the all-powerful Appropriations Committee. He was also a highly skilled parliamentarian and, drawing on both these resources, he came within a hair's breadth of derailing the compromise worked out between the Senate and Bush's staff. This was brought about by Byrd sponsoring an amendment to provide generous compensation for high-sulphur coal miners expected to be thrown out of work by the acid rain control provisions in the proposed legislation. An original estimate of costs to the taxpayer of $1.4 billion led to pressure on Byrd to modify his plan, but even $700 million was too much for the White House which let it be known that the President would veto any bill including such a provision. Byrd's amendment was eventually beaten back by a 49–50 vote, a result that turned on bad weather preventing one Senator from returning to Washington, the flightiness of a few of the votes promised to Byrd, and the veto threat.[25]

Negotiations in the House were no less fraught and the outcome was similarly threatened by numerous amendments, including a proposal approved by a vote of 274–146 calling for a $250 million programme for unemployment and retraining benefits for workers who lost their jobs. President Bush expressed his displeasure at these provisions and, during the conference stage, there were indications that they might lead to the bill being vetoed. In the event, after further negotiation on this matter with the White House, the Senate and the House approved a clear air package which was then signed into law by the President on 15 November 1990.[26]

There has been some dispute as to the significance of the Clean Air Act of 1990. The President described it as 'the most significant air pollution legislation in our nation's history' and his Counsel went even further in describing it as 'the most sweeping environmental statute in the history of the world'.[27] Elsewhere the gains from the Act were seen as marginal and the burden of costs that it imposed remained a matter of great concern to industrial interests that would resurface to damage Bush later in his presidency.

Reference to these latter sentiments provoked a typically robust response from C. Boyden Gray, the President's Counsel and a major player on the clean air issue in the Bush White House. He said: 'I'd go up against anybody that the costs were negative; that is the Clean Air Act, as it was passed, reduced costs on the American public in comparison to what it replaced. Sure it added some costs, but overall the benefits vastly exceeded the costs.' Gray went on to argue that the Clean Air Act was a truly 'great piece of reform legislation' of great benefit to the American economy. The 'ultimate' test of any reform bill:

. . . the marketplace test [was] productivity. Manufacturing productivity, service productivity, the ultimate test is productivity. [Some critics argue that such legislation] renders us unproductive, you're wasting dollars, you're not competitive. The fact of the matter is the US has uncontested the best air quality of any industrialized country on earth. Uncontested the best manufacturing productivity growth and service growth . . . [Let] the facts speak for themselves. We have the best air quality [and] we have the most competitive industry.'[28]

If the Clean Air Act is to be seen as a mark of Bush's effectiveness, of his ability to translate goals into policy realities, it has to established that it was, in a real sense, *his* bill. This too is open to dispute with some claiming that the bill 'originated in the Congress, among Democrats.'[29] There is obviously something in this argument; like any complex, controversial bill its success depended on a number of key actors both in Congress and the White House. Nevertheless, Bush's role was surely crucial as the Democratic Chairman of the Conference Committee, Senator Max Baucus of Montana, generously conceded on the Senate floor: 'George Bush turned around the previous administration's point of view. The Reagan administration was very much opposed to clean air. The Bush administration is very much in favor of clean air. George Bush deserves major credit.'[30]

There seems to be little doubt that without Bush's initiative in June 1989, his commitment and the efforts that he and his staff put into negotiating with Congress there would not have been a Clean Air Act. This was, by any standard, an impressive exercise of presidential leadership as his chief lobbyist in the House at the time later claimed. 'Congress had struggled for years . . . to re-write the Clean Air Act. They were never able to do it until they got the leadership and the cooperation out of the president. Now there were people within our party who didn't like that because they didn't want any [change] but there's no chance in the world all those disparate factions could have been brought together without the leadership of the President.'[31] Some confirmation for this accolade is provided by a more neutral observer Paul Quirk, who says that the Clean Air Act was, 'probably Bush's principal self-initiated domestic policy accomplishment', one achieved in the face of 'regional and sectoral conflicts . . . so intense and complicated that some doubted that any bill could obtain a majority.'[32]

THE AMERICANS WITH DISABILITIES ACT

The Americans with Disabilities Act, so often wheeled out by Bush and his staff as another of his greatest accomplishments, is hardly in the same league in terms of presidential input. It was not a Bush bill to the same degree as the Clean Air Act and its passage was far less problematical. In sending a clean air proposal of his own to Congress in June 1989 Bush had moved the legislative process forward in an infinitely troublesome area, whereas disability legislation was already progressing through the system when he became President.

The need for such a bill had been first advanced by the National Council on Disability in 1985 which then prevailed on the Republican Senator Lowell Weicker of Connecticut to draft the first version of the ADA bill in 1987. On Weicker's electoral defeat in 1988 sponsorship of the bill was taken up by Senator Tom Harkin, Democrat of Iowa, while, in the House, the main sponsor originally was Representative Tony Coelho, Democrat of California. After the latter's resignation responsibility for the bill in the House fell primarily to Representative Steny Hoyer, Democrat of Maryland, later commended for 'skillfully shepherding [the ADA] through substantive and procedural obstacles in 1989 and 1990'.[33]

In campaigning for the presidency Bush came out strongly in support of the ADA. In his acceptance speech at the 1988 Convention he said, 'I am going to do whatever it takes to make sure the disabled are included in the mainstream. For too long they've been left out. But they're not going to be left out anymore.' Immediately before he took up office, the President reiterated his commitment. In a speech at the Department of Health and Human Services he said, 'One step that I've discussed will be action on the Americans with Disabilities Act, in simple fairness, to provide the disabled with the same rights afforded other minorities.'[34]

Nevertheless it is evident that the Bush Administration did not originate this bill and it is not inconceivable that it would have passed even without the President's enthusiastic support. The public, for instance, appeared to be solidly behind the idea of change with a Gallup poll in 1989 establishing that 81 per cent of Americans believed that existing policies with regard to the disabled were inadequate.[35] And it was not easy for anyone to oppose such a bill, as a *Reason* editorial noted: 'The ADA is the nicest bill to come along in a long time. Only the scum of the earth would oppose protecting [the disabled] from discrimination. It wouldn't be nice.'[36]

The chances of disability rights legislation passing were also helped by the personal interest of many of the prime movers. Coelho was himself an epileptic as was Hoyer's wife. Senator Harkin had a brother who had been deaf since childhood. Senator Edward Kennedy, Democrat of Massachusetts, and Chairman of the Labor Committee, had a mentally retarded sister and a son who had lost a leg to cancer. The Minority Leader in the Senate, Senator Robert Dole, Republican of Kansas, had suffered serious injury in the Second World War and was partially disabled. Finally a daughter of George Bush's had died of leukaemia and two of his sons suffered some form of disablement.

A starting point for many of those who campaigned for changes in the law to benefit the disabled was the 1964 Civil Rights Act which made illegal discrimination in employment and public accommodations based on race, sex, religion or national origin. The ADA was modelled on the 1964 Act, but was necessarily much more far reaching. The earlier legislation was primarily directed against discriminatory practices preventing black people from obtaining employment or using restaurants, hotels, cinemas, swimming pools, etc. It was designed to correct the adverse consequences arising from racial prejudice in the white majority. The ADA, however, was concerned not just with majority attitudes, but with providing the facilities whereby disabled people could enjoy fuller lives. As Pat Wright of the Disability Rights and Education Fund put it: 'Sometimes there are barriers that prevent people from getting in to be discriminated against. The problem [for the disabled] has been getting them in the door.'[37]

Under the ADA establishments were required to make new or remodelled facilities accessible to disabled people seeking jobs or endeavouring to make use of public accommodations;

existing facilities were to be similarly modified where that was 'readily achievable'. Whereas the 1964 Act did not incur substantial costs this could not be said of the ADA:

> The bill's scope is vast. New apartment blocks and business buildings – restaurants, grocery stores, dry cleaners – must be made accessible to the disabled, for instance, with ramps and widened doorways: employers must make 'reasonable accommodations' for employees with disabilities: hotels' and car rental companies' new pick-up vans must have wheel-chair lifts; public transit must do the same, and must also provide door-to door service for people who can't get to the bus stop.[38]

The massive costs arising from these requirements provided the basis for strong opposition to the ADA by business interests and their many allies in Congress. Many of Bush's critics on the right of the Republican party moreover were deeply troubled by the additional burdens being placed on industry and commerce and pointed to the ADA (and the Clean Air Act) as 'significant drags on the country's economic recovery'.[39] At first sight there was indeed some incongurity between a President supposedly committed to the free market and his willingness to impose large additional regulatory costs on business. C. Boyden Gray, the senior White House aide principally responsible for the ADA, vigorously rebutted such allegations arguing that the legislation was entirely consistent with Bush's conservative principles.[40]

Gray claimed that the ADA was the 'greatest welfare reform ever pulled off', and a few statistics illuminate that point of view. A survey of disabled persons in 1985 showed that 66 per cent of disabled persons aged 16–64 were not working and 65 per cent of those not employed said that they would prefer to work.[41] Elsewhere it was estimated that the unemployed disabled collected 'federal disability and welfare checks, costing nearly $60 billion a year'.[42] With some reason therefore Gray argued that the largest consumer of welfare in the country was not 'the black community, not the unwed mothers drawing Aid for Dependent Children, it is the disabled.'[43]

When Gray and Michael Boskin, the President's Chairman of the Council of Economic Advisers, sat down at the beginning of the Bush Administration to ponder the implications of the ADA they focused on the question: 'How can you justify doing this if it's going to undermine your regulatory principles?' They believed they had the answer to their question after Boskin had calculated the benefits and set them against the costs. This revealed that by making it possible for disabled people to get off welfare, to earn their own living and pay taxes, the benefits 'completely dwarfed the costs of the plan and that was the basis on which we proceeded.'

Gray spoke rather bitterly of the failure of the press to give Bush credit for empowering the disabled and said further, 'It is not as much appreciated now as it will be in about ten years as the baby boom generation hit their wheelchairs and their canes and their whatever, and then people will realize as the population really ages how important it was to prepare for that eventuality.'[44] Bobbie Kilberg, Deputy Assistant to the President for Public Liaison, also stressed Bush's interest in empowerment. In an emotional address at the signing of the ADA:

He talked about giving people the opportunity to be in the mainstream economically, with a sense of self-worth . . . he believed very strongly in giving everybody a chance to participate fully in society and giving everybody a chance to earn their own way. Yes, he didn't like the idea of regulation and he's very strongly in favor of a free market, but he also had a very strong social conscience.[45]

To set against these laudatory interpretations there are the views of those on the right of the Republican party troubled by the added burden of regulations and unconvinced that such legislation made more than a marginal contribution to the pressing social problems of the United States. It is also necessary to bear in mind that despite Gray's adamant insistence that the ADA 'would not have happened without [Bush], no question about it', it can be argued, as I have suggested above, that the President's role was less important than that; his part in it was undoubtedly important, but it is far from clear that the ADA can be simply simply regarded as his accomplishment.[46]

THE POINTS OF LIGHT MOVEMENT

If there is reason to doubt just how far the ADA can be categorized as a Bush accomplishment there is no question whatsoever as to who deserves the credit for the 'Thousand Points of Light' initiative even if the ideas behind it had been aired on a number of occasions by Reagan.[47] However, this is not an achievement taken at all seriously by Bush's many critics across the political spectrum. From the start cartoonists lampooned the idea, with Herblock, for example, showing a drunk asking for a 'thousand pints of lite'; elsewhere it was assailed as a trivial, opportunist programme born out of *noblesse oblige* and unlikely to make a serious contribution to the amelioration of deep-rooted social problems.[48]

Such criticisms are, however, beside the point for the purposes of this analysis. I am not concerned here with judgements as to the desirability of Bush's policies, but with his effectiveness in the sense of gaining acceptance of those policies. In pursuing that line of inquiry it becomes very clear that while Bush's adversaries in the media and elsewhere did not think highly of the thousand points of light policy it was, for the President, of the greatest importance, as he indicated as he prepared to depart from the White House:

> If I could leave but one legacy to this country, it would not be found in policy papers or even in treaties signed or even wars won; it would be [a] return to the moral compass that must guide America through the next century, the changeless values that can and must guide change. And I'm talking about a respect for the goodness that made this country great, a rekindling of that light lit from within to reveal America as it truly is, a country with strong families, a country of millions of Points of Light.[49]

However much it was derided by Bush's critics, the points of light phrase encapsulated ideas central to his presidency. It first entered the lexicon of American politics in Bush's acceptance speech at the 1988 Republican Convention.[50] As is so often the case with catchy political slogans the meaning behind it was, at first, not at all clear. Bush made use of it in a passage of his speech apparently concerned with reaffirming the advantages of American pluralism:

We are a nation of communities, of thousands of ethnic, religious, social business, labor union, neighborhood, regional and other organizations – all of them varied, voluntary and unique. This is America: the Knights of Columbus, the Grange, Hadassah, the Disabled American Veterans, the Order of AHEPA, the Business and Professional Women of America, the union hall, the Bible study group, LULAC, 'Holy Name' – a brilliant diversity spread like stars, like a thousand points of light in a broad and peaceful sky.[51]

Elsewhere in the same speech Bush called for a 'kinder and gentler nation', deplored materialism, self-centredness and blind ambition and alluded to the merits of voluntary service.

Further elaboration of these ideas appeared in Bush's inaugural address where he noted the limited contribution that government could make to the alleviation of social problems, stressed the inherent goodness of the American people and reflected on the possibility of putting that strength to use:

I am speaking of a new engagement in the lives of others – a new activism, hands-on and involved, that gets the job done. We must bring in the generations, harnessing the unused talent of the elderly and the unfocused energy of the young . . . I've spoken of a thousand points of light – of all the community organizations that are spread like stars throughout the nation doing good . . . The old ideas are . . . timeless: duty, sacrifice, commitment, and a patriotism that finds its expression in taking part and pitching in.[52]

Several months later Bush provided the clearest statement yet of the thinking behind the thousand points of light initiative. His starting point was the high level of commitment to voluntary service already existing in the United States which had helped 'countless Americans find self-respect and dignity'. It was now necessary to extend substantially these efforts; there were limits to what government could do, it 'can't rebuild a family or reclaim a sense of neighborhood.' Throwing public money at problems had been shown to be futile in the past and the 'key to constructive change [lay in] building relationships not bureaucracies.'

The President recalled the various forms of community service that he and his wife had been involved in during their

time in Texas; he noted the sense of self-fulfilment that such
work brought, and continued: 'Today more than ever, we
need community service to help dropouts, pregnant teens,
drug abusers, the homeless, AIDS victims, the hungry
and illiterate.' To relieve the pain and isolation of such people
required the voluntary help of individual Americans as well
as schools, churches, businesses and civic groups. 'For this is
what I mean when I talked about a Thousand Points of Light:
That vast galaxy of people and institutions working together
to solve problems in their own backyard.'

Urging citizens and organizations to extend community
service to all parts of the nation, Bush stressed the non-
governmental nature of the movement being created: 'This is
not a program, not another bureaucracy.' Using a form of
words which he was constantly to reiterate in speeches during
the remaining years of his presidency, Bush said 'from now
on in America any definition of a successful life must include
serving others.' The objective of the thousand points of light
initiative as it now emerged was, the President said, 'to carry
this belief to every person in the land.'[53]

The strategies for implementing this policy were developed
by C. Gregg Petersmeyer, appointed to head a new division
within the White House, the Office of National Service.
Petersmeyer could be said to be a classic Bush appointment.
While a generation younger, Petersmeyer's background and
education was very similar to Bush's with the *New York Times*
suggesting that 'he might be described as a man not only of
kindred political views but one of kindred build, kindred blue
suits and kindred résumés.'[54]

Whereas Bush had been educated at Andover and Yale and,
as a young man, worked in the oil industry in Texas, his protégé
attended Choate, Harvard and Oxford before being employed
in the natural gas business in Colorado. Petersmeyer's father,
the head of a television station in Texas, was a Bush acquain-
tance and Petersmeyer himself first encountered the future
President when he worked as a summer intern in the Nixon
White House in 1969. Subsequently, when Bush became
Chairman of the Republican National Committee Petersmeyer
was a staff assistant in the White House, where the two men
'spent a fair amount of time together.' When Bush served in
China in the 1970s, Petersmeyer stayed with him for a month

where 'we played tennis every day, we had three meals a day together, we travelled some together.' In 1980, Petersmeyer worked briefly in Bush's campaign for the Republican nomination; he kept in touch with the Vice President when he moved to Colorado in 1982 and, at his instigation, became 'very close friends' with his son Neil; in 1988, he became Chairman of Bush's campaign in Colorado.

In terms of background, loyalty and an understanding of his thinking about politics, Petersmeyer could hardly have been better qualified to put into practice the core idea of the Bush presidency. Moreover Petersmeyer took very seriously indeed his responsibility, as a member of the White House staff, to pursue the President's agenda even though the specifics of that agenda were often difficult to discern. 'I always thought to myself, what would the President want to do here? . . . I knew him well enough to know that if he thought about what I was thinking about he'd probably want to do it this way. And so when he saw all the things I was doing he went along with them because it made sense.'[55]

From his experience of working in the Nixon White House Petersmeyer knew how valuable an independent relationship with the President could be, it gave such persons 'an extraordinary advantage in the rough and tumble of debate'. Petersmeyer had such a relationship with Bush; technically he was subordinate to the Chief of Staff, but in practice reported directly to the President. 'I was able to operate under the protection of George Bush . . . I felt I had a responsibility to him, as opposed to a responsibility to the Chief of Staff.' Thus the creation of a points of light infrastructure came about as a result of 'using the President's imprimatur without explicitly seeking or acquiring formal approval within the machinery of the White House.'[56]

Escaping in this way from the close control of policy-making otherwise exercised by John Sununu and his ally Richard Darman was facilitated by two factors, the absence of significant budgetary consequences and the Chief of Staff's lack of interest in Petersmeyer's project. 'That portion of the presidency happened to be a portion that he wasn't particularly interested in, but it was nonetheless important to George Bush.'

The high priority of Petersmeyer's work for Bush was reflected in his initial appointment as a Deputy Assistant to the President and his later promotion to an Assistant; it can also be seen in the substantial amount of time that Bush gave to the points of light enterprise throughout his presidency. Petersmeyer's task, as he saw it, was to lead:

> an effort to use the presidency to call people to a type of engagement in the most serious social problems of our time. To show people how they could do that should they want to respond to that call and to support it in certain ways. We developed a basic strategy the objective of which was, ideally, to cause every American to engage in a direct and consequential way in helping to solve these serious social problems.[57]

The strategy of the points of light movement had five components: changing people's attitudes to community service; identifying notably successful and valuable examples of individual and collective community service; discovering and encouraging leaders; establishing supporting institutions; and reducing the vulnerability of volunteers to legal liability.[58]

Bush has often been criticized for failing to make sufficient use of his office as a 'bully pulpit' and has himself conceded that this was one of his shortcomings. Under Petersmeyer's prodding, however, it seems that the President did resort to the bully pulpit on behalf of the points of life movement. In a number of ways the weight of his office was thrown behind a comprehensive effort to move the country in a particular direction. In other words, a chief executive normally sceptical of crusades did, in this area at least, embark on a wide-ranging exercise in moral leadership, striving to convince his compatriots of the value and rewards of voluntary community service.

The President's public utterances provided the linchpin of the points of light strategy with Petersmeyer assiduously injecting the 'theology' of voluntary service into as many of Bush's speeches as possible. It is estimated that during his presidency he spoke on the subject in more than 500 speeches and public pronouncements and, by constant repetition, sought to make a mantra of 'from now on in America any definition of a successful life must include serving others.'[59]

The second part of the strategy involved identifying notable contributions to voluntary service by individuals or groups, giving them presidential recognition and publicizing them through the media as examples for other Americans to emulate. In November 1989 the White House began a process whereby the President, on a daily basis, formally recognized the voluntary service efforts of an individual or group. On 22 November 1989 the first of these presidential Points of Light to be named was a newspaper *The Memphis Commercial Appeal* of Tennessee, which, in July 1989, had embarked on a series 'highlighting citizens who have made community service a central part of their lives.'[60] The 100th Point of Light to be recognized was Barbara Tomblinson, of Kansas City, Missouri who once homeless herself, had founded 'a non-profit corporation which provides transitional housing assistance for homeless families'. The final and 1020th Point of Light, identified on the day that Bush left office, was the Mariucci Inner City Hockey Starter Association of St Paul, Minnesota, an organization of 28 volunteers that 'teaches inner-city children aged six to eight to skate and play hockey.' The President met with representatives of 675 Points of Light and Vice President Quayle met with representatives of a further 103.[61]

The amount of time and effort invested by the Bush White House in the Point of Light awards was quite unprecedented. In Petersmeyer's words it was a programme of 'constant parable telling' by the President: 'it was never the most important thing happening that day, it was typically not among the top four things happening [but] it was always there. And over time it had an impact on the way people, including the hardnosed press corps, saw this President.'[62]

To publicize the awards Marlin Fitzwater, the President's Press Secretary, issued daily press releases to 45 media outlets. The White House press corps gave them little attention, but at the local level each Point of Light generated an average of four or five newspaper stories and two items on radio or television; overall, it is estimated that approximately 8000 news stories appeared.[63]

In addition to making speeches and honouring exemplary individuals and groups President Bush worked to encourage the participation of leaders in government, business, education, entertainment, sports and youth organizations. He established an independent non-profit organization, the Points of Light Foundation, to be funded 50 per cent by the private

sector and 50 per cent by Congress. This institution, initial
funding for which was included in the National and Community
Service Act of 1990, was intended to 'promote the ethic of
community service, disseminate information about successful
local activities to other communities across the Nation,
and stimulate the development of new leaders and their
community service initiatives.'[64] The foundation advertised
extensively, set up educational programmes and local
volunteer centres and provided technical assistance to corpo-
rations. The President also called for the creation of an
independent institution to provide legal advice and assistance
to volunteer programmes, an initiative that led to the setting
up of a National Center for Community Risk Management
and Insurance.

What did these and the many other activities that consti-
tuted the points of light movement actually achieve? How far,
in other words, did the President succeed in completing what
is described in a document put out over his signature as the
'defining mission' of his administration?[65]

Significant policy change normally requires the mustering
of supporting coalitions and epic struggles with the legislative
branch, but this initiative was of a different sort. Apart from
the $25 million in funding included in the National and
Community Service Act, no additional authorization legislation was required. In essence, this was a presidential campaign
trying to effect a consequential change in popular attitudes.
Rather than enlisting the aid of government on behalf of reform
this was an attempt to bring home to the American people
that there were limits to what government could do; that voluntary community service was not only essential to the eradication
of serious social problems, but was necessary to the self-fulfilment of those who became volunteers.

In this instance presidential effectiveness had little to do
with the passing of bills; it turned instead on how successful
a White House sponsored campaign of public education was.
When pressed on this point Petersmeyer alluded to Advertising
Council surveys that found that the points of light slogan 'was
recognized by an exceptionally high number of the American
people a year or two into the Bush presidency. And [found]
that there was no [significant] difference between Republicans
and Democrats in those who thought well of it.'[66]

There is also evidence of an increase in volunteerism during the Bush years. According to Gallup poll figures in 1990 54 per cent of 2727 American adults surveyed said they had done some volunteer work compared to 45 per cent who had answered similarly in 1988. In New York City, furthermore, it was estimated that inquiries about volunteer opportunities increased between 1990 and 1991 by 28 per cent; similar increases were also reported in other cities, 16 per cent in Kansas City and 20 per cent in Houston.[67]

There are several possible explanations for the new interest in volunteerism at the end of the 1980s. As the economy moved into recession social problems intensified – unemployment went up and homelessness became more common, as did as other forms of distress, creating a greater need for voluntary workers. Economic decline by putting people out of work also made them available for volunteer work in a way that they had not been hitherto. In addition, the cuts in funding for social programmes at all levels of government in the 1980s had made social service agencies more dependent on the efforts of volunteers. Having said all that experts in the field conceded that the points of light campaign had played a part of some significance in stimulating voluntary activity.[68]

CONCLUSIONS

If Bush's record in fulfilling his agenda in domestic policy is to be used for evaluative purposes it has to be said that it was, at best, mixed. In economic policy he singularly failed to build on Ronald Reagan's record as he had undertaken to do at the 1988 Republican Convention. This can be demonstrated by a few statistics. The average annual rate of growth of GNP had been 2.3 per cent during Reagan's first term and 3.2 per cent in the second, whereas for Bush's incumbency it was 0.9 per cent. Reagan had managed to cut substantially the rate of growth of domestic spending; it grew by an annual average of 0.87 per cent in his first term and 0.19 per cent in the second. During Bush's presidency, by contrast, the average annual growth rate of domestic spending was 7.54 per cent. The Reagan administration could claim to have created 18 million new jobs over two terms and Bush spoke jauntily in

1988 of '30 million in 8', but, in fact, less than a million new jobs came into being in the four years that he held office.[69] In late 1991 it was established that despite the President's supposed commitment to deregulation his administration had 'witnessed the broadest expansions of government's regulatory reach since the early 1970s.'[70] And most damaging of all, Bush proved unable to keep his most sacred campaign pledge of 'no new taxes' – a disastrous failure for his presidency discussed at length in Chapter 6.

Bush was also unable to deliver much of significance on his undertakings before taking office to improve the education system and to work for a drug-free America. Nevertheless, as we have seen, Bush did have some success in meeting his limited agenda. He spoke in 1988 of the need to 'clean the air' and submitted to Congress a bill of some importance that eventually resulted in important legislation. He had promised to do what he could to ensure that the disabled were brought into the mainstream of American life and he played a significant part in the passage of notably advanced legislation. The founding of the points of light movement meant little to Bush's critics whether on the left or the right, but for a guardian president progress in such matters was especially gratifying. Guardian presidents are also anxious to hold the line against undesirable change, another area where Bush could claim some success, as the next chapter will demonstrate.

5 'Preventing Bad Laws'

Modern presidents, whether Democrat or Republican, are expected to be activists in the White House. It is routinely argued that it is incumbent upon them to advance proposals for change and to mastermind their enactment into law. As a new president takes up office the problems of governance are reduced to activist clichés. He is advised to 'hit the ground running' and is expected to exploit fully the opportunities offered by the 'honeymoon' relationship with Congress that is is assumed will prevail during the early months of his presidency. At the end of his 'first hundred days' in office media pundits and others will calculate how successful he has been in gaining the cooperation of Congress, estimates that will be reactivated at the end of each year in office and again at the conclusion of his term. According to calculations of this type George Bush was consistently found wanting. As we saw in the previous chapter, he was accused of 'hitting the ground crawling' and of failing to take advantage of the 'honeymoon': analysts found his achievements in his first year to be slim and were similarly unimpressed by his legislative record throughout his presidency.

CONGRESSIONAL QUARTERLY SCORES

Plausible evidence of Bush's failure to impose himself on the legislature seemed to be provided by the annual presidential success scores calculated by the *Congressional Quarterly*. By examining speeches and other statements by the president, or his authorized spokesmen, CQ decides, where possible, what his position is on a given congressional roll call vote. Presidential success is then calculated by totalling the percentage of roll call votes where the chief executive had a clearly stated position and his view prevailed.

The application of these criteria to Bush's presidency present a most unflattering picture. Leaving aside the very special case of Gerald Ford, Bush's presidential success rate of 62.6 per cent in his first year in the White House was by far the worst of any president since records began in 1953. Comparable first year success rates were Eisenhower 89 per cent, Kennedy 81 per cent, Johnson 93 per cent (in 1965), Nixon 74 per cent, Carter 75.4 per cent and Reagan 82.4 per cent. On the face of it, these figures provide convincing evidence of Bush's failure to make good use of the honeymoon period.[1]

Similarly, Bush's success rate in the final year of his term at 43 per cent was 'the worst performance of any president at any point in his term since CQ began keeping score 39 years ago.'[2] Bush's success rate over the whole of his presidency averaged 51.8 per cent, the lowest of any first-term president since 1953 – by comparison Eisenhower averaged 79.7 per cent, Kennedy 84.6 per cent, Johnson 82.2 per cent, Nixon 74.4 per cent, Carter 76.6 per cent and Reagan 72.3 per cent. Again the gap between George Bush and other modern presidents was large, with even a fellow guardian like Eisenhower exceeding his average success score by a margin of 28 per cent.[3]

Congressional Quarterly scores are eagerly seized upon by commentators as concrete evidence of how a president is faring, whereas they need to be handled with care. Such figures undoubtedly do provide useful yardsticks of presidential effectiveness and those cited above contribute something to an analyis of the Bush presidency. On the other hand, such calculations, while not without relevance in the case of activist presidents, have much less to say about conservative guardians.

As a number of scholars have shown there are difficulties with CQ presidential success scores.[4] In the first place, no account is taken of the wide variations in party support in Congress; that is to say, there is no difference in treatment between presidents who encounter the perils of divided government and those who do not. This makes a mockery of simple comparisons between, say, Johnson and Nixon, or even Carter and Bush. It is also the case that success scores are based on roll-call votes alone, whereas many important questions turn on voice votes, may be decided by party leaders or in committee, or may not come to a vote at all. Thus a proposal from Bush early in his term 'to open the Arctic National Wildlife Refuge never came to the House or Senate floor, and all the 1989 tests of his clean-air proposal took place in committee.'[5]

There is also, under the CQ scoring system, no attempt to differentiate between votes, or to weight them in terms of their significance. In 1989 the highly significant vote to reject John Tower's nomination as Secretary of Defense was given the same weight as innumerable, routine, unanimous confirmations. In such calculations votes of great importance are rolled together with the trivial and, as Anthony King pointed out, that is to ignore the fact that 'some congressional outcomes matter far more to presidents than others. In 1919, Woodrow Wilson would probably have been content with a *Congressional Quarterly* support score of near zero if he could have got the Senate to ratify the Treaty of Versailles.'[6]

CQ scores moreover are liable to distortion by the inclusion of roll-call votes on matters which are non-controversial and which are decided by near unanimous votes and may therefore inflate levels of presidential support. It is also the case that there may be a multitude of votes on similar or related questions and this too may give an artificial impression of presidential support; the Senate, for instance, 'took 116 roll call votes on the 1964 Civil Rights Act.'[7]

It is, however, with regard to the veto power that limitations in CQ scores become especially pertinent in the case of guardian presidents – chief executives particularly mindful of their responsibility to amend or to prevent the passage of undesirable legislation. As Nick Calio, head of Bush's legislative liaison operation, put it: 'I think in terms of [CQ's] ratings vs. our internal ratings, there's a real difference. CQ rates every vote and there are some we don't care about. And there are some votes CQ rates as a loss, but that we considered a win because we showed veto strength. So they don't really reflect the complicated reality.' In other words, account must be taken not just of Bush's notable success in sustaining vetoes, but also of his use of veto threats to shape, or to cause the withdrawal of bills that met with his disapproval.[8]

THE VETO POWER

Conservative Republicans have attacked George Bush for being excessively conciliatory towards Congress, but such analyses take insufficient account of his veto strategy. As Richard Rose has pointed out: 'A guardian president can accept Congress being in opposition hands, whereas an expansive President depends more for success on congressional approval of White House proposals. Confronted with an activist Congress, a guardian President can fulfil his role by vetoing bills.'[9] Out of Bush's 44 vetoes only one was overridden, a level of success that no other modern president has equalled.[10] Among other enthusiastic vetoers Nixon was overridden five times in respect of 24 vetoes of 'nationally significant legislation' whereas Ford was similarly overridden on 12 vetoes out of 42 of national significance. Modern presidents (1933–81) have, on the average, had a quarter of their vetoes of nationally significant legislation overridden.[11]

The rationale underlying Bush's veto strategy was provided by Nicholas Calio, originally head of legislative liaison in the House and subsequently in overall charge of congressional relations. 'There were many things that, in our view, Congress got involved in [which] it really shouldn't – in micro managing markets, in micro managing foreign policy . . . There were a lot of things we felt needed to be stopped . . . on all sorts of issues we felt the legislation wasn't in the best interest of the country and so, to use the only tool the President had to stop it and to [thereby] "make policy" we had to use the veto.'[12] As this statement confirms, the veto power assumes particular importance for those who labour on behalf of a guardian president. And, it should be noted, there was ample support for the negativism of the guardian position, for the determination of such presidents to prevent the passing of bad laws, in the debates held at the Constitutional Convention in 1787.

The Founding Fathers were anxious to place in the president's hands some sort of veto on the actions of the national legislature for, in the words of Alexander Hamilton, such an arrangement would give the executive 'the power of preventing bad laws'. Moreover, the very fact that the veto existed and might be brought into play would act as a restraint on lawmakers:

A power of this nature will often have a silent if unperceived, though forcible, operation. When men engaged in unjustifiable pursuits, are aware that obstructions may come from a quarter which they cannot control, they will often be restrained by the bare apprehension of opposition from doing what they would with eagerness rush into if no such external impediments were to be feared.[13]

Another heavyweight in the Convention, Gouverneur Morris declared that 'the public liberty [was] in greater danger from legislative usurpations than from any other source' and the possibility that 'bad laws will be pushed' meant that 'a strong check will be necessary.'[14] The justification for a veto, according to George Mason, arose from the fact that the legislature 'must be expected to pass unjust and pernicious laws. This restraining power was therefore essentially necessary.'[15] While the veto power and the guardianship posture arouses the ire of those who favour activism in the White House, both were fully supported by those who drew up the Constitution.

The principal author of Bush's veto strategy appears to have been Roger Porter, Assistant to the President for Economic and Domestic Policy. As a political scientist who had studied the history of presidential vetoes Porter was well qualified to apprise President Bush of the possibilities inherent in the device.[16] He recognized that it could be not just a means of outright rejection, but also a tool available to presidents for shaping legislation as it moved through Congress. 'One of Porter's major beliefs was that the veto should not always be considered the end of a bill's evolution but only part of an ongoing process of compromise.'[17]

Relevant experience was another of Porter's strengths. He had served in the Ford White House where the veto had been freely used; indeed, according to Spitzer, writing in 1988, 'Ford was the only twentieth century president to design and pursue a calculated veto strategy.'[18] There were, of course, parallels between Ford and Bush; they were conservatives and guardians and in both cases their position *vis-à-vis* Congress was weak. Lacking any sort of electoral mandate and weakened further after the 1974 mid-term elections Ford was obliged to resort to a veto strategy.[19] Similarly, as we saw in the previous chapter, Bush, in 1989, had less party support in the House and Senate than any other newly elected modern president and his extensive use of veto threats could be construed as 'a sign of a weak position in Congress.'[20]

The threat of a veto makes it possible for chief executives to exercise considerable influence on the legislative process. According to one source, the Bush Administration used the veto power like a ratchet, with spokesmen privately mentioning the possibility of a veto at the committee stage of a bill; if that failed to have the desired effect White House communications staff would let it be known that a veto might occur before, where necessary, a public wielding of the veto threat by the President himself.[21] Bush moreover established a reputation for following through on his veto threats; in this respect at least, he was stronger and more effective than Reagan. According to Terry Eastland: 'In general, Reagan did not have as much veto credibility as Bush.'[22]

David Stockman, Director of the Office of Management and Budget in the Reagan Administration, complains of the reluctance of that president to use veto threats. For example, in testifying before the House Budget Committee in March 1981 Stockman said that Reagan would veto a one-year tax cut if it was passed by Congress instead of the succession of cuts over three years that the Administration was seeking. Such aggression troubled pragmatists in the White House like James Baker and Richard Darman bent on deal-making with congressional leaders. They convinced Reagan that his 'general principle of not announcing vetoes in advance' had been violated and Larry Speakes, the Press Secretary, was commissioned to disassociate the President from Stockman's comment.[23]

The exceptional effectiveness of Bush's veto strategy was highlighted in 1991 when it was reported that not only had he vetoed 21 bills without once being overridden, but, in addition, his veto threats were proving to be major factors in determining the fate of many bills.[24] On a wide range of issues, the Democratic leadership in both houses now felt obliged to accept that a veto-proof two-thirds vote, rather than a simple majority, was essential for the passage of legislation. As one Democratic leader, Representative Vic Fazio of California, ruefully commented: 'We have fallen into the trap of thinking that if we don't have a two-thirds vote we should do nothing.'[25] These were, no doubt, comforting words for a President so committed to limiting the reach of government.

Some have questioned the use of the veto as an instrument of policy rather than for constitutional purposes.[26] However, Hamilton argued that it had two purposes: the first was concerned with the Constititution and the second with the substance of policy. The primary purpose of the veto was to make it possible for the president to defend himself against the propensity of the 'legislative body to invade the rights of the executive'. The secondary purpose of the veto related to matters of policy – it would aid the president in preventing the 'passing of bad laws through haste, inadvertence or design.'[27] The use of the veto for policy purposes was also anticipated by James Madison when he said:

> It would be useful to the legislature by the valuable assistance it would give in preserving a consistency, conciseness, perspicuity and technical propriety in the laws, qualities peculiarly necessary, and yet shamefully wanting in our republican codes. It would moreover be useful to the community at large as an additional check against a pursuit of those unwise and unjust measures which constituted so great a portion of our calamities.[28]

For President Bush and his principal adviser on constitutional matters, his Counsel, C. Boyden Gray, the dangers of congressional encroachment on the rights of the executive were particularly grave in the foreign policy realm. Accordingly, four of the nine vetoes exercised in 1989 were concerned with protecting presidential prerogatives in foreign affairs. The first of these was directed at a resolution approving arrangements for the co-development with Japan of the FS-X, a fighter plane. Congress included in the resolution certain conditions which would become relevant if the plane went into production. Bush saw these conditions as infringing on his freedom to engage in negotiations with another country. 'In the conduct of negotiations with foreign governments,' the President insisted, 'it is imperative that the United States speak with one voice. The Constitution provides that that one voice is the president's.'[29]

A second foreign policy veto was cast in 1989 against a foreign aid appropriations bill, partly for reasons of policy substance, but also on constitutional grounds. Congress, in light of the Iran Contra affair, included in the legislation certain prohibitions on how aid to other countries might be used. The President and his advisers saw these restrictions as a constitutionally unwarranted encroachment on the right of the executive to conduct foreign policy. On 21 November 1989 Bush vetoed another bill with Iran Contra ramifications, that authorizing funds for the Department of State and other foreign policy agencies. Part of the bill 'prohibited executive officials from giving funds to other countries to carry out activities banned by law.' The President's legal advisers regarded such restrictions as unconstitutionally circumscribing his 'responsibility to protect national security by representing US interests abroad.'[30] Similar concerns about presidential prerogatives led Bush to veto a bill designed to waive the visa restrictions on Chinese students after the Tiananmen Square repression of June 1989. In 1990, a further three bills were vetoed in defence of the presidential prerogative in foreign affairs. Two of these were concerned with international trade, whereas the third was yet another arising from the congressional backlash against the Iran Contra débâcle.[31]

In substantive policy matters Bush used the veto power most frequently to reject abortion-related legislation. There were no less than ten such vetoes in 1989–92. In 1989 HR 2990 included provision for federal funding of abortions in cases of rape and incest where they were 'promptly reported' to the relevant authorities, language unacceptable to the President and which led to a veto. In the same year, appropriations legislation for the District of Columbia was twice vetoed because it would have made possible abortions funded out of locally raised tax revenues. The foreign aid appropriations bill referred to above was also vetoed partly because of abortion concerns.[32]

Debates on the abortion issue in the 102nd Congress (1991–92) showed evidence of movement in favour of abortion rights, but Bush repeatedly used his veto power to hold the line against further liberalization. 'In 1991, both chambers voted to jettison five separate abortion-related restrictions. But Bush vetoes and repeated veto threats prevented any policy changes.' The following year the President vetoed four bills 'because of abortion language, while abortion-related language was dropped from the final versions of three other measures to avert threatened vetoes.'[33] The Bush Administration's resourceful use of the veto to shape national policy on abortion points to the dangers of making too much of CQ scores as a measure of presidential effectiveness.

On the face of it, 43 out of 44 vetoes upheld, plus an untold number of successful veto threats would seem to represent useful evidence to set against popular perceptions of Bush as a weak and ineffectual President, incapable of imposing his priorities on Congress.[34] Some on the right of the Republican Party however, were not impressed. One of these was Charles Kolb who, as Deputy Assistant for Domestic Policy, had an inside view of the workings of the Bush White House from mid-1990 onwards.

Kolb argues that Bush's veto strategy was, in truth, ultra cautious with the Administration generally unwilling to resort to the veto except when victory was assured. The President 'would rarely veto legislation unless he knew in advance that he had the votes necessary to sustain the veto. The issue was counting heads, not standing on principle. If Fred McClure or Nick Calio, his two assistants who headed his legislative shop, told him he was shy on votes, Bush rarely applied the veto. Simple as that.'[35]

This charge was vehemently rejected by some of Kolb's senior colleagues. Calio, for instance, who was very much in the front line when it came to sustaining vetoes, questioned Kolb's claim to knowledge of decision-making at the highest level and continued: 'Putting together the votes for most of those vetoes was extremely difficult. If you look at the numbers we had available on the Republican side . . . [it is evident that] we had to rely on getting some Democratic votes as well. George Bush did not veto things when they were in the bag, George Bush vetoed things as a matter of principle, with all due respect to Charlie.'[36] David Demarest was no less scathing describing Kolb's analysis as 'staggeringly inaccurate' and insisting that Bush was a man of principle. 'We got 39 [sic] vetoes and sustained all but one. On many occasions, I'm not going to say a majority, but on a number of occasions, we were in a situation where most of us thought we could not sustain the veto and it was the President saying, "Yes we are [sic]".'[37]

James Cicconi went further in defending Bush as a man of integrity who used the veto courageously and honourably:

He wielded the veto with great success throughout his presidency on a lot of issues of principle, where in many [cases] . . . it was predicted he would easily be overridden and humiliated. I can recall when he vetoed sanctions against China. He felt extremely strongly on that issue and our legislative liaison chief said at the time that [the President] announced his decision, that we didn't have single vote, not a single vote to sustain that veto. We had to work to sustain it, but he firmly believed that the proper course of action was not to isolate China. That it would destroy so much of what we were working to achieve in the world.[38]

Nevertheless Kolb is not alone in claiming that Bush picked his veto fights rather cautiously. James Sundquist remarked that 'Bush has been careful in selecting his targets. When he knows that he is going to lose, he goes ahead and signs the bill.'[39] Yet this argument cannot be carried too far. An examination of Bush's vetoes does show that on many occasions the margin of success in sustaining them was very close, most notably in the Senate.[40]

The veto of the FS-X fighter plane was upheld by the bare minimum of 34 votes required in the Senate. The veto of the bill waiving the visa requirements of Chinese students attracted 37 votes after an intensive lobbying campaign by the White House. In May 1990, the veto of an Amtrak authorization bill was upheld with 36 votes; the following month a Hatch Act amendments veto obtained 35 votes. One of Bush's most controversial vetoes was of the 1990 Civil Rights Act, another which was upheld by the bare minimum of 34 Senators. In 1991, the veto of an unemployment benefits bill survived 'a major effort to override the veto' by a vote of 65–35.[41] Another epic struggle in 1992, that referred to by Ciconni above, saw 38 votes sustain a veto on legislation concerning MFN ('most favoured nation') status for China, and the same number of Senators prevented a veto of a 'Motor Voter' registration bill from being overturned. Several of the abortion-related vetoes in the House also only narrowly escaped being overridden.[42]

In defence of Bush's veto strategy it can also be said that he and his advisers understood that a degree of caution in wielding the veto could be a source of strength in that it gave greater credibility to his threats to veto. As the Republican Representative Steve Gunderson of Wisconsin remarked: 'When he talks veto, people take it seriously.'[43] Reagan's veto threats, by contrast, were less effective, with members of Congress able to take comfort from the fact that the President often backed down from veto threats and was overridden on a number of occasions. According to *US News and World Report*:

'Ronald Reagan vetoed only 78 bills in eight years and was overridden nine times. As his administration wore on, he made the mistake of threatening more and more vetoes, then backing off without extracting important concessions from Democrats. That damaged his credibility.'[44] In that sense Bush, it could be argued, was the stronger of the two chief executives, but such views carried little weight with conservatives like Kolb who wanted the President to be more adventurous; to be less protective of his record in sustaining vetoes and to be prepared to go down with all guns blazing where necessary.

At first sight the arguments within Republican ranks over Bush's use of the veto highlight the differences between his pragmatic, reactive, guardian style of leadership and the more ideological crusading approach of Reagan. Kolb, who is clearly a Reaganite, was appalled to find among his colleagues on the White House staff a 'real resistance to doing anything when they knew they might lose'. He wanted the Administration to take principled stands, to say simply: 'We are going to veto these appropriations bills and we don't care if we are over-ridden because they are wrong, or they are too expensive . . . why not take a position of principle and if you win it you win it, if you lose it move on to the next thing.'[45] However, we must set against such complaints the frustration that David Stockman endured in the previous administration in the face of Reagan's repeated unwillingness to use the veto against appropriations bills.[46]

Any calculation of George Bush's effectiveness in meeting his agenda needs to take account of his use of the veto power. Advised by shrewd strategists like Gray and Porter, Bush used the veto as the Founding Fathers intended, first to defend the presidency in the never-ending struggle with the legislature over prerogatives, and second as a means of shaping policy outcomes. Not just abortion, but also US policy towards China, civil rights, minimum wage, family leave and many other important issues provoked the veto. As a guardian Bush made relatively little effort to advance legislative proposals of his own, but was successful in modifying or 'preventing bad laws' emanating from his Democratic opponents. As the President said in defence of his record when he faced re-election: 'I wasn't elected to do it the way the liberal Democrats that control Congress want, and so I've had to stand up to them.'[47]

As might be expected Bush's repeated flaunting of the veto led to irate comment on Capitol Hill. 'The president is ruling the country by the rule of 33 plus one,' said Senator Dale Bumpers, Democrat of Arkansas. 'It doesn't matter what 535 people think. What matters is 34 people in the Senate.'[48] Similarly Richard Gephardt, the House Majority Leader, said: 'If you are looking for George Bush's domestic program, and many people are, this is it: the veto pen. The president's veto pen is more powerful than the votes of 66 senators and 289 representatives. He has used it to thwart the will of the American people, to defend the status quo of a declining economy, to preserve the privileges of the powerful, and to deny the positive role of government as an agent of renewal and change.'[49]

Leaving aside for a moment the partisan rhetoric, Bumpers and Gephardt were, of course, analytically correct; the veto, like the filibuster and judicial review, is a flagrantly counter-majoritarian device. In theory, 501 national legislators could be in favour of a policy, but could then be defeated by 34, a mere fragment of the whole. Less than 7 per cent of the total membership of Congress could theoretically thwart the wishes of 93 per cent Nevertheless, the use of the veto both as a self-defence mechanism and for policy-shaping purposes is fully in accord with the intentions of those who devised the Constitution. In addition, however, Bush used signing statements to protect his prerogatives and to influence policy outcomes, and this device, defined by George Edwards as a 'type of unofficial item veto', was constitutionally far more dubious.[50]

SIGNING STATEMENTS

Signing statements enable presidents to place on record their reservations about some part of a bill which they are nevertheless willing to sign. Statements allow a president to 'express the intent not to enforce a provision of the bill on the grounds that it is unconstitutional. He may state that it is against the policy of the administration. Or the president may give his interpretation of some provision of the statute.'[51] The use of signing statements is a long-established practice and was deployed, among others, by Andrew Jackson, Woodrow Wilson, Richard Nixon, Jimmy Carter and Ronald Reagan.[52]

It is charged against George Bush that he made excessive use of signing statements, turning them into 'sovereign powers for shaping or escaping laws and for governing without Congress by voiding or revising key provisions in congressional enactments.'[53] The uses of signing statements can be illustrated by the one issued by Bush when he put his signature to the National Community Service Act of 1990. The President began by expressing his pleasure at that part of the bill which provided for initial funding for one of his most favoured projects, the Points of Light Foundation, but then went on to express doubts about other parts of the Act. He was troubled by the degree to which paid rather than unpaid volunteers were to be employed in community service and he rejected as unconstitutional certain limitations on presidential appointees to a commission to be set up under the statute. In addition, Bush noted that prohibitions in the act on the transfer of funds from one account to another without congressional approval represented a legislative veto and were therefore unconstitutional.[54]

The substantive policy position expressed in this signing statement squared with the stance of a guardian president, sceptical of what government could do and reluctant to extend its reach. The statement was also consistent with Bush's determination, guided by his Counsel, the ubiquitous C. Boyden Gray, to resist what they perceived as congressional encroachments on the powers of the executive. This latter concern was particularly relevant in the realm of foreign policy. Thus in signing the Foreign Relations Authorization Act in 1990, the President referred to provisions that 'raise consitutional difficulties' and intimated that he would regard some of these as advisory rather than binding. In signing the Foreign Relations Authorization Act for Fiscal Years 1992 and 1993, the President went out of his way to make a sweeping assertion of executive power:

'Article II of the Constitution confers the executive power of the United States on the President alone. Executive power includes the authority to receive and appoint ambassadors and to conduct diplomacy. Thus, under our system

of government, all decisions concerning the conduct of negotiations with foreign governments are within the exclusive
control of the President.'[55]

Quite apart from the constitutional dubiety of such a large
claim, it is not difficult to understand why presidential signing
statements are the source of great indignation on Capitol Hill.
The signing of a bill is supposedly the concluding stage of the
legislative process – at that point a bill becomes a law. And yet,
by a signing statement a president may effectively undermine
the force of a law on either substantive or constitutional
grounds. Unlike the veto, moreover, there is no means whereby
the legislature can recoup the situation. Saving intervention
by the courts, which past precedent would suggest is unlikely,
the chief executive is given the last word in the policy-making
process and the separation of powers principle is violated.[56]
It has been argued by Charles Tiefer that, contrary to the
popular impressions of a pathetically weak President buffeted
by an unruly and partisan Congress, Bush in truth, used signing
statements, vetoes and other strategies in a flagrant effort to
govern without the legislature. That he attempted, in other
words, to bring about a 'semi-sovereign' presidency.[57] Tiefer
mounts a formidable, if distinctly one-sided case with his professional allegiance to the United States Congress as acting general
counsel to the House of Representatives, evident on every page.
For this observer Tiefer's analysis takes insufficient account of
the undeniable fact that constitutional development in America
has culminated in a situation where the responsibility for
policy-making, for national leadership, falls primarily on the
President in both domestic and foreign policy.
As Theodore Sorensen said in a book based on his experience in the Kennedy Administration: 'No one else has [the
President's] power to lead, to inspire, or to restrain the Congress
and country. If he fails to lead, no one leads . . . The nation
selects its President, at least in part, for his philosophy and his
conscientious conviction of what is right – and he need not
hesitate to apply them.'[58] All manner of obstacles are placed
in the way of presidents as they attempt to meet their responsibility to lead and the circumstances of divided government
may make their task immeasurably more difficult. In attempting
to impose himself on the policy-making process, whether to

initiate change, or to prevent change from occurring, presidents are likely to resort to whatever weapons they can lay their hands on, even those that are constitutionally suspect. While Tiefer is undoubtedly correct in arguing that the Founding Fathers were most anxious to guard against the emergence of an all-powerful executive, it is also the case that they were no less determined to resist the inevitable encroachment by the legislature on presidential prerogatives.[59]

And it is not as if members of Congress were paragons of constitutional propriety. In 1994, for instance, President Clinton's attempts to govern were constantly frustrated by the incessant use of filibuster threats: 'Under Rule 22 of the Senate the only way to close debate is to get 60 senators to concur. By using the filibuster liberally, conservative forces in the Senate have thwarted the Clinton administration's legislative agenda time and again.'[60] Just like signing statements, filibusters were used in the past selectively and infrequently, unlike their regular use today. Furthermore, the constitutionality of the filibuster is as much open to challenge as the signing statement.

President Bush has been criticized for being weak, for not providing sufficient leadership, yet Tiefer would have preferred him to have been even weaker. He should, it seems, have sat idly by while Congress seized control of the policy process and wilfully eroded presidential prerogatives. This is to ignore the fact that the legislature and the executive in the United States are engaged in a constant battle to maintain their respective positions in the 'separated system' provided for by the Constitution.[61] This was of course, anticipated by the Founding Fathers: Madison famously made reference to the 'tendency in the legislature to absorb all power into its vortex' while Gouverneur Morris worried that the executive would be so weak 'that there is the justest ground to fear his want of firmness in resisting encroachments.'[62] Similarly, Hamilton, in making the case for the veto, said that without it the president 'would be absolutely unable to defend himself against the depredations of the [legislative branch]. He might gradually be stripped of his authorities by successive resolutions or annihilated by a single vote. And . . . the legislative and executive powers might speedily come to be blended in the same hands.'[63]

The never ending struggle between the branches is, of course, liable to be even fiercer than usual in circumstances of divided government and it is surely the case that presidents are obliged to do what they can to defend their office against assaults from ambitious, parochially minded, sometimes unscrupulous and often ruthlessly partisan members of the legislature. Certainly, this has been the view of past presidents, some of whom enjoy heroic status among Democratic legislators who supposedly squirmed under the lash of the 'semi-sovereign' Bush. Thus Dean Acheson reported that Truman was moved by the passionate conviction that 'his great office was to him a sacred and temporary trust, which he was determined to pass on unimpaired by the slightest loss of power or prestige.'[64] Similarly, Kennedy's faithful aide Sorensen said that a president 'must strive always to preserve the power and the prestige of his office, the availability of his options, and the long range interests of the nation.'[64]

CONCLUSIONS

The discussion in this chapter does something to offset perceptions of Bush as a do-nothing, passive figure in the White House, incapable of imposing his leadership on the legislature. It has been argued here that CQ scores have to be treated with care and that they are especially limited in what they contribute to our understanding of the legislative leadership records of conservative, guardian presidents. Presidents, as I have repeatedly said, are entitled to be judged on their own terms and, viewed charitably, Bush's veto strategy, devised and implemented by some of the shrewdest minds on his staff, appears to have been moderately successful; allowing a 'resource poor' president to play a not insignificant part in shaping the substance of policy and to defend his prerogatives against encroachment, most notably in the realm of foreign policy.[66] In this regard at least Bush appears to have been a rather stronger chief executive than his predecessor.[67] Similarly, signing statements, while questionable constitutionally, helped to make it possible for Bush to be rather more effective in office than is sometimes suggested.

6 The 1990 Budget Crisis

The tortured efforts by President Bush and congressional leaders to agree a budget in 1990 raised fundamental questions about the American political system. The difficulties encountered exposed the extraordinary fragility of party discipline in the national legislature, emphasized the problems of divided government and once again cast doubt on the very governability of the United States. For the purposes of this study, however, the budget crisis of 1990 is especially interesting as a defining event for the presidency of George Bush, one which revealed major flaws in his style of presidential leadership.

NO NEW TAXES

At the Republican Convention in 1988 the future President, in reflecting on how economic policy would develop when he was in the White House, said: 'The Congress will push me to raise taxes, and I'll say no, and they'll push me again, and I'll say to them, "Read my lips; no new taxes".' Bush had been under pressure to make such a commitment for some time. During the primaries he had resisted the entreaties of campaign advisers like Lee Atwater and James Pinkerton that he should sign an anti-tax pledge to help him fend off the challenges of Jack Kemp and Robert Dole.[1] Such reluctance was understandable, for while Bush was a conservative, instinctively resistant to tax increases and had been a meticulously loyal Vice President, he had never been a devotee of Reaganomics. Unlike his predecessor, he bracketed an enthusiasm for low taxes with a belief in government. As one unnamed close adviser later explained: 'Some days he gets up and says "Jesus Christ, you know we ought to hold taxes down." Next day he gets up and finds out that we got to cut funding to some special education program and he gets all worked up.'[2]

This lack of certainty had caused Bush to haver on the tax issue prior to the 1988 Convention; on some occasions he had taken a hard anti-tax line, while on others he appeared to be unwilling to rule out tax increases in some circumstances. Such shilly-shallying troubled members of his staff either because of their own supply-side inclinations or for strategic reasons, with some convinced that signing up to an anti-tax pledge would help dispose of allegations that Bush was an ideological wimp lacking in firm convictions and would sharply define his candidacy. Others like Craig Fuller, the Vice President's Chief of Staff, worried that a fixed position on taxes would detract from Bush's ability to govern if elected. Similarly, Richard Darman, recognizing that whoever was elected would have to deal with the burgeoning budget deficit, decried the irresponsibilty of making such a pledge.[3] Charles Kolb suggests that initially Darman concealed his opposition to the pledge for opportunistic reasons, but leaving that aside, there is little doubt that he was against it from the beginning.[4] These concerns were overridden by those whose focus was campaigning rather than governing with Peggy Noonan, at the urging of Jack Kemp, incorporating the pledge in Bush's acceptance speech and vigorously fending off attempts to remove it.[5]

Immediately the election was over the President came under pressure to go back on his 'no new taxes' promise. Initially, the National Economic Commission was the main source of that pressure. Established in 1987, the NEC was a high-powered, bipartisan body set up to consider how the ever-growing federal deficit should be dealt with. The commission had devised a deficit reduction scheme including both spending cuts and tax increases, and on 7 December 1988 an outline of the proposal was placed before the President-elect. At this stage Bush flatly refused to countenance tax increases reportedly saying: 'There's no possibility I can even consider this. I'll have no credibility with the American public, if before I even get sworn into office, I support a program that increases taxes.'[6]

By early 1990, however, the situation had changed. The economy was looking less healthy with the budget deficit set to become even larger than anticipated and the possibility looming of swingeing cuts in government expenditures becoming necessary under the provisions of the Gramm-Rudman-Hollings legislation. This law, otherwise known as the Balanced Budget and Emergency Deficit Control Act of

1985, established maximum deficit levels and required across-the-board spending cuts if those targets were not reached. No one was more conscious of these problems than Richard Darman, now Director of the Office of Management and Budget and in the process of becoming one of the three most influential members of the White House staff, the others being John Sununu, the Chief of Staff, and Brent Scowcroft, the National Security Adviser.

RICHARD DARMAN

From the outset opposed to the 'no new taxes' pledge, Darman had, for some months, been working behind the scenes to convince the President of the adverse consequences of an ever-increasing budget deficit. He argued that the situation could only be brought under control by striking a deal with Congress requiring cuts in government expenditures coupled with increased taxes. As James Cicconi put it: 'Our Budget Director became entranced with the notion of being able to do a deal to help cure the problem on the deficit . . . and set about over the course of the better part of a year . . . to convince the President, gradually step by step, that a budget deal involving taxes was really the only way to deal with the problem and essential to the well-being of the nation.'[7] Charles Kolb also claims that Darman talked Bush into the budget deal.[8]

Other senior members of Bush's staff have testified to the extraordinary influence that Darman came to exert over the President in the making of economic policy. Two factors that help to explain Darman's hold over Bush and his dominant position within the White House were his exceptional intelligence and his extensive experience of working in the upper echelons of previous Republican administrations. One presidential aide estimated that the Budget Director was about '30 IQ points forward of Bush'.[9] Another spoke of him as a 'brilliant, brilliant man' while C. Boyden Gray noted that Darman's cleverness, in conjunction with his superior understanding of the system, allowed him to manipulate situations to his advantage: 'If you are as smart and as clever and experienced as Darman you can manipulate the process to control it to your political end, or your programmatic end.'[10]

Deputy Chief of Staff, Andrew Card, provided an illumi-
nating description of Darman's dazzling ability to monopolize
information and thereby dominate the domestic policy decision-making process in the Bush White House:

> Dick Darman is very bright and he does his homework; he
> is probably the most diligent person I've met in govern-
> ment. He does his own work, he is not staff-dependent; he
> reads, he understands; he is also very opinionated. He also
> knows that information is power . . . and he disseminates
> that information when he wants to. It used to be frustrating
> because sometimes he would blindside everybody else in
> the room with his information. He would pull out this little
> document in a policy reading with the President, and nobody
> else in the room would have seen the information he put
> on the table, but they didn't want to say 'Dick, I haven't
> seen that before, where did you get that?' And you didn't
> have the information to attack the document so therefore
> the document stood. I think the President maybe some-
> times was swayed towards Dick Darman's bias because of
> the way [he] managed the information.[11]

A similar, if slightly different, slant on Darman's influence
over Bush was provided by Clayton Yeutter, another of the
genuine heavyweights in the Administration, who had known
and worked with the Budget Director since the Nixon years.

> Darman is so skilful at making himself appear indispens-
> able. He's been around in government so many years that
> he's just good. He's smart, clever, sometimes ruthless, and
> he knows that knowledge is power. There is no better
> knowledge base than the Office of Management and Budget,
> and he used it skilfully to persuade President Bush of his
> indispensability. No one is indispensable, of course, but the
> perception thereof made Dick Darman one of the most
> powerful people in the executive branch for many years.[12]

Even the Chief of Staff, John Sununu, who possessed an
intelligence and a self-confidence no less formidable than
Darman's, seems to have succumbed to the idea that the Budget
Director was indispensable. In conversation with Bobbie
Kilberg Sununu explained: 'The President needs Dick, he's
the only one with a coherent [budgetary] policy.' With rare

modesty Sununu denied that he could perform such a role himself saying 'No, I don't have the knowledge, Darman has.' Kilberg concluded that 'even as brilliant as Sununu was he was cowed a little bit by Darman's knowledge of the budgetary process.'[13]

By mid-1990 the Director of OMB and the Chief of Staff, whose egos had been widely expected to clash, were working closely with one another and had together become the principal arbiters of domestic policy. As Sununu's deputy saw it, 'while people thought they would do battle with each other [they] ended up becoming real allies.'[14] This gave Darman access to the power he craved while allowing the relatively inexperienced Sununu to benefit from the Budget Director's understanding of the labyrinthine workings of the federal government and, in particular, his mastery of the budgetary process.[15]

THE 1990 BUDGET DEAL

In May 1990, the President, in calling on congressional leaders to participate in a summit with Administration officials designed to address the budget deficit, let it be known, through his press secretary, that discussions would start with 'no preconditions' and would proceed 'unfettered with conclusions about positions taken in the past'. This was, not surprisingly, interpreted as a signal that Bush would now countenance tax increases, a conclusion which Sununu tried surreptitiously to dispel by saying that 'no preconditions' meant that the Democrats were at liberty to propose tax increases, but 'it's our prerogative to say no. And I emphasize the no.'[16]

The Chief of Staff's statement alarmed Democratic leaders suspicious of being manoeuvred into a situation where they would have to take the blame for any increases in taxation. In subsequent meetings with Bush the Democratic leadership insisted that he clarify his position on taxes.[17] This led to a statement drafted by Darman and issued in the name of the President which said, in part:

> It is clear to me that both the size of the deficit problem and the need for a package that can be enacted require all of

the following: entitlement and mandatory program reform, *tax revenue increases*, growth incentives, discretionary spending reductions, orderly reductions in defense expenditures and budget process reform, to assure that any bipartisan agreement is enforceable and that the deficit problem is brought under responsible control.[18] [My italics]

By those three italicized words Bush jettisoned the defining issue between the parties, horrified many members of his own party in Congress, appalled conservative Republicans in general, shattered morale among White House staff and sowed the seeds of his defeat in 1992. For the moment, however, Bush's concession made it possible for budget negotiations between congressional leaders and Administration officials to proceed behind closed doors. These continued fitfully for three months with agreement on a package of cuts and tax increases, largely orchestrated by Richard Darman, finally being reached on 30 September.

This deal, it was claimed, would reduce government borrowing by approximately $500 billion over five years. Defence and domestic discretionary spending were to be cut by $182 billion; entitlements such as Medicare and farm subsidies were to be reduced by $106 billion; interest payments on the national debt would be reduced by $65 billion and new taxes and user fees for government services were expected to raise $148 billion.[19] While the agreement included a whole range of tax increases covering commodities such as gasoline, tobacco, alcohol and heating oil it did not include an increase in income tax, the one thing the Adminstration was most anxious to avoid.[20]

The President and his staff now lobbied members of Congress hard and Bush, on 2 October, made a nationally televised address to the people to urge support for the package. He described the budget deficit as 'a cancer gnawing away at our nation's economic health' and, while he accepted that the bipartisan budget agreement was less than perfect, it was 'the best . . . that can be legislated now.' Bush admitted that the agreement included tax increases which he was not 'a fan' of, but income taxes would not go up and those tax increases that were included 'should allow the economy to grow' by reducing the deficit and allowing interest rates to be lowered. The

President warned, 'if we fail to enact this agreement our economy will falter, markets may tumble and recession will follow' and concluded by making a direct appeal to the American people:

'I ask you to understand how important and, for some, how difficult this vote is, for your congressmen and senators. Many worry about your reaction to one part or another. But I want you to know the importance of the whole. And so I ask you to take this initiative: Tell your congressmen and senators you support this agreement . . . Your senators and congressmen need to know that you want this deficit brought down.'[21]

Despite these dire warnings and exhortations the House of Representatives refused by a large margin to ratify the budget compromise that had been worked out between the White House and congressional leaders. The House as a whole voted it down on 5 October by 254–179; the Democrats opposed it 149–108 while the Republicans voted against 105–71. Many Democrats opposed the agreement because they saw it as being balanced unfairly against their natural constituents. They were troubled by cuts in Medicare and welfare progammes and believed that the suggested tax increases would hit the middle class and and the poor hardest while leaving the wealthy relatively unscathed. Conservative Republicans on the other hand were mortified by the President's willingness to renege on his repeated pledge to not increase taxes.[22]

In the days immediately following this humiliating set-back President Bush, in an abortive effort to frighten Congress into submission, vetoed a continuing resolution designed to prevent the shutting down of essential government services now that authority for spending money had elapsed. After a further three weeks of negotiation and adjustments a budget resolution was cleared by the House and the Senate on 27 October.

This new package passed largely because it had now been made more 'progressive' and thereby more palatable to congressional Democrats. More of the burden of reducing the deficit, in other words, was to be placed on those of means and the pressure relaxed somewhat on the less well off. Thus the top marginal income tax rate was increased from 28 per cent to 31 per cent; Medicare cuts were to be less swingeing;

proposed increases in gasoline taxes were almost halved and a new tax on home heating oil was eliminated altogether.[23]

Overall, however, the final version of the Omnibus Budget Reconciliation Act of 1990 differed little from the earlier deal.[24] It was designed to reduce the deficit by $492 billion over five years – $137 billion of that was to be realized by revenue increases, $99 billion would be obtained by cuts in entitlements and other mandatory spending programmes, while $184 billion would come from cuts in other appropriations. The remainder was to be realized by savings on interest payments on the national debt.[25] Most significantly perhaps the 1990 legislation also included important procedural changes designed to make a reality of attempts to reduce the deficit. The much derided Gramm-Rudman-Hollings legislation was, in effect, repealed and in an effort to contain increases in spending it was now agreed that appropriations bills would have to stay within specific caps for discretionary spending. There would be one such cap for defence, one for foreign aid and a third for domestic expenditures. New spending under either of these headings would have to be offset by decreases elsewhere under the same heading. 'Bills exceeding the caps would be out of order for floor consideration.'[26] Despite the inauspicious circumstances of its birth the budget finally agreed in 1990 was seen as a modest but not unimportant step towards bringing the deficit under control.[27]

A CRISIS OF GOVERNABILITY

The budget débâcle of 1990 can be seen as a crisis of governability, demonstrating not just the fallibility of Bush and other leaders, but also revealing structural defects in the American political system. As Janet Hook said in writing at the time of the defeat of the first budget deal: 'It is a seismic political event that exposes the architecture of power in Washington, unsettling the relationship between political leaders and their followers, between the two parties, and between Congress and the public.'[28]

The fact of divided government obviously contributed to this crisis and yet that is only part of the explanation. In the 1950s, despite divided government, President Eisenhower enjoyed a reasonably constructive relationship with Congress, whereas close to 40 years later the conditions were markedly different. Congress had now become an intensely individualistic institution where the old adage 'to get along go along' associated with the legendary former Speaker Sam Rayburn had become outmoded, where an ethos of 'every man for himself' prevailed.[29]

By the 1990s the proliferation of direct primaries and the ever-expanding role of television in electoral politics had turned congressional campaigns into personal rather than party affairs, and legislators elected almost entirely by their own efforts were bound to be less susceptible to party discipline. A former member of the House, Perkins Bass of New Hampshire, in referring to the budget crisis said: 'When I was in Congress we had a lot of party discipline. There's no discipline I can see today. Congress can't take on the entitlements, or the other tough budget choices, because there's no discipline.'[30]

This situation had arisen in part as a consequence of congressional reforms introduced in the 1970s, which had sharply tilted the balance of power in favour of the rank and file while making party leaders and committee chairmen weaker than they had ever been before.[31] As another former congressman, Joel Pritchard, a Republican from the state of Washington, said: 'In Congress today everyone runs for office as a political entity of his own. Without a strong party connection, there's no coherent philosophy for them to connect to; it's everyone for himself.'[32] During the budget crisis the Minority Leader in the House, Robert Michel, spoke of his role in terms that would have appalled congressional titans of previous eras, 'You just have to keep begging and begging and begging.'[33]

Given the line-up of party forces in the House of Representatives, passage of the first bipartisan budget agreement required that the leaders of each party obtain the support of half their followers – 130 Democratic votes and 89 on the Republican side. The fact that neither came close to these modest objectives with only 108 Democrats and 71 Republicans voting with the leadership provides dramatic testimony of the weakness of party in Congress. This was, after all, a critical issue, and one where Bush and congressional leaders lobbied hard and yet they failed to convince even 50 per cent of their followers to support a bipartisan package.

Among the Democrats only 14 out of 27 standing committee chairmen voted Yea while a mere six out of 13 appropriations sub-committee chairmen voted in favour of the deal.[34]

The most serious divisions, however, were among the House Republicans where the conservative wing led by the Minority Whip, Newt Gingrich, was in open revolt against the President's reversal of his 'no new taxes' undertaking. For a long time the Republican Party had been divided between devotees of supply side economics and those with more traditional views as Gingrich himself explained: 'There is a clear difference between those of us who believe passionately in growth incentives and those with the traditional view that reducing the deficit is more important. It's a debate that has been going on for 15 years.'[35] Initially, it seemed unlikely that conservative Republicans in the House would go so far as to humiliate their own President on such a critical issue, but party loyalty was, in the end, strained beyond reasonable limits by the insensitive tactics of the principal White House negotiators. The President's televised appeal to the voters to pressure their representatives into compliance backfired and the defection by Gingrich was crucial. He was the second-ranking Republican leader in the House and, as Minority Whip, was normally responsible for marshalling votes behind the party leadership, whereas on this occasion, he actively undermined Michel's capacity to deliver the votes of half of his party colleagues.

In defence of the Bush Administration, it can be said that the budgetary crisis of 1990 was, in part, brought about by systemic problems. It was a victim of the chronic individualism that now characterizes the national legislature in the United States. It failed also because of the astonishing fragility of American parties, with the Republican Party in the House on this occasion revealing profound divisions over the direction of economic policy. On the other hand, it is difficult to avoid the conclusion that this crisis might have been avoided by more skilful leadership from the White House.

A CRISIS OF LEADERSHIP

The President himself, his Chief of Staff and his Director of the Office of Management and Budget must bear the heaviest responsibility for the budget débâcle of 1990. The dominant role of Sununu and Darman in the making of domestic policy in the Bush Administration has been attested to by a number of insiders. As Edie Holiday put it, the two men 'were very powerful; they were able to basically command the domestic agenda.'[36] The Assistant to the President for Communications argued similarly that after about three months 'Sununu and Darman were wielding tremendous influence, not only in the shaping and the direction of the President's policies, but also in how he advanced those policies . . . in terms of having a complete picture of what was going on they were the only two that had that.'[37]

Earlier, I touched on some of the reasons why these two aides were so influential in the Bush White House. Sununu's intellect, his tough cop demeanour and his links with conservative Republicans complemented the President's patrician, ideologically agnostic and more decorous approach. Darman, for his part, had made himself seemingly indispensable by dint of his lengthy experience in government, the sharpness of his intellect and his mastery of the arcane mysteries of the budgetary process. However, none of these factors would have counted for so much if the President had not been so disinterested when it came to matters of domestic policy.

With characteristic transparency Bush blurted out his preference for foreign policy at a press conference during the budget crisis: 'When you get a problem with the complexities that the Middle East has now, and the Gulf has now, I enjoy trying to put the coalition together and keep it together . . . I can't say I just rejoice every time I go up and talk to Rostenkowski about what he's going to do on taxes.'[38] John Keller, Director of Presidential Advance and a dedicated Bush loyalist, spoke of the difficulty of engaging the President's interest when it came to domestic issues. 'Getting him excited about agriculture and things like that was like pulling teeth; you could see it when you did those sort of events . . . he was doing it [only] because he had to do it.'[39] The same point was made by Clayton Yeutter who contrasted the President's responses in press conferences to questions on foreign policy with those on domestic matters: '[With] an international question, his eyes would sparkle, his voice would get stronger, he would answer it in a persuasive way . . . When it got to a domestic policy question it was sort of "Jeez, do I have to answer this God awful thing".'[40]

This all too evident lack of interest in domestic affairs by the chief executive created a vacuum that Sununu and Darman eagerly sought to fill. In budgetary matters Darman was allowed to become the prime mover. Aided and abetted by Sununu, he manoeuvred to marginalize other senior figures in the White House who otherwise might have acted as counterweights in this area – notables such as Nicholas Brady, Secretary to the Treasury and a close friend of the President; Michael Boskin, Chairman of the Council of Economic Advisers, and Roger Porter, Assistant to the President for Economic and Domestic Policy.

Both Bush loyalists and Reaganite conservatives in the White House have pointed the finger at Darman as an over-bearing, unprincipled manipulator who led the hapless George Bush into the budget quagmire. Thus the infinitely loyal Bobbie Kilberg found Darman to be 'extraordinarily bright but arrogant'; David Demarest believed the Budget Director was 'too brilliant for his own good' and according to Andrew Card the President 'was politically, poorly served by Dick Darman'.[41] Among the conservatives Connie Horner deplored Darman's penchant for wheeling and dealing and his lack of attachment to principles. She accused him of favouring 'deals rather than standing fast to ideas . . . he did not believe in the no new taxes pledge. He thought it was a stupid idea and was quite happy to draw the President into a repudiation of it.'[42] Another conservative, Charles Kolb, devotes much of his book to the excoriation of Darman and charges that Bush's 'apostasy on taxes was the result of a palace coup orchestrated by Darman. By convincing Bush that the chief threat to the economy was the budget deficit, Darman managed to con Bush away from the one message that had sustained and galvanized Republicans since 1978: economic growth through lower taxes.'[43]

The many critics of the Budget Director within the Bush Administration may have overstated their case and there is much to be said for William Kristol's more measured view. He perceived Darman as 'a very shrewd operator who had his own views on what should be done, but at the end of the day he was doing what the President wanted him to do and what other forces in the White House wanted him to do.'[44] James Pinkerton argued similarly that Darman's budget deal strategy 'appealed to Bush's anti-Reagan instincts' and believed that the President was taken in by the Budget Director, effectively saying: 'If you leave all this to me, I will take care of it and all you've got to worry about is foreign policy.'[45]

It seems that not all the blame for this crisis of leadership can be heaped on Darman, and his close ally Sununu. As a guardian President Bush was only too pleased to have the opportunity to concentrate on what he saw as his primary responsibility, the conduct of foreign and national security policy. This became even more the case after 2 August 1990 and the invasion of Kuwait by Iraqi forces. Unquestionably Darman was on the pragmatic rather than the ideological wing of the Republican Party, but so was Bush. The President moreover shared his Budget Director's scepticism about Reaganomics and almost certainly made the no new taxes pledge more for electoral reasons rather than out of economic policy convictions. Darman had a proclivity for elite deal-making away from the public view, a style of decision-making that Bush himself preferred. Rather than the President being brainwashed and manoeuvred into the budget deal by Darman and Sununu there is good reason to believe that they doing what he wanted them to do.

For all that, the Chief of Staff and the Director of the budget office were deeply implicated in several strategic errors of great consequence. As Bush's most influential advisers on domestic policy they appear to have done him a major disservice by allowing the fateful reversal of his no new taxes pledge to dribble out via a five-line statement pinned to the White House press office bulletin board. According to one source there was no attempt to 'staff' properly this enormously significant announcement. 'Did it go through Boyden [Gray]? No. Did it go through Jim Cicconi? No. Did it go through "speech"? No. Did it go through Marlin Fitzwater? No. Did it go through anybody but Sununu and Darman? No.'[46]

Other senior White House staff were deeply shocked by the manner of Bush's U-turn on taxes, by what Cicconi described as 'cavalierly reneging on a pretty sacred commitment.' In expounding on the nature of that commitment Cicconi said,:

There are very few pledges that have been made in American politics that have been made so clearly and with such obvious intent that it be taken as much more than a typical political promise. When you not only say 'I am not going to raise taxes' but you [also] say 'read my lips' it was as if he'd said, 'I really mean this' and 'I can be believed'. To renege on that after only a year and a half, no matter what the rationale, was fated to divide the party and alienate the American people, and that is exactly the effect that it had.[47]

John Keller took a more relaxed view of the President going back on his pledge, but despaired of the failure of the Administration to 'spin' the issue effectively:

[The President] made a decision which actually was probably the right thing to do for the American people, for the economy, for the country. He realized, although this never came out, that one cannot always be held to campaign promises. You cannot predict the future, or how current events are going to affect your decision-making . . . [Unfortunately there] were no road trips, no events, no spin, no anything around that whole thing. We just got eaten alive; it was like making an announcement and then sitting in the Oval Office and waiting for them to chew you up, which they did.[48]

In an earlier chapter I noted how Nick Calio, the Administration's head of legislative liaison in the House of Representatives, received no forewarning of the abandonment of the tax pledge, even though this development was bound to make his job immeasurably more difficult. After the announcement had been made however, Calio participated in the debate in the White House on how the President should now proceed. Like Keller, Calio argued that the President needed to actively and publicly sell the change of policy:

He should have gone on TV immediately and said 'Look this is something I don't want to do. I said no new taxes, but here is where our economy is and here is what we think needs to be done – the deficit is the problem . . . I know this will hurt me politically, but I am supposed to be your leader and, as your leader, I am going to say I made a mistake to say never. But now we have to go forward; here is why we are doing this. If you are going to take it out on me politically you are welcome to, but I have to do what I think is best for the country and I hope you will come with me'.[49]

Instead of following Calio's excellent advice the President, in the middle of a press conference, 'made some kind of short statement that nobody picked up at all, and was meaningless in terms of the public relations that needed to be done.'[50] One cabinet member subsequently placed the blame for this presentational disaster primarily on Darman, who would not:

> ... admit that it was a mistake, because Darman didn't make mistakes ... But what Darman missed was how damaging it would be to break that ... pledge ... [He] totally missed the political significance of that. So did the other executive branch participants ... And they were totally nonchalant about it. They really thought nobody would pay any attention; that this was just another campaign promise and nobody pays any attention to campaign promises.[51]

These critics from within the Administration, all of them Bush loyalists, surely made, admittedly with the benefit of hindsight, a number of telling points. Darman and Sununu should have recognized that the no new taxes pledge was far more than an ordinary campaign promise; they should have seen that the cavalier abandonment of such a 'sacred commitment' was bound to outrage conservative Republicans and to damage significantly the President's standing in the country. It could be argued that the deterioration in economic circumstances since the election made necessary a change of course, but the rationale for such an important change needed to be spelled out in detail to the public by the President. By openly and courageously facing up to the fact that he had made a mistake and explaining why the good of the country required a budget including increased taxes, Bush would have stood a far better chance of minimizing the damage to his party and retaining the trust of the American people.

The President and his closest advisers were also badly mistaken in adopting a strategy of putting together a budget by deal-making with congressional leaders behind closed doors. This attempt to take the politics out of intensely political matters was ill-advised. The fiercely democratic spirit that infuses the

American system makes elitist decision-making arrangements particularly inappropriate and neither the public, nor rank and file members of Congress, were pleased to be presented with a *fait accompli* on such a politically sensitive matter. At a press conference, after the first budget deal had been rejected, the President was asked whether the behind closed doors strategy had not been a mistake: 'Don't you think though, the secrecy was an impediment? [The budget deal] fell like a lead balloon . . . So had you not negotiated more in public, more public dialogue, more debate, don't you think you would have been better off?'[52]

The President blandly brushed this criticism aside doubting that anyone opposed to raising gasoline taxes would have been more likely to accept them if the matter had been the subject of public debate. This was an especially revealing response, indicating a lack of faith in what can be accomplished through the democratic process.

Dealing with highly contentious matters in secret was also unwelcome to members of Congress of both parties. Thus a California Republican in the House, Bill Thomas, in commenting on the rejection of the first budget deal said 'What this vote proved was that closed door sessions don't work; the whole process should begin and end with full public debate.'[53]

Another House Republican, Arthur Ravenel of South Carolina asked his colleagues: 'Are we in charge as we were sent here to be, or have we become a house of political eunuchs?' On the Democratic side Benjamin Cardin of Maryland observed: 'Even if we weren't happy with what was going on, we'd be a lot more comfortable if we knew what was going on.'[54] Meanwhile his party colleague, Dan Glickman of Kansas, said: 'Eight men met in secret for several weeks to prepare this budget, that is not the democratic way to do business.'[55]

To add to the resentment provoked by the Administration's strategy of secrecy the handling of the legislature by Sununu and Darman was, in other ways, insensitive if not inept. Neither man was well liked on Capitol Hill. The Budget Director was well known for brash intolerance of those he deemed to be his intellectual inferiors, an attitude that made him less than popular among conservative Republican representatives who, in any case, doubted his ideological credentials. Rightly enough, they regarded Darman as a traditional Republican, with little time for the tax pledge or the supply-side faith. The Chief of Staff was less vulnerable on ideological grounds, but his brutish behaviour towards legislators had been a liability before and now proved, once again, to be counterproductive.

Republican members of the House, already smarting from having been excluded from the budget discussions that had gone on through the summer of 1990, might have expected some quiet diplomacy from a White House badly in need of their support when the first budget deal came to the floor of the House. The President's lobbying was suitably low key, but Sununu after a moderate beginning, adopted a different approach. In addressing the House Republican Conference, the Chief of Staff outraged his listeners by saying: 'By the way, none of you guys want to have the President come to your district, to be on a platform with him with a big audience of constituents and have him turn and say, "Why aren't you with me on this deal?" '[56] One indignant Congressman responded, 'I know George Bush, and he would never do anything like that', leading Sununu to reply, 'George Bush is a much nicer guy than I am.'[57]

These acrimonious exchanges badly damaged the President's cause. In the first place Sununu's threat was seen as an empty one that merely served to alienate potential supporters. As we saw earlier, Bush, arising from his own service in the House and the friends he still had there, had adopted a conciliatory approach to Congress and there was no reason to suppose that this was now to be abandoned. Moreover, the Chief of Staff's abrasive comments helped to drive moderate Republicans into the arms of conservatives already appalled by the President's reversal on taxes. A senior Republican member of the House reportedly said of Sununu's intervention: 'I bet you that of the 176 members of the conference, at least 100 of them were undecided at that point. You could feel the tide turn. All of those people who wanted to help shifted to "no" and it was downhill from there.'[58] Another Republican said 'Sununu insulted the conference. Some of us who felt bad about voting against the President before the conference now feel good about it.'[59] In these new circumstances, Newt Gingrich, the leader of the conservatives, felt sufficiently emboldened to go public with his opposition to the budget deal, a defection of the greatest consequence.

The President's most influential advisers on the budget also erred in insisting on keeping information on the budget negotiations even from senior White House colleagues. From the outset of the Bush Administration there had been a downplaying of the role of those who worked in Communications, Legislative Affairs and Public Liaison and now their exclusion from discussions on the budget deal proved to be a costly mistake.

Several senior staff expressed their indignation at being totally shut out of the negotiations . Bobbie Kilberg reported that 'the only people with any idea of what was in the budget deal in the White House were Sununu and Darman.'[60] James Cicconi observed that 'virtually the entire senior staff were kept in the dark on this; the only people that really knew what was going on were Sununu and Darman.'[61] The dangers in such an approach were pinpointed by Edie Holiday; she noted that 'Dick Darman wanted total control over those issues and didn't want anybody to know what they were doing,' and went on to say 'as a result there was not an apparatus working to prepare the necessary public relations or communications strategy, that would have helped to sell the reasons' why the budget deal was necessary.[62]

The same point was elaborated in some detail by Kilberg who, as one of the two people in charge of the Office of Public Liaison, was responsible for maintaining healthy relationships with business and other interest groups sympathetic to the Administration. These organizations could be expected to play a pivotal role in ensuring public and congressional acceptance of any budget agreement. However, as Kilberg explained, during the budget negotiations Public Liaison was placed 'in an absolutely impossible position because we were totally cut out of the loop . . . Darman let nobody know what was going on, absolutely nobody. [Consequently], we could not defuse anger, help build coalitions, help get support for what was going on, because we didn't have the foggiest notion of what was going on, and neither did any of the interest groups.'

Kilberg went on to recount how she was summoned to the White House on the Sunday morning when the budget deal was to be announced. After the announcement was made in the Rose Garden:

'Sununu turned to me and said 'Sell it.' I said 'Sell what? How am I going to sell this when for the last three months I have been stonewalling all of these people? Telling them that we couldn't have their input; telling them they weren't part of the game. And now you want me to turn around and tell them to start selling this. What do I do?' And he said, 'Just do it.'

Having outlined the impossible situation in which Public Liaison had been placed Kilberg nevertheless tried to meet her responsibilities by turning to Darman and saying 'OK here is a piece of paper [listing] all the groups we need to touch base with between now and Tuesday. And between now and Tuesday I need you here for this briefing and there for that briefing.' Darman, however, declined to be so instructed saying, before turning away,'I will brief when I care to brief on what I care to brief about and you will not direct me.'[63] This arrogant, wilful refusal to draw on the expertise, the contacts and the relationships nurtured by Kilberg and her colleagues was another reaction most unhelpful to the acceptance of the budget agreement.

President Bush suffered a humiliating setback when he urged the American people, during his 2 October television address, to call upon their representatives to support the first budget deal. In the event, far greater numbers of constituents appear to have demanded rejection rather than support for the agreement. According to Kilberg the calls from constituents to their members of Congress ran something like six to one against the budget deal.[64] Part of the explanation for this humiliating rebuff surely lies in the failure to prepare the ground adequately for the President's appeal. Again according to Kilberg, neither she, her boss David Demarest, Assistant to the President for Communications, or Nick Calio, the President's chief of legislative affairs in the House, had any advance warning that the President's address would include such an appeal and it appears that the relevant wording was only added to the text of the President's speech shortly before Bush spoke. With some feeling Ms Kilberg said: 'No other White House would ever have done that without having decided it at least a day before, without having told public liaison, without having public liaison all organized and ready to go.' Immediately after the President had spoken the Office of Public Liaison began working the phones, but 'our association folks were so mad they couldn't see straight. They said, "You're on your own on this one. Forget it. You tell us after the speech that this is what you're expecting us to do just days ahead of the vote." I said, "I didn't know." They said, "How could you not know?" I said, "Nobody knew." They said, "How is that possible?" '[65]

It is evident that George Bush, in 1990, was poorly served by his Budget Director and his Chief of Staff. Their obsessive determination to monopolize information, to keep details of the budget negotiations secret from rank and file members of Congress, from the public, and even from their senior White House colleagues, was a fundamental and damaging mistake. Sununu and Darman failed abysmally to anticipate the political fallout that was bound to arise from the President going back on a constantly reiterated, specific promise that formed the centrepiece of his 1988 campaign.

Both men, moreover, had difficulty in concealing their contempt for Congress, and the Chief of Staff's abrasive tactics in dealing with legislators were especially ill-judged. Sununu acted as if he was still the governor of a small state with a part-time legislature rather than the agent of a chief executive facing a Congress with formidable powers in divided government circumstances. As one Republican House member said of Sununu: 'He's an extraordinarily bright and intellectual man. But his basic problem is that was effective as a governor dealing with people who were part-time legislators. Frankly, you can bully them around. You don't get anywhere in this town by bullying people around. That lesson has not quite soaked through.'[66]

It should also be noted that the White House includes specialists in communications, in legislative liaison and in public liaison; these groupings of staff possess expertise, resources and contacts invaluable to a president as he struggles to gain acceptance of his policies. It was foolhardy in the extreme for Sununu and Darman to go out of their way to cut such people out of the 'loop', to exclude these specialists from the decision-making process, to deny them the opportunity to make use of their expertise and to prepare the ground for the announcement of the budget deal.

'THE BUCK STOPS HERE'

Harry Truman famously placed on his desk a sign which said 'The buck stops here', a slogan that should be kept in mind by all those Bush loyalists inclined to heap blame on senior advisers for his failures.[67] To be sure, Sununu and Darman had their shortcomings, but Bush selected them in the first place and persisted in keeping them on despite the mounting evidence of their inadeqacies. Sununu only left after the 'Air Sununu' scandal had made his position untenable and Darman remained until the very end. According to one source, when Samuel Skinner replaced Sununu as Chief of Staff, he 'tried to get Bush to get rid of Darman . . . but Bush wouldn't do it and he should have, that was a big mistake.'[68]

The selection of competent staff is one of the tests of effective leadership and if the White House functioned imperfectly during the budget crisis of 1990 the responsibility for that rests ultimately with George Bush. As is the case with any president, Bush's staff and the organization of the White House were reflections of his character and his style of leadership. Richard Darman was a pragmatist and an elitist; he disdained ideology and delighted in making deals behind the scenes with other members of the elite. This type of leadership was all of a piece with the President's patrician, managerial approach. He too had a penchant for 'cutting deals with other leaders. His is the insider game. His weakness is in sensing outside perspectives and in extending the ambit of discussion. This is not because, like Reagan, Bush has strong passions about the substance, but because his style of operation is fundamentally boardroom politics and brokerage among "proper gentlemen".'[69]

As I argued earlier, it was the President's extravagant lack of interest in domestic policy that created the vacuum that his two egotistical, belligerent aides leapt to fill. It was his lack of engagement that allowed them to act without inhibition, monopolizing information, offending legislators and cutting out of the decision-making process other senior White House staff. If Bush had been more 'hands-on' in this area, in the way that he was in matters of foreign policy, it is probable that neither Sununu nor Darman would have been appointed. Or if they had managed to secure appointment we may presume that their displacement would have been less; conceivably, they would have been less able to exclude other staff from the decision-making process, and their removal would have become highly likely when their behaviour became damaging to the President's purposes.

The widespread belief that Bush was not interested in domestic policy tended to feed the suspicion that he was a man without deeply held views on economic policy. These concerns were especially prevalent among those on the right of his party who had not forgotten his denunciation of supply side theory during the 1980 primaries as 'voodoo economics'. This notably significant comment revealed the fault line in Bush's party that has for years divided the Reaganites from more traditional, more pragmatic Republicans. The former had been reassured by Bush taking the tax pledge in 1988, whereas their worst fears were confirmed by his apparently casual abandonment of that undertaking. It does not make sense to exonerate Bush from responsibility for taking a step that disastrously divided his party, and ultimately destroyed his presidency, on the grounds that he was talked into it by Richard Darman for, in the end, it was the President's decision and his alone.

Several Bush loyalists whom I spoke to robustly defended him against the charge that his willingness to renege on taxes was evidence of his lack of convictions. One of those who worked closely with the President and knew him well, James Cicconi, insisted that the no new taxes promise was made sincerely; when he 'made that pledge he meant it and he fully intended to keep it.' Eventually, however, he succumbed to Darman's persuasion, accepting that:

> A budget deal involving taxes was really the only way to deal with the [deficit] problem and was essential to the well-being of the nation. George Bush does have an inner core of conviction [one] that is rooted in doing what is right for the country regardless. The Budget Director understood this and was able to appeal to that gradually over time to swing him around to the notion that this was the only way to help the country . . . In George Bush's mind it probably amounted to "Look, you can either adhere to your commitment for the sake of foolish consistency, or you can do what

is right for the country and seize the moment for an historic agreement with Congress that will finally get the deficit under control and ensure future generations of prosperity." . . . The George Bush I know probably said to himself, "I am willing to take the heat for reneging if it is in the best interest of the nation." . . . There are many occasions on which he stood up to political heat because of that integral conviction. I don't think the budget deal showed him to be cynical. Certainly a lot of the American public concluded that, but I don't think it was a correct conclusion.[70]

This explanation presents Bush as a man of principle forced to change course out of a concern for the national interest. It is also the case that Bush's change of tack was entirely consistent with a guardianship approach to presidential leadership. As Chapter 1 made clear, guardian presidents have no preordained plan for change; they take the view that presidents should be skilled managers who deal with problems on an *ad hoc* basis. Such an approach presupposes pragmatic flexibility rather than the sort of ideological certainty associated with Bush's predecessor. However, it is surely the case that making an iron-clad commitment in the first place was inconsistent with a guardian style of leadership, and the fact that George Bush nevertheless did so serves to reinforce the allegation that the pledge was made principally for electoral reasons.

Further reason to question the President's motives and to doubt the quality of his leadership in domestic policy was provided by his weaving back and forth on the capital gains issue during the budget crisis. Since the beginning of his presidency, Bush had been pressing on Congress the case for a reduction in capital gains tax. In addressing a joint session on 9 Febuary 1989 he had said: 'I propose that we cut the maximum tax rate on capital gains to increase long-term investment. History is clear. This would increase revenues, help saving and create new jobs'.[71]

During the budget negotiations capital gains had been a central issue, but the Democrats had been been resistant to a reduction in the rate which they saw as a windfall for the wealthy. They would only countenance such a cut if it was offset by higher rates of income tax on those with large incomes. The negotiators failed to reach agreement on this matter in the summer ultimately because the Republicans' aversion to an income tax increase outweighed their enthusiasm for a capital gains tax reduction. After the defeat of the first budget deal on 5 October the possibility of some such trade-off was reopened.

At a press conference on the morning of 9 October the President was asked whether he was willing to contemplate a higher income tax rate for the wealthy in an exchange for a capital gains cut. He replied: 'That's on the table. That's been talked about. And if it's proper, if it can be worked in the proper balance between the capital gains rate and the income tax changes, fine'.[72] Later that day, however, 17 Republican senators descended on the White House to put it to the President that any such deal was not possible in the short term; their virtually unanimous advice was, according to Senator Pete Domenici of New Mexico, 'Get it off the table.' Senator Bob Packwood of Oregon emerged from the meeting to announce: 'The President agreed, our unified position was we will not go up on the rate, not 1 per cent, not 2 per cent, not one penny . . . we will leave the rates where they are, drop capital gains and do nothing about the rates.' The following morning Robert Dole, the Senate Minority Leader, put a different gloss on Bush's position: '[He] did not make any decision yesterday, even though that was reported. He listened to us. He did not announce his position at all. He did not acquiesce in what we said.'[73]

When asked, on a trip to Florida, to clarify the confusion that had arisen, Bush most unhelpfully said: 'Let Congress clear it up.' Rather more damagingly, when out jogging, the President, on being asked whether he was ready to give up on a capital gains cut, pointed to his backside and said: 'Read my hips.'[74] On his return to Washington Bush met with a delegation of House Republicans on 11 October after which Congressman Bill Archer of Texas reported to the press that the President was ready to accept a tax increase in return for a capital gains cut: 'He is willing – and I think he will speak to you today about this – he is willing to equalize or level the rate at 31 per cent . . . in exchange for a 15 per cent capital gains rate . . . I'm telling you that he told us today that he has been consistently for this all the way through.' Within hours, however, the President's position changed again, when he said through his press spokesman that 'he did not believe that such a compromise was now possible'.[75]

To summarize the foregoing fiasco, in the course of two days the President appeared to make several U-turns on a central issue of economic policy. He began on 9 October by saying that a trade-off between capital gains and income tax rates was 'on the table'. After meeting later that day with Republican senators he left those like Packwood with the clear impression that no deal was possible. The following morning, Dole inferred that, in fact, the President was undecided on the matter and Bush, when pressed to resolve the confusion, made only flippant response. Subsequently, he gave congressmen reason to believe that a deal was back on the table only to deny that this was so later the same day.

Not surprisingly, this display of 'rampant indecision' brought about many unflattering newspaper headlines across the country, precipitated a sharp fall in the President's public opinion poll ratings and further damaged his standing in Congress with one Democrat in the House, Thomas Downey of New York gleefully observing: 'Our president has now taken more positions on taxes than Nadia Comaneci.'[76] Meanwhile, conservative Republicans like Gingrich were appalled by the President making a wisecrack about what they looked upon as a sacred campaign commitment and regarded his behaviour during this episode as further proof of his lack of any settled beliefs in economic matters.

President Bush's leadership during the 1990 budget crisis was shown to be badly flawed; not only was he chronically indecisive, throughout he failed to make effective use of his office as a bully pulpit. In an earlier chapter I commented on Bush's disinclination to use rhetorical appeals in support of policy objectives and this weakness now became glaringly apparent. As a good loyalist, Edie Holiday faulted other senior staff for not impressing on Bush the need to go to the country to explain why it was necessary to go back on no new taxes, but this is surely disingenuous.[77] An experienced leader like Bush should have seen for himself that if he was to abandon such a central and often repeated undertaking, a programme of public education beforehand would be required.

As Stuart Eizenstat, chief domestic policy adviser in the Carter White House, noted in a rather prescient article written in

June 1990 before the budget had become a crisis issue, presidents had broken campaign promises before and survived relatively unscathed. FDR, for instance in the 1932 campaign promised to reduce spending and to balance the budget and then did precisely the opposite in office. However Bush needed to understand that 'the people will forgive a breach in a major campaign commitment if the president can convincingly demonstrate that external circumstances have changed.' Roosevelt had done this impressively in 1936 and gone to win re-election in a landslide. 'In Bush's case, circumstances have indeed changed, but not in ways that are immediately evident to the average citizen. That's why it is essential that if the president does agree to raise taxes, he explain to the people why new circumstances have required it. Otherwise he risks provoking a degree of public cynicism that could be dangerous to his presidency.[78]

As I indicated earlier, there were some in the upper reaches of the Bush White House who urged the President to go to the country to explain why it was necessary to renege on his promise, but he chose to ignore such voices. He did so presumably because such advice was unpalatable to him, because he had little talent for public speaking, had no faith in what it could accomplish and, in any case, did not see such activity as an essential role for presidents. Even though it should ideally have come months earlier it is not inconceivable that inspired use of the bully pulpit after the first budget deal might have saved Bush and his colleagues from disaster. Instead the President made a brief, insipid television address that was unaccompanied by any careful preparing of the ground and had all the effect, according to one source, of a 'whisper in a hurricane'. Indeed, the *Congressional Quarterly* reported that: 'Unexpectedly, those selling the budget found momentum slowed in the 24 hours after Bush's speech. Far from producing a groundswell of support, it seemed to have increased constituents' awareness of its painful provisions.'[79]

Even ardent Bush loyalists in the White House agreed that, irrespective of the merits of the budget deal, its presentation to the public was a disaster. Ron Kaufman said: 'It wasn't the deal itself, it was the way it was sold . . . It wasn't what we did, it's how we did it; it's not what you say, it's how you say it.' Similarly, Andrew Card said: 'We did a lousy job of communicating to the public as to why we were where we were and what the consequences of failure were.' According to the Cabinet Secretary, Edie Holiday: 'I saw it as a failure of communications as opposed to a policy failure . . . [we could] have managed the policy change had it been conducted properly.'[80]

The inability of Bush and his Administration to communicate effectively with the American people and to mobilize support behind his budgetary policy in 1990 stands in stark contrast with the high professionalism in such mattters of Ronald Reagan and his colleagues. Not only was Reagan himself a master communicator, his staff, when crucial votes were at stake, worked tirelessly to organize support for his policies in the country – contacting interest groups and campaign contributors to get them to bring pressure to bear on members of Congress.[81] This was precisely the sort of input that Bush's communications staff could have provided if he had not allowed them to be sidelined by Sununu and Darman.

Unlike Bush, Reagan was devastatingly effective in making set-piece speeches on television and testimony to his ability to use that medium to bring members of Congress into line was provided by former Senator Laxalt: 'While Reagan very often could not convince [legislators] on given major policy issues,' Laxalt said, 'they'd better not cross him because he'd get on television and appeal to their constituencies and build up enormous constituent pressure . . . On issue after issue, I saw Reagan change the complexion of Congress on key votes because he had that capability.'[82] By his own admission, Bush lacked that capability and his ability to gain support for his policies in Congress was further eroded by his insider, kid-glove style in dealing with senators and representatives. 'George Bush might be too nice for his own good' Norman Ornstein suggested during the budget crisis.'Every one of those House Republicans knows that if they defied him on this vote the president would be real unhappy, but within a couple of weeks they'd each get a handwritten thoughtful note saying let "bygones be bygones." Nobody out there really feared any serious consequences from this.'[83]

If a president's ability to achieve his policy objectives is the criterion by which he may be legitimately assessed, Bush, in 1990, failed by some margin to meet this test. He was first forced to abandon a hallowed campaign commitment with grave consequences for the unity of his party. He then suffered humiliation when, despite his televised appeal for its acceptance, the first budget deal was rejected. A second budget deal then only became possible after the President had given further ground to his opponents. To put it another way, the budget crisis was a defining event for the Bush presidency demonstrating several deficiencies in his approach to leadership. His choice of Sununu and Darman for key roles was mistaken, as was his willingness to allow them wide-ranging freedom of action. No modern president can afford to be as disinterested in domestic policy as George Bush was and his preference for insider decision-making, out of the public view, was ill-advised in domestic affairs. His indecisiveness and his evident lack of convictions when it came to economics, and in domestic policy generally, badly undermined his credibility. Finally, Bush's presidency was crippled by his reluctance to mount the bully pulpit and his uninspired performances when he grudgingly did so.

In reflecting on their experience in the Bush White House various senior people have identified the budget imbroglio of 1990 as a pivotal occurrence. Vice President Quayle observed: 'If you want to look for the place where things first went wrong, I'd pick the "budget summit" of 1990.'[84] Much the same point was made by James Cicconi: 'In our White House there is a dividing line between what happened before the budget agreement and what happened after . . . the budget agreement, in many ways was one of the seminal events of the Bush presidency. In my view, his defeat in the 1992 elections flowed directly from the budget agreement.' In reviewing the reasons for Bush's loss in 1992 the conservative Pinkerton mentioned the ending of the Cold War, 'the dry rot of twelve years in power . . . and the budget deal.'

Several of those who were there have confirmed how the atmosphere inside the White House itself was dramatically, if not disastrously, transformed by the budget deal. It shattered 'staff morale in the White House to an extraordinary degree' according to Cicconi, while also destroying the 'collegiality' that existed for the first year and a half of the Bush Administration. This was confirmed by Ms Kilberg: 'After the budget deal the whole domestic White House operation changed dramatically, everybody was suspicious of everybody and everybody started doing their own thing.' In this new atmosphere where 'staff were shocked and more than a little rebellious' the Chief of Staff and his ally the Budget Director, those who had fostered the budget deal, were driven into 'a death embrace with each other. It became them against the world, them against the rest of the staff.'[85] The prevalence of this distinctly unhealthy state of affairs has been remarked upon by Charles Kolb: 'After the deal was concluded, Darman and Sununu became locked together in a fraternal death embrace. Anyone who criticized their deal or who proposed policies even slightly at odds with the legislation was treated as a leper. Policy-making ground to a halt.'[86]

The President's conduct during the budget crisis severely damaged his credibility as a leader and eroded respect for his competence in economic policy. The budget deal 'undermined [Bush's] credibility' in the words of Nick Calio, a view Vice President Quayle and many other Americans shared.[87] According to a *Time*/CNN poll taken on 10 October 1990, Bush's approval rating slumped to 59 per cent from 74 per cent on 23 August, while only 34 per cent now thought he was doing a good job in handling the economy compared to 56 per cent who thought he was doing a poor job.[88].

To add to all this, the rebuffs that Bush suffered over the budget in 1990 did immense harm to his 'professional reputation' defined by Richard Neustadt as the standing of a president in the 'Washington community'. That community comprised not only members of Congress and those within the administration, but also 'governors of states, military commanders in the field, leading politicians in both parties, representatives of private organizations, newsmen of assorted types and sizes, foreign diplomats (and principals abroad)'.[89] In Washington itself the defeat of the first budget deal sparked off ruminations by leading politicos on the possibly dire consequences for the President. Robert Strauss, a former Chairman of the Democratic National Committee, remarked to the press: 'You know and I know that when they smell blood in the water, they go in this town.' Meanwhile Jody Powell, who, as President Carter's press secretary, had first-hand experience of the weakening of a presidency, said: 'Any time you get beat, it makes people inclined to think they can beat you again.'[90]

Another seriously adverse result of the budget débâcle was the heavy damage inflicted on Republican Party unity. The White House 'ideas man', Pinkerton spoke of the agreement on the budget breaking 'the spine of the Republican Party's morale'; Calio referred to it as 'undermining party unity' and Cicconi reported that the 'party was clearly divided on this issue.'[91] The candidacy of Patrick Buchanan in the 1992 primaries was a direct result of the divisions in the party brought about by the budget deal.

Bush's reactions under the pressure of a significant threat to his renomination added weight to the suspicions of those inclined to doubt whether he was a man of convictions. In a radio broadcast in the spring of 1992 the President described his abandonment of the no new taxes pledge as the worst mistake of his presidency. What was remarkable, however, was the stress Bush laid on political considerations in explaining why the change of course was a mistake: 'Listen, if I had to do that over, I wouldn't do it. Look at all the flak its taking.' The President admitted that Republican voters were 'just overwhelmed by the fact that I went for a tax increase' and were giving him 'political grief' as a consequence.[92] Elsewhere he said: 'If I had it to do over, I wouldn't do what I did then, for a lot of reasons, including political reasons.'[93]

These admissions provide an example of Bush's tendency, on occasion, towards transparent honesty, but they also reveal the misplaced distinction he was inclined to make between campaigning and governing. In addition, they gave renewed currency to the allegation that he was a political wimp. As one of his most senior and loyal advisers frankly observed: 'He explained [the mistake] on the basis of all the flak he was getting, not on the substance of the issue. The importance of the issue was his credibility and that of his administration. He should have taken it like a man. He should have said "This was wrong. [If] the President of the United States makes major campaign promises [he's] got to live up to them. I didn't, I was wrong, and if I am re-relected in 1992 I'm going to live up to campaign promises".'[94]

Over the long term, one of the most damaging repercussions arising from the budget deal was the dimunition of the American people's trust in George Bush, a critical factor in his 1992 defeat. To lose ground on trust in a contest with a candidate notoriously vulnerable on this score was especially galling for presidential staff, denied what would have been a potent campaign weapon. With understandable bitterness David Demarest claimed that the budget deal 'deprived us of two key arguments that Republicans make – you can trust us [and] we won't raise taxes. It killed us on trust and it killed us on taxes.' It was particularly frustrating to be hurt on the issue of trust 'given Bush's inherent strengths; because if you looked at the poll data, one of his strengths was that this is a decent and honorable man.' That same frustration was apparent in James Cicconi's remark, 'We were not able to take advantage of the far larger questions of trust that revolved around Clinton because we ourselves were vulnerable on that issue.'[95] After the 1992 election, exit polls showed Bush ahead of Clinton on the trust issue, but without the budget deal we may assume the margin would have been far greater, sufficient, perhaps, to have brought electoral success.[96]

7 Guardianship and Foreign Policy

In domestic policy guardian presidents are unambitious if not passive. They are reluctant to take initiatives and are keenly conscious of the limits of the power of government. In dealing with foreign and national security issues, by contrast, they adopt a more activist stance, as Richard Rose has noted: 'A guardian President wants to be more influential abroad than at home.'[1] This was certainly true in the case of George Bush, yet for all that there were parallels between his style of leadership on the domestic front and in international affairs.

In managing foreign policy Bush made much use of private diplomacy, a style not unlike his penchant for behind-the-scenes negotiations with other leaders that he used at home. In domestic policy he was at pains to 'do no harm' and his foreign policy stewardship was similarly marked by prudence, caution and pragmatism. An emphasis on limited government at home was reflected by a limited role for the United States abroad. In both arenas, there was the same inclination to discourage people from expecting Washington to provide solutions to their problems. People should 'look to private organizations for domestic problems, and [should] settle their own problems abroad before expecting the United States to take a hand in imposing a settlement.'[2]

In domestic policy Bush's inadequacies as a communicator were a notable source of weakness and for his critics, this deficiency was also a liability in international affairs. He was to be faulted for failing to articulate a memorable response to the destruction of the Berlin Wall and for not spelling out a convincing rationale to the American people for massive intervention in the Persian Gulf.

Bush was accused of lacking vision in international affairs no less than in domestic policy, but he was unrepentant, seeing no need for a conceptual framework for dealing with foreign policy problems. As he saw it, it was more important that he possessed the experience, the contacts and the understanding necessary for dealing with developments on a case-by-case basis. Consequently, his Administration spawned no grand strategy comparable to containment or detente; there was to be no Bush doctrine to place alongside the Truman doctrine, or the Reagan doctrine. An early attempt to enunciate a strategy of 'beyond containment' was derided in the media, a fate which also befell attempts to define a 'new world order' in the wake of the Gulf War.[3]

The key words distinguishing Bush's approach to foreign policy were prudence, moderation and pragmatism. In the same way that he had no plan for restructuring America at home, he entertained no grand schemes for reordering the world outside. He responded cautiously to the tumultuous changes that occurred on his watch, constantly warning of the dangers of instability and upredictability. Instinctively, he favoured the status quo and often, to the chagrin of conservatives in his party, displayed a preference for dealing with established elites rather than encouraging dissenters.

In January 1993 Lawrence Eagleburger, by then Secretary of State, denied that Bush's foreign policy had been unduly reactive and lacking in vision; he insisted that:

> There was a strategy behind the President's conduct of foreign policy . . . [it] was characterized by pragmatism and flexibility . . . [Admittedly] our approach was often ad hoc [but] a certain degree of ad hockery is a virtue, not a vice, when you are dealing with a world in crisis and in chaos, one in which it is impossible to be certain of anything six months ahead . . . for a long time to come, we will be in a post-revolutionary transitional period which will require of us an ability to react quickly to events. In these circumstances, good instincts are as invaluable as a good plan.[4]

The strategy apparently was, in essence, to not have a strategy at all, but to be ready to respond quickly, and on an *ad hoc* basis, to events as they unfolded. This is not to say that Bush had no foreign policy objectives even though they undoubtedly differed from those of his predecessor. Unlike Reagan, who was an ideologue and an often strident advocate of change, Bush and the circle of policy advisers close to him were moderates and pragmatists, troubled by the rapidity of change while they were in office and convinced that the interests of the United States would be best served by cautiously conservative policies that encouraged stability and minimized departures from the status quo. As one senior member of the National Security Council staff explained it: 'This administration is not ideological. It is conservative with a small "c". It is trying to preserve what is working, not embracing departure for departure's sake. We prefer what is, as opposed to the alternative. We don't want to reinvent the world. This is not an administration that is hellbent on change.'[5]

While the Bush Administration has been criticized for being unadventurous in the international arena, there is a sense in which the President's management of foreign policy was far from timid. He had no doubt that the conduct of foreign policy was an executive responsibility and he and his colleagues vigorously resisted attempts by Congress to encroach on his prerogatives in this area. As I explained in Chapter 5, he did this by resolute use of the veto, by extensive use of National Security Directives and, as will become apparent, most significantly of all, by wide-sweeping and controversial interpretations of his constitutional role in warmaking.

FOREIGN POLICY ADVISERS

In sharp contrast to his marked lack of interest in domestic policy, Bush regarded foreign and national security policy as his forte and there was no possibility of his ceding control over decision-making to senior staff in this area. His closest advisers on such matters were James Baker, his Secretary of State, and his Assistant for National Security, Brent Scowcroft. As might be expected, both men had longstanding and close relationships with the President. No one outside his family was closer to Bush than Baker who had been a friend and confidant for more than thirty years. Baker had managed Bush's unsuccessful Senate campaign in 1970 and on the latter's recommendation was appointed Under Secretary for Commerce in the Ford administration. Subsequently, Baker ran Ford's 1976 campaign and then did the same for Bush in 1980. He served as a notably successful Chief of Staff during Reagan's first term, before becoming Secretary of the Treasury in 1985; he was Bush's campaign manager again in 1988.[6]

The President's relationship with Scowcroft extended back to the days of the Nixon Administration. A former Air Force lieutenant general and holding a PhD in international relations, Scowcroft worked in the Nixon White House as a military aide and became Henry Kissinger's deputy at the National Security Council. Scowcroft became National Security Adviser himself in the Ford Administration and it was at this point that Bush became Director of the Central Intelligence Agency and Scowcroft provided the channel through whom he reported to the President.[7]

For a President bent on keeping the control of foreign policy in his own hands, Baker and Scowcroft were excellent choices. Their loyalty was unquestioned and their world views reflected that of George Bush. To take the Bush-Baker relationship first, the President had far greater knowledge of international affairs than his friend whereas Baker's reputation rested on his astute political sense. Essentially, however, these two men were strikingly similar in their approaches to politics. Neither was remotely interested in ideas and they prided themselves on their unremitting pragmatism. Thus Bush pronounced: 'I am a practical man. I like what's real. I'm not much for the airy and the abstract. I like what works. I am not a mystic, and I do not yearn to lead crusades.' His friend Baker meanwhile, said: 'I'm more interested in the game than in philosophy.'[8]

As Chief of Staff and then Secretary of the Treasury in the Reagan Administration, Baker had been seen as the 'ultimate pragmatist', respected for his problem solving skills and his acute political sense, but also criticized by conservatives for his readiness to strike deals rather than to hold out for the whole loaf of Reagan's ideological agenda and 'for lacking an overall conceptual design'.[9] The same sort of complaints surfaced when Baker became Bush's Secretary of State. Thus a 1989 magazine article with the title 'Vision Problems at State . . .' quoted Frank Gaffney, director of the conservative Center for Security Policy, as saying that Baker 'believes in success for its own sake and often finds specific goals inconvenient. That's not leadership or vision.'[10]

Three years later, the same publication in a piece headed 'Boldness Without Vision' praised Baker for the problem-solving capability he had shown in working out an agreement with Congress on Nicaragua, and for putting together the massive coalition necessary for the war against Iraq, but nevertheless found his performance wanting. 'In a fragmented and challenging new world American foreign policy needs a conceptual overhaul, the kind of coherent vision that it got in a simpler past from such men as Dean Acheson and George Kennan. A seat-of-the-pants approach to international relations, even with its share of short-term successes, will not preserve American leadership.'[11]

While Baker was always one of those closest to the President his duties required him to travel abroad extensively and it was the knowledgeable, experienced, self-effacing Scowcroft who was constantly at Bush's side, aiding and advising him on foreign and national security matters. The President's reasons for selecting Scowcroft as his National Security Adviser are apparent from his autobiography, published in 1987. In that book, Bush noted the tendency, apparent since the presidencies of Kennedy and Johnson, for National Security advisers to stray from their original purpose to 'advise the President with respect to the integration of domestic, foreign and military policies relating to the national security'.

Beginning in the early 1960s, NSC chiefs had assumed a role in the policy-making process that had never been intended; they had become rivals for influence over the conduct of foreign policy with the Secretary of State. However, Scowcroft's conduct during his brief tenure as Ford's National Security Adviser had been exemplary, providing 'a model that every future American president ought to follow in choosing and properly using a national security adviser. Scowcroft scrupulously adhered to the NS charter, seeing to it that the views of all the council members were accurately and objectively reported to the President. He didn't try to make the NSC into a policy-making agency.'[12]

As a member of the Tower Commission set up to investigate the Iran Contra scandal, Scowcroft had been shocked by the evidence uncovered of the misuse of the National Security Council during the Reagan presidency.[13] According to Richard Haass, one of Scowcroft's principal aides, the idea of the National Security Adviser as an honest broker had been lost sight of in the previous administration. Under Reagan the NSC 'was both too weak and too strong. It was too weak at what it was supposed to do and too strong at what it wasn't supposed to do.' In other words, advisers had neglected to be honest brokers, turning themselves into policy advocates and allowing NSC staff to adopt operational roles. 'Scowcroft wanted to bring back a fairly orderly system, much like he had under Ford. Not to go back to Kissinger's heavily controlled thing, but much more of a Ford-like system, where multiple advocacy would be the closest model; where he would play the broker role.'[14]

Scowcroft began by reducing the number of NSC staff from 200 to 150 and by defining his own role in limited terms: 'The President runs the government. He has expert advice from State and Defense, and it is my job to ensure the integration of that advice, to fill in where there are holes, and hopefully to help provide a strategic concept which covers the whole field of national security.'[15] Leaving day-to-day management of NSC staff to his deputy Robert Gates, Scowcroft became, in effect, the President's personal counsellor on foreign and national security policy.[16]

As a political scientist by training who observed Scowcroft in action at close range, Richard Haass had some insightful comments to make about how the National Security Adviser perceived his responsibilities. Those who had studied presidential decision-making had argued that White House policy advisers should be honest brokers. They needed to be close to the President, but should be low-profile individuals without policy management responsibilities, capable of detachment and finding 'satisfaction in pulling the strands of a problem together or in laying out a complex issue for someone else's judgment.'[17] Haass, drawing on his experience of working with Scowcroft, noted that National Security Advisers were somewhat more than honest brokers even though that was their most important role. It might be more appropriate to characterize the adviser as an 'honest balancer'. The brokerage role required them 'to ensure that the options get to the President; that they are well staffed; that the analysis is rigorous; that everyone who wants and deserves to be a player gets to play; that decisions are made and that they're carefully communicated and implemented.' In addition, however, the Assistant for National Security Affairs was obliged to offer the president 'advice and counsel' to be both a 'referee and a protagonist'. This had been how Scowcroft operated, as had Haass himself, and it was up to to others to judge 'whether we did that fairly or rigorously and whether our counselling ever got in the way of our facilitating.'[18]

Even if Baker knew relatively little about foreign policy issues when he became Secretary of State, his Washington experience caused him to be well versed in the political manoeuvring and deadly infighting that had, in the past, detracted from presidential control of the foreign policy process. From the beginning Baker made clear his determination not to become a captive of the career professionals in the State Department; it was his intention to be 'the President's man at State and not State's man at the White House.'[19]

To further that overriding aim, Baker brought with him to the State Department a praetorian guard of senior aides who had worked elsewhere for him before. These were Margaret Tutwiler, who became Assistant for Public Affairs, Robert Kimmit, Under Secretary for Political Affairs, Dennis Ross, director of policy planning and Robert Zoellick counsellor and Under Secretary for Economic and Agricultural Affairs. These four officials formed an inner circle around the Secretary of State: 'They alone had direct access to Baker and were familiar with most of what went on.'[20] Inevitably this attempt by Baker to insulate himself from the wiles of career professionals led to resentment. 'He's running a mini NSC, not State,' a senior diplomat complained. 'We learn what our policy is when we read it in the newspapers.'[21] Ultimately other observers saw Baker's shutting out of State Department specialists while heavily relying on an inner sanctum of advisers as a mixed blessing. 'This management style enhanced his control over policy, but also left him vulnerable to missed opportunities.'[22]

NICARAGUA

The new administration's quite different approach to the management of foreign policy was demonstrated at an early stage by Baker's orchestration of a deal with Congress over aid for the Nicaraguan Contras. In the previous administration, US policy in Central America had been the subject of bitter contention between the White House and Capitol Hill. In President Reagan's mind there was no doubt that Nicaragua was potentially a second Cuba and as such a serious threat to the national security of the United States. The Reagan doctrine entailed supporting anti-Soviet counter-revolutions and, in line with this strategy, Reagan sought to provide military aid to Contra rebels against the Sandinista regime. This had provoked the ire of many Democrats in Congress who succeeded in passing a number of amendments designed to curtail the provision of such aid. It was Reagan's attempts to evade these restrictions that led to the Iran Contra affair, the greatest crisis of his presidency and the most acrimonious episode in executive-legislative relations since Watergate.

In the 1988 campaign Bush called for the renewal of military aid to the Contras, but after the election congressional leaders made it clear that any request to provide such aid would meet with rejection out of hand.[25] Shortly afterwards the five Central America presidents who had for some time been trying to bring about peace and reconciliation in the area, drew up the Tesoro Beach agreement. This allowed for the 'demobilization, repatriation or relocation' of the Contras matched by an undertaking by the Nicaraguan government to provide the conditions for free and fair elections in the near future. In the United States this agreement had a mixed reception with President Bush welcoming the 'positive elements', namely the promise of democratic elections, but questioning whether the Sandinistas could be relied on to honour that pledge once the Contras had disbanded.

Nevertheless, in response to the Tesoro Beach accord and the solid congressional resistance to military aid for the Contras, a new American policy with regard to Nicaragua now began to take shape. Masterminded by James Baker, the Secretary of State, this emphasized the promotion of democracy by diplomatic rather than military means, involved a renewal of humanitarian aid for the Contras and called for the use of sticks and carrots as a means of keeping the pressure on the Sandinistas to deliver on their promise of free elections. 'Carrots could include lifting the trade embargo, improving diplomatic relations, and even restoring US aid to Nicaragua. Sticks could include a tightening of the embargo, further curtailment of diplomatic relations, or if the Sandinistas refused to hold free elections, a possible renewal of military support for the Contras.'[23]

A bipartisan agreement with Congress in line with the above policy was eventually hammered out by Baker after several months of private discussions and 22 days of intense negotiation on Capitol Hill.[24] It was agreed that non-military aid of nearly $50 million would go to the Contras subject to three conditions insisted on by Democrats in the House of Representatives – no Contra funds were to be used for offensive military operations, no funds would go to any Contra human rights violators and aid would not continue beyond 30 November 1989 unless approval was given by four relevant congressional committees.

By adopting a pragmatic approach and engaging in some accomplished deal-making Baker thereby defused an issue that, for some years, had poisoned relations between President Reagan and Congress and adversely affected the conduct of American foreign policy. Some questioned the validity of such case-by-case problem-solving, but the most important criticism in the short term came from within the White House itself.[25]

As I have said, while Bush tried where possible to be conciliatory and accommodating towards the legislature he simultaneously resisted with resolution any encroachment on his constitutional powers. C. Boyden Gray, the White House Counsel, assumed particular responsibility for protecting presidential prerogatives and he took exception to that part of the Contra aid agreement that allowed congressional committees to prevent the President from spending appropriated funds.[26] As Gray saw it, this would be tantamount to an 'unconstitutional legislative veto and set a dangerous precedent for congressional checks on presidential power in foreign affairs.' [27]

On this occasion, Gray was rebuked by the President for speaking out publicly yet his clash with Baker threw light on tensions within the White House.[28] Gray was a conservative and a constitutionalist and, for the moment, he was outgunned by a master pragmatist and deal-maker. The nature of the deal that led to the congressional veto was frankly explained by one of the Secretary of State's lieutenants: 'It was the last little blood out of the turnip. It's the price we had to pay to get the job done, to get a deal. It was a tradeoff. We decided it was time we got our act together so we could do what we need to do on the ground in Central America without being distracted by bureaucratic and political fights up here in Washington.'[29] While the formidable Gray was forced to give ground on this occasion he persisted to the end in vigorous defence of the President's position *vis-à-vis* Congress in the making of foreign policy

PANAMA

Panama and its military dictator General Noriega represented another piece of unfinished business in Central America left behind by the Reagan Administration. Rather embarrassingly for the United States, Noriega had been recruited by the CIA as long ago as 1967 and had been a purveyor of intelligence material to Washington on Cuba and Nicaragua for some years. Indeed, he had been on the books of the agency when Bush himself was the Director of the CIA. The disenchantment of the American government with Noriega began in 1987 and, in early 1988, he was indicted on drugs charges in two US federal courts.

Two months later, President Reagan imposed economic sanctions on Panama and the removal of Noriega from office became a priority of American foreign policy. In 1989, Bush continued in the same vein, renewing sanctions and providing covert support for the opposition when elections took place in May. These were massively fraudulent, with the pro-Noriega coalition claiming to have won by 2:1 while the Panamanian Catholic Church made its own count and estimated that, in fact, the opposition had won by a margin of 3:1.[30] Noriega's continuance in power and his brutal putting down of opposition demonstrations outraged both the Bush Administration and Congress. On 3 October 1989, however, a coup attempt by disaffected members of the armed forces in Panama was crushed by Noriega loyalists with the US military in the country remaining largely on the sidelines, providing only minimal support to the rebels.

The failure of the Bush Administration to support the attempted coup was the subject of fierce criticism in Congress and the media. Many observers saw it as a damning indictment of the President's management of foreign policy. It was charged that he and his advisers had carried caution to excess, thereby wasting an excellent opportunity to unseat a dangerous adversary. Critics focused also on Bush's obsessive concern with secrecy and his tendency to deal with such matters informally, conferring only with a small and exclusive group of advisers while failing to draw on the expertise of the bureaucracy.[31]

It was not long however, before Bush was gifted the chance to redeem his earlier failure. The killing, in mid-December 1989, of a US military officer by members of the Panamanian Defence Forces, in conjunction with the roughing up of a US Navy officer and the sexual harassment of his wife, provided Bush with a pretext for launching a massive military operation against Panama involving 24 000 US troops.[32] Ostensibly, the purposes of Operation Just Cause were to protect the lives of 35 000 Americans, to defend democracy, to combat drug trafficking by taking Noriega into custody and to secure the Panama Canal.

Abroad, the incursion into Panama was widely seen as an exercise in American imperialism. The Organization of American States voted 20–1, with five abstentions, in favour of a resolution condemning the intervention and calling for the immediate withdrawal of US troops. A similar resolution brought before the General Assembly of the United Nations passed 75–20, with 40 abstentions.[33] These condemnations had little consequence within the US where the President's standing in public opinion polls rose sharply and Congress, with a few exceptions, eagerly applauded his decisive action.[34] The Senate Majority Leader, George Mitchell, said that the invasion 'was made necessary by the reckless action of General Noriega', while his counterpart in the House, Speaker Tom Foley, despite some concerns, felt that the President's actions were 'justified'.[35] Such reactions by opposition leaders and others in Congress helped Bush escape condemnation for an action that, some have argued, was both contrary to international law and a flagrant violation of the Constitution.[36]

The invasion of Panama brought to light the hardline influences at work in the Bush White House; those unwilling to concede an inch to Congress in the never-ending struggle between the executive and the legislature over the conduct of American foreign policy. On this occasion, as on others, President Bush effectively treated the War Powers Resolution of 1973 with contempt. That legislation, designed to reassert the war power of Congress, sought 'to insure that the collective judgment' of both branches was drawn on when US forces were to be committed to armed conflict. In furtherance of that end presidents were required to consult with Congress 'in every possible instance' before taking such actions and were then obliged to report to the legislature within 48 hours.

Bush complied with the latter provision, but the decision to commit troops in the first place was, in no sense, an outcome of 'collective judgment'. In fact, the President typically made his decision in circumstances of the utmost secrecy with only a small group of the most senior officials including Baker, Vice President Quayle, Secretary of Defense Cheney, William Webster, the Director of the CIA and General Colin Powell, the Chairman of the Joint Chiefs of Staff, privy to the plan.[37]

There was, of course, no meaningful consultation with Congress whatsoever. The President did inform congressional leaders, but only after the decision to invade had already been taken. A document published in the name of the US House of Representatives Committee on Foreign Affairs mentioned that a few members of Congress were troubled by the constitutional ramifications, yet also limply observed: 'The US intervention in Panama did not raise the issue of the War Powers Resolution in Congress. This was largely because Congress was not in session during the intervention and because the action was supported by most Members of Congress and by US public opinion.'[38]

Such blithe capitulation to the executive branch, principally on the grounds that the end justifies the means, has taken place repeatedly throughout the history of the United States. It allowed Lincoln's reputation to remain unscathed by his violations of the Constitution in defence of the Union, and similar arguments were applied to FDR's several consitutionally dubious actions in the run up to the entry of the US into the Second World War. This is all very understandable, but it does seriously undermine the validity of furiously indignant complaints about unconstitutional behaviour that follow when some members of Congress and some segments of the public decide that the President's ends are not justifiable.[39]

ENDING THE COLD WAR

Caution is the hallmark of guardian presidents. They are at pains not to arouse expectations that cannot be fulfilled and are much concerned to 'do no harm'. They disdain ideology and are disinclined to engage in florid rhetoric; by definition, they harbour no grand schemes for reordering the world and see themselves as reactive leaders, as pragmatists responding to situations as they arise.

For many, however, the Bush Administration was from the beginning marked by an excess of caution.'Ever since he took office, critics at home and abroad have lambasted Bush for what they describe as a halting and reactive approach to the historic changes afoot in the Soviet Union.'[40] Initially wary of of Gorbachev, Bush's staff embarked on a painstaking, five month long, policy review. The Soviet leader meanwhile was pushing ahead with perestroika and glasnost; separatism was on the march in Georgia, the Ukraine and the Baltics; free elections had been agreed in Poland, and the lowering of the Iron Curtain had been set in train by Hungary beginning to dismantle its barbed wire border with Western Europe.

The unprecedented opportunities now on offer and in danger of being neglected by undue caution were stressed by various luminaries. Ronald Reagan was reliably reported to be becoming uneasy about the foreign policy indecisivevness of his successor.[41] Henry Kissinger, a former Secretary of State, said: 'We face an opportunity – the greatest in 40 years – to bring an end to the Cold War. International factors have rarely been so fluid. The one thing that cannot occur is a continuance of the status quo.'[42] Very similarly, James Schlesinger, formerly Director of the CIA, observed: 'For the [US] to appear both passive and impassive to Gorbachev is a problem. One needs to strike a balance between caution . . . and responsiveness to the changes going on in the Soviet Union.'[43]

In reply to the allegation that the Bush Administration did not, in those early months, strike the right balance in reacting to developments in the Eastern part of Europe, Brent Scowcroft explained to this author:

> That may be true, but one of the things you have to remember is that President Bush and I, and Cheney and, to some extent,

Baker, had gone through the detente period and the euphoria that was created in the US and Europe during that period, [and] for which we paid a fairly heavy price in the late 70s and early 80s. We were very reluctant to have that sort of thing happen again. So maybe we were over-cautious – perhaps, perhaps. I think it was because we were watching Gorbachev's actions rather than [listening to] his rhetoric. In 1989 he was running around Europe trying to outpromise things in arms control and so forth. It looked like typical Soviet tactics [designed to] split the West.[44]

Gorbachev's reforms within the Soviet Union, however, had had repercussions in the Warsaw Pact countries – setting off opposition movements and leading, during Bush's first year in office, to the overthrow of communist regimes in Poland, Hungary, East Germany, Czechoslovakia, Bulgaria and Romania. The fact that these extraordinary changes occurred relatively peacefully owed much to the restraint displayed, on the one hand, by Gorbachev and, on the other, by Bush. The Soviet leader effectively renounced the Brezhnev doctrine of intervening in satellite countries to put down revolutions while Bush avoided the temptation to make political capital out of the disintegration of the Soviet empire.

Before leaving for a trip to Eastern Europe in July, Bush told his speechwriters: 'Whatever this trip is, it's *not* a victory tour, with me running around over there pounding my chest. [In my speeches] I don't want it to sound inflammatory or provocative. I don't want what I do to complicate the lives of Gorbachev and the others . . . I don't want to put a stick in Gorbachev's eye.'[45] On that same trip, both in Poland and Hungary, the President exercised caution again by appearing to be intent on emphasizing stability at the expense of the forces of change; he seemed to prefer dealing with existing elites rather than encouraging dissident elements. Thus Bush gave succour to the Communist President of Poland, General Jaruzelski, by encouraging him to run for re-election. The President then bestowed his support on Hungarian Communist leaders while telling representatives of the noncommunist opposition: 'Your leaders are moving in the right direction. Your country is taking things one step at a time. That's surely the prudent thing to do.'[46]

A few months later, the caution that pervaded the Bush Administration was reflected in the President's subdued, inarticulate reaction to the pulling down of the Berlin Wall. This was the source of much critical comment in the media and in Congress.[47] The Majority Leader in the House, Congressman Richard Gephardt, said: 'Even as the walls of the modern Jericho come tumbling down, we have a president who is inadequate to the moment.'[48] There was, however, according to Bush's staff, a purpose to the President's reticence; he knew that excessive celebration of the Wall's collapse might well create a backlash by the military and other conservative elements in both East Germany and the Soviet Union. As Andrew Card, the Deputy Chief of Staff explained the President was being urged to:

> Go stand in front of the Wall, [but] he had to say 'Wait a minute. That's smart short-term politics, but it is dumb diplomacy. Let's see how Helmut Kohl reacts. Let's see how Gorbachev reacts. This is a tricky time for Gorbachev; he's probably being pressured by the generals to go in and take East Germany back. Let's step back. Let the world celebrate the Wall coming down. I am celebrating too, but I don't have to be there waving the flag.'[49]

It was while he was in Europe that Bush appears to have decided that Gorbachev was a man he could do business with and that it was time for an informal meeting with the Soviet leader. This led to the Malta summit in December 1989, a crucial event in the process of ending the Cold War. This meeting gave Bush the opportunity to deploy his personal diplomacy skills and to forge a highly productive relationship with Gorbachev. As we saw earlier, Scowcroft had reservations about Gorbachev and was, reportedly, wary of the summit before it took place.[50] Nevertheless when I spoke to him he confirmed how important the meeting had been: 'They did establish then a personal relationship which continued and helped to cut through the enormous encrustation of bureaucracy to bureaucracy, the way the dialogue had taken place up until then.' Scowcroft also went out of his way to stress the importance of Eduard Shevardnadze as a highly desirable influence on Gorbachev at this point.[51]

In one-on-one meetings in Malta, Gorbachev assured Bush that he was determined to avoid the use of force against the breakaway Baltic countries of Estonia, Latvia and Lithuania. In return, Bush made it clear that while the US had never recognized the annexation of these countries by the USSR, provided Gorbachev kept his promise, the American side would act with restraint in making public statements.[52] As testimony to the central importance of the good personal relationship established between the two presidents at Malta, Shevardnadze's deputy, Alexander Bessmertnykh, said two years later: 'If it were not for Malta, the Soviet Union would never have so smoothly surrendered its control of Eastern Europe and the Baltics.'[53] George Bush's taste for personal diplomacy had, on this occasion, proved to be a formidable asset.

In early 1990 US policy towards the Baltics was a highly sensitive matter for all those cold warriors on the right of the Republican party, but Bush, advised by the ultra cautious Scowcroft, was determined to move carefully, taking account of the fragility of Gorbachev's position and fearful of a backlash by hardliners within the Soviet Union.[54] Some of the flavour of the advice Scowcroft was providing at this stage was revealed later when he explained to me:

> What we sought to do in Eastern Europe was to move the process as fast as possible without creating an explosion like that of Hungary in 1956 or even like that in Czechoslovakia in 1968. [We feared] creating a reaction from the Soviet Union which would stop it all . . . What we wanted to do was to establish a pace that could be sustained [although] we certainly didn't see it moving as rapidly as it did.[55]

In line with Scowcroft's counsel, Bush, at a White House meeting, was reported as saying: 'I don't want to do something that would inadvertently set back the progress that has been made in Eastern Europe . . . And so it is delicate . . . I'm old enough to remember Hungary in 1956 where we exhorted people to go to the barricades, and a lot of people were left out there alone.'[56]

The caution that was so much a feature of the Bush Administration's reaction to events in Eastern Europe was evident in their handling of Gorbachev. Initially, Bush and his foreign policy team doubted the Soviet leader's motives and sought to keep him at arm's length, whereas later the President came under attack, particularly from the right, for clinging to the Soviet leader too long, and to the disadvantage of Boris Yeltsin. 'Fearing instability in the Soviet Union almost as much as Gorbachev does, Bush has hitched his star to the Soviet president, believing that only Gorbachev can keep the USSR from spinning out of control.'[57]

As General Scowcroft explained it to me, the Administration's rationale for remaining with Gorbachev so long was that even though the Soviet leader's commitment to democracy was questionable, he was moving the USSR in the right direction; he was, moreover, able to carry the military with him. This was essential to one of the most significant developments of all in this period, the reunification of Germany, while also keeping it within NATO. Gorbachev achieved that, whereas it was doubtful whether Yeltsin could have done likewise:

> [He] wasn't a very polished politician at that time. Could he have brought the military along? I don't know, but I guess we were very pragmatic . . . We are frequently criticized for sticking with Gorbachev too long, but nobody I have read has said what would have happened had we turned on him, or what that would have meant, and what the consequences would have been.[58]

A similar defence of Bush's reluctance to abandon Gorbachev in favour of Yeltsin, as so many on the right of his party urged, was provided by James Cicconi:

> If he had [done so] the odds are that the 1991 coup in the Soviet Union would probably have succeeded, and the hardliners would have come back into control. If we had not stuck with Gorbachev, I think it's very arguable that none of these changes would have transpired, or at least been brought to fruition. Certainly not the unification of Germany and probably not the collapse of the Warsaw pact which were strategically the two most salient events.'[59]

With the advantage of hindsight and the evidence available to us now, moreover, the case for questioning Yeltsin's reliability has been reinforced.

It is difficult to apply the central test of statecraft, a leader's fulfilment of his or her agenda, to this part of the analysis. As Eagleburger suggested in the quotation at the beginning of this chapter, Bush had no agenda as such for dealing with the extraordinary occurrences taking place in Europe during his presidency, he was reacting to events. Measured by results, however, it is difficult to deny Bush's achievement in helping to bring the Cold War to a conclusion in a manner that served well the interests of the United States. Massive change of a nature that his predecessors could only dream of took place while he was in office. The arch enemy communism was vanquished with no American lives lost and democratic, capitalist values began to take root in a large area of the world. How far all this can be attributed to Bush and his advisers will remain a matter of endless dispute. It clearly is the case that he was not a prime mover in the sense that Reagan and Gorbachev could be said to be, but that does not detract from his role in managing the change that their actions, in conjunction with other factors, had set in motion. It was not unreasonable for Brent Scowcroft to claim in reviewing Bush's part:

> The fact that these earthshaking developments all took place within about a three year period – Eastern Europe was freed, Germany was unified and stayed within NATO, and the Soviet Union collapsed [all] without a shot being fired – it was pretty remarkable. Fifteen years ago, if you had forecast that people would have said 'You are crazy, you are crazy!' The only way this could happen is in the context of another war. So, I am content to let history speak for itself. These things were going to happen sooner or later, that's clear, but the way they happened, President Bush had an enormous amount to do with it.[60]

The 1988 election placed George Bush in overall charge of the management of the West's response to the massive upheavals already underway within both the Soviet Union and the countries of the Warsaw Pact, and historians are likely to accord him a large part of the credit for a peaceful, mainly successful conclusion to a notably fraught and dangerous period in world history. It can hardly be argued, moreover, that such an outcome was a foregone conclusion. As another senior member of the White House explained, there were many hazards involved: 'There were a lot of predictions that if the Soviet empire ever came to the brink of collapse, if communism ever came to the brink of collapse . . . that could trigger a nuclear war . . . believe me, while I don't think things ever got to that point, there were very hairy moments in the whole process.'[61] As to Bush's methods, many commentators worried about his caution, his obsessive concern with doing nothing imprudent, his penchant for secrecy, his fondness for stability and his preference for dealing with elites rather than going public. Many have argued, however, that these tactics were appropriate for the moment, that this was not the time for ideological clamour or strident appeals, but for the quiet, cautious diplomacy that Bush was so well qualified to provide.[62]

8 The War in the Gulf

George Bush's second year in office provided the two defining events of his presidency, the budget crisis and the war in the Gulf. The former was a leadership débâcle whereas the latter showed President Bush in a far more favourable light, particularly if the analysis is concentrated primarily, as it will be here, on the seven months between Iraq's invasion of Kuwait at the beginning of August 1990 and the cease fire agreed at the end of Febuary 1991. During this critical period Bush's foreign policy leadership is not easy to fault if it is measured simply by the fulfilment of goals. At an early stage the President decided that Iraq's aggression had to be reversed and seven months later he presided over the triumphant achievement of that objective. On this occasion, far from being excessively cautious, Bush came across as a bold and resolute leader who kept his nerve in the face of many dangers and uncertainties.

THE CHRONOLOGY

To review in bare outline the chronology of this crisis. On the evening of 1 August 1990 (early morning on 2 August in the Middle East), word reached Washington that Iraqi forces had moved into Kuwait. The President issued a statement condemning the invasion as 'naked aggression' and calling for 'the immediate and unconditional withdrawal of all Iraqi forces'. Later that night, Bush signed executive orders banning all trade with Iraq and freezing both Iraqi and Kuwaiti assets. Meanwhile Thomas Pickering, the US Ambassador to the United Nations, was instructed to call an emergency session of the Security Council. At that meeting, which went on through the night, a resolution condemning the invasion and calling for immediate and unconditional withdrawal was agreed to by a vote of 14–0 with Yemen abstaining.[1]

This was the first of a remarkable series of resolutions relevant to the crisis in Kuwait passed by the Security Council in the period between 2 August 1990 and 29 November 1990. Of twelve resolutions, five were agreed to unanimously by the

177

15 members of the Council; three passed by 13–0 with Cuba and Yemen abstaining; one was agreed by 14–1 with Cuba voting against; one received a vote in its favour of 13–2 with Cuba and Yemen voting against, and one passed by a vote of 12–2 with Cuba and Yemen voting against, while China abstained.[2]

At 8 a.m. on 2 August the National Security Council came together and before the meeting began the President told reporters in front of television cameras: 'We're not discussing intervention . . . we're not considering any military option . . . I am not contemplating such action.' Later that day in Colorado Bush appeared to shift his position, saying to the press: 'We're not ruling any options in, but we're not ruling any options out.'[3]

On his return to Washington from Camp David on 5 August, the President, in speaking to the press, spoke of 'Our determination to reverse out this aggression – this will not stand, this will not stand this aggression against Kuwait.'[4] On 6 August the UN Security Council agreed by a vote of 13–0 to impose sanctions against Iraq. On the same day King Fahd indicated his willingness to accept foreign forces to assist in the defence of Saudi Arabia. Two days later President Bush appeared on television to announce to the nation the deployment of American troops to the Middle East saying that 'the sovereign independence of Saudi Arabia is of vital interest to the United States.' The President also stressed however, that 'The mission of our troops is wholly defensive.'[5] This force in support of 'Operation Desert Shield' was to grow to 230 000 men and women by late October 1990. On 25 August the UN Security Council voted 13–0 in favour of a resolution effectively authorizing military action to enforce the sanctions against Iraq agreed earlier. This was the first occasion in the history of the UN that individual countries were authorized 'to enforce an international blockade, an extraordinary diplomatic victory for the administration.'[6]

At the beginning of October the US Congress gave overwhelming support to the Bush Administration's efforts so far to deter Iraqi aggression – the House by a vote of 380–29, and the Senate by a vote of 96–3. On 8 November the President at a news briefing announced that the size of US forces committed to 'Operation Desert Shield' was to be increased –

reportedly by 200 000 – 'to ensure that the coalition has an adequate offensive military option should that be necessary to achieve our common goals.' Three weeks later the Security Council adopted Resolution 678 authorizing the use of 'all necessary means' to enforce Iraq's removal from Kuwait, unless Iraq complied with UN resolutions and withdrew by 15 January 1991.[7]

On 5 December, 54 Democratic members of the US House of Representatives sought a federal court injunction that would have prevented the President from embarking on offensive, military action without first obtaining explicit congressional authorization. This suit was dismissed by US Federal District Court Judge Harold Greene on 13 December on the grounds that there was 'lack of evidence of an imminent clash between the executive and legislative branches, lack of evidence that either the administration is on the verge of launching a war, or that a majority of Congress deems a declaration of war imprudent.'[8]

While never admitting that Congress had a formal role in the ultimate decision to go to war President Bush on 8 January 1991 requested a congressional resolution authorizing the use of force. The Senate on 12 January approved by a vote of 57–42, a resolution that gave the President authority to use military force against Iraq in order to achieve the implementation of the various relevant Security Council resolutions. Later the same day, the House voted 250–183 in favour of an identical resolution.[9] The war against Iraq – Operation Desert Storm – began on 17 January with a bombing campaign. The coalition ground attack was launched on 24 Febuary and ceased on 28 Febuary, following President Bush's televised announcement: 'Kuwait is liberated. Iraq's army is defeated. Our military objectives are met.'[10]

THE WOODWARD BOOK

Early judgements in the media regarding Bush's leadership in the Gulf War tended to be highly favourable.[11] Subsequent analyses have been much more critical and, in most cases, have drawn heavily on material presented in Bob Woodward's *The Commanders*.[12] The latter is an important source, but it needs to be treated with care. There are no footnotes for the many interviews conducted by Woodward and his assistants, and the fact that the book began as a study of the Pentagon needs to be borne in mind.

It has been said of Woodward's account that notwithstanding any doubts about its credibility, it 'has not been publicly disputed by any major figure he quotes.' However, this may come later when all the memoirs have been written.[13] When asked what he thought of Woodward's book, General Scowcroft, the President's closest adviser during this crisis, replied:

> I don't think too much of it. Woodward's typical practice is to start with something that is pretty well accepted fact and then spin from that conclusions and run it out to a degree that it ends up being pure supposition. He does that over and over again, so that you are captured by the fact that he starts with something [accurate] but then he [reaches] unwarranted conclusions'.[14]

Another of those closely involved in the decision-making process was somewhat more charitable, but drew attention to the incompleteness of Woodward's analysis:

> What is there . . . based on my recollection, is fairly accurate [although] not a hundred percent accurate. My problem with the book is what is not there. It [has] a fairly narrow take on things and it's heavily influenced by what I infer, if I use the word carefully, to be his sources, which were heavily from the Pentagon . . . it is just an incomplete story; it doesn't have the way it often looked from the White House, or the State Department.'[15]

Eliot Cohen has also suggested that Woodward's perspective is largely that of the Pentagon with 'James Baker, Brent Scowcroft and even George Bush . . . chiefly heard as offstage voices in a drama that centers on Colin Powell and Dick Cheney.'[16]

NO TIME TO GO WOBBLY

It has been suggested that far from displaying resolute and decisive leadership throughout this crisis, Bush dithered at the outset before weakly allowing himself to be hustled into a belligerent response by Mrs Thatcher and Brent Scowcroft.[17] This does not accord with Scowcroft's version of events. He reports that when the invasion of Kuwait first took place some of the President's advisers threw up their hands and said: 'Well, it's a tragedy, but what [can] you do? Let's make sure [the Iraqis] don't get any further into Kuwait.' Bush, however, was not content to leave matters there; from the beginning he said: 'No. This is an unacceptable move.'[18]

There is, moreover, ample evidence to refute the widely prevalent supposition that President Bush only concluded that Saddam Hussein must be ejected from Kuwait after Mrs Thatcher had stiffened his resolve when they met in Aspen, Colorado, on the day after the invasion. Jean Edward Smith, for instance, heads his chapter on this period with the quotation 'Remember, George, this is no time to go wobbly' and dates it 3 August. It was at this juncture, moreover, that the Prime Minister supposedly performed a 'backbone transplant' on the President.[19] However, some witnesses with powerful claims to know what actually occurred in Aspen have categorically denied the thrust of such stories. Accompanied by his National Security Adviser, the President met with the British Prime Minister who had with her Charles Powell, her Private Secretary. Subsequently, Powell observed: 'It has been said that Mrs Thatcher had to put backbone into the President. That is just wrong. They both arrived there absolutely determined that this was something that could not be tolerated. The genuine sense of outrage on the part of both of them is the thing that I remember.'[20]

With some vigour, Richard Haass, Scowcroft's principal aide for the Middle East, insisted that 'Bush was not wobbly when he went out [to Colorado] . . . I was with him both before and afterwards . . . the idea that somehow she gave him an infusion of backbone . . . I see nothing that supports that thesis.'[21]. Similarly, Scowcroft talked of 'a meeting of minds between Mrs Thatcher and the President . . . they were both heading in the same direction . . . they tended to reinforce each other.'[22]

The Prime Minister did use the 'no time to go wobbly' expression nearly three weeks later, but in a totally different context. Towards the end of August the National Security Council had to decide how to respond to Saddam's flouting of the sanctions against Iraq agreed on 6 August. Some took the view that the US should unilaterally enforce the blockade if necessary, whereas others were more cautious. In the words of James Baker: 'The question was whether we should proceed under Article 51 [of the UN Charter], which we were all agreed we had the full legal right to do. Or whether, in order to keep the coalition together, we should take a little bit longer and try to get another resolution from the Security Council in order to authorize the use of force to enforce the embargo.'[23]

This clearly became a fiercely contested issue in NSC meetings. As Brent Scowcroft remembered it, it was necessary to decide: 'Would we intervene unilaterally, or would we go to the UN not knowing whether we would get authority? We were divided on the issue; I wanted to move [unilaterally] and Secretary Baker did not.' The State Department was particularly conscious of the fact that the Iraqis were actively attempting to separate the USSR from the US and Baker recalled 'counselling [the President] to see at least if we could not bring the Soviets along.'[24]

The Secretary of State rather than the National Security Adviser won this particular battle for the President's ear and, once convinced, Bush moved to bring Mrs Thatcher around to the same view. The Prime Minister's conversion was not achieved without difficulty, for conscious of her own problems with the UN over the Falklands she 'felt that the Security Council Resolution which had already been passed, combined with our ability to invoke Article 51 of the UN Charter on self-defence, was sufficient.' And despite the changes wrought by the ending of the Cold War 'the fact remained that if one could achieve an objective without UN authority there was no point in running the risks attached to seeking it.'[25] Notwithstanding her reservations, Mrs Thatcher finally fell into line and it was this point according to Scowcroft that she famously said: 'all right George, all right, but this is no time to go wobbly.'[26]

As we have seen, a resolution was successfully obtained from the Security Council on 25 August and, in retrospect, it was surely just as well that this additional authorization was sought. The success of the allied cause was ultimately much dependent on keeping an inherently fragile coalition together and if the Soviet Union had broken away the consequences might well have been disastrous.

PERSONALIZATION AND POLICY-MAKING ON THE HOOF

The President's National Security Adviser rejected the allegation given currency in several studies of the war that Bush personalized this conflict excessively and made far too much of supposed parallels between Saddam Hussein and Adolf Hitler.[27] As Scowcroft explained it, when these events were taking place Bush was immersed in a book on the Second World War. He was reading about:

> . . . the invasion of Poland at the outset of the war and the horrors that the Nazis perpetrated [there]. That was where he started calling Saddam Hussein a fascist and [suggesting that he] was like Hitler . . . It came right out of that book and him seeing the similarities of the two. But it was not personalized in any deep sense. [His reaction] was based on what he felt was an important movement not only against the US national interest, but as a destabilizing factor in a world which was getting into a turmoil.[28]

Scowcroft agreed that the parallels between Hussein and Hitler were overdrawn, and admitted that 'some of us worried a little bit about that', but excused these lapses on the grounds that they were rhetorical clichés of the sort that Bush, like any politician, was likely to use out on the campaign trail. Finally, in answering the charge of personalization, Scowcroft insisted that 'if in fact it had been a personalized issue the President never would have stopped when he did.' The implication being that Bush would have permitted US forces to go on to Baghdad, not stopping them, as he did, short of Hussein's removal.[29]

Critics of Bush's leadership during the Gulf War have argued that the processes of decision-making were unstructured with the President prone to make policy on the hoof without sober consideration and appropriate consultation with the military and other specialists. Woodward, for example, makes much of the Chairman of the Joint Chiefs of Staff, Colin Powell, feeling obliged to inform himself of changes in US policy by keeping abreast of the President's public utterances: 'It was his habit to excavate Bush's public statements. The Chairman had to know the President's policy, and this President tended to lay out at least some of his thinking in speeches and comments to the press. Sometimes the policy came out carefully and incrementally. Other times Powell discovered surprises.'[30.]

In the early days of the crisis, if Woodward is correct, Powell was deeply troubled by the President in his public remarks appearing to move policy goalposts without consulting with senior advisers like himself. Initially, on 2 August, the President had told the press that military intervention was not under consideration. There had then been discussions within the Administration, which Powell had been privy to, regarding the possibility of committing US forces to the Middle East as a defensive measure to prevent any attempt by the Iraqis to move into Saudi Arabia. But then on 5 August, Powell, we are told, was stunned to see the President on television arriving at the White House from Camp David and angrily saying 'This will not stand' in reference to the the aggression against Kuwait. 'There had been no NSC meeting, no debate. The Chairman could not understand why the President had laid down this new marker, changing radically the definition of success. It was one thing to stop Saddam from going into other countries like Saudi Arabia; it was very much another thing to reverse an invasion that was accomplished.'[31] The impression created by comments such as these that Powell was 'out of the loop' when crucial decisions were made was crisply and flatly denied by Scowcroft: 'I don't think that [Powell] was ever out of the loop at all.'[32]

More detail was provided by Richard Haass. He did not accept that the military could reasonably claim to be unpleasantly surprised by Bush's public remarks on 5 August: 'People had their day in court and the military was often asked their views. Even if they were not specifically asked for, they were sitting at the table and could have offered them.' Prior to Sunday, 5 August, there had already been three meetings of the NSC on Thursday, Friday and Saturday to discuss the crisis: 'We were all there; you had a chance to talk about these things. People were given the chance to talk about what we should do . . . Everyone was basically saying we have got to resist . . . So when the President said "This will not stand" on

Sunday . . . [while] he was very emotional . . . the policy ought not to have come as a surprise to anyone.'[33]

THE DECISION-MAKING PROCESS

Not surprisingly, General Scowcroft was unimpressed by suggestions that the crisis had not been properly handled within the White House. One source for instance claims that 'rational' procedures were notably absent and argues that the President and his National Security Adviser 'alone determined' the crucial steps towards war with Iraq. Another critic meanwhile claimed that:

> Throughout the crisis, Bush acted with a small coterie of subordinates. Expert opinion was screened out, and the NSC rarely met in structured fashion. Means and ends were never reconciled, policy alternatives were not canvassed, structured analysis was not rendered. The executive branch of the government moved at the President's command and no institutional checks were provided.[34]

These charges were countered by Scowcroft: 'The analysis was very dispassionate and the conclusions were [arrived at] calmly and analytically. The objectives and the means to achieve them [were worked out] in what, to me, is a model way. [We] had to understand what the problem was. What we thought we wanted to do about it, and after we had done it would we be able to get out.' The Administration's first concern was to 'get some force over there and to send a strong signal to Saddam Hussein that we would defend Saudi Arabia. We tried very hard to send that message.' The second decision taken was 'that the conquest of Kuwait would not be allowed to stand. [This] did not immediately translate into a plan for a military operation; it was originally translated into a general force build up that would allow us to keep our options open.'

In the early weeks it was necessary to decide how big a force would be required to defend Saudi Arabia; the advice from General Schwarzkopf, the field commander, was that 100 000 troops would be needed and this provided the basis for the first military build-up. Then the President said: 'We need to keep our options open beyond that. That is the minimum that we have to do for now, [but] what does it take to keep our options open.' It was this that led to a continuation of the build-up far beyond the early prognostications, given that Hussein continued to put forces into the area.

None of this precluded the possibility of a diplomatic solution to the crisis, although Scowcroft, by his own admission, always doubted that Saddam would leave Kuwait peaceably. In defence of the Administration's decision to not let sanctions run indefinitely Scowcroft said this grew out of a careful consideration of which side 'would be favored by a long drawn out deadlock.' The military consensus had been:

> . . . that we needed to act before Ramadan . . . that a military operation late in the spring and into the summer would be a very, very difficult operation. So unless sanctions operated in the very short term, in a matter of a few months, we would have almost a year to wait. In a year the outrage and the cohesiveness of the Arab world was likely to erode . . . therefore we had a time window basically between August, when the attack was launched, and some time in March.[35]

The criticism given the widest currency in the literature on the Gulf War is the claim that policy-making was restricted to an inner circle that quickly developed a consensus on a military solution and gave scant consideration to alternative courses of action.[36] While accepting that decision-making was limited to a small group Scowcroft made no apology for that: 'It included basically everyone who would have attended a National Security Council meeting . . . all of the principal national security decision-makers participated. The meetings were not large . . . since staff were informed only to the minimal amount.' The latter restriction was deemed necessary for reasons of security. 'We felt it was important when we began planning for a military solution that it should stay closely held so that we would not signal to Saddam Hussein what it was we actually had in mind.'[37]

Given his background as a political scientist, Richard Haass's perspective on matters of process is of particular interest. He agreed that decision-making had been restricted to 'a fairly small group', but went on to explain that 'there was a multi-layered cake.' There were 'lots of people at the lower level';

then there was a small group of deputies at the intermediate level. This included Haass himself, Robert Gates, the Deputy National Security Adviser; CIA Deputy Director, Richard Kerr; Robert Kimmit, Undersecretary for Political Affairs at the State Department; Admiral David Jeremiah, Deputy Chairman of the Joint Chiefs of Staff; and Paul Wolfowitz, Under Secretary for Policy at the Department of Defense. At the top, the number of National Security Council principals varied. There 'could be a few, could be as many as nine or ten, it was often eight. But the principals had a chance to influence the deputies and the deputies had a chance to influence the principals.' When the crisis was at its height the deputies 'met every day; often several times a day, either personally or electronically [via a video link].'[38]

As he was one of those involved and had been particularly 'responsible for dispensing good process a lot of the time' Haass recognized that he might be thought to be biased. Nevertheless he was dismissive of the allegations that a proper airing of alternative courses of action had not taken place, that adhocracy rather than multiple advocacy had occurred. Academic students of decision-making have stressed the value of ensuring that a suitably wide range of viewpoints are properly represented in the process, that major participants are given a full hearing and that all options are thoroughly considered – multiple advocacy, it has been argued, is essential. If a president draws advice from only a small group of intimates there arises a danger of 'groupthink'; the consideration of options is likely to be incomplete and an artificial consensus behind one course of action may develop.[39]

Haass was aware of this literature, but denied that it was relevant in this case. 'This was very clear multiple advocacy. This was not adhocracy . . . I have trouble thinking of a more carefully managed process . . . When I add up all the meetings the deputies had and then all the meetings the principals had, there was an extraordinary amount of interaction and of structured consideration.' This was the case in the process leading up to the war and for 'most of the pursuit of the war' even if things got 'messier' toward the end. During these later stages the process was 'not quite as deliberative as it might have been because things happened rather suddenly' and as 'everybody was on the road in different places it was difficult to pull things together.' After the war's end, in coping with events occurring in northern and southern Iraq, decision-making 'got a little less tidy . . . but it was still considered, it was still deliberative [even if] it wasn't quite as formally done as in some of the earlier sessions.'[40]

In answer to those critics who claim that all the options were not fully aired, Scowcroft said:

> There was a strong debate about all these issues . . . [even if] we all came down generally in the same place . . . [there were differences with] me out in front on the military side and Colin Powell maybe on the other end . . . [However,] President Bush put together a national security team that was generally like-minded. They were not poles apart. That was one of the reasons we were effective; because we did have a general consensus. We were all facing in the same direction on national security issues. While we had hours of vigorous debate, it was not visceral or ideologically motivated. It was analytical. 'Can we do this?' 'Is this the right way to go?' It was practically oriented, rather than emotionally or ideologically.

The value of a vociferous naysayer, or devil's advocate comparable to George Ball in the Johnson White House, was lost on Scowcroft.[41] The fact that 'we all came to a common conclusion doesn't seem to me to be a bad [thing]. I don't think you have to have somebody that says you are a fool and that you cannot go that way to have a thoughtful conclusion.' Of Colin Powell's role Scowcroft said: 'He was I think the most reluctant of the [decision-making] group and the least willing to entertain the military option. I think that was clear.' When asked whether it was true that Powell had not stated his reservations particularly strongly, Scowcroft replied: 'No, he did not. And as a matter of fact I think he never spoke of them directly to me.'[42]

The National Security Adviser discounted suggestions that the President's inner circle made insufficient use of outside experts in its decision-making during the Gulf War.[43] 'Did we have every Middle East expert in the world [in]? Not at all. But we did draw on [such] people. We had one or two groups of outside Middle East experts in with the President. We had them talk about Saddam Hussein [and] about Iraq. To talk

[also] about what was going on in the Iraqis' mind, and what was the impact throughout the Arab and the Muslim world.' According to Scowcroft's account there were also fairly regular discussions with Congress: 'We consulted quite frequently with the Congress, both individually and in groups. While the general tenor of the Congress was negative, we got key support from some members [such as Les Aspin, the Chairman of the Armed Services Committee in the House] that gave us a lot of confidence that we were going the right way.'[44]

Both Scowcroft and Haass, however, agreed that the Administration had erred in not keeping Congress informed about the decision, at the end of October 1990, to double the number of US troops in Saudi Arabia. Bush waited until the mid-term elections were safely past before announcing that he had 'directed the Secretary of Defense to increase the size of US forces committed to Desert Shield to ensure that the coalition has an adequate offensive military option should that be necessary to achieve our common goal.'[45] This was a crucial decision, for given this level of commitment, war became a virtual certainty, short of a most unlikely total withdrawal by Iraq. Congress however, had no foreknowledge of this decision, even though congressional leaders had been regularly briefed on the Gulf crisis by the White House. As Tom Foley, the Speaker of the House, explained: 'There was a call from Secretary Cheney in the morning – not very elaborate, just an announcement – the Administration was doubling the forces – this, of course, had never been discussed with the congressional leadership group that had been visiting the White House in recent weeks.'[46]

In accepting that the Administration had made a mistake in not keeping Congress better informed on the doubling of forces Scowcroft said that he thought that the President had made it sufficiently clear that 'we were going to put enough force in there to keep our options open.' Nevertheless, in retrospect he could see 'we were inadequate in our briefings to Congress to prepare them for that.' Richard Haass went further, describing the doubling decision as 'probably the worst handled piece of decision-making of the crisis . . . it was clumsily done particularly in the consultative area with the Congress.' Partly this was because Baker was away drumming up support for what eventually became UN Security Council Resolution 678, that which authorized the use of force, but the doubling decision 'was a bit rushed through and it created more problems with Congress than necessary.'[47]

It is argued in one of the most fiercely critical studies of the Gulf War that George Bush adroitly brought public opinion along with him; first in support of the defence of Saudi Arabia and then behind the decision to launch an offensive to eject Saddam Hussein from Kuwait. 'By any standard it was a superlative performance.'[48] This is not a widely shared view, with various commentators remarking on Bush's failure to make clear what was at stake and what would be gained by going to war against Iraq.[49] In November 1990 Jim Hoagland of the *Washington Post* wrote of the 'need for a clear and ideally inspirational statement to the nation to explain the goals of the potentially bloody conflict we may be approaching.'[50]

A review of the 'road to war' in late January 1991 noted that Bush on 10 November, baffled by declining support in the polls asked close advisers 'What am I doing wrong', only to be told that 'he had to get out every day and explain why he was there. He said he had made his case over and over.'[51] The fact that the Gulf War, in the short term at least, was seen as a fabulous success for the Administration should not obscure the fact that Bush's chronic inability to articulate his purposes, his failure to make good use of the bully pulpit, was a major disadvantage in this crisis as it was in others.

SUMMARY OF BUSH'S LEADERSHIP DURING THE CRISIS

To summarize this discussion of Bush's leadership during the Gulf crisis. Valuable though Woodward's book is as source, it has perhaps been relied on too heavily by others who have written about these events. As several have emphasized, Woodward's picture is incomplete and his perspective is largely that of the Pentagon. In this analysis, I have attempted to give an airing to rather different recollections from within the White House.

The notion that Mrs Thatcher gave Bush a backbone 'transplant' at the beginning has been shown to be without foundation. The complaints about the President's tendency to

personalize this conflict need to be set against Scowcroft's explanation, particularly the fact that Bush, in the end, did not seek
Saddam's removal from office.

The allegations that decision-making was unstructured and
lacking in rationality, that the President made policy on the
run and sprang surprises on the military is contested by NSC
sources. They insist that decision-making was orderly and
rational, that many meetings took place and contentious
issues were vigorously debated. There is no disagreement
with the claim that the crucial policy decisions were made by
an inner circle of largely like-minded individuals, but this is
not seen to be a source of weakness. The advice of outside
Middle East experts was sought and multiple advocacy, we are
told, did occur. It is also reliably reported that ample opportunities were available to those who dissented from the
developing consensus.

Briefly stated, that consensus embraced an early agreement
that the invasion of Kuwait could not be allowed to stand, but
before that objective could be pursued steps had to be taken
to ensure that Saddam Hussein did not move into Saudi Arabia.
Once the defence of Saudi Arabia had been assured by the
arrival of sufficient troop numbers and sanctions had been
brought into play, it was deemed essential to increase substantially the number of troops in order to keep open the option
of freeing Kuwait by force, while continuing to explore the
possibility of a diplomatic solution.

The consensus began to fray somewhat over the question of
when to resort to force, with a majority convinced that sanctions were only plausible as a basis for policy for a few months
given the fragility of the allied coalition. As Richard Haass put
it to me, there were 'legitimate differences about how long to
let sanctions work, but the purpose of a decision-making system
is not to eliminate those differences, it is simply to resolve
them. That is what Bush did.' Colin Powell's reservations
were evident, but the President finally had to decide: 'That is
what political leaders do. [They] ought to be making the big
decisions. The president sets general policy after deliberation
with his principal advisers.'[52]

Powell, it should be noted, has said much the same himself:
'There was no disagreement . . . We hoped sanctions would
work.' As time passed, however, doubts grew within the inner

circle of decision-makers as to whether sanctions would actually work and, as the Chairman of the Joint Chiefs saw it, it was his responsibility to ensure 'that we knew what the military component was for whatever policy choice [the President] made . . . what military strategy and force structure associated with the continuing sanctions would be and what military and force structure associated with going on the offensive would be. And we talked about it. We talked about the pros and cons. And we talked about at what point we should shift the strategy.'[53]

This hardly supports the suggestion that the military were shut out of the crucial decision to move to a resolution of the crisis by the use of force. Better than some of the critics, Powell had a good understanding of what his role should be: 'It was clear to me by late December that the sanctions were not working, . . . [but] What I said was: How long sanctions should be allowed to go is essentially a political question, whether it be six, twelve, eighteen, twenty-four months. It's a policy and political judgment . . .'[54] In other words, the Chairman gave his advice and made his recommendations, but the critical decisions about whether and when to go to war finally rested with the President.

THE WAR POWERS DEBATE

As we have seen, there was some modest recognition from within the White House that consultation with Congress could have been better handled. On the other hand, there is much evidence to support the conclusion that Bush himself was quite prepared to go to war without congressional approval if that should prove necessary.[55] On this, as on other occasions where his constitutional authority was at stake, Bush was a tough and uncompromising president determined to defend his prerogatives. His doubling of US forces in the Gulf in the fall of 1990 without consulting Congress, not surprisingly alarmed members of the legislature concerned that an irreversible momentum towards military action was building up which placed in jeopardy the congressional war power.

The President, however, supported as always on such issues by his chief legal adviser C. Boyden Gray, remained utterly convinced that he, as Commander in Chief and repository of

the executive power of the government, had the constitutional right to take whatever action he thought necessary to
defend the vital interests of the United States. More than once
Bush made it clear that if forced into it he would embark on
military action, even in the face of unanimous congressional
opposition and hostile public opinion: 'If I have to go, it's not
going to matter to me if there isn't one congressman who
supports this, or what happens to public opinion. If it's right,
it's gotta be done.'[56] Despite such statements George Bush
worried about the political consequences of going to war
without Congress behind him. As Scowcroft explained, while
the President had no doubt about his right to take military
action without congressional approval, he was conscious of
Lyndon Johnson's desperate difficulties during the Vietnam
war and recognized the value of having Congress 'on board'.[57]
Vice President Quayle confirms that while Bush was glad to
get congressional authorization for the use of force, 'I am
convinced [he] would still have made war against Saddam
Hussein without it.'[58]

The question of whether the President should seek congressional authorization for the use of force became a hotly
debated issue within the Administration. According to Gray,
several members of the inner circle, including Cheney, Baker,
Scowcroft and Sununu, were against going to Congress because
they feared Bush would lose such a vote: 'There were three
people who felt differently and the only one who mattered,
of course, was Bush, but Bush, Vice President Quayle and I
were the three people who felt that he had to go and get
authority from Congress . . . that it would be a disaster without
it.'[59]

In light of his recent background as Minority Whip in the
House, Richard Cheney's membership of the group willing to
resort to force without first obtaining congressional agreement is particularly noteworthy. He explained his position after
the war:

> The concern was that if we went to Congress and asked for
> a vote and they voted no, that would weaken our position.
> We always believed that the President had the constitu-
> tional authority to go forward and to send the troops into
> combat and liberate Kuwait and that we did not need an

additional vote from Congress. You had the Truman precedent. In 1950 Harry Truman committed forces to Korea,
to liberate Korea after the North had attacked; he did so
under the UN Charter which was a treaty ratified by the
US Senate. The President had all the authority he needed
to act in this case . . . There was no legal requirement for
us to go to Congress.[60]

Despite this highly controversial view, anathema to many of
his former colleagues in the legislature, Cheney joined with
other senior figures in the Administration in a lobbying blitz
in support of a congressional resolution authorizing the use
of force. This passed, but only by small margins with voting
taking place largely on party lines. In the Senate, all but two
Republicans voted yea, while on the Democratic side 45 voted
no, with 10 voting yea; this made possible a vote of 52–47 in
favour. In the House, only three Republicans voted no while
164 voted yea. The Democrats split 86 in favour and 179 against
and the overall vote was 250–183 in favour of the resolution.[61]

While Bush got the resolution he asked for from Congress
supporting his use of force he had no intention of conceding
the constitutional point, as he explained in a signing statement: 'As I made clear to congressional leaders at the outset,
my request for congressional support did not, and my signing
this resolution does not constitute any change in the long
standing positions of the executive branch on either the
President's constitutional authority to use the Armed Forces
to defend vital US interests or the constitutionality of the War
Powers Resolution.'[62]

The implications of this statement were, of course, unacceptable to many members of Congress, 56 of whom, as we
saw earlier, had attempted to get the Supreme Court to prohibit
the President from going to war without a declaration of war
from the legislature. Most scholars side with Congress in such
disputes over the meaning of the Constitution, although the
pros and cons of this never-ending debate are evenly balanced
and coming down on one side or another tends to follow
partisan affiliation.

While understanding the enormous symbolic significance
of the Constitution itself and acknowledging the great wisdom
of those who drew it up, it is surely the case that distant histor-

ical precedents and literal interpretations of a document drawn up more than two centuries ago have only a limited relevance to modern situations. There is no doubt that the Founding Fathers intended to give the war power to Congress; however, when they, rather briefly, considered these matters at Philadelphia they conceded that it was necessary to allow the President the 'power to repel sudden attacks'.[63] In those days, protecting the nation's vital interests was a relatively straight-forward matter; it primarily entailed securing the country's borders against imperialist predators, dependent on sailing ships. Yet if those who drew up the Constitution had been able to envisage the future place of the United States in a complicated, interdependent, highly technological world, they might well have modified their position even further.

Antique definitions of the nation's vital interests are hardly appropriate now and there was some logic to Bush's claim on 15 August 1990 when he said: 'Our jobs, our way of life, our own freedom and the freedom of friendly countries around the world would suffer if control of the world's great oil resources fell into the hands of Saddam Hussein.'[64] Moreover, despite the dangers, it cannot be denied that presidents are normally in a better position than legislators to judge when the national security is threatened, although this is, of course, no guarantee of that their judgements will be wise.

It is also the case that there have now been many instances where presidents have successfully claimed the right to commit American forces without meaningful consultation with Congress. The list is long and encompasses some of the greatest names in the history of the United States – Lincoln, Theodore Roosevelt, Wilson, FDR, Truman, Kennedy, Johnson, Nixon, Carter, Ford, Reagan, Bush and Clinton. When considering this roll call, members of Congress and scholars alike are prone to be selective – to approve, or at least to acquiesce in, some violations of the Constitution and to disapprove of others.

The basis upon which such distinctions are made often has little to do with constitutional law and everything to do with partisan affiliation. Much also turns on whether the military conflcit in question is crowned by success. In the euphoria of victory, constitutional concerns tend to be forgotten, a pheno-menon that, in itself, points to the limited relevance of such considerations when the national security is deemed to be under threat.

Having said all that it is nevertheless the case that Bush and his advisers pushed to the very outer limits, and beyond, the case for presidential primacy in war-making. They placed far more weight on the Commander-in-Chief clause in the Constitution than it could reasonably bear and argued spuriously that UN resolutions superseded congressional constitutional responsibilities. Furthermore, this crisis could hardly be said to fall within the President's constitutional right to 'repel sudden attacks'. The situation was not comparable to, say, the Cuban Missile Crisis where swift decision-making was, arguably, imperative. The war with Iraq did not begin until four and a half months after the invasion of Kuwait and there had, therefore, been ample time for extensive consultation with Congress. The Administration rode roughshod over the rights of Congress and it is highly questionable whether the assault on Kuwait really represented the large threat to American interests claimed by the President and his spokesmen. In these matters, Bush was quite unlike that other guardian president Dwight Eisenhower, who was, by comparison, a meticulous constitutionalist.

STATECRAFT AND GOOD FORTUNE

Initially, George Bush was the beneficiary of much post-war euphoria. He was rapturously received when he addressed a joint session of Congress at the end of the war, while among the public, those approving of his conduct of the presidency soared to 92 per cent in one poll, the highest figure ever recorded.[65] As an exercise in leadership Bush's performance in response to the Gulf crisis was, in many respects, undeniably impressive. The contrasts with the last occasion when the US had despatched massive military force abroad – the war in Vietnam – could hardly have been more striking. Lyndon Johnson's lack of experience in international affairs had been a grave disadvantage and the Vietnam conflict turned into a long drawn-out affair bedevilled by uncertain objectives, bringing heavy US casualties and conducted in the face of widespread international opprobrium. Rather than immediately committing large forces to Vietnam, Johnson had begun by sending relatively small numbers which were subsequently surreptitiously escalated over several years until they reached half a million plus. Johnson had also made the mistake of immersing himself in the detail of military planning.

George Bush and his advisers were keenly aware of Johnson's mistakes as well as those made by President Carter during the Iranian hostage crisis of 1979–81. They also assumed that, particularly after the trauma of Vietnam, the American people lacked the stomach for a long drawn-out conflict. If there was to be a war, it needed to be short and sharp and, to accomplish that, a whole-hearted commitment of troops on a massive scale was required. Saddam Hussein made a most plausible enemy and, as a short-term objective, the intention of ejecting him from Kuwait was undeniably clear-cut. The UN threw its support behind the United States from the start and President Bush was able to draw on his experience in putting together a vast, disparate anti-Saddam alliance. The President made no attempt to micro manage the war, which, in any case, lasted for only a few weeks and incurred few American casualties.[66]

Even the most severe critics of the Bush Administration's conduct of the Gulf War have been obliged to concede that the diplomatic skills of the President and his Secretary of State played a vital part in securing what was ultimately an impressive victory.[67] The contacts with leaders overseas that Bush had built up over the years and his mastery of telephone diplomacy now proved to be formidable assets enabling him to fashion an extraordinary international coalition.[68]

> The intimate knowledge of world leaders and world politics that he had acquired during his years as ambassador to the UN, envoy to Beijing and CIA director helped him forge an unprecedented international alliance. Throughout, Bush . . . displayed an exquisite sensitivity to diplomatic nuance and the need for subtle compromise – and sometimes outright bribes – required to bring together such mutually suspicious bedfellows as Syria, Israel, Iran and the Soviet Union. His performance went beyond competence to sheer mastery.[69]

Any assessment of Bush's leadership during this crisis, however, needs to include recognition that his achievements were much dependent on the fortuitous conjunction of circumstances that existed in 1990. The UN, for instance, was now in a position to play a part in pressurizing Saddam Hussein and in cementing the international coalition that made possible his ejection from Kuwait. It had, however, only recently become possible for the UN to take on such a role. For the previous four decades it had been racked by ideological division with the Soviet Union routinely using its veto in the Security Council to defeat Western initiatives, and vice versa. The General Assembly, meanwhile, had, by the 1970s, become a bastion of Third World and other powers generally hostile to the United States. As a consequence, many Americans, particularly conservatives, remained deeply sceptical of the value of the United Nations. One who held these views in the late 1980s was Vice President George Bush, as he made clear in his autobiography: 'Clearly, the United Nations has much to be said for it, but it still has a long way to go before it can ever achieve its early promise as "the world's best hope for peace".'[70] By 1990, however, the Cold War was at an end, the Warsaw Pact had disintegrated and Soviet–American relations had never been more amicable. In these new circumstances the Bush Administration was able to utilize the UN fully in its efforts to drive Iraq out of Kuwait.

In the past the Middle East had been a region of intense superpower rivalry and any move made by presidents from Truman to Reagan had to take careful account of how the USSR might respond. No such difficulty attended the Gulf crisis. Notwithstanding the Soviet Union's earlier support for Iraq it now gave US policy-makers a free hand. This new posture can hardly be explained as simply a result of Bush's diplomacy and the efforts of his Secretary of State – it arose in large part from the fortuitous accession of Gorbachev and the internal and external weakness of the Soviet Union, all developments which pre-dated the Bush presidency. The end of the Cold War furthermore, made it possible for the Administration to respond to General Schwarzkopf's insistence that if Saddam Hussein was to be driven from Kuwait, he would need the VII Corps, the centrepiece of US ground defence in

Europe. This was an extraordinary request that could not possibly have been met only a year previously.[71]

President Bush was also fortunate to face a crass and incompetent foe in Saddam Hussein. The Iraqi invasion was instantly the subject of condemnation throughout the world and there must be doubts about the competence of a national leader who causes his country to become such a pariah in the international community. Even Nazi Germany was never as isolated as Iraq became in 1990–91 with overwhelming votes against it not only in the Security Council, but also in the General Assembly where, for example, it was condemned by a vote of 132–1 on 3 December 1990 and by 144–1 on 18 December 1990.[72]

Bush and his advisers knew that it was important that the United States not become bogged down in a long Vietnam-type war with heavy casualties. However, contrary to the pre-war hype regarding the might and prowess of the Iraqi army, it soon became apparent that Bush and his allies had the good fortune to be facing military forces much smaller than anticipated and singularly lacking in the will to fight. Various sources have suggested that far from 'a million man army', as Secretary of Defense Cheney and others maintained, Saddam may have had less than 200 000 troops in the field facing coalition forces in excess of 550 000 and in possession of vast technological superiority. When the war got under way the ill-equipped, demoralized, ramshackle army of an impoverished Third World country was, not surprisingly, no match for the overwhelming weight of the American-led coalition.[73]

It is evident from the above that President Bush enjoyed a considerable amount of luck during this crisis. In addition, any complete assessment of his leadership must go beyond the sequence of events that extended from the invasion at the beginning of August to the cessation of hostilities at the end of the following February. It has, for instance, been argued that the Bush Administration failed to heed many warning signs of a crisis developing throughout the first half of 1990 and even gave Saddam Hussein reason to believe that the US would not intervene if he attacked Kuwait.[74] Such an attack had been a possibility for some time. Although the two countries were temporarily allied during the Iraq/Iran war there were longstanding areas of dispute between them.[75] The mutual border was arbitrarily, and none too precisely, drawn by the British in the 1920s and, in particular, two islands, Warba and Bubiyan, controlling Iraq's access to the sea had been given to Kuwait. For years this had rankled with the Iraqis and after the Iraq/Iran war ended relations with Kuwait deteriorated even further. In May 1990, Saddam Hussein complained bitterly that Kuwait, by grossly exceeding its OPEC oil production quota, had severely depressed the price of oil with disastrous consequences for Iraq: 'You are wrecking our means of sustenance,' Saddam told the Kuwaitis, 'and if you cut people's means of sustenance, it is equivalent to cutting their neck and killing them.'[76]

Aggrieved by longstanding border disputes and the violation of OPEC rules Saddam, in 1990, made numerous belligerent statements, but the Bush Administration, preoccupied with events elsewhere in the world, gave mixed signals in response. Thus eight days before the Iraqi invasion Ambassador April Glaspie, in a meeting with Saddam, assured him that the United States wanted better relations with Iraq and went on: 'We have no opinion on the Arab–Arab conflicts, like your border disagreement with Kuwait.'[77] Ms Glaspie later claimed that she also said that the US would protect its interests in the area and that Saddam had asked her to assure President Bush that he had no intention of attacking Kuwait.[78] Nevertheless, the comments of Glaspie and other Administration spokespeople at this time suggested that the US would not interfere if Iraq seized Kuwait. It is arguable, in other words, that a more alert Administration might have taken steps to prevent the invasion before it occurred, thereby preventing a conflict which, while it ended in success for the US and its allies, had disastrous consequences for the Iraqi people, including an enormous loss of life.

With the advantage of hindsight it is easy to be critical of Bush's management of the Persian Gulf crisis: to question the validity of the decision-making process, to emphasize the elements of good fortune while downplaying the hazards that had to be negotiated and the desperately difficult choices that the President alone was ultimately responsible for. Nevertheless during this, the greatest challenge of his presidency, Bush appears to have been strong, resolute and decisive. He stated his objective in early August: 'This will not stand this aggression against Kuwait' and drove unflinchingly towards it, declining to be deflected by those who looked for compromise, wanted more time for sanctions to work, or shrank from the probability of large-scale bloodshed. In this instance at least Bush was, within limits, a highly effective leader. Irrespective of the merits of the policy that he and his advisers developed, the President was, without doubt, successful in imposing his priorities and in moving the nation in the direction in which he sought to take it. Having said that it is the case that this was a narrowly focused demonstration of statecraft which, to be seen in its best light, has to be isolated from what went before and what has happened since.

9 Conclusions

It has been argued throughout this book that presidents are entitled to be judged on their own terms rather than on those preferred by their political opponents, media pundits or academics. As a guardian president Bush expressed boundless faith in the American political and economic system.[1] Furthermore, in contrast to reforming presidents of the past like Wilson, the two Roosevelts and Johnson, he regarded extensions of the role of government without enthusiasm. He shared Eisenhower's belief that presidents had a responsibility 'to restrain and limit government, not to force it to fulfil any great mission or obligation.'[2]

In the early weeks of his presidency Bush was reported to have installed a portrait of Theodore Roosevelt in the Cabinet Room and to have told a visitor: 'I'm an Oyster Bay kind of guy . . . Maybe I'll turn out to be a Teddy Roosevelt.'[3] This was never more than a fanciful suggestion for while not unlike TR in his origins, Bush's style in office was far removed from that of his aggressively proactive predecessor. The first Roosevelt was a combative, creative leader and is remembered particularly for his mastery of the bully pulpit; in domestic policy he was anything but an unambitious near-passive leader, abjuring rhetorical appeals and responding to problems as they arose on a case-by-case basis, in the manner of guardians like Eisenhower, Ford and Bush. The parallels between Roosevelt and Bush are somewhat more meaningful in foreign policy where both vigorously asserted presidential prerogatives and compiled records of achievement.

RECORD OF ACHIEVEMENT

It seems likely that Bush's place in history will be determined almost entirely by his accomplishments in foreign policy. As we saw in Chapter 7, US policy in Central America had been a disaster area for the Reagan Administration and the Iran Contra affair had damaged severely executive relations with the legislature. James Baker as Bush's Secretary of State skilfully mended fences with Congress and developed a bipartisan policy that relied on diplomacy in contrast to the military emphasis of the previous administration. In early 1990 this approach was apparently vindicated by the electoral defeat in Nicaragua of the governing Sandinistas and the election as president of Violeta Chamorro.[4] Further success for the Bush Administration in Central America came with the eventual invasion of Panama and the removal from the area of the troublesome Manuel Noriega.

Earlier, in reviewing Bush's contribution to the end of the Cold War, I indicated that this would remain a matter of some dispute for a long time to come. Nevertheless, for the moment, it is interesting to consider the early verdicts of some specialists in this field who could in no way be described as political allies of the President. Michael Mandelbaum, for instance, observed that Bush was gifted the 'greatest geopolitical windfall in the history of American foreign policy' when the communist regimes of Eastern Europe fell apart; however, the President is praised for his handling of the situation, for ensuring that the United States stayed on the sidelines while these extraordinary events occurred. The President's restraint 'served America's interests well . . . the qualities most characteristic of [his Administration] – caution, modest public pronouncements and a fondness for private communications – were admirably suited to the moment.' There was nothing inevitable about the relatively smooth ending of communism in Europe; there were many hazards and possible disasters, but Bush is credited with managing to avoid them all.[5]

Michael Elliott, the diplomatic editor of *Newsweek*, applauds in particular Bush's commitment to a unified Germany in the face of resistance from Mrs Thatcher and François Mitterrand. He commends also his refusal to engage in triumphalism at Gorbachev's expense, thereby ensuring that the new Germany would stay within NATO.[6] Two other students of these matters, Michael Beschloss and Strobe Talbott, who later became Deputy Secretary of State in the Clinton Administration, while questioning Bush's extravagant representation of himself at the 1992 Republican convention as some sort of hero in the struggle to end communism, are willing to concede that he 'made an indispensable contribution to the Cold War's end. From January 1989 through December 1991, he coaxed the Soviet

Union toward worldwide surrender. He did so largely by exercising restraint and refraining from pushing the Soviet government too hard, thus never giving Moscow a pretext to reverse course.'[7]

Bush's leadership during the crisis created by Saddam Hussein's invasion of Kuwait will obviously be central to any consideration of his historical significance. Leaving aside the alleged inadequacies of American foreign policy that arguably helped to bring this crisis about, George Bush's conduct during these most testing moments of his presidency is not easy to fault. It is, however, the case that in the Gulf War, as with the ending of the Cold War, Bush's strength was in managing change rather than in charting a new course. He made his contribution by dealing skilfully with problems on an *ad hoc* basis, in engaging in transactional rather than transformational leadership, a style of leadership particularly appropriate to the situations he faced.[8]

The North American Free Trade Agreement finally adopted by Congress in 1993 can also be counted among President Bush's foreign policy achievements. The idea of such an agreement first emerged during the Reagan years when it was seen as a natural outgrowth of the free trade agreement negotiated in 1987 between the US and Canada. In September 1990, Bush informed Congress of his intention to negotiate a free trade pact with Mexico and announced in Febuary 1991 that Canada would join the talks. Under the terms of the 1988 Trade Act the President was given authority for three months to negotiate a trade agreement that would then be submitted for congressional approval under 'fast-track' procedures. These gave Congress 90 days to act once an agreement was concluded and protected it from amendments.

An extension of the President's negotiating authority for two years became the subject of intense political debate in 1991 with opponents of a free trade agreement in both houses of Congress seeking to pass resolutions disapproving an extension. If either of these had passed the effect would have been to terminate the fast-track process and to wreck the negotiations. The Bush Administration fought vigorously and successfully against the resolutions, thereby making it possible for the negotiations to proceed and leading eventually to the signing of NAFTA in December 1992.[9]

Far more comfortable with foreign policy-making and instinctively doubtful of the efficacy of governmental action in domestic policy, Bush, as we saw in Chapter 4, nevertheless felt obliged to have an agenda at home. Asked by journalists, late in his term, to identify the most significant domestic initiatives that he had 'originated, promoted and seen through to fruition' the President referred to education, child care, the Americans with Disabilities Act, revision of the Clean Air Act and appointments to the federal bench.[10]

During the 1988 campaign Bush had vowed to be 'the education president' and in September 1989 he followed this up by holding an education summit with state governors where a number of educational goals were agreed. In the first Congress of his presidency, however, Bush failed to secure passage of legislation that would have provided some first steps towards the fulfilment of those goals.[11] In 1991 the Administration initiated 'America 2000', an education reform programme including voluntary national testing; merit pay for teachers; reductions in regulations; and the establishment of innovative schools financed by business and the federal government. A voucher scheme for low and middle income families was subsequently added to this list of proposals, but none of these various initiatives became law and there is little hard evidence to support Bush's inclusion of education as an area of significant achievement.[12]

In 1990, Bush signed into law major child care legislation and he had campaigned on the issue in 1988. On the other hand, important though his commitment was, Bush was by no means alone in pressing the case for this measure. According to the *Congressional Quarterly*, the $22.5 billion package eventually passed represented the culmination of a 'three year effort by a coalition of child care advocacy groups, organized labor and educators.'[13] Similarly, as I argued earlier, while Bush was undoubtedly an enthusiastic supporter of the ADA there were many others involved in that cause and it might well have passed without the President's help. The 1990 Clean Air Act also had a complex legislative history, but Bush's claim to a significant role in its fashioning is less open to dispute than it is in the cases of the ADA and child care legislation.

For Bush's many critics on the right of his own party the clean air and aid for the disabled bills were, in any case, distinctly

dubious accomplishments for a president supposedly dedicated to deregulation. As Vice President, Bush had been
chairman of Reagan's Task Force on Regulatory Relief and
had been notably successful in reducing the burden of government regulations. With Bush in the White House the situation
appeared to change radically with regulation substantially
increasing.[14] The pages of new regulations in the *Federal Register*
had totalled 50 997 in the final year of Reagan's first term and
53 376 in the last year of his presidency whereas in the concluding year of Bush's term the figure rose to 67 716.[15] Moreover,
after adjustment for inflation, 'the amount that the government [spent] on its regulatory activities [was] 22% higher in
fiscal 1991 than in Carter's last year.'[16] Conservatives outraged
by the increase in regulation during the Bush years were
much inclined to hold the ADA and the clean air legislation
especially responsible.[17]

None of this helped Bush's chances of re-election, but, aside
from that, it can hardly be denied that his legislative record
was thin. I discussed the unprecedented paucity of his presidential success scores in Chapter 5, although I also drew
attention to the inadequacy of such measures when applied
to guardian presidents. While the latter are obliged to labour
in an activist ethos they take very seriously indeed their
responsibility, in Hamilton's words, for 'preventing bad laws'
and, as we saw, Bush deftly wielded the veto power and
signing statements to shape or to prevent the passage of laws
he found wanting.

It was not unreasonable for George Bush to place his judicial appointments among his most noteworthy domestic policy
accomplishments. His predecessor had shown that by careful
screening of nominations to the federal courts it was possible
to exercise a crucial influence in policy areas of particular
importance to conservative presidents such as abortion, affir-
mative action, religious freedom and the rights of criminal
defendants.[18] In the Bush administration the conservative C.
Boyden Gray, Counsel to the President and one of his closest
allies, took charge of the judicial selection process and insti-
tutionalized the elaborate arrangements for screening
candidates begun under Reagan.[19] Out of this process emerged
a preponderance of relatively young, white males 'true to the
key tenets of the conservative agenda'.[20]

During the course of his presidency Bush appointed 185 federal district and circuit court judges, nearly a quarter of the federal bench.[21] He also had the opportunity to appoint two US Supreme Court justices, David Souter and Clarence Thomas. Little was known of Souter's views when he was appointed in 1990, but, to the chagrin of right-wing Republicans, he has joined with Sandra Day O'Connor and Anthony Kennedy to form an alliance of moderate conservative justices 'responsible for preventing a reversal of the court's long-held positions on abortion, school prayer and, in one key case, prisoners' rights.'[22] Thomas, on the other hand, has consistently voted with the hardline conservatives Antonin Scalia and Chief Justice William H. Rehnquist.[23] Overall, while Bush has been fiercely criticized by conservatives in his party for other reasons, his efforts to carry on Reagan's mission of moving the federal bench to the right have met with approval; in July 1992 it was reported that in this regard at least: 'The conservative community is extremely pleased.'[24]

C. BOYDEN GRAY

The fact that Bush's judicial appointments largely satisfied conservatives owed much to the efforts of C. Boyden Gray, without question one of the most influential members of the White House staff. The role of the president's Counsel, or legal adviser, has varied from one adminstration to another, but Gray, with good reason, came to be indentified as Bush's *éminence grise*.[25] The two men had not met before Gray was interviewed in 1981 for the post of Counsel to the Vice President. However, their backgrounds gave them much in common. Both were from wealthy Eastern establishment families and were educated at private schools and elite universities, Yale in Bush's case and Harvard in Gray's. The President's father, Prescott Bush, had been a United States Senator from 1953 until 1962 and was a friend of Gray's father, Gordon Gray, Army Secretary in the Truman Administration and National Security Adviser to President Eisenhower. Both fathers and sons became members of the Alibi Club, one of the most exclusive clubs in Washington.[26]

After eight years on Vice President Bush's staff, C. Boyden

Gray became Counsel to the President in 1989 with special responsibility for monitoring ethical standards among administration officials, overseeing the judicial nomination process and protecting the constitutional prerogatives of the presidency.[27] Gray's closeness to the President, his unquestionable loyalty, his intellect and his forceful personality allowed him to emerge as a major player in the upper reaches of the Bush Administration, someone able to 'go in and talk to the President on any issue he chooses.'[28] Involved not only in judicial selections, but in all nominations, Gray also had a role in policy formulation and was one of the prime movers behind both the clean air legislation and the ADA. Beyond that, Gray advised the President on his exercise of the veto and was the principal architect of the strategy of using signing statements to defend presidential prerogatives, most notably in the realm of foreign policy. Gray was clearly a figure of some weight in the Bush White House and his influence was particularly evident on those occasions when the President displayed some mettle in his dealings with Congress.

LEGISLATIVE LEADERSHIP

The acid test of presidential leadership is widely believed to be a chief executive's capacity to fashion a productive relationship with Congress. For activist presidents this is obviously imperative, and while it is less essential for guardians, given their limited agendas, they also require cooperation from the legislature. I referred in Chapter 2 to Bush's initial adoption of a conciliatory approach towards Congress. Some conservatives were troubled by this stance from the beginning, but Roger Porter, Assistant to the President for Economic and Domestic Policy, felt that Bush had little option to do otherwise in light of the configuration of party strength in the legislature. Porter also vigorously rebutted the suggestion that Bush's record of achievement in domestic policy was weak and emphasized the successes of his veto strategy.[29]

Gray, while recognizing that the President's violation of his no new taxes pledge 'will dog him through the rest of time' thought 'he did rather well with a hostile Congress.' Despite the machinations of the Democratic leader in the Senate,

George Mitchell, Bush had 'revolutionized' the enforcement of environmental controls, 'triggered educational reform', 'cleaned up the savings and loan mess', obtained passage of the ADA and left behind an economy 'as good as any left to anybody in American history'. As Porter did, Gray laid great stress on the fact that Bush had to deal with a Congress controlled by the Democrats by large margins. Reagan, the yardstick against which Bush was so often measured, had enjoyed a Senate controlled by the Republicans for six of his eight years. Consequently, the Senate was like an echo chamber for Reagan. He would make pronouncements and present policies which would then be sympathetically heard whereas Bush's initiatives were promptly subject to partisan mutilation, a disadvantage the importance of which 'could not be emphasized too much.'[30]

Despite these rationalizations it surely is the case that Bush's early strategy of conciliation towards the legislature was ill-judged. As he said himself towards the end, he 'held out the hand of friendship . . . and these old mossbacks bit it off.'[31] That this would happen was entirely predictable. At the best of times, Congress is packed with ruthless adversaries who revel in creating difficulties for the man in the White House and they were unlikely to be much impressed, in the long term, by honeyed words and gestures of friendship.

As several observers noted in reflecting on Bush's approach, presidents cannot afford to be unduly accommodating in their dealings with legislators. A veteran of the Reagan White House said: 'Presidents do well when the people on the Hill have a healthy regard for them – verging on fear.'[32] A House Democratic leadership aide made the same point when he noted that Bush 'did not generate the raw political fear that Mr Reagan had in his glory years . . . there isn't any cost to crossing him.'[33] Authoritative confirmation of the inadvisability of Bush's 'kinder gentler' style was provided later by one the most experienced and hard-headed members of his Administration, Clayton Yeutter: 'Bush was never sufficiently aggressive with the Congress. He just didn't want to do it that way. He never realized that those folks were doing him in. He had so many good friends over there, and, on a one-on-one basis, they all loved George Bush and he loved them and it was marvellous. But he was never able to separate the personal relationships with the Congress from the political relationships. He couldn't comprehend that those who were great friends of his were doing him in politically every day of the week.'[34]

GOING PUBLIC

As Bobbie Kilberg, among other members of the Communications division of the White House staff, discovered, Bush had neither the capacity nor the inclination for 'going public', for appealing to the American people over the heads of his old friends in Congress.[35] He was not, in short, a particularly good mass communicator and saw no need to become one. This was surely one of the gravest weaknesses in Bush's style of leadership, providing a key to an understanding of why his presidency ultimately failed, on the domestic front at least.

In 1988 he had campaigned on the strength of his CV, boasting of being 'Ready from day one to be a great president', but, in truth, he was not fully qualified to meet the demands of the US presidency in the late twentieth century. As Samuel Kernell has demonstrated, the American political system has undergone change in recent decades. As recently as the 1960s, in the circumstances of 'institutional pluralism', it had been appropriate to focus on bargaining as the principal means whereby coalitions were formed and policies were agreed. In Congress there had been party and committee leaders of consequence allowing presidents to cut deals, largely behind the scenes, to advance their programmes. In such conditions, insiders thrived and the influence of public opinion was relatively limited in normal circumstances. By the 1980s, however, institutional pluralism had decayed and been replaced by 'individualized pluralism'. Parties had weakened and centrifugal tendencies in Congress had intensified; there were now hardly any leaders of significance in the legislature with whom a president could negotiate and the ethos of 'To get along, go along' had been replaced by rampant individualism.[36] Success in the White House now increasingly required a capacity the part of chief executives for going public, for 'forcing compliance from fellow Washingtonians by going over their heads to appeal to their constituents'.[37]

The various activities associated with going public – making trips around the country, visits overseas, prime-time addresses, televised news conferences and ceremonial occasions – all made for situations where Bush did not perform particularly well. His fractured syntax, his unwillingness to take direction from media advisers, his 'hot' rather than 'cool' persona, his obvious discomfort in front of television cameras and his oratorical limitations combined to make him a less than effective communicator. As one presidential scholar, Thomas Cronin, said of the President: 'He is rhetorically and oratorically a handicapped man.'[38] The President's 'tone deafness' was remarked on by another critic, the conservative commentator, Robert Novak, who went on to say: 'Of all successful politicians Bush has the least feel for language . . . [he] lacks an essential weapon of politics: the ability to stir the nation with words.'[39]

Even more telling was the rueful awareness among Bush's senior staff of his weakness as a communicator. Andrew Card, Deputy Chief of Staff and later Secretary for Transportation, declared that Bush was 'a great President' and 'a great leader for the world' and yet he was not 'a great communicator [and] he was not good on television.'[40] According to James Ciccone, Bush singularly lacked Reagan's 'quite extraordinary' talent for communicating with the public. Not only did he 'distrust the power of rhetoric' he also displayed a 'lack of comfort in front of the media.'[41]

Even the ultra-loyalist C. Boyden Gray, who in the course of two long interviews hardly let a word critical of the President pass, accepted that as a communicator Bush was not in the same league as his predecessor: 'Reagan had a capacity to exploit the bully pulpit; he was a masterful public speaker [whereas] Bush just did not have that very awesome talent.' The no less loyal Gregg Petersmeyer spoke of Bush being 'not particularly warm with the camera lens' and, in contrast to Reagan 'he never thought about the presidency in wholesale terms versus retail terms.' In other words, while Bush was a master of retail politics, in dealing with people one on one, he had no feel for 'projecting to large numbers of people'.[42]

Several members of Bush's staff drew my attention to the President's often impressive performances at press conferences in contrast to Reagan's inadequacies in that setting. Bush, moreover, held far more press conferences than his predecessor.

However, Terry Eastland has written perceptively about the limitations of press conferences, as compared to set speeches, as techniques for marshalling support behind policy proposals:

> [P]ress conferences are a poor means of presenting a legislative policy and offering a coherent argument on its behalf. The President must share time with reporters who ask questions that can bounce from one subject to another or who wish to 'pin' him down on a matter he would not care, or is not prepared, to talk about . . . a President who so prefers press conferences that he neglects the public argument he can make through well-considered speeches is underemploying the presidential office.[43]

In the late twentieth century, effective communication with the American public, largely through the medium of television, has become an essential prerequisite for success in the White House. Behind the scenes leadership and bargaining skills are not enough in the present age and, in that sense, Bush was less well qualified for the presidency than he and others recognized. None of the jobs he had held in the past had prepared him for the demands of going public, and he lacked both the talent and the inclination for mass communication – major handicaps in an era of individualized pluralism.

Outside of those brief periods when he was in what he described as his 'campaign mode', Bush seemed to have an aversion to selling himself and the policies he espoused. Several of his senior staff expressed their frustration at his failure to understand that it was not sufficient for him to work hard and to pursue the correct policies. The President's naivety in these matters bemused John Keller, the Director of Advance, and a devoted Bush admirer. 'He thought that you should be able to just work your ass off and people would love you. You really do get into some genuine innocence if he really thought that, but he did!'[44] Similarly, Nicholas Calio believed that Bush was mistaken in believing that 'you didn't need to communicate through sound bites or creating perception.' This was to ignore the fact that if the people 'don't understand what you're doing, you're going to have a problem accomplishing what you want to achieve', whereas Bush erroneously 'assumed that the American public would understand perfectly well what he was doing.' It was also matter of regret for Calio, as a legislative liaison chief, that Bush's disinclination to go public, as a means of framing the debate on contentious issues, often resulted in his being upstaged by the Democrats in Congress. In this regard, there were two exceptions :the fight to obtain fast-track authority for the North American Free Trade Agreement and the Persian Gulf war. 'In both [of those] cases he went very public, got right behind it, communicated specific messages and brought the public along. That normally didn't happen.'[45]

Few would question that foreign policy was an area of achievement for President Bush, but whatever success he enjoyed in that realm turned primarily on personal diplomacy. Here too he often appeared to believe that as long as his policies were sound the public would understand, an attitude that exasperated Scowcroft's aide Richard Haass, who was of the view that the administration should have:

> gone public more in arguing why it was we were doing things the way we were and not doing things the way some of our critics wanted . . . it isn't enough just to do the right things and have them turn out right, you have to go out and sell and explain policy. I think Bush's sense of stewardship was 'I will do the right things and they will turn out well and the people will see that and they will reward me for it.' And that is just inadequate.[46]

AN ABSENCE OF VISION

George Bush's weakness as a communicator bears on his alleged lack of vision. Presidents who have vision are blessed with a clear sense of direction, and they come into office with a master plan, or blueprint, that can be readily communicated to the people. No one ever accused Ronald Reagan of being without vision and he famously entered office with a preconceived plan. For years he had been traipsing around the country exalting the advantages of lower taxes, less government and stronger defence – stark and simple aims that were relatively easy to communicate, that clearly differentiated him from his political opponents and that ultimately gave coherence and direction to his presidency. The constant insistence by critics on the right that he too exhibit vision baffled George Bush. In his autobiography he reluctantly addressed the complaint by wheeling out a few vapid references to freedom, justice, opportunity, minimal government and economic freedom before saying: 'My "vision" – it was all there in everything I'd said as a candidate and done in nearly twenty years of public life.'[47]

This dismissive comment is particularly revealing; those who wished to find out what Bush stood for could be left to work it out for themselves by examining his record. Such things were to be divined rather than articulated by the man himself who was 'not comfortable with rhetoric for rhetoric's sake'.[48] There is an elitist ring to Bush's persistent insistence that he should not have to explain himself and it is at odds with Reagan's more populist approach. For the latter, the establishment of a dialogue with the people, explaining what he was trying to do, and why, was a matter of the first priority.

While Bush himself remained unconvinced of the need for vision, for any sort of master plan, this could not be said of some of his senior staff. One of those closest to him, Gregg Petersmeyer, regretted his 'failure to project a vision for America . . . people expect of leaders just two things: they expect to be told where we are going and how we are going to get there,' but Bush had been found wanting on both counts.[49] Sununu's executive assistant, Ed Rogers, put it differently; as he saw it the problem was that: 'Nobody knew if Bush was a dictator what he would do about anything. If he was a dictator, what would he do about our education problem, what would he do about our crime problem, what would he do about our economic problems?'[50]

In the same vein Constance Horner noted that in domestic policy:

The big picture wan't there in the President's mind . . . He had good particulars that he was committed to, and in fact achieved through legislation, but there was no articulation of a grand design that would compel other people's attention. There was therefore, no basis for determining what was important from day to day in domestic policy . . . I think President Bush would view a grand design as a burden to be avoided, as a potential embarrassing conflict with what daily reality required.

As Ms Horner said, this was 'quite different from Reagan' and her analysis neatly distinguishes Bush as a reactive, pragmatic leader from the proactive, ideological president who preceded him.[51]

Given the nature of the American political system, there are clearly advantages to be derived from a chief executive working to a grand design. Such a strategy makes for coherence and gives direction to the administration in a polity marked by chronically weak political parties and a centrifugal structure of power. As Charles Kolb emphasized, Reagan's political appointees took up their posts with a clear sense of what they were expected to do, whereas the Bush Administration was encumbered by 'an aimless agenda nursed along by thousands of clueless appointees wondering what they were hired for.'[52]

Such scorn was to be expected from a conservative and a Reaganite like Kolb, yet Clayton Yeutter said something very similar: 'Reagan was very skilful in laying out the things that were fervently important to him. He did that better than any president in my lifetime . . . He did it year in and year out for 40 or 50 years [*sic*] . . . He had four or five major objectives and everybody in the United States understood them. That helped in governing too because people within his own administration understood what the priorities were . . . Bush was never that clear in what his presidential objectives were.'[53]

Yeutter understood that a president stood a better chance of being successful if he had some sense of direction. On the other hand he also appeared to recognize how unusual Reagan was in possessing vision, in having a master plan that gave coherence and direction to his presidency. Indeed, as I argued earlier, Bush's style of leadership was, in some respects, far more typical than Reagan's – visionless, non-ideological, pragmatic presidents have been the norm, historically.[54] Vision is synonymous with ideology loosely defined, but the political context in the United States has never encouraged ideological approaches to leadership. Furthermore, it is difficult to recall any president other than Reagan who could be said to have had vision. Certainly that infinitely influential, master of statecraft Franklin Roosevelt does not qualify. Far from being any sort of visionary, FDR was, in the words of Theodore Lowi: 'a broker, an eclectic, a pragmatist, an improviser, one

who lived comfortably with great inconsistencies.'[55] Those
activist presidents nursing the ambition to follow in Roosevelt's
footsteps such as Truman, Kennedy, Johnson, Carter and
Clinton may have had far more extensive agendas than
guardians like Eisenhower, Ford and Bush, but it is questionable whether their lists of proposals have been bound together
by intellectual coherence sufficiently to merit use of the term
vision.

While there are obvious advantages in a president having
some sort of grand design there is also a downside. At its
worst, it demands simple-mindedness rather than sophistica-
tion in decision-making. Charles Kolb, one of those within the
White House most severely critical of Bush's lack of an overall
plan, made much in conversation with me of the fact that
what Reagan stood for could be summarized in six words, a
test that his successor certainly could not meet.[56] Unquestionably it was one of the strengths of Reagan's presidency
that what he was trying to accomplish could be stated so
briefly: 'lower taxes, less government, stronger defense.'[57] Yet,
as I noted earlier, simple clear-cut goals, while beneficial for
communication purposes, may not do justice to the complexity
of the issues.[58]

Environmental protectionism was one such issue. In
accepting the Republican nomination in 1988 Bush committed
himself to improving the environment: 'We must clean the air.
We must reduce the harm done by acid rain.' Those who
worried about such matters were subsequently encouraged by
the appointment of a conservationist, William Reilly, to head
the Environmental Protection Agency and by the
Administration's crucial role in the passage of the 1990 Clean
Air Act, discussed in more detail in Chapter 4 above. Late in
Bush's term, however, he came under attack from environ-
mentalists for failing to implement clean air legislation with
sufficient resolution.[59] At the same time, conservatives
complained bitterly about the mounting regulatory burdens
being placed on industry by the Administration-sponsored
Clean Air Act and the Americans with Disabilities Act.

As Bush prepared to face the voters in 1992 it appeared
that he favoured both deregulation and environmental protection, a posture which his critics derided as symptomatic of the
absence of vision: 'It is a real dichotomy. On one hand, he is

too "green"; on the other hand he is not "green" enough. It all goes back to the idea of leadership and vision. We don't know what his vision really is. He wants the best of two conflicting worlds – to be green and to deregulate.'[60] Bush's straddling of both positions moreover was reflected in conflict within his Administration, with Reilly finding himself engaged in a constant struggle with prominent conservatives in the White House like John Sununu and Dan Quayle, who did not share his concerns.

For the purposes of communication, unity within the Administration and effective leadership in general, it would have been far better if Bush had set aside the complexities and come down firmly on one side or the other of the issue – if he had committed himself firmly to environmental protection or deregulation; there had, of course, been no such ambiguity about Reagan's position – he had consistently resisted clean air proposals.

A charitable interpretation of Bush's stance, however, requires some recognition of the fact that environmental protectionism raises complex questions that are not susceptible to easy answers. There is surely a case for being simultaneously a green and an advocate of deregulation; the centrist position may well be sounder and more intellectually honest than either of the two extremes.[61] Much the same could also be said of other contentious issues that troubled Bush such as abortion, civil rights and management of the economy. None of this was likely to impress the President's many critics on the right who interpreted his ambiguities and uncertainties as nothing more than a lack of convictions 'as the incoherence that afflicts a public person operating without a public philosophy'.[62]

A LACK OF CONVICTIONS?

Throughout his presidency Bush was haunted by the widely held perception that he was a man without convictions; that he really did not believe in anything very much and sought office, at best, out of sense of duty to serve, or at worst, merely for 'the honor of it all'.[63] Some of Bush's staff indignantly rejected such allegations. As I recorded earlier, James Cicconi attributed noble motives to the President, claiming that he had 'an inner core of conviction that was rooted in doing what's right for the country regardless [of the consequences] . . . there are many occasions when he stood up to the political heat because of that integral conviction'. [64] David Demarest was equally dismissive of the 'no convictions' charge seeing it as a cover for the argument 'he's not on our team 100%' and for the complaint that Bush was not 'really a true believer'.[65]

Despite such protestations, there is a lot of evidence tending to support the contention that Bush, to an unusual degree, lacked settled beliefs. He is, to put it another way, vulnerable to the charge of political opportunism, appearing, on a number of occasions, to shift his ground on the issues for reasons of political expediency. Thus my discussion of the 1990 budget crisis in Chapter 6 drew attention to Bush's, ultimately fatal, havering on economic policy. He denounced supply-side economics in the 1980 primaries as 'voodoo economics' but then swiftly became a 'born-again supply sider' once he had become Reagan's running mate.[66] When he ran for the presidency in his own right he repeatedly promised 'no new taxes', a pledge that seems to have been born out of electoral considerations, with Bush's advisers convincing him that such an undertaking was necessary to shore up conservative support and to exorcize the 'wimp' allegation.

His lack of serious commitment to the pledge was revealed by his cavalier reneging on it when it was deemed necessary; a manoeuvre executed with hardly a word of explanation or justification. Moreover, during the crisis that followed, Bush swung back and forth with dizzying speed on a central issue of economic policy – the question of whether he would agree to an increase in income tax in return for a reduction in capital gains tax. The President's several U-turns, within a few days, on this matter further damaged his collapsing credibility as economic policy manager.

Over a much longer time scale, Bush appeared to undergo a number of changes of position on one of the most vexed issues of domestic policy, civil rights, even though this was categorically denied by that most forcefully loyal member of his senior staff, C. Boyden Gray. When I referred to Bush's alleged inconsistencies in this area outlined in newspaper articles Gray retorted: 'I dont think that is true. They just don't understand what they are talking about.'[67] Nevertheless, there do seem to have been a number of shifts in Bush's position on these matters over the years.

In 1948 Bush's liberalism on the race issue was apparently reflected in his leadership of the United Negro College fund drive at Yale University.[68] Yet his first run for public office in 1964, when he sought a seat in the Senate, found him supporting Goldwater without reservation and inveighing against the legislation that would eventually become the Civil Rights Act of 1964.[69] Elected to the US House of Representatives in 1966, Bush shed the conservative position he had taken earlier to join the moderate wing of the Republican Party.

In 1968, Bush voted in favour of a civil rights bill, the Open Housing Act and, subsequently, at a meeting with constituents outraged by this vote, he cited Edmund Burke's theory of representation in his defence before going on to say: 'Sometimes it seems fundamental that a man should not have a door slammed in his face because he is a Negro or speaks with a Latin American accent.' Open housing, Congressman Bush declared, offered a ray of hope for minorities 'locked out by habit and discrimination'. The subject of catcalls initially, Bush was finally given a standing ovation and, in recalling the occasion in his autobiography, observed: 'More than twenty years later I can truthfully say that nothing I've experienced in public life, before or since, has measured up to the feeling I had when I went home that night.'[70]

As Ruth Marcus has shown, however, the background to this incident is revealing. In the first place Bush's electoral position was so safe that he was re-elected without opposition; secondly, in running for election in 1966 he had spoken out against open housing legislation; thirdly, the crucial vote on the bill in question was not on final passage, when Bush voted in favour, but on the procedural question of whether to send the bill back to the conference committee, a manoeuvre that would have almost certainly killed the bill off. This earlier critical vote found Bush siding with the forces hostile to civil rights.[71]

Nevertheless, between 1966 and 1980, Bush generally took liberal positions on civil rights, but as Reagan's Vice President he appeared to move to the right on this, as on other issues. He made no more than modest attempts to counter the anti civil rights thrust of the Reagan Administration and his record in this area was further tarnished in 1988 by the racial undertones of the infamous Willie Horton advertisement. In office Bush, despite having spoken out in favour of quotas twenty years earlier, found it necessary to veto the 1990 civil rights bill on the grounds that it would lead to quotas.[72]

The 1990 bill arose from concern among congressional Democrats at the consequences of a number of decisions by the US Supreme Court, most notably *Wards Cove Packing Company* v. *Antonio* (1989). This overruled the precedent set by *Griggs* v. *Duke Power Company* (1971) when the Court ruled that employment practices that led to discrimination were unacceptable even if there was no discriminatory intent. Under the *Griggs* ruling, moreover, the statistical underrepresentation of minorities in the workforce of a company could, in itself, be the source of litigation, with the onus of proof placed on the employer to show that the employment practices being used were not discriminatory.[73] *Wards Cove* reversed the *Griggs* decision with the Court now arguing that statistical evidence of underrepresentation was not enough to justify proceeding with a prima facie case against an employer, while also shifting the burden of proof from the employer to the worker. 'Instead of employers having to show that a legitimate business necessity existed for challenged practices workers were required to prove that there was not.'[74]

Conservatives, appalled by *Griggs* because they believed that it obliged employers to use quotas, enthusiastically welcomed *Wards Cove*, whereas it horrified Senator Edward Kennedy and Congressman August Hawkins who co-sponsored the 1990 civil rights bill designed to reinstate the essence of the *Griggs* judgment. In vetoing the bill, Bush confusingly indicated his wish to sign a civil rights bill and, in 1991, he duly signed a bill which most observers regarded as an only slightly modified version of that which he had vetoed the year before.[75] In explaining why Bush was willing to sign the 1991 bill, commentators were quick to point to the furores created by the nomination of Clarence Thomas to the Supreme Court and the candicacy of the former Klansman David Duke for the governorship of Louisiana. Political expediency, in other words, supposedly led Bush to sign.[76] But whatever the reasons it had become difficult to say where Bush stood on quotas; he favoured them in 1970, denounced them in 1990 but, a year later seemed willing to accept them.

Bush's position on another of the great contemporary issues, abortion, was similarly marked by inconsistency. Jefferson Morley has carefully documented Bush's enthusiastic support for family planning as a congressman in the late 1960s. During this period he became the chairman of a House Republican Task Force on Earth Resources and Population Planning which recommended revising abortion laws 'to eradicate the increasing number of unlicensed and unqualified practitioners who jeopardize the health and safety' of women seeking abortions.[77] For the next decade Bush remained pro-choice and, as late as the spring of 1980, was prepared to express publicly his support for *Roe* v. *Wade*, the abortion rights decision.[78]

A few months later he became Reagan's running mate and quietly abandoned his pro-choice stance; by the time he was ready to compile his autobiography Bush found it possible to say, without a word of explanation of his dramatic change of mind: '*Abortion*. I oppose abortion, except in cases of rape, incest, or when the life of the mother is at stake. Reagan and I both disapproved of the Supreme Court ruling in *Roe* v. *Wade*; we agreed that some form of constitutional amendment was needed to overturn the decision.'[79]

When challenged on his U-turn on abortion Bush argued that the enormous increase in abortions had caused him to reconsider. He also replied tartly to one questioner: 'Have you ever changed your mind? That's one thing about intellectual honesty.'[80] These were perfectly reasonable responses; the number of abortions did increase massively between the 1960s and the 1980s. On both sides of the abortion question there are those who take the view that the answers are self-evident and clear-cut with no place for refinement, doubt or reconsideration. However, such dogmatic certainty on complicated matters is of dubious merit and there is something to be said for politicians being willing to change their minds in the light of further thought and new circumstances.

Having said that, there are two considerations that add weight to the charges of political opportunism laid against George Bush. The first of these concerns the timing of his shifts in his positions on the issues – time and again he seemed to move at moments when it was politically expedient to do so. The second relates to his tendency, on occasion, to be extraordinarily transparent and naive in explaining his inconsistencies.

Thus, in defence of the pro-Goldwater stance he had taken in running for the Senate in 1964 he told the minister of his church: 'You know, John, I took some of the far right positions to get elected. I hope I never do it again. I regret it.'[81] This was a remarkably frank admission of tailoring political views to meet the needs of campaigning for office.

As I noted in Chapter 6 Bush was still blurting out the unthinkable in the closing months of his political career. In 1990 he had abandoned his 'no new taxes' pledge and insisted that the budget deal including a tax increase was essential to American prosperity, but then in early March 1992 he declared the budget compromise to be the worst mistake of his presidency: 'Listen, if I had to do that over, I wouldn't do it. Look at all the flak it's taking.' In explaining why this had been such a terrible mistake the President focused not on considerations of economic policy, but on the adverse consequences for his chances of re-election – Republican voters were 'just overwhelmed by the fact that I went for a tax increase' and were giving him 'political grief' as a result.[82] As one commentator remarked, this was to virtually admit 'that cynical political calculations had dictated the latest U-turn.'[83]

A few weeks later Bush laid himself open to the charge of rampant political opportunism all over again when he was asked why he was now making much of welfare reform when he had ignored the issue for the previous three years. The President replied: 'The politics drives some things . . . a lot of the issues we're talking about . . . they get much more clearly in focus every four years, and then you go ahead and try to follow through and do something about them.'[84] This was yet another statement of astonishing frankness with the President, in effect, confessing that his domestic policy was driven by political expediency.

FINALE

The most conclusive evidence of Bush's failure as President is to be seen in the result of the 1992 election. In 1988 Bush had defeated Dukakis 53 per cent to 45 per cent in the popular vote, whereas after the votes were counted in 1992 the President with 38 per cent was 15 per cent down on his 1988 total; Clinton secured victory with 43 per cent and Perot obtained 19 per cent.[85] In accounting for this result it is first necessary to acknowledge that the timing was to the incumbent's considerable disadvantage; it is inconceivable that Clinton, with his record of avoiding the draft and protesting against the Vietnam war, could have beaten Bush prior to 1992. In other words, the ending of the Cold War, which, of course, Bush had helped to bring about, was crucial to his defeat.[86]

Foreign policy was, without question, Bush's strongest suit in the 1992 campaign, but unfortunately for him, this was not an issue area concerning many American voters at that moment. A *Time*/CNN poll at the end of August 1992 asked: 'Which of these is the main problem the candidates should be addressing?' and of the suggested answers 2 per cent opted for foreign policy while 60 per cent indicated the economy.[87] Later, exit polls, used to determine which issues mattered most to voters in deciding whom to vote for, found that only 8 per cent mentioned foreign policy with 87 per cent of those voting for Bush, 8 per cent for Clinton and 5 per cent for Perot.[88]

Strong on the major issue that mattered least, Bush was weak on many of the concerns troubling voters the most, in particular the weakness of the economy. For much of the Bush presidency the economy was in the doldrums, and it remained 'sluggish throughout 1991 and the first half of 1992'.[89] As the voters went to the polls in November 1992 the economy was recovering rapidly, but this came too late to influence the result.

Seymour Martin Lipset in commenting on the failure of Raymond Fair's economic model to predict the result of the 1992 election noted that, comparatively speaking, the state of the economy was not all that bad during the Bush years: 'The 1991–92 downturn was more moderate than the Reagan 1981–82 recession, or the Carter 1977 decline, while the misery index – unemployment plus the inflation rate – was much worse in 1979–80.' However, Bush's problem was that the American people thought that the economy was much worse than it actually was and 'perception is more important than reality.'[90]

Senior White House staff attributed popular misconceptions about the health of the economy to media bias: 'To hear the press talk about 1992 it was the worst year since the Great Depression.'[91] While there may be some justification for such complaints it is also surely the case that Bush's credibility suffered badly from his obvious lack of interest in domestic policy, and his unwillingness to act in response to the widely held belief that the economy was in trouble. As we saw in Chapter 1, Bush, as a guardian president was instinctively resistant to intervention in the economy, believing that recessions arose from business cycles and that there was little the government could do to control them.[92] Public concern at the state of the economy, coupled with the President's disinclination to attempt corrective action, helps to account for Gallup poll figures in 1992 where 80 per cent disapproved of Bush's handling of the economy.[93]

The outcome of the 1992 presidential election can, in part, be explained by the weakness of the Republican campaign. Confirmation of just how inadequate it was has been provided by some authoritative sources including Dan Quayle and Ed Rollins, the Republican strategist, who presided over the Reagan landslide in 1984. In his memoirs, the former Vice President remarks: 'This was the most poorly planned and executed incumbent presidential campaign in this century.'[94] Meanwhile Rollins went further, declaring on a number of occasions that this was 'the worst campaign ever seen'.[95]

The gross inadequacies of the 1992 campaign had much to do with the personality and leadership style of the candidate himself. There is more than a little evidence from within the White House that Bush found campaigning distasteful; that he regarded it as an activity that he was obliged to participate in from time to time, but which he regarded as an unwelcome, unseemly distraction from the really important work of governance. Paul Bateman commented on the President's dislike for campaigning and his belief that it was undignified.[96] The Secretary to the Cabinet, Edie Holiday, observed that Bush 'much preferred governing to campaigning . . . and felt that was what he was elected to do was to govern, not to be out campaigning.' She referred also to the President's resistance to advisers trying to get him to turn his attention to campaigning for re-election, even as early as the Gulf War.[97]

Clayton Yeutter, at the time Chairman of the Republican National Committee, was firmly of the view that Bush erred in not getting his campaign under way earlier than he did. He recalled writing to the President in July 1991 to urge him to decide who would be on his campaign staff: 'When you head out to Kennebunkport in August put your feet up on your desk . . . figure out who's going to do what and announce them right after Labor Day.' But as Yeutter records, while 'that would have been the ideal scenario . . . he wouldn't buy it; he thought that was too early.'

The same vastly experienced member of the President's staff put his finger on the underlying cause of Bush's aversion to campaigning:

> What he was saying to the American public was 'I have just done a heck of a good job as President of this country; I deserve a second term and I shouldn't have to go through all this hassle to get there. The American public ought to be able to perceive that I have done a fine job . . .' He just didn't feel that he should be compelled to go and present his case before the American public in a campaign setting. It was almost as if it was belittling at this stage in his life and at this stage in his distinguished career. He felt that his track record accumulated over several decades was there for everybody to behold.[98]

Yeutter's revealing insights bring us back to that major flaw in Bush's makeup, his shortcomings as a communicator. He not only lacked any feel for words, he seemed unable to grasp that effective communication with the people is indispensable to presidential leadership – necessary not just for winning elections, but for governance itself. The need to explain himself or to marshall public support for his policies appears to have escaped George Bush. Those who doubted whether he had vision could be left to examine his record, and it was not necessary for him to explain in any detail his policy reversals on 'no new taxes', abortion or anything else. And when it came to re-election, the American public ought to be able to see for themselves what a fine job he had done without him having to suffer the grubby processess of campaigning. Meanwhile, he would get on with the business of government, reacting to problems, parleying with other leaders and making decisions, and not engaging in 'rhetoric for rhetoric's sake'.

According to Lipset, Bush made the mistake of not adhering to the Franklin Roosevelt model of governance: 'The Roosevelt approach is the way to run the presidency, i.e. as a continuing campaign. Some like Jimmy Carter and George Bush never understood this. Ronald Reagan did, as he noted when he said repeatedly that he modelled himself on Roosevelt.'[99] In some respects such analysis runs counter to mine. As I have argued throughout this book, presidents are entitled to be judged on their own terms. At no point did Bush aspire to be another FDR, he was not even trying to be another Reagan.

As a guardian in the White House, Bush was not attempting to advance a large programme of reform legislation, nor was he bent on fundamental change. It makes little sense therefore to judge him according to standards set by predecessors with quite different aims. Nevertheless, however modest a chief executive's ambitions may be, he cannot avoid having some sort of agenda. Furthermore, even a guardian president's success in office will, to some extent, turn on his capacity for speaking to the American people, a skill that George Bush singularly lacked and was never disposed to acquire.

Notes

INTRODUCTION

1. See, for example, Stephen Graubard, *Mr Bush's War: Adventures in the Politics of Illusion* (London: I.B. Tauris, 1992) and Jean Edward Smith George Bush's War (New York: Henry Holt, 1992).
2. Theodore Sorensen, *Decision-Making in the White House* (New York: Columbia University Press, 1963), p. xii.
3. For example, Richard Nixon, *In the Arena* (New York: Pocket Books, 1990), pp. 80–81 and Edwin Meese, *With Reagan: The Inside Story* (Washington DC: Regnery Gateway, 1992), p. 332.
4. 'Politics of the Professoriate' *The American Enterprise*, Vol. 2, No. 5, July/August, 1991 pp. 86–87.
5. Christopher J. Bosso, 'Congressional and Presidential Scholars: Some Basic Traits', (PS: *Political Science and Politics*, December, 1989, pp. 839–848.
6. Walter B. Roettger and Hugh Winebrenner, 'Politics and Political Scientists', *Public Opinion*, September/October, 1986, pp. 41–44.
7. Robert Murray and Tim Blessing, *Greatness in the White House: Rating the Presidents* (University Park, Penn. The Pennsylvania State University Press, 1994), p. 164.
8. I have developed this argument elsewhere – see David Mervin, *Ronald Reagan and the American Presidency* (London and New York: Longman, 1990) and David Mervin, 'Ronald Reagan's Place in History', *Journal of American Studies*, Vol. 23, No. 2, 1989, pp. 269–286.
9. Murray and Blessing, op. cit., pp. 141, 142, 144, 145, 147, and 149. As *Time* magazine sharply commented when the results of the Murray/Blessing poll were first made public, 'Such a harsh and inclusive indictment will raise further questions about the partisanship and competence of the historians as well as about Reagan' (International edition, 15 April 1991, p. 39. See David Mervin, 'Political Science and the Study of the Presidency', *Presidential Studies Quarterly* (forthcoming).
10. William Leuchtenburg, *In the Shadow of FDR* (New York: Cornell University Press, 1983), p. x.
11. Richard Neustadt, *Presidential Power and the Modern Presidents* (New York: John Wiley and Sons, 1960). In subsequent editions Neustadt has done very little backtracking from his earlier harshness towards Eisenhower. In the 1976 edition he wrote somewhat defensively: 'To write in Eisenhower's time after serving under Truman was to writhe with impatience at the President's concern for his extraordinary public standing, his hero's prestige, hoarding not risking it, being not doing. Especially during his second term, Eisenhower's quietude seemed more conservative in terms of policy than I, for one, deemed prudent. So I still think it was. We paid a price for damming up

reform until the flood of the mid-sixties. Still, it also was conservative in institutional terms, identifying man and office to the office's advantage. Looking back after Nixon, that seems a more impressive contribution than it did before.' *Presidential Power and the Modern Presidents* (New York: The Free Press, 1990), pp. 190–191. This offsets very slightly some of the earlier criticism although Eisenhower is also condemned all over again for failing to adopt the presidential style of a liberal Democrat, for not being another Roosevelt. See also ibid, pp. 295–301 for another modest rethinking of Eisenhower's presidency.

12. Fred J. Greenstein is the most notable of the revisionists: see *The Hidden-Hand Presidency: Eisenhower as Leader* (New York: Basic Books, 1982.

13. Michael Oakeshott, *Rationalism in Politics* (London: Methuen, 1962), p. 191.

14. Richard Rose, 'Evaluating Presidents', in George Edwards, John Kessel and Bert Rockman (eds), *Researching the Presidency* (Pittsburgh: University of Pittsburgh Press, 1993,) p. 473. Murray and Blessing, op. cit., p. 57.

15. Charles O. Jones, *The Presidency in a Separated System* (Washington DC: The Brookings Institution, 1994), p. 11.

16. Federalist No. 73, Clinton Rossiter (ed.) *The Federalist Papers* (New York: New American Library, 1961), p. 444.

17. Margaret Coit (ed.), *John C. Calhoun* (New Jersey: Prentice Hall, 1970), p. 21.

18. Terry Eastland, *Energy in the Executive: The Case for the Strong Presidency*, (New York: The Free Press, 1992), p. 31.

19. Nixon, op. cit., p. 42 and p. 132.

20. Alonzo Hamby, essay on Truman, in Fred Greenstein (ed.), *Leadership in the Modern Presidency* (Cambridge: Harvard University Press, 1988), p. 43.

21. Ibid.

22. Robert Ferrell (ed.), *The Eisenhower Diaries* (New York: W.W. Norton, 1981), pp. 246–247.

23. Michael Duffy and Dan Goodgame, *Marching in Place: The Status Quo Presidency of George Bush* (New York: Simon & Schuster, 1992), p. 65.

24. For the guardian concept of presidential leadership see Rose, op. cit., p. 473–80. Also Richard Rose, *The Postmodern President* (Chatham, New Jersey: Chatham House, 1991), pp. 48–49 and pp. 307–309.

25. Oakeshott, op. cit., p. 184.

26. Emmet Hughes, *The Ordeal of Power* (London: Macmillan, 1963), p. 58.

27. Rose, *The Postmodern President*, op. cit, p. 46.

28. Bert Rockman, *The Leadership Question: The Presidency and the American System* (New York: Praeger, 1984), p. 12. A similar emphasis on effectiveness as the hallmark of presidential leadership is to be found in Barbara Kellerman's *The Political Presidency* (New York: Oxford University Press 1984), p. x, who writes: 'When I speak of an effective presidency, or effective presidential leadership, I am speaking

here in terms of functional criteria only. I am not asking if the leadership was, for example, courageous, wise or moral, or if it led the country down the proper path. I am asking only if it was effective in the sense that the president was able to accomplish what he wanted to accomplish.' Similarly, Aaron Wildavsky portrays Ronald Reagan as 'a superb political strategist' successful in the sense of effectively moving the nation in the directions in which he chose to take it, but who goes on to say: 'Nothing is implied about the desirability of the directions chosen, for then (such) politicians could be (successful) strategists only by being in accord with the preferences of the analyst. *Society*, May/June 1987, pp. 56–62.

29. John Hart, *The Presidential Branch* (New York: Pergamon Press, 1987), p. 127.
30. Ibid, p. 104.
31. Lyn Ragsdale, *Presidential Politics* (Boston: Houghton Mifflin, 1993), p. 225.
32. Charles Kolb. *White House Daze: The Unmaking of Domestic Policy in the Bush Years* (New York: The Free Press, 1994), p. xii.

CHAPTER 1 THE MAKING OF A GUARDIAN PRESIDENT

1. Robert Shogan, *The Riddle of Power: Presidential Leadership from Truman to Bush* (New York: Dutton, 1991), p. 259.
2. Michael Oakeshott, *Rationalism in Politics* (London: Methuen, 1962), p. 184.
3. George Bush (with Victor Gold), *Looking Forward* (London: The Bodley Head, 1988), p. 81.
4. Ibid, pp. 39–40.
5. Ibid, p. 44.
6. Ibid.
7. Fitzhugh Green, *George Bush: An Intimate Portrait* (New York: Hippocrene Books, 1991), p. 78.
8. Shogan, op. cit., p. 270.
9. Donnie Radcliffe, 'The Bush in the Background', *Washington Post National Weekly Edition*, 13–19 June 1988, pp. 10–11.
10. Bush, op. cit., p. 25.
11. See Donald Matthews, *US Senators and their World* (New York: Vintage Books, 1960).
12. Green, op. cit., p. 9.
13. Kerry Mullins and Aaron Wildavsky, 'The Procedural Presidency of George Bush', *Political Science Quarterly*, Vol. 107, No. 1, 1992, pp. 31–62.
14. David Hoffman, 'Patrician with a Common Touch', *Washington Post National Weekly Edition*, 14–20 November, 1988, pp. 6–7.
15. Bush, op. cit., p. 46.
16. Green, op. cit., pp. 63–64.

17.   Michael Barone, 'George Bush: Not So Much a Preppie as a Pioneer', *Washington Post National Weekly Edition*, 4–10 July, 1988, p. 29.
18.   See Shogan, op. cit., pp. 259–268.
19.   John Newhouse, 'Profiles: The Tactician', *New Yorker*, 7 May, 1990, pp. 50–82.
20.   Nicholas King, *George Bush: A Biography* (New York: Dodd Mead, 1980), p. 53.
21.   See Barbara Kellerman, *The Political Presidency: Practice of Leadership From Kennedy Through Reagan* (New York: Oxford University Press, 1984), p. 38.
22.   See Fred Greenstein, 'Ronald Reagan's Presidential Leadership', in Ellis Sandoz and Cecil Crabb (eds), *Election 84: Landslide Without a Mandate?* (New York: New American Library, 1985), p. 78.
23.   See William Adams, 'Recent Fables About Ronald Reagan', *Public Opinion*, Vol. VII, No. 5, October/November 1984.
24.   Interview with James Cicconi, 8 November 1993.
25.   Interview with John Keller, 18 November 1993.
26.   Interview with Gregg Petersmeyer, 16 November 1993.
27.   Interview with Gail Wilensky, 14 November 1993.
28.   Peggy Noonan, *What I Saw at the Revolution: A Political Life in the Reagan Era* (New York: Ivy Books, 1990), p. 313.
29.   Interview with C. Boyden Gray, 10 November 1993.
30.   Interview with Andrew Card, 15 November 1993.
31.   Interview with David Demarest, 12 November 1993. See also Kristin Clark Taylor, *The First to Speak* (New York: Doubleday, 1993), *passim*.
32.   For a different perspective on Bush's 'niceness' see Michael Kinsley, 'Is Bush Nice? A Contrarian View', *Time* (International edition),16 July, 1990.
33.   David Hoffman, 'George Bush and the Power of the Thankyou Note', *Washington Post National Weekly Edition*, 21–27 August, 1989, pp. 22–23.
34.   Ruth Shalit, 'What I Saw at the Devolution', *Reason*, 9 March, 1993, pp. 27–33.
35.   Interview with Gregg Petersmeyer, op. cit.
36.   Hoffman, 'Patrician with the Common Touch', op. cit.
37.   Richard Brookhiser, 'A Visit with George Bush', *Atlantic Monthly*, August 1992, pp. 22–28.
38.   *Time* (International edition), 20 March, 1989, p. 38.
39.   Mullins and Wildavsky, op. cit. p. 31 and Charles Kolb, *White House Daze: The Unmaking of Domestic Policy in the Bush Years* (New York: Free Press, 1994, p. 314.
40.   See Bush, op. cit., pp. 94–95.
41.   Ronald Elving, 'House Service Set Course for New President', *Congressional Quarterly Weekly Report*, 14 January, 1989, pp. 55–57.
42.   When he first ran for the presidency in 1979, Bush 'referred to his House service with an ironic joke, implying that it had been too brief to be a liability.' Ibid.
43.   Walter Pincus and Bob Woodward, 'The Bumpy Years of Bush, From UN Ambassador to CIA Head', *Washington Post National Weekly Edition*, 29 August–4 September, 1988, p. 12.

44. Ibid. and Green, op. cit., pp. 119–120.

45. Ibid, p. 141.

46. Ibid, p. 153.

47. Pincus and Woodward, op. cit.

48. Apparently a sanitized version of what Garner actually said.

49. Jules Witcover, *Crapshoot: Rolling the Dice on the Vice Presidency* (New York: Crown, 1992), p. 59.

50. See H.R. Haldeman, *The Haldeman Diaries* (New York: G.P. Putnam's Sons, 1994), pp. 52–53 and 106.

51. Joseph Pika, 'A New Vice Presidency', in Michael Nelson (ed.), *The Presidency and the Political System*, 2nd edn. (Washington DC: The Congressional Quarterly Press, 1988).

52. C. Boyden Gray, 'The Coordinating Role of the Vice Presidency' in James Pfiffner and Gordon Hoxie (eds) *The Presidency in Transition* (New York: Center for the Study of the Presidency, 1989), pp. 427–428.

53. Bush, op. cit., p. 234.

54. Gray, op. cit., p. 426. See also Pika, op. cit., p. 475 for details of significant foreign travel by Bush as Vice President.

55. Witcover ,op. cit., p. 327.

56. Arthur Schlesinger Jr, *The Cycles of American History* (London: André Deutsch, 1986), pp. 363 and 365.

57. Gail Sheehy, *Character: America's Search for Leadership*, revised edition (New York: Bantam Books, 1990), p. 198.

58. Witcover, op. cit., p. 319 and David Stockman, *The Triumph of Politics: Why the Reagan Revolution Failed* (New York: Harper & Row, 1986), p. 86.

59. Michael Duffy and Dan Goodgame, *Marching in Place: The Status Quo Presidency of George Bush* (New York: Simon & Schuster, 1992), pp. 38–39 and Michael Barone, 'The Vice President's Problem', *Washington Post National Weekly Edition*, 1622 June 1988, p. 28.

60. David Hoffman, 'George Bush Takes Up the Baton', *Washington Post National Weekly Edition*, 16–22 January 1989, pp. 6-8.

61. For the Vice President's conviction that he was amply qualified see Bush, op. cit., pp. 192–193.

62. Duffy and Goodgame, op. cit., p. 21, Kolb, op. cit., pp. 5–6; and John Podhoretz, *Hell of a Ride: Backstage at the White House Follies 1989–1993*, (New York: Simon & Schuster, 1993), p. 129.

63. George Will, 'A National Embarrassment', *Washington Post National Weekly Edition*, 3–9 October 1988, p. 33.

64. Theodore Lowi, 'Ronald Reagan – Revolutionary?', in Lester Salamon and Michael Lund (eds) *The Reagan Presidency and the Governing of America* (Washington DC, The Urban Institute Press, 1984).

65. Hoffman, 'Patrician With a Common Touch', op. cit.

66. Nomination acceptance speech, Republican National Convention, New Orleans, 18 August 1988.

67. Emmet Hughes, *The Ordeal of Power* (London: Macmillan, 1963), p. 60.

68. See James Cicconi as quoted in Kolb, op. cit., p. 95.

69. Duffy and Goodgame, op. cit., p. 56.
70. Interview with William Kristol, 23 March 1994.
71. See especially Richard Neustadt, *Presidential Power and the Modern Presidents* (New York: Free Press, 1990).
72. Stephen Ambrose, *Nixon, Volume Two: The Triumph of a Politician 1962–1972* (New York: Simon & Schuster, 1989), p. 26.
73. Richard Nixon, *In the Arena* (New York: Pocket Books, 1990), p. 43.
74. David Broder, 'The Chief Myth-Maker', *Washington Post National Weekly Edition*, 27 May–2 June 1991, p. 4.
75. Mullins and Wildavsky, op. cit., p. 47. See also Bush, op. cit., p. 193 for his faith in the American system.
76. Quoted in John Yang, 'Who is George Bush?', *Washington Post National Weekly Edition*, 24 Febuary–1 March 1991, pp. 9–10.
77. Inaugural address.
78. See Fred Greenstein, *The Hidden-Hand Presidency: Eisenhower as Leader* (New York: Basic Books, 1982).
79. Interview with Edward Rogers, 3rd November 1993.
80. Duffy and Goodgame, op. cit., p. 65.
81. Ann Devroy, 'The Reluctant Activist; Domestically, Bush Tries to Recast Himself', Washington Post National Weekly Edition, 17 August 1992.
82. Joseph Califano, *A Presidential Nation* (New York: W.W. Norton, 1975), p. 20.
83. Broder, op. cit.
84. Inaugural address.
85. Duffy and Goodgame, op. cit., p. 283.
86. Michael Beschloss and Strobe Talbott, *At the Highest Levels: The Inside Story of the End of the Cold War* (Boston: Little Brown, 1993), p. 21. 87. ibid. p. 205.
88. Devroy, op. cit.
89. Interview with Bobbie Kilberg, 19 November 1993.
90. Devroy, op. cit.
91. Interview with James Cicconi, op. cit.
92. See David Hoffman, 'Zip My Lips: George Bush's Penchant for Secret Decisions', *Washington Post National Weekly Edition*, 15–21 January 1990, p. 23.
93. Quoted in Ann Devroy, 'There's No Homecoming For Bush', *Washington Post National Weekly Edition*, 17–23 June 1991, p. 12.
94. For others sharing this view see Kolb, op. cit., pp. 187–88.

CHAPTER 2 STRATEGIES OF LEADERSHIP

1. Martin Anderson, *Revolution* (New York: Harcourt Brace Jovanovich, 1988) p. 204.
2. Edwin Meese, *With Reagan: The Inside Story* (Washington DC: Regnery Gateway, 1992), pp. 87–88.
3. Hedrick Smith, *The Power Game* (New York: Random House, 1988), pp. 475–476.

4. David Hoffman, 'At Last, a President Who Ran as an Insider, Not an Outsider', *Washington Post National Weekly Edition*, 26 December–1 January 1989, p. 31.

5. Burt Solomon, 'Bush's Lack of Ambitious Policies . . . Makes His Plans Seem Thin Gruel', *National Journal*, 6 May 1989, No. 18, p. 1102.

6. James Pfiffner *The Managerial Presidency* (Pacific Grove, Calif. Brooks/Cole, 1991), p.12.

7. 'Establishing the Bush Presidency', *Public Administration Review*, January/Febuary 1990, pp. 64–72.

8. Interview with Constance Horner, 10 November 1993.

9. Richard Ben Cramer, *What It Takes* (New York: Random House, 1992), p. 153. See also David Hoffman, 'George Bush and the Power of the Thankyou Note', *Washington Post National Weekly Edition*, 21–27 August 1989, pp. 22–23.

10. Maureen Dowd, 'Bush's Fierce Loyalty Raises Debate On Whether It Hinders His Judgment', *New York Times*, 10 March 1989, B6.

11. Kenneth Thompson, *Presidential Transitions: The Reagan to Bush Experience* (Lanham,MD: University Press of America), p. 95.

12. Pfiffner, 'Establishing the Bush Presidency', op. cit.

13. Interview with Ronald Kaufman, 19 November 1993.

14. Ibid.

15. Ibid.

16. 'With 115 Nominations Awaiting Votes, Fingers Point Fast and Furious', *New York Times*, 28 August 1989, p. A13.

17. Interview with Constance Horner, op. cit.

18. Maureen Dowd, 'Transformation of Bush: His Own Man', *New York Times*, 21 January 1989, p.1.

19. Bob Woodward and Walter Pincus, *Washington Post National Weekly Edition*, 15–21 August 1988, p. 8.

20. Kerry Mullins and Aaron Wildavsky, 'The Procedural Presidency of George Bush', *Political Science Quarterly*, Vol. 107, No. 1, 1992, pp. 31–62 and Michael Duffy and Dan Goodgame, *Marching in Place: The Status Quo Presidency of George Bush* (New York: Simon & Schuster, 1992), p. 51.

21. Maureen Dowd, 'Kindness is Foundation as Bush Builds Bridges', *New York Times*, 6 Febuary 1989, p. A13.

22. Bradley Patterson, *The Ring of Power: The White House Staff and Its Expanding Role in Government* (New York: Basic Books, 1988), p. 210.

23. Interview with Bobbie Kilberg, 19 November 1993.

24. Charles Kolb, *White House Daze: The Unmaking of Domestic Policy in the Bush Years* (New York: Free Press, 1994), p. 5.

25. Interview with Bobbie Kilberg, op. cit.

26. Ibid.

27. Interview with William Kristol, 23 March 1994.

28. See Chapter 5 below.

29. See Samuel Kernell, *Going Public* (Washington DC: Congressional Quarterly Press, 1986), *passim*. Also William Kerr Muir, *The Bully Pulpit: The Presidential Leadership of Ronald Reagan* (San Francisco: Institute for Contemporary Studies, 1992) and David Mervin, 'The Bully Pulpit', *Presidential Studies Quarterly*, Vol. XXV, 1995, pp. 19–23.

30. Interview with Clayton Yeutter, 22 March 1994.
31. Interview with C. Boyden Gray, 10 November 1993.
32. Interview with Gregg Petersmeyer, 16h November 1993.
33. Interview with Constance Horner, 10 November 1993.
34. Interview with James Cicconi, 8 November 1993.
35. Interview with John Keller, 18 November 1993.
36. Interview with Betsey Anderson of the Bush Office of Policy Development, 28 March 1994.
37. Interview with Bobbie Kilberg, 19 November 1993.
38. Interview with Clayton Yeutter, 22 March 1994.
39. Interview with William Kristol, op. cit.
40. Interview with David Demarest, 12 November 1993.
41. Ibid.
42. Peggy Noonan, *What I Saw at the Revolution: A Political Life in the Reagan Era* (New York: Ivy Books, 1990), p. 356.
43. Eleanor Randolph, 'The Newly Polite Press', *Washington Post National Weekly Review*, 20–26 March 1989, pp. 14-15.
44. Maureen Dowd, 'Basking in Power's Glow: Bush's Year as President', *New York Times*, 31 December 1989, p. A1
45. David Hoffman, 'What Bush Lacks in Style He Makes Up for in Method', *Washington Post National Weekly Edition*, 2–8 April 1990, p. 24; David Ignatius, 'After Reagan, the Media Miss Being Manipulated', *Washington Post National Weekly Edition*, 15–21 May 1989, p. 23–24; and John Cassidy, 'America Loves Its Inaction Man', *Sunday Times* (London), 16 April 1989, p. B7.
46. Maureen Dowd, 'Journalists Debate the Risks as President Woos the Press', *New York Times*, 2 April 1989, p. A1.
47. Edwin Diamond, Adrian Marin and Robert Silverman, 'Bush's First Year: Mr Nice Guy Meets The Press', *Washington Journalism Review*, Vol. XII, 1990, pp. 42–44.
48. Interview with John Keller, op. cit.
49. Interview with C. Boyden Gray, op. cit.
50. Interview with David Demarest, op. cit.
51. Interview with Gail Wilensky, 14 November 1993
52. Noonan, op. cit., p. 148
53. Ignatius, op. cit.
54. Andrew Rosenthal, 'President Seeks a Way to Adapt His Cool Persona to a Hot Medium', *New York Times*, 22 November 1989, p. B6.
55. Interview with Nicholas Calio, 19 November 1993.
56. Interview with John Keller, op. cit.
57. See, for example, Peter Goldman and Tom Mathews, *The Quest for the Presidency: The 1988 Campaign* (New York: Simon & Schuster, 1989), pp. 190–196.
58. 'What Bush Lacks in Style He Makes Up for in Method', *Washington Post National Weekly Edition*, 2–8 April 1990, p. 24.
59. Interview with Barbara Kilberg, op. cit.
60. Cramer, op. cit., p. 27.
61. Green, op. cit., p. 79.
62. Ibid.

63. Duffy and Goodgame, op. cit., pp. 44-45. For the fractured syntax see especially Maureen Dowd, 'The Language Thing', *New York Times Magazine*, 29 July 1990, pp. 32 and 48.
64. Green, op. cit., p. 16.
65. Green, op. cit., pp. 26–27.
66. Duffy and Goodgame, op. cit., p. 46.

CHAPTER 3 ORGANIZING THE PRESIDENCY

1. Richard Neustadt, *Presidential Power and the Modern Presidents* (New York: Free Press, 1990), p. xx.
2. John Ehrlichman, *Witness to Power* (New York: Pocket Books, 1982).
3. John Hart, *The Presidential Branch* (New York: Pergamon Press, 1987), p. 125.
4. Ibid.
5. Fred Greenstein, *The Hidden Hand Presidency: Eisenhower As Leader* (New York: Basic Books, 1982), p. 115.
6. James Pfiffner, *The Modern Presidency* (New York: St. Martin's Press, 1994), p. 116. See also Bradley Patterson, *The Ring of Power* (New York: Basic Books, 1988), p. 29.
7. According to Pfiffner, ibid., 'President Bush was one of the few modern presidents who did not promise cabinet government in campaigning for the Presidency.' One source did suggest that Bush was 'seeking to use the concept of Cabinet government to run his administration.' Gerald Boyd, 'On Bush's Team, Key Word in Assistant to the President Will Be Assistant', *New York Times*, 20 January 1989, Section A10, p 10.
8. Interview with David Bates, 17 November 1993. The words quoted are from an interview with Edith Holiday, 11 November 1993.
9. Ibid. Eliot Richardson and James Pfiffner noted that Bush would hear at Cabinet meetings 'what all recent Presidents have heard: a briefing on the budget, a Vice Presidential travelogue or a review of pending legislation. Big issues are seldom debated, much less decided.' 'Our Cabinet System Is a Charade', *New York Times*, 28 May, 1989, Section IV, p. 15.
10. Dan Quayle, *Standing Firm* (New York: Harper Collins, 1994), pp. 99–100.
11. Interview with Edith Holiday, op. cit.
12. Colin Campbell and Bert Rockman (eds), *The Bush Presidency: First Appraisals* (Chatham, New Jersey: Chatham House, 1991), p. 211 and Burt Solomon, 'In Bush's Image', *National Journal*, 7 July 1990, p. 1642.
13. Pfiffner, *The Modern Presidency*, op. cit., p. 116.
14. James Pfiffner, 'Establishing the Bush Presidency', *Public Administration Review*, January/Febuary 1990, pp. 64–72.
15. Bernard Weinraub, 'White House: The President has a Cabinet that is (a) runaway (b) powerful. (Choose one.)', *New York Times*, 19 May 1989, p. A14.

16. David Hoffman and Ann Devroy, 'The Open Oval Office Door', *Washington Post National Weekly Edition*, 14–20 August 1989, pp. 6–7.

17. Burt Solomon 'When the Bush Cabinet Convenes . . . Its a Gathering of Presidential Pals', *National Journal*, 1 July 1989, No. 26, pp. 1704–1705. Also Solomon, 'In Bush's Image' op. cit., and Ann Reilly Dowd, 'How Bush Manages the Presidency', *Fortune* 27 August 1990, pp. 38–43.

18. The title of an article by Burt Solomon, *National Journal*, 10 June 1989, pp. 1402–1403.

19. Interview with Edward Rogers, 3 November 1993.

20. Interview with Edith Holiday, op. cit.

21. Ibid.

22. Interview with Andrew Card, 15 November 1993.

23. Interview with James Pinkerton, 8 November 1993.

24. *United States Government Manual* (Washington DC: US Government Printing Office, 1990). p. 83.

25. Patterson, op. cit., labels one of his chapters 'Crisis Management: Command Center at 1600 Pennsylvania Avenue'.

26. Interview with Nicholas Calio, 19 November 1993.

27. Interview with James Cicconi, 8 November 1993.

28. Patterson, op. cit., p. 85.

29. Lyn Ragsdale, *Presidential Politics* (Boston: Houghton Mifflin, 1993), p. 223.

30. 'Panetta goes in goal', *The Economist*, 2 July 1994, p. 44. For Rockman quotation see Juan Williams, 'John Sununu, The White House Chief of Gaffe', *Washington Post National Weekly Edition*, 2–8 December 1991, pp. 22–23. For other negative views of Sununu's tenure see Michael Duffy and Dan Goodgame, *Marching in Place* (New York: Simon & Schuster, 1992), Ch. 5, Pfiffner, *The Modern Presidency*, op. cit., Chapter 3, and 'The President's Chief of Staff: Lessons Learned', *Presidential Studies Quarterly*, Vol. XXIII, No. 1, 1993, pp. 77–102.

31. Peter Goldman, *The Quest for the Presidency: The 1988 Campaign* (New York: Simon & Schuster, 1989), pp. 258–262.

32. Kristin Clark Taylor, *The First to Speak* (New York: Doubleday, 1993), p. 190.

33. Kolb, op. cit., p. 183, and interview with John Keller, 18 November 1993.

34. Interview with C. Boyden Gray, 10 November 1993.

35. Interview with Andrew Card, 15 November 1993.

36. Interview with Nicholas Calio, 19 November 1993.

37. Interview with James Cicconi, op. cit.

38. At an early stage Sununu said rather revealingly to a journalist: 'The staff is beginning to realize that they don't have to prepare a 15 page memo for me. They can wander in and raise an issue and I can give them a decision by the President either at 4.45 or the next morning. You get rapid feedback.' Bernard Weinraub, 'Sununu, the Staff Chief, Is Learning the Ropes the Hard Way', *New York Times*, 6 February 1989, p. A12.

39. Interview with Roger Porter, 23 November 1993.

40. Maureen Dowd, 'The "Impossible" Happens to Bush: He is Isolated, Associates Say', *International Herald Tribune*, 30 October 990, p. 1.
41. David Hoffman and Ann Devroy, 'The White House Tough Guy', *Washington Post National Weekly Edition*, 5–11 Febuary 1990, pp. 6–7.
42. According to some sources Bush's original preference for the post was Frederic Malek, a former Nixon Administration official with a reputation for toughness. Ibid.
43. See p. 68 above.
44. Dan Goodgame, 'Bush's Big Bad Cop', *Time* (International Edition), 28 May 1990, p. 42.
45. For the lightning rod concept see Greenstein, op. cit., pp. 238–239.
46. Hoffman and Devroy, 'The White House Tough Guy', op. cit.
47. Interview with Constance Horner, 10 November 1993.
48. Williams, op. cit.
49. Interview with Ed Rogers, op. cit.
50. Interview with James Pinkerton, op. cit.
51. Hoffman and Devroy, 'The White House Tough Guy', op. cit.
52. Interview with Ed Rogers, op. cit.
53. Interviews with Bobbie Kilberg, 19 November 1993, and Clayton Yeutter, 22 March 1994.
54. Hoffman and Devroy, 'The White House Tough Guy', op. cit.
55. Eleanor Randolph, 'The Man Washington Loves to Hate', *The Washington Post National Weekly Edition*, 17–23 December 1990, pp. 6–7.
56. R.W. Apple, 'Emotions in Check, Intellect Not, Sununu Wins Reluctant Respect in Capital', *The New York Times*, 13 September 1989, p. A18.
57. Hoffman and Devroy, 'The White House Tough Guy', op. cit.
58. Randolph, op. cit.
59. Duffy and Goodgame, op. cit. p. 120.
60. Interview with Bobbie Kilberg, op. cit.
61. Interview with Ed Rogers, op. cit.
62. On the 'Air Sununu' matter see, for example, Edwin Yoder Jr., 'Puritan in Babylon', *The Washington Post National Weekly Edition*, 29 April–5 May 1991, p. 28.
63. Burt Solomon, 'George Bush's Congressional Crew Has an Oar or Two Out of Sync', *National Journal*, 24 June 1989, pp. 1650–1657.
64. Boyd, op. cit.
65. Solomon, 'George Bush's Congressional Crew . . .' , op. cit.
66. Bernard Weinraub, 'White House Staff Makes Series of Tactical Errors', *New York Times*, 1 March 1989, IV, p. 4.
67. Calio interview, op. cit.
68. Sununu made the comment to a Conservative Leadership Conference meeting in Washington on 9 November 1990. Duffy and Goodgame, op. cit., p. 82.
69. See p. 34 above.
70. Interview with Nicholas Calio, op. cit.
71. Interview with David Demarest, 12 November 1993.
72. See Patterson, op. cit., p. 87 and *passim*.
73. Interview with David Demarest, op. cit.

74. See, for example, John Podhoretz, *Hell of a Ride: Backstage at the White House Follies 1989–1993* (New York: Simon & Schuster, 1993), pp. 81–82 and Charles Kolb, *White House Daze: The Unmaking of Domestic Policy in the Bush Years* (New York: The Free Press, 1994), p. 5.
75. Interview with David Demarest, op. cit.
76. See Patterson, op. cit., pp. 209–210.
77. Interview with Bobbie Kilberg, op. cit.
78. Podhoretz, op. cit. p. 94.
79. Interview with Bobbie Kilberg, op. cit.
80. On 8 August 1991 the paid staff of the Office of Public Liaison was 16, eleven of whom were women. Source White House document kindly provided by Bobbie Kilberg in the author's possession.
81. Interview with Bobbie Kilberg, op. cit.
82. For example, interviews with Edie Holiday, Clayton Yeutter and Betsy Anderson, all op. cit.
83. Interview with Bobbie Kilberg, op. cit.
84. Quoted in Bernard Weinraub, 'How the President lost his tongue, or, the Bush speechwriters leave a mess', *New York Times*, 7 April 1989, p. A14.
85. Interview with Clayton Yeutter, op. cit.
86. David Broder described Skinner as 'one of the best people President Bush has brought to Washington – an energetic, intelligent, politically skillful manager committed to doing a job, not just filling an office.' 'The Man, the Plan, the Pothole', *The Washington Post National Weekly Edition*, 19–25 March 1990, p. 4.
87. Interview with Nicholas Calio, op. cit.
88. Interview with Bobbie Kilberg, op. cit.
89. Interview with John Keller, op. cit.
90. Interview with Edith Holiday, op. cit.
91. Interview 3.5.
92. Don Phillips and Bob Woodward, 'An Ambitious Pragmatist Takes Over', *The Washington Post National Weekly Edition*, 9–15 December 1991, p. 9.
93. Marjorie Williams, 'An Eagle Scout Gets His Wings Clipped', *The Washington Post National Weekly Edition*, 15–21 June 1992, pp. 6-9.
94. Interview 3.5.

CHAPTER 4   A GUARDIAN'S AGENDA

1. Stephen Hess, *Organizing the Presidency*, 2nd edn. (Washington DC: The Brookings Institution, 1988), p. 55.
2. David Hoffman, 'One Hundred Days of Solicitude', *Washington Post National Weekly Edition*, 8–14 May 1989, p. 13.
3. Acceptance speech, Republican Convention, New Orleans, 1988.
4. Ibid.
5. Marshall Ingwersen, 'Bush Lags at Setting Agenda!', *Christian Science Monitor*, 25–31 May 1989 pp. 1–2.

6. David Hoffman, 'Setting the Pace for the Bush Presidency', *Washington Post National Weekly Edition*, 23–29 January 1989, p. 11.
7. Roger Davidson and Walter Oleszek, *Congress and Its Members*, 4th edn. (Washington DC: Congressional Quarterly Press, 1994), p. 457.
8. Acceptance speech.
9. *Roosevelt: The Lion and the Fox* (New York: Harcourt Brace and World, 1957), p. 186.
10. *Congress and the Nation*, Vol. VIII, 1989–1992 (Washington DC: Congressional Quarterly Press, 1993), p. 339.
11. George Church, 'Is This Goodbye?', *Time* (International edition), 6 March 1989, pp. 10–14.
12. Ibid.
13. *Congress and the Nation*, op. cit., p. 340.
14. Charles O. Jones, *The Presidency In A Separated System* (Washington DC: The Brookings Institution, 1994), p. 11.
15. Gerald Boyd, 'Bush Aides Play Him Up As 100-Day Mark Nears', New York Times, 22 April 1989, p. 1.
16. See, for example, Chuck Alston, 'Rules of Political Navigation Altered by Bush Centrism, *Congressional Quarterly Weekly Report*, 6 May 1989, pp. 1017–1019.
17. Editorial, 'President Bush's Hundred Days', *New York Times*, 23 April 1989, Section V, p. 22.
18. Janet Hook, 'Bush Inspired Frail Support For First-Year President', *Congressional Quarterly Weekly Report*, 30 December 1989, pp. 3540–3545. Helen Dewar and Tom Kenworthy, 'Putting Off Till Tomorrow What They Could Have Done Today', *Washington Post National Weekly Edition*, 4–10 December 1989, p. 13.
19. 'The Can't Do Government', *Time*, (International Edition) 23 October 1989, p. 22–25.
20. Interviews with Edie Holiday, C. Boyden Gray, Katharine Super, Roger Porter, Nicholas Calio, et al.
21. *Congress and the Nation*, op. cit., p. 474.
22. Michael Weisskopf, 'Environmental Impact', *Washington Post National Edition*, 17–23 October 1988.
23. Editorial, 'The President's Clean Air Plan', *Washington Post National Weekly Edition*, 19–25 June 1989, p.26.
24. *Congressional Quarterly Almanac, 1990* (Washington DC: Congressional Quarterly Press, 1991), p. 232.
25. Ibid., pp. 236–237.
26. Ibid., pp. 242–243 and 279.
27. Ibid. Interview with C. Boyden Gray, 10 November 1993.
28. Ibid.
29. Michael Duffy and Dan Goodgame, *Marching in Place: The Status Quo Presidency of George Bush* (New York: Simon & Schuster, 1992), p. 88.
30. *Congressional Quarterly Almanac*, op. cit., p. 278.
31. Interview with Nicholas Calio, 19 November 1993.
32. 'Domestic Policy: Divided Government and Cooperative Presidential Leadership' in Colin Campbell and Bert Rockman, *The Bush Presidency: First Appraisals* (Chatham, NJ: Chatham House, 1991), pp. 69–91.

33. Michael Barone and Grant Ujifusa, *The Almanac of American Politics 1994* (Washington DC: National Journal, 1993), p. 584.

34. *Congressional Quarterly Almanac*, op. cit., p. 448.

35. Stephen Percy, *Disability, Civil Rights and Public Policy* (Tuscaloosa: University of Alabama Press, 1992) p. xi.

36. 'The Disabilities Act', *CQ Researcher*, 27 December 1991, Vol. I, No.32 pp. 993–1016.

37. *Congressional Quarterly Almanac*, op. cit., p. 447.

38. Jonathan Rauch, 'The Regulatory President', *National Journal*, 30 November 1991, Vol. XXIII, pp. 2902–2906.

39. Charles Kolb, *White House Daze: The Unmaking of Domestic Policy in the Bush Years* (New York: The Free Press, 1994), p. 70.

40. Interviews with C. Boyden Gray, 10 November 1993 and 21 March 1994.

41. Percy, op. cit., p. 8.

42. 'The Disabilities Act', op. cit.

43. Interview with C. Boyden Gray, 21 March 1994.

44. Ibid.

45. Interview with C. Boyden Gray, 30 March 1994.

46. Interview with C. Boyden Gray, 21 March 1994.

47. William Kerr Muir, *The Bully Pulpit: The Presidential Leadership of Ronald Reagan* (San Francisco: Institute for Contemporary Studies, 1992), pp. 61–63.

48. Duffy and Goodgame, op. cit., pp. 209–12.

49. Remarks at a Celebration of the Points of Light, The White House, 14 January 1993, in *Public Papers of the Presidents of the United States, 1992–1993* (Washington DC: Government Printing Office, 1993), Book II, p. 2251.

50. See Peggy Noonan, *What I Saw at the Revolution* (New York: Ivy Books, 1990), Chapter 17.

51. Acceptance speech, 1988 Republican Convention.

52. Inaugural address.

53. Remarks in New York City, 22 June 1989, in *Public Papers of the Presidents of the United States, 1989* (Washington DC: Government Printing Office, 1990), Book I, p. 785.

54. '"Thousand Points" as a Cottage Industry', *The New York Times*, 29 May 1991 p. 1.

55. Interview with Gregg Petersmeyer, 16 November 1993.

56. Ibid.

57. Ibid.

58. *The Points of Light Movement: The President's Report to the Nation*, January 1993, in the author's possession, p. 7.

59. Ibid., p. 9.

60. Ibid., p. 48.

61. Ibid., p. 11.

62. Interview.

63. *The Points of Light Movement*, op. cit., pp. 10–11.

64. Statement on Signing the National and Community Service Act of 1990, 16 November 1990 in *Public Papers of the Presidents of the United*

States, 1990 (Washington DC: Government Printing Office, 1991), Book II, p. 1613.

65. *The Points of Light Movement*, op. cit., p. 3.
66. Interview with Gregg Petersmeyer, op. cit.
67. J. Pederzane, 'As Society's Need Increases, So Does Volunteerism', *New York Times*, 6 January 1992, p. A1.
68. Ibid.
69. Pierre Kim, 'From Carter to Reagan to Bush', *Policy Review*, Winter 1993, pp. 18–19.
70. Rauch, op. cit.

CHAPTER 5 'PREVENTING BAD LAWS'

1. *Congressional Quarterly Almanac,1992* (Washington DC: Congressional Quarterly Press, 1993), p. 9B.
2. Ibid., p. 3B.
3. Ibid., p. 4B.
4. See especially George Edwards, 'Measuring Presidential Success in Congress: Alternative Approaches', *Journal of Politics*, Vol. 47, 1985, pp. 667–685.
5. Janet Hook, 'Bush Inspired Frail Support For First Year President', *Congressional Quarterly Weekly Report*, 30 December 1989, pp. 3540–3545.
6. Anthony King, 'A Mile and a Half Is a Long Way', in Anthony King, *Both Ends of the Avenue: The Presidency, the Executive Branch and Congress in the 1980s* (Washington DC: American Enterprise Institute, 1983), pp. 246–273.
7. Edwards, op. cit.
8. *Congressional Quarterly Almanac*, op. cit., p. 5B.
9. Richard Rose, *The Postmodern President*, 2nd edn (Chatham, NJ: Chatham House, 1991), p. 313.
10. 'Presidential Vetoes, 1989–1992', *Congress and the Nation, Vol. VIII, 1989–1992* (Washington DC: Congressional Quarterly Press, 1993), pp. 1181–1182.
11. Richard Watson, *Presidential Vetoes and Public Policy* (Lawrence: University of Kansas Press, 1993), p. 146.
12. Interview with Nicholas Calio, 19 November 1993.
13. Federalist Papers, Number 73, *The Federalist Papers* (New York: New American Library, 1961), pp. 443 and 446.
14. Max Farrand (ed.), *The Records of the Federal Convention of 1787* (New Haven, Conn.: Yale University Press, 1937), Vol. II, p. 76.
15. Ibid., p. 78.
16. Interview with Roger Porter, 23 November 1993.
17. Kenneth Walsh, 'Bush's Veto Strategy', *U.S. News and World Report*, 2 July 1990, pp. 18-20.
18. Robert Spitzer, *The Presidential Veto: Touchstone of the American Presidency* (Albany: State University of New York Press, 1988), p. 85.
19. Paul Light, *The President's Agenda* (Baltimore, Md.: Johns Hopkins University Press, 1982), p. 113.

20. Janet Hook, 'President's Mastery of Veto Perplexes Hill Democrats', *Congressional Quarterly Weekly Report*, 27 July 1991, pp. 2041–2045.
21. Michael Duffy and Dan Goodgame, *Marching in Place: The Status Quo Presidency of George Bush* (New York: Simon & Schuster, 1992), p. 78.
22. Terry Eastland, *Energy in the Executive: The Case for the Strong Presidency* (New York: The Free Press, 1992), p. 73.
23. David Stockman, *The Triumph of Politics* (New York: Harper & Row, 1986), pp. 234, also 157 and 337.
24. Hook, 'President's Mastery . . .' op. cit.
25. Ibid.
26. Eastland, op. cit., p. 71, discusses and rejects Charles Black's insistence that the veto should be used only rarely and not as a means of policy control.
27. Federalist Papers, Number 73, op. cit., p. 443.
28. Farrand, op. cit., Vol. II, p. 74.
29. *Congress and the Nation*, op. cit., p. 355.
30. US House of Representatives, 101st Congress, *Congress and Foreign Policy, 1989* (Washington DC: US Government Printing Office, 1990), p. 9.
31. US House of Representatives, 101st *Congress, Congress and Foreign Policy, 1990* (Washington DC: US Government Printing Office, 1991), pp. 17–19.
32. *Congress and the Nation*, op. cit., pp. 1181–1182.
33. Ibid., p. 598.
34. See Spitzer, op. cit., on the value of veto threats, pp. 100–103.
35. Charles Kolb, *White House Daze; The Unmaking of Domestic Policy in the Bush Years* (New York: The Free Press, 1993), p. 11.
36. Interview with Nicholas Calio, op. cit.
37. Interview with David Demarest, 12 November 1993.
38. Interview with James Cicconi, 8 November 1993.
39. Hook, 'President's Mastery . . . , op. cit.
40. *Congress and the Nation*, op. cit., pp. 1181–1182.
41. Robert Spitzer, 'Presidential Prerogative Power: The Case of the Bush Administration and Legislative Power', *PS: Political Science and Politics*, March 1991, pp. 38–42.
42. *Congress and the Nation*, op. cit., p. 721.
43. Hook, 'President's Mastery . . op. cit.
44. Walsh, op. cit.
45. Interview with Charles Kolb, 29 March 1994.
46. Stockman, op. cit., p. 371
47. 'Excerpts From Interview With Bush on First Term and Future', *New York Times*, 25 June 1992, p. A24.
48. Hook, 'President's Mastery . . . , op. cit.
49. Duffy and Goodgame, op. cit., pp. 79–80.
50. Edwards, op. cit.
51. Watson, op. cit.
52. Ibid., pp. 167–168, Spitzer, op. cit., p. 139; and Louis Fisher, *Constitutional Conflicts Between Congress and the President* (Princeton, NJ: Princeton University Press, 1985), pp. 154–162.

53. Charles Tiefer, *The Semi-Sovereign Presidency: The Bush Administration's Strategy For Governing Without Congress*, (Boulder, Colo.: Westview Press, 1994), p. xi.

54. Statement on signing the National and Community Service Act of 1990, 16 November 1990 in *Public Papers of the Presidents of the United States, 1990* (Washington DC: US Goverment Printing Office, 1991) Book II, p. 1613.

55. US House of Representatives, 102nd Congress, *Congress and Foreign Policy, 1991* (Washington DC: US Government Printing Office, 1992), p. 17.

56. See Tiefer, op. cit., pp. 153–158.

57. Ibid., *passim*.

58. Theodore Sorensen, *Decision-Making in the White House* (New York: Columbia University Press, 1963), pp. 83–84.

59. See Federalist Papers, Number 73.

60. Thomas Geoghegan, 'Bust the Filibuster', *Washington Post National Weekly Edition*, 12–18 September 1994, p. 25.

61. See Charles O. Jones, The Presidency in a Separated System (Washington DC: Brookings, 1994).

62. Farrand, op cit. ,Vol II, pp. 74 and 76.

63. Federalist Papers, Number 73, p. 442.

64. Dean Acheson, *Present at the Creation* (New York: W.W. Norton, 1987), p. 415.

65. Sorenson, op. cit., p. 84.

66. The phrase quoted is from Barbara Sinclair, 'Governing Unheroically (and Sometimes Unappetizingly): Bush and the 101st Congress', in Colin Campbell and Bert Rockman (eds), *The Bush Presidency: First Appraisals* (Chatham, NJ: Chatham House, 1991).

67. See Eastland, op. cit., *passim*, for a conservative commentator's criticisms of Reagan's failure to make good use of the veto.

CHAPTER 6 THE 1990 BUDGET CRISIS

1. Bob Woodward, 'Origin of the Tax Pledge; In '88, Bush Camp Was Split on "Read My Lips" Vow', *Washington Post*, 4 October 1992, pp. A1, A22.

2. Bob Woodward, 'Primary Heat Turned Deal Into a "Mistake"; Disappointed Darman Offered to Resign', *Washington Post*, 6 October 1992, pp. A1, A14–A15.

3. Woodward, 'Origin of the Tax Pledge . . . op. cit.

4. Charles Kolb, *White House Daze: The Unmaking of Domestic Policy in the Bush Years* (New York: The Free Press, 1994), p. 57.

5. Peggy Noonan, *What I Saw at the Revolution* (New York: Ivy Books, 1990), p. 319.

6. Bob Woodward, 'No-Tax Vow Scuttled Anti-Deficit Mission', *Washington Post*, 5 October 1992, pp. A1, A8–A9.

7. Interview with James Cicconi, 8 November 1993.

8. Kolb, op. cit., p. 56.

9. Interview with James Pinkerton, 8 November 1993.
10. Interviews with David Demarest., 12 November 1993, and C. Boyden Gray, 10 November 1993.
11. Interview with Andrew Card, 15 November 1993.
12. Interview with Clayton Yeutter, 22 March 1994.
13. Interview with Bobbie Kilberg, 19 November 1993. For Darman's influence over both Sununu and Bush see Dan Quayle, *Standing Firm* (New York: Harper Collins, 1994) p. 107.
14. Interview with Bobbie Kilberg, op. cit.
15. Burt Solomon, 'In Bush's Image', *National Journal*, 7 July 1990, pp. 1642–1647.
16. George Church, 'Ignore My Lips', *Time* (International Edition), 21 May 1990, pp. 44–46.
17. Woodward, 'Primary Heat . . . op. cit.
18. *New York Times*, 27 June 1990, Section B, p. 6.
19. *Congress and the Nation*, Vol. VIII, 1989–1992 (Washington DC: Congressional Quarterly Press, 1993), p. 55.
20. Woodward, 'Primary Heat . . . op. cit.
21. *New York Times*, 3 October 1990, Section A, p. 1.
22. See articles by George Hager, Pamela Fessler, John Cranford and Janet Hook, *Congressional Quarterly Weekly Report*, 6 October 1990, pp. 3189–3195.
23. John Yang and Steven Mufson, 'The End of Self-Delusion: Congress makes a modest beginning at paring the deficit', *Washington Post National Weekly Edition* 5–11 November 1990, pp. 6–7.
24. James Pfiffner, 'The President and the Postreform Congress', in Roger Davidson (ed.), *The Postreform Congress* (New York: St. Martin's Press, 1992).
25. *Congress and the Nation*, op. cit., pp. 58–59.
26. Ibid., p. 57.
27. See, for example, Richard Lacayo, 'Dose of Reality', *Time* (International edition), 5 November 1990, pp. 30–32 and Yang and Mufson op. cit.
28. Janet Hook, 'Budget Ordeal Poses Question: Why Can't Congress Be Led?' *Congressional Quarterly Weekly Report*, 20 October 1990, pp. 3471–3473.
29. John Yang, 'Is George Bush Casting Fiscal Stones From A Glass House', *Washington Post National Weekly Edition*, 27 August–2 September 1990, p. 13.
30. David Broder, 'Take It From Those Who Know Best: Congress is a Wreck', *Washington Post National Weekly Edition*, 14–20 January 1991, p. 24.
31. See, for example, Thomas Mann and Norman Ornstein (eds) *The New Congress* (Washington DC: American Enterprise Institute, 1981); Hedrick Smith, *The Power Game* (New York: Random House, 1988); and Davidson, op. cit.
32. Broder, op. cit.
33. Hook, op. cit.
34. Janet Hook, 'Anatomy of a Budget Showdown: The Limits of Leaders' Clout', *Congressional Quarterly Weekly Report*, 6 October 1990,

pp. 3189–3191.
35. As quoted in *Congressional Quarterly Weekly Report*, 29 September 1990, p. 3096.
36. Interview with Edith Holiday, 17 November 1993.
37. Interview with David Demarest, 12 November 1993.
38. Dan Goodgame, 'Read My Hips', *Time* (International Edition) 22 October 1990, pp. 54–56.
39. Interview with John Keller, 18 November 1993.
40. Interview with Clayton Yeutter, op. cit..
41. Interview with Andrew Card, op. cit.
42. Interview with Constance Horner, 10 November 1993.
43. Kolb, op. cit., p. 95.
44. Interview with William Kristol, 23 March 1994.
45. Interview with James Pinkerton, 8 November 1993.
46. Interview with David Demarest, op. cit.
47. Interview with James Cicconi, op. cit.
48. Interview with John Keller, op. cit.
49. Interview with Nicholas Calio, 19 November 1993.
50. Ibid.
51. Interview 3.5.
52. As quoted in *Congressional Quarterly Weekly Report*, 13 October 1990, p. 3447.
53. As quoted in Terry Eastland, *Energy in the Executive* (New York: The Free Press, 1992), pp. 56–57.
54. *Congressional Quarterly Weekly Report*, 29 September 1990, p. 3094.
55. Ibid. 20 October 1990, p. 3472.
56. Bill Whalen, 'For Republicans, a House Divided', *Insight*, 12 November 1990, pp. 8–13.
57. Laurence Barrett, '1,000 Points of Spite', *Time* (International Edition), 15 October 1990, p. 24.
58. Whalen, op. cit.
59. *Congressional Quarterly Weekly Report*, 6 October 1990, p. 3189.
60. Interview with Bobbie Kilberg, op. cit.
61. Interview with James Cicconi, op. cit.
62. Interview with Edith Holiday, op. cit.
63. Interview with Bobbie Kilberg, op. cit.
64. Ibid. See also Goodgame, op. cit.
65. Interview with Bobbie Kilberg, op. cit.
66. Dan Balz and Ann Devroy, 'Sununu and Darman Give the Hill the Screaming Meanies', *Washington Post National Weekly Edition*, 15–20 October 1990, pp. 7–8.
67. See, for example, interviews with Bobbie Kilberg and Edie Holiday, both op. cit. Also Quayle, op. cit., pp. 94–95.
68. Interview 3.5.
69. Bert Rockman, 'The Leadership Style of George Bush', in Colin Campbell and Bert Rockman, *The Bush Presidency: First Appraisals* (Chatham, NJ: Chatham House, 1991), p. 18.
70. Interview with James Cicconi, op. cit.
71. *Congress and the Nation*, op. cit., p. 1189.

72. As reported in *Congressional Quarterly Weekly Report*, 13 October 1990, p. 3447.
73. George Hager, 'Parties Angle For Advantage As White House Falters', *Congressional Quarterly Weekly Report*, 13 October 1990, pp. 3389–3398.
74. Goodgame, op. cit.
75. Hager, op. cit.
76. Ibid.
77. Interview with Edie Holiday, op. cit.
78. Stuart Eizenstat, 'What Bush Should Do About Taxes', *Washington Post National Weekly Edition*, 25 June–1 July 1990, p. 29.
79. Hook, op. cit.
80. Interviews. Also interviews with Nicholas Calio, Roger Porter and Clayton Yeutter.
81. Smith, op. cit., p. 476.
82. *Miller Center Report*, Vol. 6, No. 4, Winter 1990.
83. As quoted in Whalen, op. cit.
84. Quayle, op. cit., p. 203.
85. Interviews with Bobbie Kilberg.
86. Kolb, op. cit., p. 95.
87. Interview with Nicholas Calio, op. cit., and Quayle, op. cit, p.202.
88. Goodgame, op. cit.
89. Richard Neustadt, *Presidential Power and the Modern Presidents* (New York: The Free Press, 1990), p. 50.
90. Thomas Edsall, 'The Gridlock of Government', *Washington Post National Weekly Edition*, 15–21 October 1990, p. 6.
91. Interviews.
92. Martin Walker and Simon Tisdall, 'Bush Says Sorry for Tax U turn', *Guardian* (London) 4 March 1992, p. 1.
93. Quoted in Dan Balz, 'Hussein Made Him Break the Tax Pledge – Yeah, That's It', *Washington Post National Weekly Edition*, 3–9 August 1992, p. 15. *Note*: Balz effectively disposes of the claim raised, more than once, by Vice President Quayle that the tax increase in 1990 was forced upon the President by the crisis created by the Iraqi invasion of Kuwait. As Balz points out, and Quayle concedes in his memoirs, Bush broke the tax pledge well before the invasion took place. See Quayle, op. cit., pp. 195–196.
94. Interview 3.5.
95. Interviews.
96. Michael Nelson (ed.), *The Elections of 1992* (Washington DC: CQ Press, 1993) p. 81. *Note:* On the other hand, as James Pfiffner pointed out to me without the budget deal the deficit would have been larger and the health of the economy probably even worse than it was in fact.

CHAPTER 7 GUARDIANSHIP AND FOREIGN POLICY

1. Richard Rose, *The Postmodern President*, 2nd edn (Chatham, NJ: Chatham House, 1991), p. 308.

2. K. Thompson (ed.), Presidential Transitions: The Reagan to Bush Experience (Lanham, MD: University Press of America, 1993), p. 19.
3. Michael Beschloss and Strobe Talbott, *At the Highest Levels: The Inside Story of the End of the Cold War* (Boston: Little Brown, 1993), pp. 7071.
4. 13 January 1993, Official Text, USIS, US Embassy, London.
5. David Hoffman, 'The Politics of Timidity', *Washington Post National Weekly Edition*, 23–29 October 1989, p. 67.
6. John Newhouse, 'Profiles: The Tactician', *New Yorker*, 7 May 1990, pp. 5082.
7. Henry Allen, 'The Quintessential Establishmentarian', *Washington Post National Weekly Edition*, 9–15 January 1989.
8. The first quotation is from John Yang, 'Who is George Bush?', *Washington Post National Weekly Edition*, 24 Febuary–1 March 1991, pp. 910; the second quotation is from Newhouse, op. cit.
9. Don Oberdorfer, 'It Helps to Have a Buddy in the White House', *Washington Post National Weekly Edition*, 14–20 November 1988, p. 15.
10. Christopher Ogden, 'Vision Problems at State . . . *Time* (International Edition), 25 September 1989 p. 36.
11. Richard Lacayo, *Time* (International Edition, 9) March 1992 pp. 34–35.
12. George Bush, *Looking Forward* (London: The Bodley Head, 1987), p. 174. See also Bradley Patterson, *The Ring of Power* (New York: Basic Books, 1988), Chapter 7, for the various functions of the Assistant to the President for National Security Affairs.
13. Tower Commission Report (New York: Bantam Books, 1987).
14. Interview with Brent Scowcroft, 28 March 1994.
15. Christopher Madison, 'No Sharp Elbows', *National Journal*, 26 May 1990, pp. 1277–1281, and Andrew Rosenthal, 'National Security Adviser Redefines the Role, Drawing Barrage of Criticism', *New York Times*, 3 November 1989 p. A16.
16. Hoffman, op. cit.
17. Roger Porter, *Presidential Decision Making: The Economic Policy Board* (New York: Cambridge University Press, 1980), p. 216.
18. Interview with Richard Haass, 24 March 1994.
19. Ogden, op. cit.
20. Newhouse, op. cit.
21. Ogden, op. cit.
22. David Hoffman, 'James Baker's Determination To Put the New World in Order,' *Washington Post National Weekly Edition*, 24–30 August 1992, p. 31.
23. US House of Representatives, 101st Congress, *Congress and Foreign Policy 1989* (Washington DC: Government Printing Office, 1990), p. 58.
24. Don Oberdorfer, 'Behind a Bipartisan Announcement, a Long Trail of Secret Meetings', *Washington Post National Weekly Edition*, 3–9 April 1989, p. 14.
25. Rochelle Stanfield, 'Cutting Deals', *National Journal*, 8 April 1989 p. 889.
26. Robert Pear, 'Unease Is Voiced On Contra Accord', *New York Times*, 26 March 1989, p. 1.

27. Jeremy Rabkin, 'At the President's Side: The Role of the White House Counsel in Constitutional Policy', *Law and Contemporary Problems*, Vol. 56, No. 4, Autumn 1993, pp. 63–98.

28. Bernard Weinraub, 'White House Rebukes Counsel on Pact', *New York Times*, 28 March 1989, p. A6.

29. Pear, op. cit.

30. *Congress and Foreign Policy 1989*, op. cit., p. 76.

31. Hoffman, 'The Politics of Timidity' . . . op. cit.

32. Bob Woodward, *The Commanders* (New York: Simon & Schuster, 1991), p. 164.

33. *Congress and Foreign Policy 1989*, op. cit., p. 86.

34. Bush's already high standing in the polls – 68 per cent approval according to Gallup – rose to 80 per cent after the invasion and the surrender of Noriega. Paul Brace and Barbara Hinckley, *Follow the Leader: Opinion Polls and the Modern Presidents* (New York: Basic Books, 1992), p. 110.

35. *Congress and Foreign Policy 1989*, op. cit., p. 85.

36. George McGovern, 'A Betrayal of American Principles', *Washington Post National Weekly Edition*,22–28 January 1990, p. 29.

37. David Hoffman and Bob Woodward, 'This Guy Is Not Going to Lay Off', *Washington Post National Weekly Edition*, 25–31 December 1989, p. 6.

38. *Congress and Foreign Policy 1989*, op. cit., p. 86.

39. For example, Lyndon Johnson's massive escalation in Vietnam and Nixon's incursion into Cambodia.

40. David Hoffman, 'The President's New Stand Towards Gorbachev: No More Wait and See', *Washington Post National Weekly Edition*, 19–25 March 1990, p. 11.

41. Lou Cannon, 'Reagan Is Concerned About Bush's Indecision', *Washington Post National Weekly Edition*, 15–21 May 1989, p. 28.

42. Don Oberdorfer, *The Turn: From the Cold War to a New Era* (New York: Simon & Schuster, 1992), p. 346.

43. Editorial, *Christian Science Monitor*, 'What's Bush's Vision?', 11–17 May 1989, p. 20.

44. Interview with Brent Scowcroft, op. cit.

45. Beschloss and Talbott, op. cit., p. 86.

46. Ibid., p. 92.

47. Oberdorfer, *The Turn* . . ., op. cit., p. 364, and Beschloss and Talbott, op. cit., p. 135.

48. Ibid.

49. Interview with Andrew Card, 15 November 1993.

50. Oberdorfer, The Turn . . ., op. cit., p. 367.

51. Interview with Brent Scowcroft, op. cit.

52. Beschloss and Talbott, op. cit., p. 163–164.

53. Ibid., p. 165.

54. Dan Quayle, Standing Firm (New York: Harper Collins, 1994) p. 175.

55. Interview with Brent Scowcroft, op. cit.

56. Beschloss and Talbott, op. cit. p. 205.

57. Kim Holmes, 'In Search of a Strategy', *Policy Review*, Winter 1991, pp. 72–75.
58. Interview with Brent Scowcroft, op. cit.
59. Interview with James Cicconi, 8 November 1993.
60. Interview with Brent Scowcroft, op. cit.
61. Interview with James Ciconni, op. cit.
62. See, for example, Michael Mandelbaum, 'The Bush Foreign Policy', *Foreign Affairs*, Spring 1991, Vol. 70 pp. 5–22.

CHAPTER 8 THE WAR IN THE GULF

1. *The Gulf Crisis: A Chronology, July 1990–July 1991*, USIS, US Embassy, London, 1991, p. 2. Subsequently cited as Chronology.
2. Dilop Hiro, *Desert Shield to Desert Storm: The Second Gulf War* (London: Harper Collins, 1992), Appendix 1.
3. Bob Woodward, *The Commanders* (New York: Simon & Schuster, 1991), pp. 225 and 231.
4. *The Washington Version*, television documentary on the Gulf crisis decision-making process made by the American Enterprise Institute and the BBC, 1991. Commended to the author as 'a pretty good primary source' by one of those close to these events. Interview with Richard Haass, 24 March 1994.
5. *Chronology*, p. 3.
6. Woodward, op. cit., p. 285.
7. *Chronology*, pp. 15 and 18.
8. Ibid., p.21.
9. *Congress and the Nation*, Vol. VIII, 1989–1992 (Washington DC: Congressional Quarterly Press, 1993), pp. 309 and 1061.
10. Ibid., p. 315.
11. Dan Balz and Ann Devroy, 'Bush Became a Leader When It Mattered Most', *Washington Post National Weekly Edition*, 11–17 March 1991, p. 9. Dan Goodgame, 'What if we do nothing?', *Time* (International Edition) 7 January 1991, pp. 14–15.
12. For example, Jean Edward Smith, *George Bush's War* (New York: Henry Holt, 1992); Alex Roberto Hybel (foreword by James Rosenau), *Power Over Rationality: The Bush Administration and the Gulf Crisis* (Albany: State University of New York Press, 1993); Roger Hilsman, *George Bush Versus Saddam Hussein* (Novato, CA: Presidio Press, 1992); James Pfiffner, 'Presidential Policy-Making and the Gulf War', in Marcia Lynn Whicker, James Pffifner and Raymond Moore, *The Presidency and the Persian Gulf War* (Westport, Conn.: Praeger, 1993).
13. Ibid. p. 20.
14. Interview with Brent Scowcroft, 28 March 1994.
15. Interview 3.8.
16. 'In DOD We Trust', *New Republic*, 17 June 1991, pp. 29–35.
17. See especially Smith, op. cit., Chapter 2.
18. Interview with Brent Scowcroft, op. cit.
19. Smith, op. cit., p. 68. See also Hilsman, op. cit., p. 45.

20. *Washington Version*, op. cit.
21. Interview with Richard Haass.
22. *Washington Version*, op. cit.
23. Ibid.
24. Ibid.
25. Margaret Thatcher, *The Downing Street Years* (London: Harper Collins, 1993), p. 821.
26. *Washington Version*, op. cit.
27. See, for example, Smith and Hilsman, both op. cit. Also Stephen Graubard, Mr Bush's War: Adventures in the Politics of Illusion (New York: I.B. Tauris, 1992).
28. Interview with Brent Scowcroft, op. cit.
29. Ibid.
30. Woodward, op. cit., p. 234.
31. Ibid., p. 261.
32. Interview with Brent Scowcroft, op. cit.
33. Interview with Richard Haass.
34. The first source is Hybel, op. cit., p. 8; the second is Smith, op. cit., p. 255.
35. Interview with Brent Scowcroft, op. cit.
36. Smith, Hybel and Pfiffner, all op. cit. Also Elizabeth Drew, 'Letter From Washington', *New Yorker*, 4 Febuary 1991, pp. 82–90.
37. Interview with Brent Scowcroft, op. cit.
38. Interview with Richard Haass.
39. Alexander George, 'The Case for Multiple Advocacy in Making Foreign Policy', *American Political Science Review*, Vol. 66, September 1972, pp. 751–785. Irving Janis, *Victims of Groupthink* (Boston: Houghton Mifflin, 1972).
40. Interview with Richard Haass.
41. See Pfiffner and Drew, both op. cit.
42. Interview with Brent Scowcroft, op. cit.
43. For example, Hybel, op. cit., p. 8.
44. Interview with Brent Scowcroft, op. cit.
45. *Washington Version*, op. cit.
46. Ibid.
47. Interviews with Brent Scowcroft, op. cit., and Richard Haass.
48. Smith, op. cit., p. 161.
49. See Terry Eastland, *Energy in the Executive* (New York: The Free Press, 1992), p. 133.
50. Jim Hoagland, 'Wanted: A Clear Statement Of Purpose', *Washington Post National Weekly Edition*, 12–18 November 1990, p. 23.
51. Tom Mathews, 'The Road to War', *Newsweek*, 28 January 1991, p. 34–45.
52. Interview with Richard Haass.
53. David Roth, *Sacred Honor: Colin Powell* (New York: Harper Collins, 1993), p. 262.
54. Ibid., p. 263.
55. For some of the objections to the constitutionality of this position see especially Louis Fisher, 'The Power of Commander in Chief', in

Whicker, Pfiffner and Moore, op. cit. Also Michael Glennon, 'The Gulf War and the Constitution', *Foreign Affairs*, Spring 1991, Vol. 70, pp. 84–101.

56. Matthews, op. cit.
57. Interview with Brent Scowcroft, op. cit.
58. *Standing Firm*, op. cit., p. 227.
59. Interview with Boyden Gray, 21 March 1994.
60. *Washington Version*, op. cit.
61. *Congress and the Nation*, op. cit., p. 310.
62. US House of Representatives, 102nd Congress, *Congress and Foreign Policy 1991* (Washington DC: US Government Printing Office, 1992), p. 17.
63. Max Farrand (ed.), *The Records of the Federal Convention of 1787* (New Haven, Conn.: Yale University Press, 1937), Volume II, p. 318.
64. Hilsman, op. cit., p. 48. For other Administration justifications of the US intervention see Colin Campbell and Bert Rockman (eds) *The Bush Presidency: First Appraisals* (Chatham, NJ: Chatham House, 1991), p. 117.
65. Richard Marin, 'George Bush Could Set A Record', *Washington Post National Weekly Edition*, 16–22 March 1990, p. 37.
66. Roth, op. cit., p. 231.
67. On Baker's role see David Hoffman, 'Jim Baker: Global Dealmaker', *Washington Post National Weekly Edition*, 19–25 November 1990, pp. 6–7.
68. According to one source between 2 August 1990 and Febuary 1991 the President made 231 phone calls to other heads of state. David Lauter and James Gerstenzag, 'The Clutch President', *Los Angeles Times Magazine*, 14 July 1991, p. 12.
69. Goodgame, op. cit.
70. George Bush, *Looking Forward* (London: The Bodley Head, 1988), p. 120.
71. Woodward, op. cit., p. 310.
72. *Chronology*, pp. 19 and 23.
73. Theodore Draper, 'The True History of the Gulf War', *New York Review of Books*, 30 January 1992, pp. 38–45.
74. Don Oberdorfer, 'The War No One Saw Coming', *Washington Post National Weekly Edition*, 18–24 March 1991, pp. 6–10.
75. Theodore Draper, 'The Gulf War Reconsidered', *New York Review of Books*, 16 January 1992, pp. 46–53.
76. Oberdorfer, 'The War No One . . . op. cit.
77. Draper, 'The Gulf War . . . op. cit.
78. For a robust response to the allegation that the Bush Administration 'coddled' Saddam Hussein see Brent Scowcroft, 'We Didn't "Coddle" Hussein', *Washington Post National Weekly Edition*, 19–25 October 1992, p. 29.
79. Terry Diebel, 'Bush's Foreign Policy: Mastery and Inaction', *Foreign Policy*, No. 84, Fall 1991, pp. 3–23.

CHAPTER 9 CONCLUSIONS

1. See, for example, George Bush, *Looking Forward* (London: The Bodley Head, 1988), p. 193.
2. Alan Brinkley, as quoted in Robert J. Samuelson, 'There's Good Reason To Like Ike,' *Washington Post National Weekly Edition*, 22–28 October 1990, p. 31.
3. R.W. Apple, 'In the Capital', *New York Times*, 29 March 1989, p. A16.
4. *Congress and the Nation*, Vol. VIII, 1989–1992 (Washington DC: Congressional Quarterly Press, 1993), pp. 218–219.
5. Michael Mandelbaum, 'The Bush Foreign Policy', *Foreign Policy*, Spring 1991, Vol. 70, pp. 5–22.
6. Michael Elliott, 'The Gipper vs the Evil Empire', *Washington Post National Weekly Edition*, 22–28 August 1994, p. 35.
7. Michael Beschloss and Strobe Talbott, *At the Highest Levels: The Inside Story of the End of the Cold War* (Boston: Little Brown, 1993), p. 469.
8. See James MacGregor Burns, *The Power to Lead* (New York: Simon & Schuster, 1984), p. 16.
9. Committee on Foreign Affairs, US House of Representatives, 102nd Congress, *Congress and Foreign Policy 1991* (Washington DC: US Government Printing Office, 1992), pp. 103–117.
10. 'Excerpts From Interview With Bush on First Term And Future', *New York Times*, 25 June 1992, p. A24.
11. *Congress and the Nation . . .*, op. cit. p. 657.
12. See ibid., pp. 643–658. It is the case however, that spending for the Head Start programme went up by 22 per cent a year during the Bush presidency and federal expenditures on elementary and secondary education increased by 11 per cent per year. Robert Pear 'Social Programs Grow, But Largely By Neglect', *New York Times*, 2 August 1992, p. 1.
13. *Congress and the Nation . . .*, op. cit., p. 611.
14. See Jonathan Rauch, 'The Regulatory President', *National Journal*, 30 November 1991, pp. 2902–2906 and Matthew P. Weinstock, 'Running On His Record', *Occupational Hazards*, October 1992, Vol. 54, pp. 75–79.
15. Pierre Kim, 'From Carter to Reagan to Bush', *Policy Review*, No. 63, Winter 1993, pp. 18–19.
16. Rauch, op. cit.
17. See Charles Kolb, *White House Daze: The Unmaking of Domestic Policy in the Bush Years* (New York: The Free Press, 1994), p. 73, and John Podhoretz, *Hell of a Ride: Backstage at the White House Follies 1989–1993* (New York: Simon & Schuster, 1993), p. 227.
18. See David O'Brien, 'The Reagan Judges: His Most Enduring Legacy', in Charles O. Jones, *The Reagan Legacy* (Chatham NJ: Chatham House, 1988).
19. Interview with C. Boyden Gray.
20. Neil A. Lewis, 'Selection of Conservative Judges Insures a Presidential Legacy', *New York Times*, 1 July 1992.
21. *Congress and the Nation . . .*, op. cit., p. 776.
22. Joan Biskupic, 'The Reagan-Bush Court Is Back To Keep The Nation

Guessing', *Washington Post National Weekly Edition*, 12–18 October 1992, p. 32.

23. Ruth Marcus, 'It's All in the Interpretation for Justices Souter and Thomas', *Washington Post National Weekly Edition*, 13–19 July 1992, p. 31.
24. Lewis, op. cit.
25. Jeremy Rabkin, 'At the President's Side: The Role of the White House Counsel in Constitutional Policy', *Law and Contemporary Problems*, Vol. 56, No. 4, Autumn 1993, pp. 63–98. John E. Yang and Sharon Lafraniere, 'George Bush's Eminence Grise', *Washington Post National Weekly Edition*, 2–8 December 1991, p. 14.
26. Charles Tiefer, *The Semi-Sovereign Presidency* (Boulder, Colo.: Westview Press, 1994), p. 34.
27. Ibid., p. 35.
28. Neil Lewis, 'Turning Loyalty and Service to Bush Into Power as Presidential Counsel', *New York Times*, 12 December 1990, p. B12.
29. Interview with Roger Porter, 23 November 1993.
30. Interview with C. Boyden Gray.
31. David Broder, 'Getting Government Moving Again', *Washington Post National Weekly Edition*, 7–13 September 1992, p. 4.
32. David Broder, 'Bush Showed He Can Fight, but Does He Know How to Lead', Washington Post National Weekly Edition, 20–26 March 1989, p. 23.
33. Robin Toner, 'For Bush and Congress, Some Spirited Battles But No Full Scale War', *New York Times*, 9 August 1989, p. B6.
34. Interview with Clayton Yeutter, 22 March 1994.
35. See p.158 above.
36. Samuel Kernell, *Going Public: New Strategies of Presidential Leadership* (Washington DC: CQ Press, 1986), Chapter 2 *passim*.
37. Ibid., p. 1.
38. Quoted in Andrew Rosenthal, 'Bush in a World Remade', *New York Times*, 25 June 1992, p. A1.
39. Robert Novak, 'How George Bush May Snatch Defeat From the Jaws of Victory', *Washington Post National Weekly Edition*, 24–30 August 1992, p. 23.
40. Interview with Andrew Card, 15 November 1993.
41. Interview with James Cicconi, 8th November 1993.
42. Interviews with C. Boyden Gray and Gregg Petersmeyer.
43. Terry Eastland, *Energy in the Executive* (New York: The Free Press, 1992), pp. 53–54.
44. Interview with John Keller, 18 November 1993.
45. Interview with Nicholas Calio, 19 Novemer 1993.
46. Interview with Richard Haass.
47. Bush, *Looking Forward*, op. cit., p. 204.
48. Ibid., p. 205.
49. Interview with Gregg Petersmeyer, 16 November 1993.
50. Interview with Ed Rogers, 3 November 1993.
51. Interview with Constance Horner.
52. Kolb, *White House Daze*, op. cit., p. 242.

53. Interview with Clayton Yeutter, op. cit.
54. See Chapter 1.
55. Theodore Lowi, *The Personal Presidency* (Ithaca, NY: Cornell University Press, 1985), p.59.
56. Interview with Charles Kolb, 29 March 1994.
57. For the advantages of simplicity in political rhetoric see John Lewis Gaddis, *The United States and the End of the Cold War* (Oxford: Oxford University Press, 1992), p. 131.
58. See Chapter 2.
59. Keith Schneider 'Bush on the Environment: A Record of Contradictions', *New York Times*, 4 July 1992, p. A1.
60. Weinstock, op. cit.
61. For some of the arguments in favour of balance in such matters see C. Boyden Gray and David B. Rivkin, 'A "No Regrets" Environmental Policy', *Foreign Policy*, No. 83, Summer 1991, pp. 47–65.
62. George Will, 'A Figure of Genuine Pathos', *Washington Post National Weekly Edition*, 3–9 August 1992, p. 29.
63. Michael Duffy and Dan Goodgame, *Marching in Place: The Status Quo Presidency of George Bush* (New York: Simon & Schuster, 1992), Chapter 1.
64. Interview with James Cicconi, op. cit.
65. Interview with David Demarest, 12 November 1993.
66. Gail Sheehy, *Character: America's Search for Leadership* (New York: Bantam Books, 1990), p. 198.
67. Interview with C. Boyden Gray. The articles in question were Ruth Marcus, 'What Does Bush Really Believe?; Civil Rights Record Illustrates Shifts', *The Washington Post*, 18 August 1992, p. A1, and Jefferson Morley, 'Bush and the Blacks: An Unknown Story', *New York Review of Books*, 16 January 1992, pp. 19–26.
68. Bush, Looking Forward, op. cit., p. 91.
69. Morley, op. cit.
70. Bush, *Looking Forward*, op. cit., pp. 92–93.
71. Marcus, 'What Does Bush Really Believe?', op. cit.
72. See Morley, op. cit., on Bush's advocacy of quotas in 1970. In fairness it should be said that Bush is by no means the only prominent public figure to change his mind about the desirability of quotas.
73. Kolb, op. cit., pp. 248–249.
74. *Congress and the Nation*, op. cit., p. 78.
75. Dan Goodgame, 'Trumpeting Victory in Retreat', *Time* (International Edition), 2 December 1991, pp. 68–69. William Raspberry, 'Bush's Missing Drummer', *Washington Post National Weekly Edition*, 2–8 December 1991, p. 29. Kolb, op. cit., p. 258. For the opposite view that the Democrats 'beat a total retreat on quotas' see C. Boyden Gray, 'Civil Rights: We Won, They Capitulated', *Washington Post National Weekly Edition*, 18–24 November 1991, p. 29.
76. Raspberry, op. cit., and Kolb, op. cit., p. 257.
77. Morley, op. cit.
78. Duffy and Goodgame, op. cit., p. 282.
79. Bush, *Looking Forward*, op. cit., p. 207.
80. Duffy and Goodgame, op. cit., p. 91.

81. Robert Shogan, *The Riddle of Power: Presidential Leadership From Truman to Bush* (New York: Dutton, 1991), p. 264.

82. Quoted in Martin Walker and Simon Tisdall, 'Bush Says Sorry For Tax U-turn', *The Guardian* (London), 4 March 1992, p. 1.

83. Michael Duffy, 'Is Bush Getting a Free Ride', *Time* (International Edition), 27 April 1992, pp. 43–45.

84. 'The Other Character Question', Editorial, *Washington Post National Weekly Edition*, 27 April–3 May 1992, p. 26.

85. Seymour Martin Lipset, 'The Significance of the 1992 Election', *PS: Political Science and Politics*, March 1993, pp 7–16.

86. See Joshua Muravchik 'Why the Democrats Finally Won', *Commentary*, Vol. 95, January 1993, pp. 17–22.

87. John Mueller, *Policy and Opinion in the Gulf War* (Chicago: University of Chicago Press, 1994), p 336.

88. Michael Nelson (ed.), *The Elections of 1992* (Washington DC: CQ Press, 1993), p. 81.

89. Ibid., p. 61.

90. Lipset, op. cit.

91. Interview with C. Boyden Gray, 10 November 1993.

92. See p. 34 above.

93. Mueller, op. cit., p. 185.

94. Dan Qyale, *Standing Firm* (New York: Harper Collins, 1994), p. 355.

95. Maureen Dowd, 'A Presidency Lost: Bush and Campaign Were Out of Touch', *International Herald Tribune*, 6 November 1992, p. 1.

96. Interview with Paul Bateman, 15 November 1993.

97. Interview with Edith Holiday, 17 November 1993.

98. Interview with Clayton Yeutter, op. cit.

99. Lipset, op. cit.

Bibliography

Dean Acheson, *Present at the Creation* (New York: W.W. Norton, 1987).

Chuck Alston, 'Rules of Political Navigation Altered by Bush Centrism, *Congressional Quarterly Weekly Report*, 6 May 1989, pp. 1017–1019.

Stephen Ambrose, *Nixon, Volume Two: The Triumph of a Politician 1962–1972* (New York: Simon & Schuster, 1989).

Martin Anderson, *Revolution* (New York: Harcourt Brace Jovanovich, 1988).

Michael Barone and Grant Ujifusa, *The Almanac of American Politics 1994* (Washington DC: National Journal, 1994).

Michael Beschloss and Strobe Talbott, *At the Highest Levels: The Inside Story of the End of Cold War* (Boston: Little Brown, 1993).

Christopher Bosso, 'Congressional and Presidential Scholars: Some Basic Traits', *PS: Political Science and Politics*, December 1989, pp. 839–848.

James MacGregor Burns, *The Power to Lead* (New York: Simon & Schuster, 1984).

James MacGregor Burns, *Roosevelt: The Lion and the Fox* (New York: Harcourt Brace and World, 1957).

George Bush (with Victor Gold), *Looking Forward* (London: The Bodley Head, 1988).

Joseph Califano, *A Presidential Nation* (New York: W.W. Norton, 1975).

Colin Campbell and Bert Rockman (eds), *The Bush Presidency: First Appraisals* (Chatham, New Jersey: Chatham House, 1991).

Margaret Coit (ed.), *John C. Calhoun* (New Jersey: Prentice Hall, 1970).

Committee on Foreign Affairs, US House of Representatives, 101st Congress, *Congress and Foreign Policy, 1989* (Washington DC: US Government Printing Office, 1990).

Committee on Foreign Affairs, US House of Representatives, 102nd Congress, *Congress and Foreign Policy, 1991* (Washington DC: US Government Printing Office, 1992).

Congress and the Nation, Vol. VIII, 1989–1992 (Washington DC: Congressional Quarterly Press, 1993).

Congressional Quarterly Almanac, 1990 (Washington DC: Congressional Quarterly Press, 1991).

Congressional Quarterly Almanac, 1992 (Washington DC: Congressional Quarterly Press, 1993).

Richard Ben Cramer, *What It Takes* (New York: Random House, 1992).

Roger Davidson (ed.), *The Postreform Congress* (New York: St. Martin's Press, 1992).

Roger Davidson and Walter Oleszek, *Congress and Its Members*, 4th edn (Washington DC: Congressional Quarterly Press 1994).

Terry Diebel, 'Bush's Foreign Policy: Mastery and Inaction', *Foreign Policy*, No. 84, Fall 1991, pp. 3–23

'The Disabilities Act', *CQ Researcher*, 27 December 1991, Vol. I, No. 32, pp. 993–1016.

Ann Reilly Dowd, 'How Bush Manages the Presidency', *Fortune*, 27 August 1990, pp. 38–43.

Theodore Draper, 'The Gulf War Reconsidered', *New York Review of Books*, 16 January 1992, pp. 46–53.

Theodore Draper, 'The True History of the Gulf War', *New York Review of Books*, 30 January 1992, pp. 38–45.

Elizabeth Drew, 'Letter from Washington', *New Yorker*, 4 February 1991, pp. 82–90.

Michael Duffy and Dan Goodgame, *Marching in Place: The Status Quo Presidency of George Bush* (New York: Simon & Schuster, 1992).

Terry Eastland, *Energy in the Executive: The Case for the Strong Presidency* (New York: The Free Press, 1992).

George Edwards, 'Measuring Presidential Success in Congress: Alternative Approaches', *Journal of Politics*, Vol. 47, 1985, pp. 667–685.

George Edwards, John Kessel and Bert Rockman (eds) *Researching the Presidency* (Pittsburgh: University of Pittsburgh Press, 1993).

John Ehrlichman, *Witness to Power* (New York: Pocket Books, 1982).

Ronald Elving, 'House Service Set Course for New President', *Congressional Quarterly Weekly Report*, 14 January 1989, pp. 55–57.

Max Farrand (ed.), *The Records of the Federal Convention of 1787* (New Haven, Conn.: Yale University Press, 1937), 3 vols.

Louis Fisher, *Constitutional Conflicts Between Congress and the President* (Princeton: Princeton University Press, 1985).

Louis Fisher, 'The Power of Commander in Chief', in Marcia Whicker, James Pfiffner and Raymond Moore, *The Presidency and the Gulf War* (Westport, Conn.: Praeger, 1993).

John Lewis Gaddis, *The United States and the End of the Cold War* (Oxford: Oxford University Press, 1992).

Alexander George, 'The Case for Multiple Advocacy in Making Foreign Policy', *American Political Science Review*, Vol. 66, September 1972, pp. 751–785.

Michael Glennon, 'The Gulf War and the Constitution', *Foreign Affairs*, Spring 1991, Vol. 70, pp. 84–101.

Peter Goldman and Tom Mathews, *The Quest for the Presidency: The 1988 Campaign* (New York: Simon & Schuster, 1989).

Stephen Graubard, *Mr Bush's War: Adventures in the Politics of Illusion* (New York: I.B. Tauris, 1992).

C. Boyden Gray, 'The Coordinating Role of the Vice Presidency', in James Pfiffner and Gordon Hoxie (eds) *The Presidency in Transition* (New York: Center for the Study of the Presidency, 1989).

C. Boyden Gray and David B. Rivkin, 'A "No Regrets" Environmental Policy', *Foreign Policy*, No. 83, Summer 1991, pp. 47–65.

Fitzhugh Green, *George Bush: An Intimate Portrait* (New York: Hippocrene Books, 1991).

Fred Greenstein, *The Hidden-Hand Presidency: Eisenhower as Leader* (New York: Basic Books, 1982).

Fred Greenstein, 'Ronald Reagan's Presidential Leadership', in Ellis Sandoz and Cecil Crabb (eds), *Electon 84: Landslide Without a Mandate?* (New York: New American Library, 1985).

The Gulf Crisis: A Chronology, July 1990–July 1991, USIS, US Embassy, London, 1991.

George Hager, 'Parties Angle For Advantage As White House Falters', *Congressional Quarterly Weekly Report*, 13 October 1990, pp. 3389–3398.

H.R. Haldeman, *The Haldeman Diaries* (New York: G.P. Putnam's Sons, 1994).

John Hart, *The Presidential Branch* (New York: Pergamon Press, 1987).

Stephen Hess, *Organizing the Presidency*, 2nd edn (Washington DC: The Brookings Institution, 1988).

Dilys Hill and Phil Williams (eds), *The Bush Presidency: Triumphs and Adversities* (London: Macmillan, 1994).

Roger Hilsman, *George Bush Versus Saddam Hussein* (Novato, Calif: Presidio Press, 1992).

Dilop Hiro, *Desert Shield to Desert Storm: The Second Gulf War* (London: HarperCollins, 1992).

Kim Holmes, 'In Search of a Strategy', *Policy Review*, Winter 1991, pp. 72–75.

Janet Hook, 'Bush Inspired Frail Support For First-Year President', *Congressional Quarterly Weekly Report*, 30 December 1989, pp. 3540–3545.

Janet Hook, 'Anatomy of a Budget Showdown: The Limits of Leaders' Clout', *Congressional Quarterly Weekly Report*, 6 October 1990, pp. 3189–3191.

Janet Hook, 'Budget Ordeal Poses Question: Why Can't Congress Be Led?', *Congressional Quarterly Weekly Report*, 27 July 1991, pp. 2041–2045.

Emmet Hughes, *The Ordeal of Power* (London: Macmillan, 1963).

Alex Roberto Hybel (foreword by James Rosenau), *Power Over Rationality: The Bush Administration and the Gulf Crisis* (Albany: State University of New York Press, 1993).

Irving Janis, *Victims of Groupthink* (Boston: Houghton Mifflin, 1972).

Charles O. Jones, *The Presidency In A Separated System* (Washington DC: The Brookings Institution, 1994).

Barbara Kellerman, *The Political Presidency: Practice of Leadership From Kennedy Through Reagan* (New York: Oxford University Press, 1984).

Samuel Kernell, *Going Public: Strategies of Presidential Leadership*, (Washington DC: Congressional Quarterly Press, 1986).

Pierre Kim, 'From Carter to Reagan to Bush', *Policy Review*, No. 63, Winter 1993, pp. 18–19.

Anthony King, 'A Mile and a Half Is a Long Way', in Anthony King, *Both Ends of the Avenue: The Presidency, the Executive Branch and Congress in the 1980s* (Washington DC: American Enterprise Institute, 1983).

Charles Kolb, *White House Daze: The Unmaking of Domestic Policy in the Bush Years* (New York, The Free Press, 1994).

William Leuchtenburg, *In the Shadow of FDR* (Ithaca, NY: Cornell University Press, 1993).

Paul Light, *The President's Agenda* (Baltimore: Johns Hopkins University Press, 1982).

Seymour Martin Lipset, 'The Significance of the 1992 Election', *PS: Political Science and Politics*, March 1993, pp. 7–16.

Theodore Lowi, *The Personal Presidency* (Ithaca, NY: Cornell University Press, 1985).

David McKay, 'Presidential Strategy and the Veto Power: A Reappraisal', *Political Science Quarterly*, Vol. 104, no. 3, Fall 1989, pp. 447–461.

Christopher Madison, "No Sharp Elbows', *National Journal*, 26 May 1990, pp. 1277–1281.

Michael Mandelbaum, 'The Bush Foreign Policy', *Foreign Affairs*, Spring 1991, Vol. 70, pp. 5–22.

Thomas Mann and Norman Ornstein (eds), *The New Congress* (Washington DC: American Enterprise Institute, 1981).

Donald Matthews, *US Senators and their World* (New York: Vintage Books, 1960).

David Mayhew, *Divided We Govern: Party Control, Lawmaking and Investigations, 1946–1990* (New Haven, Conn.: Yale University Press, 1991).

Edwin Meese, *With Reagan: The Inside Story* (Washington DC: Regnery Gateway, 1992).

David Mervin, *Ronald Reagan and the American Presidency* (London and New York, Longman, 1990).

David Mervin, 'Ronald Reagan's Place in History', *Journal of American Studies*, Vol. 23, No. 2, August 1989, pp. 269–286.

David Mervin, 'The Bully Pulpit', *Presidential Studies Quarterly*, Vol. XXV, 1995, pp. 19–23.

Jefferson Morley, 'Bush and the Blacks: An Unknown Story', *New York Review of Books*, 16 January 1992, pp. 1–26.

John Mueller, *Policy and Opinion in the Gulf War* (Chicago: University of Chicago Press, 1994).

William Kerr Muir, *The Bully Pulpit: The Presidential Leadership of Ronald Reagan* (San Francisco: Institute for Contemporary Studies, 1992).

Kerry Mullins and Aaron Wildavsky, 'The Procedural Presidency of George Bush', *Political Science Quarterly*, Vol. 107, No. 1, 1992, pp. 31–62.

Joshua Muravchik, 'Why the Democrats Finally Won', *Commentary*, Vol. 95, January 1993, pp. 17–22.

Robert Murray and Tim Blessing, *Greatness in the White House: Rating the Presidents* (University Park, Penn.: The Pennsylvania State University Press, 1994).

Michael Nelson (ed.), *The Elections of 1992* (Washington DC: CQ Press, 1993).

John Newhouse, 'Profiles: The Tactician', *New Yorker*, 7 May 1990, pp. 50–82.

Richard Neustadt, *Presidential Power and the Modern Presidents* (New York: The Free Press, 1990).

Richard Nixon, *In the Arena* (New York: Pocket Books, 1990).

Peggy Noonan, *What I Saw at the Revolution: A Political Life in the Reagan Era* (New York: Ivy Books, 1990).

Michael Oakeshott, *Rationalism in Politics* (London: Methuen, 1962).

Don Oberdorfer, *The Turn: From the Cold War to a New Era* (New York: Simon & Schuster, 1992).

David O'Brien, 'The Reagan Judges: His Most Ensuring Legacy', in Charles O. Jones, *The Reagan Legacy* (Chatham, NJ: Chatham House, 1988).

Bradley Patterson, *The Ring of Power: The White House Staff and its Expanding Role in Government* (New York: Basic Books, 1988).

Stephen Percy, *Disability, Civil Rights and Public Policy* (Tuscaloosa: University of Alabama Press, 1992).

James Pfiffner, 'Establishing the Bush Presidency', *Public Administration Review*, January/February 1990, pp. 64–72.

James Pfiffner, *The Managerial Presidency* (Pacific Grove, Calif. Brooks/Cole, 1991).

James Pfiffner, 'The President and the Postreform Congress', in Roger Davidson (ed.), *The Postreform Congress* (New York: St. Martin's Press, 1992).

James Pfiffner 'The President's Chief of Staff: Lessons Learned', *Presidential Studies Quarterly*, Vol. XXIII, No. 1, 1993, pp. 77–102.

James Pfiffner, 'Presidential Policy-Making and the Gulf War', in Marcia Lynn Whicker, James Pfiffner and Raymond Moore, *The Presidency and the Persian Gulf War* (Westport, Conn.: Praeger, 1993).

James Pfiffner, *The Modern Presidency* (New York: St. Martin's Press, 1994).

James Pfiffner and Gordon Hoxie (eds), *The Presidency in Transition* (New York: Center for the Study of the Presidency, 1989).

Joseph Pika, 'A New Vice Presidency' in Michael Nelson (ed.), *The Presidency and the Political System*, 2nd edn (Washington DC: The Congressional Quarterly Press, 1988).

John Podhoretz, *Hell of a Ride: Backstage at the White House Follies 1989–1993* (New York: Simon & Schuster, 1993).

The Points of Light Movement: The President's Report to the Nation, January 1993, in the author's possession.

'Politics of the Professoriate', *The American Enterprise*, Vol. 2, No. 5, July/August 1991, pp. 86–87.

Roger Porter, *Presidential Decision Making: The Economic Policy Board* (New York: Cambridge University Press, 1980).

Dan Quayle, *Standing Firm* (New York: Harper Collins, 1994).

Jeremy Rabkin, 'At the President's Side: The Role of the White House Counsel in Constitutional Policy', *Law and Contemporary Problems*, Vol. 56, No. 4, Autumn 1993, pp. 63–98.

Lyn Ragsdale, *Presidential Politics* (Boston: Houghton Mifflin, 1993).

Jonathan Rauch, 'The Regulatory President', *National Journal*, 30 November 1991, pp. 2902–2906.

Bert Rockman, *The Leadership Question: The Presidency and the American System* (New York: Praeger, 1984).

Bert Rockman, 'The Leadership Style of George Bush', in Colin Campbell and Bert Rockman, *The Bush Presidency: First Appraisals* (Chatham, NJ: Chatham House, 1991).

Walter Roettger and Hugh Winebrenner, 'Politics and Political Scientists', *Public Opinion*, September/October 1986, pp. 41–44.

Richard Rose, *The Postmodern President,* 2nd edn (Chatman, NJ: Chatham House, 1991).

Richard Rose, 'Evaluating Presidents', in George Edwards, John Kessel and Bert Rockman (eds), *Researching the Presidency* (Pittsburgh: University of Pittsburgh Press, 1993).

Clinton Rossiter (ed.), *The Federalist Papers* (New York: New American Library, 1961).

David Roth, *Sacred Honor: Colin Powell* (New York: Harper Collins, 1993).

Arthur Schlesinger Jnr, *The Cycles of American History* (London: André Deutsch, 1986).

Gail Sheehy, *Character: American's Search for Leadership*, revised edition (New York: Bantam Books, 1990).

Robert Shogan, *The Riddle of Power: Presidential Leadership From Truman to Bush* (New York: Dutton, 1991).

Steven Shull, *A Kinder Gentler Racism? The Reagan-Bush Civil Rights Legacy*, (New York: M.E. Sharpe, 1993).

Barbara Sinclair, 'Governing Unheroically (and Sometimes Unappetizingly): Bush and the 101st Congress', in Colin Campbell and Bert Rockman (eds), *The Bush Presidency: First Appraisals* (Chatham, NJ: Chatham House, 1991).

Hedrick Smith, *The Power Game* (New York: Random House, 1988).

Burt Solomon, 'Bush's Lack of Ambitious Policies . . . Make His Plans Seem Thin Gruel', *National Journal*, 6 May 1989, No. 18. p. 1102.

Burt Solomon, 'George Bush's Congressional Crew Has an Oar or Two Out of Sync', *National Journal*, 24 June 1989, pp. 1650–1651.

Burt Solomon, 'When the Cabinet Convenes . . . It's Gathering of Presidential Pals', *National Journal*, 1 July 1989, No. 26, pp. 1704–1705.

Theodore Sorensen, *Decision-Making in the White House* (New York: Columbia University Press, 1963).

Robert Spitzer, *The Presidential Veto: Touchstone of the American Presidency* (Albany: State University of New York Press, 1988).

Robert Spitzer, 'Presidential Prerogative Power: The Case of the Bush Administration and Legislative Power', *PS: Political Science and Politics*, March 1991, pp. 38–42.

Rochelle Stanfield, 'Cutting Deals', *National Journal*, 8 April 1989, p. 889.

David Stockman, *The Triumph of Politics: Why the Reagan Revolution Failed* (New York: Harper & Row, 1986).

Kristin Clark Taylor, *The First to Speak* (New York: Doubleday, 1993).

Margaret Thatcher, *The Downing Street Years* (London: HarperCollins, 1993).

Kenneth Thompson, *Presidential Transitions: The Reagan to Bush Experience* (Lanham, Md.: University Press of America, 1994).

Charles Tiefer, *The Semi-sovereign Presidency: The Bush Administration's Strategy For Governing Without Congress* (Boulder, Colo.: Westview Press, 1994).

Tower Commission Report (New York: Bantam Books, 1987).

The Washington Version. Television documentary on the Gulf crisis made by the American Enterprise Institute and the BBC, 1991.

Richard Watson, *Presidential Vetoes and Public Policy* (Lawrence: University of Kansas Press, 1993).

Matthew P. Weinstock, 'Running On His Record', *Occupational Hazards*, October 1992, Vol. 54, pp. 75–79.

Marcia Lynn Whicker, James Pfiffner and Raymond Moore, *The Presidency and the Persian Gulf War* (Westport, Conn.: Praeger, 1993).

Jules Witcover, *Crapshoot: Rolling the Dice on the Vice Presidency* (New York: Crown, 1992).

Bob Woodward, *The Commanders* (New York: Simon & Schuster, 1991).

Index

bumped

MEGAN McCAFFERTY

CORGI BOOKS

BUMPED
A CORGI BOOK 978 0 552 56539 4

First published in Great Britain by Corgi,
an imprint of Random House Children's Books
A Random House Group Company

This edition published 2011

1 3 5 7 9 10 8 6 4 2

The Random House Group Limited supports The Forest Stewardship Council®
(FSC®), the leading international forest certification organisation. All our titles that
are printed on Greenpeace approved FSC® certified paper carry the FSC® logo. Our
paper procurement policy can be found at www.randomhouse.co.uk/environment.

MIX
Paper from
responsible sources
FSC® C016897

Set in Bembo

Corgi Books are published by Random House Children's Books,
61–63 Uxbridge Road, London W5 5SA

www.**kidsatrandomhouse**.co.uk
www.**randomhouse**.co.uk
www.**totallyrandombooks**.co.uk

Addresses for companies within The Random House Group Limited can be found at:
www.**randomhouse.co.uk/offices**.htm

THE RANDOM HOUSE GROUP Limited Reg. No. 954009

A CIP catalogue record for this book is available from the British Library.

Printed and bound in Great Britain by CPI Bookmarque, Croydon, CRO 4TD

For Caitlyn, Carly, Cailey, and Zoë
– when you're old enough.

FIRST

The United States of America once ranked above all industrialized nations in the realm of teen pregnancy. We were the undisputed queens of precocious procreation! We were number one before, and we can be number one again!
     —President's State of the Union Address

melody
harmony

I'M SIXTEEN. PREGNANT. AND THE MOST IMPORTANT PERSON
on the planet.

According to the Babiez R U ad, anyway.

"You're knocked up," sings the girlie chorus. *"Ready to
pop. Due to drop."* The sixty-second jingle loops continu-
ously in the dressing room.

I check the MiNet to make sure no one I know is
shopping in this wing of the Meadowlands Mallplex. Most
of my friends are still in bed sleeping off last night's Tocin
hangovers. I'm safe.

"Do the deed. Born to breed."

Free from neggy eyes, I could act just like the fat and
happy models in the commercials. I could shout, I could
shimmy, I could show off every pound of my, um, *abundant*

awesomeness. Such gushing doesn't come as naturally to me as it does to other girls. I have to work harder at it, the way my friends struggle to solve calculus equations that are easy for me. Preparing to pregg is a full-time job with no days off—but I don't have a choice. Not when there's so much at stake.

Rubbing my spectacularly distended belly, I want to try out an expression just to hear how it sounds coming out of my mouth.

"I'm . . ."

Egging. Preggiiing . . .

"Fertilicious?"

My whole body sags under the weight of my sigh. I'm supposed to *own* my pregnancy because my *extra sixty is oh so sexy,* but I'd die of embarrassment if anyone I know caught me striking poses like this—especially Zen. So I guess it's a good thing that my best friend has made no effort to see me lately.

"Went forth and multiplied. Fightin' the omnicide . . ."

I check once more for anyone I know, then blind my MiNet with a blink-left-right-left-wink-double-blink. The song is wrapping up—*"You're the most important person on the plaaaanet. . . . Babiez R U!"*—when I'm startled out of my reverie by the sound of my own voice.

"Well!"

I jump.

I've been so focused on my own expectant spectacle, I forgot that I'm not alone in the dressing room. Standing directly behind me is Harmony. Until a few weeks ago, we had never spoken. And until a few hours ago, we had never met in person.

She's my identical twin.

harmony
melody

I LOVE THE MEADOWLANDS MALLPLEX!

It's fast and loud and bright and buzzing with temptation but that's why I love it. I love it because there's no better place for me to do the work I was born to do: to spread the Word. Everyone in Goodside is already on message, but here there's an endless supply of sinners going down the wrong path. It's dizzying trying to decide who to witness to first. Or rather, next. After Melody.

I'm here because I lost my best veil. It was so silly, really. I didn't tell Melody the whole story because I was afraid she'd laugh at me, or compare me to a happy puppy as Angel did after she calmed down when she saw that my stunt on the bridge hadn't done anyone any harm.

Angel is the driver I called to take me to Otherside. I

don't know if that's her name or not, but I like to think that it is. I had seen the billboard on Route 381 a few months ago, the last time it was my turn to leave Goodside to sell my fruit preserves at the Fayatte County Farmers' Market.

Angel Cab Company

1–800–GOD–TRIP

The LORD will watch over your coming and going.

Psalm 121

A pair of wings sprouted from the shoulders of the *A* in "Angel." It wasn't difficult to commit the ad to memory, though I'm not sure why I did. At the time, I didn't know about Melody and had nowhere else to go.

Angel isn't in the Church but she does have God, which is as blessed as you can get in Otherside. She pulled up promptly at four a.m. and was full of the spirit despite the short notice, early hour, and her advanced age. Her white hair was cropped like a newly shorn lamb's, her skin the warm brown of a biscuit ready to be taken out of the oven. With her crinkling eyes and ready smile, I trusted her immediately. Even more so when she asked, "Are you ready to let go and let God?"

I liked that. It reminded me that I wasn't leaving my faith behind, it's always here with me.

"I am!" I said, buckling myself into the backseat.

If paying someone to take me from Goodside to

Princeton sounds indulgent, you're right. But I don't know how to drive and have no access to mass transit maps and schedules and once I decided to leave I really didn't have any time to waste on figuring it all out. I made the right choice because Angel said it would've taken me sixteen hours and four transfers (bus, bus, train, train, shuttle bus) to travel three hundred miles. I might have made it past the Goodside gates, but probably not much farther than that before someone took notice of the Church girl traveling all by herself. Angel Cab traveled the same distance in just over three. I was halfway to Princeton before first light, and arrived on my sister's doorstep in time for a breakfast prayer! The one-way fare cost all the money I had in the world, but that's just one of many worries I'm choosing not to bother myself with right now.

I've taken missionary trips to other mallplexes with my prayerclique, but I've always had a chaperone and traveled on the Church bus. I suppose I could have asked Melody to MiBuy me a veil—it isn't *quite* as important to try them on as I led her to believe—but I want to make the most of my time with her. I want to go out and see the world beyond Goodside. I want to reach as many people as possible. If I serve well, this could be a life-changing experience for both of us.

It has to be.

When Melody suggested we browse at Babiez R U, I got nervous. I knew it wasn't a place of righteousness. Stores like this make a mockery out of Heaven's greatest gifts and my housesisters testify all the time about how bad company ruins good habits, which is why I'm so lucky to have them in my life. But I have complete faith in my faith. There's no reason to be afraid of anything I see here.

I pray that by joining Melody in this store, we will finally twinbond. It's been a month since our miraculous reunion and she has yet to call me sister. In fact, she has yet to say much to me at all, unless I ask her directly. Melody has been open about herself but uncurious about me, answering ten times the number of questions that she has asked, a tally that stands at three: "What are you doing here?"; "Why didn't you tell me you were coming?"; and "I don't think you'll need another veil while you're here but if it's that important to you then I guess we can go to the Mallplex, okay?"

Despite her reticence, just standing next to my sister is as exhilarating as cruising across the Benjamin Franklin Bridge, over the Delaware River, the cab taking me out of one state and into the next just as the sun crowned the horizon. . . .

That's how I lost my best veil.

I longed to merge with this glorious landscape! I longed to unite with the majestic skyline! I longed to revel in His goodness at a hundred miles per hour. I lowered the window and stuck out my head, and shouted out.

"Hallllleeeeeelllluuuuuujaaaaaaaaaaaah!"

Angel screamed, swerved, screeched the breaks, and screamed some more. We were blessed that there aren't too many cars on the road at sunrise.

Once I was safe back inside the car, she prayed about my recklessness before saying she was surprised to see such behavior out of a Church girl like me.

"You don't need to return to His kingdom *right now*, do you, love?"

She was right. I didn't need to meet my Maker today. Especially after I'd gone through so much trouble to get here.

I'll never forget the sight of my veil in the split seconds after it freed itself from my tangled hair, soaring, up, up, upward, closer to Heaven, a dazzling flash of white against the pink and blue sky.

melody
harmony

I CAN'T GET A CLEAR LOOK AT HARMONY'S FACE. IT'S THAT veil.

I tried to talk her out of wearing it in public but she's not having it. In her defense, I guess it makes sense because why would she wear her veil in *private*? Harmony managed to lose her "best" veil during the ride to my house—this one is her backup—and she begged me to take her to Plain & Simple ("Modest Clothing for Modest Youth") to shop for a replacement. The veil is the official excuse for why we hauled all the way out to the Meadowlands Mallplex; the unofficial excuse is that I couldn't handle another minute trapped in the house with her as she went into raptures (not to be confused with *the* Rapture, which is one of her favorite topics) over the miracle of me. Of *us*.

I detoured at Babiez R U because I thought she would be a good audience for rehearsing the enthusiasm I need to pull off if I have any chance of taking over as president of the Pro/Am Pregg Alliance when my other best friend, Shoko Weiss, goes on birthleave.

The vice president and would-be successor, Malia Arroyo, is on what they call an indefinite leave of absence.

Speaking as her friend, I miss her.

But as her peer birthcoach, that's all I'm legally permitted to say on the subject.

Ventura Vida is running against me. She's new, so I've got seniority, but she's flaunting a twenty-four-week bump that is just too perfect and adorable not to vote for. Her family put her in private school when the public districts starting making all preggers drop out of regular high school to attend a special school where they're all brainwashed into keeping their deliveries. Gah. It's not quite as bad as Harmony having to get *married*, but can you imagine? Ventura aspires to be the first Southeast Asian–American woman elected president of the United States and views tomorrow's vote as the first of many on the path to the White House. All of this should make her an interesting person that I would otherwise want to get to know if it weren't for the unfortunate circumstance of her being a total powertrippy bitch.

Harmony is almost a welcome distraction from what I have to look forward to at school tomorrow. Just thinking about all the drama gets my tubes in a twist.

Harmony takes a deep breath, the veil sucking up her nose, then murmurs something to herself—a go-to inspirational verse, probably—before making a go at talking.

"Well!" Harmony repeats brightly. "How many weeks is . . . ?" She points in the general direction of my belly.

"Forty. And twins."

"Twins! Like us!"

"It makes a bold statement," I say, rotating in front of the mirrors. "A twin having twins."

Harmony sucks in another lungful of air. "So true, sister!"

I cringe from the inside out whenever she says that word. I can't change the fact that Harmony is my identical twin, but I don't know if I'll ever call this stranger my sister. Special emphasis on the strange part. I know Churchies are expected to fill their conversion quotas and all, but it was still a shock when Harmony asked if I had God within ten seconds of me answering the door.

"Do I have Him, like, in my *pocket*?" I had laughed, still stunned by her unannounced arrival.

"No, sister," she had said without a trace of irony. "In your *heart*."

I had gotten used to MiChatting with her a few times a week. Though she had extended countless invitations for me to visit her in Goodside—a trip I just wasn't ready to make—she had made no mention of crossing into Otherside to see me.

So this was just too much. I mean, how do you think

you'd feel if you opened the door at seven o'clock in the morning to see your exact double standing on your front porch, dressed all in white, clutching a shiny Bible in one hand and a banged-up suitcase in the other? I'm lucky I didn't terminate right then and there. For serious.

It wasn't until she hugged me ("Sister!") that I realized I wasn't hallucinating from a secondhand dose of Tocin. It really was Harmony on my doorstep. I wouldn't have been so neggy if Harmony had *asked* to visit me. I don't know the protocol for long-lost twin reunions or anything but at the very least she could have warned me.

All things considered, I think I've been handling things pretty well. I've come a long way since our first MiChat, when I barely managed to ask, "Harmony *who*? I'm your *what*?" I immediately quikiwikied the birth certificates that proved it wasn't a phishy scam and she really was my identical twin named Harmony who had set out to find her bioparents but found me instead. It's not like I *never* wanted to meet her in person, I'm just not up for making major media right now, and being a monozygotic twin always attracts attention even when they're not nearly as reproaesthetical as I am. (I mean, *we* are.)

I'm not being braggy. It's fact. I'm everything I'm supposed to be—attractive and intelligent, athletic and artistic, social and so on—only better. Ash and Ty, my parents, can't take credit for my natural-born assets but they do deserve recognition for all the time, money, energy, and effort they put into perfecting them. Even their surname—Mayflower—boosts my brand. And yet, these pluses can only go so far. What a relief it was when the results of my YDNA test confirmed that I am indeed *the* dying breed of a dying breed, rare and highly valued in certain Eurosnobby circles.

Harmony too.

That's another reason I was so put off this morning. It was one thing to hear her (my!) voice, but it was an entirely different thing to experience Harmony face-to-face. I eyeballed her blond hair and blue eyes, full lips and wide eyes, pert nose and high cheekbones, and panicked.

She's counterfeiting me!

Then I took in her white veil and neck-to-ankle gown and unclenched. The Church is extreme even by *ordinary* God-having standards, so Harmony is off market. I wanted to make sure.

"So you're set up," I said, "like, to be a wife and mother."

Harmony looked down at her gloved hands before answering. "Yes."

"That's great news," I answered, because it was—for me.

I could be living a totally different life right now. Harmony and I could—and probably should—have been raised together. We don't have many details, but from what we do know, it's pretty clear our biomom was damaged goods by the time she dropped us off. The musical names she picked out for us are proof enough of her pharmaceutically addled mind. We were born addicted to whatever junk she was on, and came out such sickly, shrieky preemies that the counselors from Good Shepherd Child Placement Services thought we had a better chance of being snapped up as singletons than as a janky twosome. Harmony was in worse shape than I was, and was taken in by the Church several weeks after I was placed with Ash and Ty.

My parents are beyond intense, but Harmony's off-grid upbringing has made me so thankful that mine adopted me and hers adopted her. With its ancient ivy-covered buildings, Princeton may not be the moddest hub on the Northeast Corridor but at least it just opened up an Underground All-Sports Arena and an Avatarcade. Harmony has spent her whole life in Goodside, Pennsylvania. She shares 6,500 square feet with three other families in one of the Starter Castles for Christ, those half-built McMansions in the never-finished gated enclaves bought dirt cheap by the Church in the late '00s. Harmony claims it's the largest settlement of its kind, which really isn't saying much when there's only a dozen or so in existence. The Church refers to the world beyond the Goodside gates as Otherside because it's subtle like that.

One thing I appreciate about Harmony is that I don't have to worry about encryption. Her immediate intentions are totally clear: She's here to make me get religion. And not just any religion, of course, but hers. If I'm married along with the rest of her housesisters by the end of the month, I think she scores some major bonus angel points toward a heavenly set of wings or a halo or something. Despite her invitations, I know I'm not welcome in Goodside and it's not because they fear HPSV. The Church is far more threatened by the possibility that I'll infect their minds with sin. I could flash my lab results proving that the damage has already been done to my reproductive system and there's no chance of catching the Virus from me, but they wouldn't even care. I was shocked when Harmony told me that they don't even *test* for the Virus in Goodside, because, as she explained, there is only one who can open and close the womb, and He flicks the switch from His heavenly throne. It's no mere coincidence then, as she also explained, that there are more women pregging in their twenties and thirties on her side of the gates than on mine.

Well. How can you argue against that?

harmony
melody

MELODY AND I CAME INTO THIS LIFE TOGETHER AND I'LL DO
whatever it takes to see her in the next one. But, my grace,
she's not making it easy.

I was surprised that she didn't even consider searching
for her (our!) birthparents as soon as she came of age. That
was my first order of business when I turned sixteen. She
claims that she never sought the truth about our birthparents because it could bring more bad news than good.

"You weren't the least bit curious about who brought
us into this world?"

"I've got the YDNA test results, and that's all I need
to know," she replied. "Ash and Ty made me the person I
am today."

I didn't understand this reaction at all. I've *always* felt the need to know the truth about my birthparents. I thought knowing them would help me better understand myself. Please don't think I'm disrespecting the Smith family by saying this. I don't remember when I was told that I was adopted, I can only say that I don't remember a time when I *didn't* know I was adopted. The Church has a long tradition of taking in the neediest infants—as it still does—and I was one of them. My parents were the angels entrusted with my care and protection and I'm forever grateful He chose them for me.

Always worried about my health, Ma never let me roughhouse and always lured me toward more meditative pursuits like baking and crafting. These skills, she knew, would serve me well when I turned thirteen and was picked for marriage in my Blooming. She taught me everything I know about what it means to be a good wife and mother, nourishing me with all the fruits of the spirit: joy, peace, kindness, faithfulness, and gentleness. What's happened to me since then isn't her fault. She did the best she could.

I wish more than anything I could tell her that right now.

Despite Ma's efforts, I've never felt . . . complete. I prayed and prayed and prayed. I asked why my birthparents had surrendered me and I got frustrated with Him for not answering. Until I knew, I would always feel like something—or someone—was missing no matter how hard or long or often I called on Him for help. Finally, after a difficult and dark period in my early Blooming, Ma took me aside and told me something I'll never forget.

"Prayers are answered in one of four ways," she said. *"Yes. No. I have something else in mind. And . . ."*

She paused long enough for my impatience to show. "And what's the fourth answer?"

"Wait," she said.

I realized that maybe I wasn't ready for the answers God had in store for me.

And so I patiently waited until my sixteenth birthday when it was legal for me to unseal my birth documents.

HARMONY DOE
Placement: SMITH
Born: 05-02-2020 (approximate)
Birth Father: UNKNOWN
Birth Mother: UNKNOWN
Relations: MELODY DOE [See: MAYFLOWER]
Notes: Infant twin females born at approximately 32 weeks; required NICU intervention for detoxification and other development issues associated with preterm delivery; anonymously given up to Princeton Medical Center professionals in compliance with the New Jersey Safe Haven Act with handwritten note reading: "Forgive me, Harmony and Melody"; placed into permanent custody by the Good Shepherd Family Placement Services.

I had a twin.

A twin.

The Heavens opened for me at that moment. A twin! What a revelation! I made a choice right then and there not to mourn for the unknown parents I had lost, but to celebrate the sister I had found. My whole life I thought I was praying for my birthparents. Suddenly I knew who I was really praying for: my twin. My sister. My other half. Though I didn't know my sister named Melody, I loved her already. Ma and Pa were never told about Melody and were even more stunned to find out about her than I was. Ma saw an opportunity to spread the Word.

"This is your purpose in life," Ma said. "Putting your sister on the right path for the next one."

I'm taking Ma's advice. Can I redeem myself if I bring Melody to Otherside to receive the sacraments? Despite her protests, I see the truth: Melody isn't sure of her decision to go pro. I know it. And if she spends more time in my company, perhaps she'll want to follow me in faith. And she, in turn, just might give me strength to be the wife and mother I've so far failed to be.

"Am I fertilicious?" she asks. "Or what?"

I love my sister unconditionally—even if she makes it difficult to like her. Watching her as she unabashedly admires herself in the mirror, I realize that I have a long, hard road ahead of me. If only my relationship with Melody was as effortless as my relationship with God. Talking to God isn't a chore. I can let my true self shine in front of God.

melody

harmony

"DO YOU KNOW WHO ELSE MAKES A BOLD STATEMENT?"
Harmony asks.

"God?" I try.

"Inspired answer, sis—!" Harmony stops herself short.
"Melody!"

It's Harmony's mission in life to put the "fun" back in
fundamentalism. She's never happier than when she's bragging on God. I'm about to tell her that she might want to
dose down a bit when the Babiez R U salesclerk ducks her
head through the pink-and-blue gingham curtains. Name
tag: TRYNN.

"You're glowing!" Trynn gushes.

I caress my stretchy belly with pride.

"God-mocking," chimes Harmony with cheery confidence.

Trynn is a skilled saleswoman and won't be put off by Churchy negs on her trade. She puts two hands on my tumescent tummy. "Can you feel the kicking?"

I can.

"And you'll note the tiny, tasteful stretch marks," she continues, lifting my brand-new expandable-contractable MyTurnTee.

Trynn looks to Harmony. "Are you interested in trying something on?"

Harmony primly pats her shoulder-length veil. "It's against my religion."

"Really? I wouldn't have guessed," Trynn says, stifling a snicker.

The clerk takes a step back to eye Harmony's ivory veil, which matches the crisp cotton cap-sleeved ball gown with a sweetheart neckline and brush-the-floor train. She'll wear a similar, if slightly fancier, gown on her wedding day, after which she'll wear green gowns symbolizing fertility, followed by pink or blue gowns—depending on the sex of her first child—to announce the fulfillment of her "feminine promise," as she put it.

Only engaged girls wear veils, which is supposed to deflect unwanted male attention. That might work in Goodside, but here it has the opposite effect. She gets more attention all covered up than I would if I went around flashing my breedy bits all day long.

"Oh, yes," says Harmony from behind the tulle scrim. "I'm just visiting. . . ." She tugs on the elbow-length glove covering her left hand.

"Is there a ring under there?"

Harmony stiffens for a moment then says, "Of course I'm wearing a ring!"

"Can we see it?" Trynn and I ask simultaneously.

"No," Harmony says curtly. It's a voice I haven't heard before. "Showing off is the sin of pride. . . ." Her voice trails off.

"What's his name?" I ask, realizing just now that in our MiChats Harmony gushed on and on about God, but didn't say one word about her fiancé.

"Ephraim," Harmony says

"Ephraim?" Trynn asks. "That's an unusual name."

"Not where I'm from. There are four Ephraims in our settlement. It means 'doubly fruitful.'"

"Like you!" Trynn points at my belly.

"Everyone calls him Ram."

"Ram, huh?" Trynn licks her lips. "That's a breedy name if I've ever heard one!"

I'm not sure if Trynn is mocking Harmony or not. The trubie gear makes her an easy target for anyone but especially for bitter obsolescents. Just when I'm starting to feel sorry for the salesclerk's squandered reproductivity, Trynn says something totally barren to Harmony.

"That engagement gown is so *pure*," she says gently.

22

"But aren't you, like, too *mature* to wear white? Shouldn't you be in the pink or blue by now?"

Harmony yelps from behind her veil. I can't see, but I imagine the blood draining from her face, until her pallid complexion matches her colorless dress. There's no way Trynn knew about the color-coded gowns without looking it up on the quikiwiki. She did it just to be neggy.

My face glows red with anger, which is weird because I barely know Harmony. I mean, we don't have anything in common, you know, besides our genetic material. I agreed to let her stay with me for a few days because Ash and Ty swear up and down that my heart-stopping story about long-lost twinbonding will help get me into Global U., a university so notoriously selective it makes Princeton look like a safety school. That's the only reason I didn't send her straight back to the farm this morning.

I know it's a scandal to say something like that, with multis like us being so prized and all. But the more Harmony talks, the more it becomes clear that the Church isn't giving much of a choice in the matter of marriage and motherhood. Zen says that she's trapped by her own false consciousness, which, by the way, is the nerdish kind of comment that could get a guy's ass kicked at our school—if that ass was anyone's but Zen's.

He's the only one who knows I've been in contact with Harmony. For as much as he loves to talk, he is surprisingly tight-lipped when he needs to be. As such, he's the keeper of many of Princeton Day Academy's deepest secrets. Of course, that doesn't stop him from privately warning me that coming into identical twinhood at sixteen will for seriously damage my fragile psyche or whatever. But it hasn't. *Harmony's* the one who stalked our bioparents. She's the one having the identity crisis, not me. These days the majority of deliveries in this country aren't raised by their bioparents, and they should all follow my example by having the same attitude.

Don't fit me for a veil or anything because I can be sympathetic to Harmony and still have issues with her way of life. But before I have a chance to put the salesclerk in her place, Harmony breaks the awkward silence.

"I was engaged at thirteen years old."

What?! She never said a word about her starter engagement! At thirteen I wasn't even close to making my own commitment, no matter how much parental pressure I was under. Which was a *lot*.

"But God had another plan!" Harmony adds a bit too eagerly. "I keep telling my sis—" She stops herself. "I keep telling *Melody* that it's not too late for her to get a husband. There are plenty of eligible bachelors in Goodside."

I snort-laugh. Harmony is just too funny. Sometimes I wonder if Church leaders are slipping Tocin or some other prescription-strength love drug into the sacramental wine.

Trynn turns to me. "I assume *you're* here for nostalgia's sake," she says, still hoping to make the sale. "Let me guess. You're in between bumps and want to relive the best nine months of your life?"

I reluctantly flash back to Malia.

"The worst nine months of my life!" she howled. *"For what?"*

I hate thinking of her in that state.

I open my mouth but nothing comes out.

Harmony mutters another prayer and hooks an arm around my shoulder. And as much as I know that she's doing this just to prove that she's the kindhearted twin, I'm comforted by the gesture.

"My extra thirty is oh so flirty!" chirp voices outside the dressing room.

A tweenage trio comes swaggering into the dressing room. The tweens accessorize their sparkly Ts with matching First Curse Purses, the menarche must-have for stashing the pads and tampons they'll need *any minute now*. The target demo for Babiez R U, they steal Trynn's attention.

"I see you're considering the Preggerz FunBump with real skinfeel and in-uterobic activity!" she says to the one with red hair holding up the fake belly she's ready to try on. The front of the redhead's T reads: DO THE DEED. As she hops around in excited circles, I catch the phrase on the back: BORN TO BREED.

Indeed.

"She's wearing size Forty-Week Twins," Trynn continues, pointing to my distended stomach. "That's way too big for you! Size Twenty-four-Week Singleton is perfect for a girl your age. . . ."

I think of Ventura Vida's adorable six-month bump and a wave of nausea rolls right over me. Harmony can't pass up another opportunity to get preachy.

"When I was your age," she offers, "I was leading my own prayerclique!"

The twelve-year-olds giggle nastily.

That's it. I terminate. I skulk behind the curtains, strip off the Preggerz FunBump, and hang it on the wall hook. I had come here today hoping that the experience would help me feel breedier than I did before Malia's meltdown, but all I've done is remind myself just how far behind I am. Unburdening myself of the fake belly does little to improve my state of mind. The MyTurnTee shrinks to fit my taut abdominals and my mood shrivels with it.

Harmony peeks behind the curtain. "Can we please head over to Plain & Simple now?"

"Sure thing." And before I can stop myself: "Maybe there's a sale on tasteful straitjackets."

It was a for seriously pissy thing to say. I don't know why I'm taking out my frustration on her.

Harmony clasps her hands and quietly sighs behind the veil. "Oh my grace."

She lifts her veil so I can see her face. It takes my breath away whenever she does this. It's surprisingly easy to forget that there's another person on the planet who was born looking *exactly* like me, only frecklier. Harmony gestures for me to lean in closely to hear what she has to say.

"Pursue faith and love and peace," she says in a quiet

26

but confident voice. "Enjoy the companionship of those who call on the Lord with pure hearts."

Harmony lets the veil fall back over her face, pulls the curtains together, and leaves me alone to consider her biblical wisdom.

The FunBump squirms against the back of the dressing-room wall, and one of the twins' elbows or maybe a knee pokes out of the bogus belly. What felt like an organic extension of my own body just moments ago now makes me more squeamish than my worst case of Sympathetic Morning Sickness. I stab my finger deep into the belly on/off button more aggressively than necessary and the Fun-Bump goes limp.

"You're knocked up," sing the little girls along with the incessant Babiez R U theme song. *"Ready to pop, due to drop."*

It's hard not to get jealous of these nubie-pubies who—if they're pretty enough, smart enough, and healthy enough—should already be getting wooed by RePro Representatives. Those were the *best* times, when I was still all promise and potential. Because right now I'm definitely *not* the most important sixteen-year-old on the planet. Not even ish. I'm just another prebumped girl dangerously close to wasting her prime reproductivity.

Since the nubie-pubies caught me by surprise, I check my MiNet. I'm not expecting to spot anyone I know when—gah!—I get a positive MiD.

harmony
melody

I'M BEING PATIENT, KEEPING AN OPEN HEART, FORGIVING Melody for her participation in the buying and selling of blasphemous synthetic blessings when she comes running out of the dressing room blind-wild as a beheaded chicken.

"I can be anywhere but here!" she cries in a mad dash for the door.

Praise the Lord. Could it be I'm already having a positive influence on her?

"Wait for me!" I'm struggling to keep up with her, briefly regretting my decision to wear this particular gown. It's difficult to walk, let alone run. Such are the challenges when one is expected to serve as a powerful example of faith and female purity.

"Melody!"

I'm starting to think that I will never catch up when I hear a tenor voice behind me calling the same name.

"Melody!"

A whiplike figure streaks past me, quickly overtakes my sister, and stops right in her path. She screeches to a halt in front of an archway of red, white, and blue balloons. It's clear even at a distance that this boy with big hair and even bigger grin has done what I couldn't: made her burn with embarrassment.

I catch up to them at the patriotic display at the entrance to the U.S. Buff-A.

"The Meadowlands Mallplex has five million square feet of commercial enterprise and destination entertainment," the boy says, waving his arms at the stores all around us. "What are the odds of me *randomly* stumbling into your facespace?"

"None." She's pressing her lips together to stop herself from catching the boy's contagious grin. I'm smiling at him and I don't even *know* him. "I haven't seen you for, like, *ever*, and now all of a sudden you get stalky on me? How did you even find me here anyway? I blinded my MiNet."

The boy's smile gets bigger. And so does mine.

"Your MiNet blind is an insult to hackers everywhere."

"You hacked my MiNet?" She sounds more amazed than annoyed. "Again?"

The boy and Melody are exactly the same height, though the tips of his hair—dark and spiky like sprigs of blackrot rosemary—give him an extra few inches. He only has to take a step toward her to look her straight in the eyes.

"Blink-left-right-left-wink-double-blink," as his eyes follow those same commands. Melody gasps, squeezes her eyes tight, and sighs in resignation. He, having made the desired impact, takes a step back and thumbs in my direction. "Is that *her*?"

"No," Melody says drily. "That's the third sister, Symphony. And there are two more at home who look just like her named Rhythm and Tempo."

"When did she get here?" he asks. "Why didn't you tell me she was coming?"

"I didn't tell you because I didn't know she was on her way. And also because you've been too busy to reply to any of my messages."

"Oh."

"Yeah."

"Sorry."

The boy looks at me, then back at Melody.

"You must be blinked."

"You think?"

I am waiting patiently to share my own feelings about seeing my twin for the first time, but no one is asking.

"How long will she be in town?" He asks this as if I've got limited seating, like when Brother Moses' Traveling Ministry finally came to Goodside.

"We're still . . . um . . ." She coughs and casts me a sidelong glance. "Working out the details."

I've told Melody I'm willing to stay with her until she's ready to return to Goodside with me. She was so overwhelmed by emotion that she choked on her reply.

"Welcome to Otherside!" The boy sweeps his arms through the air. "I'm Zen Chen-Chavez." He extends his hand.

I tug on my gloves, fixing my fingers inside the satin. "I'm . . . Harmony."

"You hesitated," Zen says, wiggling the fingers on his still-extended hand. "Is it against the rules to touch me?"

Zen is certainly observant. I admit that I am a bit leery of making physical contact with a free male because such touching *is* against Church Orders. But I'm not in Goodside, am I? And it's not like I'm touching skin to skin!

I answer Zen by taking his hand in mine and giving it a firm shake.

"Tell me," he says, giving me his full attention now. "How do you feel about all the premarital sex and sin?"

I'm supposed to think he's showing off for my benefit, but I can tell that it's really for Melody. And yet I can't find a way of answering his question.

"I don't know," I finally say.

"You could have learned a lot from watching the Cheerclones and the Ballers in action last night," he says.

"Ugh. MasSEXtinction parties are nasty," Melody says, scrunching her nose. "Those amateurs are so desperate."

Zen clucks his tongue. "How can you be the next Pro/Am president if you neg any girl who doesn't have a contract? You have to promote positive pregging in *all* forms."

"Yeah, yeah, I know," Melody says dismissively. "I still can't believe you went last night."

"*Someone* had to be the designated driver," he says. "I was the only one who didn't get dosed."

"So," Melody says, avoiding Zen's gaze. "Does that mean you were the only one on the sidelines during the group grope?"

If Zen notices the strain in her voice, he doesn't let on.

"You of all people know I hold myself up to the highest standards," he says. "Unfortunately, this means I'll never bump with any girl who is desperate enough to bump with me."

This makes my sister laugh-snort-laugh, which makes me laugh-snort-laugh because—PTL!—we share the same laughy-snorty laugh!

Both Zen and Mel turn to me with surprised expressions, as if they'd forgotten I was standing right beside them.

"How do you feel about wearing that gown?" Zen asks. "Can you take off your veil?"

I remember being faced with such unenlightenment in my previous trips to Otherside with my prayerclique. For a group who clings so desperately to facts, seculars like Zen and Mel understand so very little about the Church. I cherish this chance to witness because there are so few opportunities to do so in a settlement where everybody—well, *almost* everybody—is already saved. It's vital for me to approach this in the right way so I don't scare him off.

"Oh my grace, those are inspired questions," I reply, mindful of my tone. "Before I answer, may I ask you a question first?"

"Sure," Zen says. "I love questions."

"Do you have God?"

He answers with uncommon directness. "I don't."

I had anticipated that response, but all witnessing must begin with the basics.

"Now that I've answered your question," Zen says, "I hope you'll answer mine."

"Well," I say, smoothing over the wrinkles in my dress, "I'm proud to serve as a powerful example of faith and female purity." I wince, worried about sounding vain. "And, yes, I'm allowed to take off my veil whenever I want."

"Why don't you take it off right now?" Zen asks.

"Because I don't want to."

I really don't. I have full control over my words but my positive messaging is often undone by negative facial expressions. This has become more clear to me since joining Melody's company. I see her pursed lips, flared nostrils, or arched eyebrows on our shared face, revealing her true feelings as they would certainly reveal mine. Meeting Melody has convinced me that wearing the veil was the right thing.

"I don't blame you for not taking it off. Some people say

the lower rates of HPSV in your community are because you get extra protection from the veils and gloves," he says, looking down at his hands. "Maybe we'd all be fertile into our twenties and thirties if we wore them."

"Or maybe it's all the *prayer* that keeps the Virus at bay," Melody offers sarcastically.

That's exactly what the Church Council claims.

"It's just a shame you won't take it off," Zen says to me with a shrug. "It would have been such a pleasure to be seen with *two* reproaesthetical girls."

"Careful, Zen, you're talking to a soon-to-be-married woman here." Melody is trying to sound lighthearted, but, as always, her face gives her away.

"I guess I'll just have to settle for half the pleasure," Zen says, ignoring her warning.

"For serious, Zen. Harmony's fiancé is named Ram."

Zen stares in disbelief. "Ram?"

"Ram. And he's a genuine agriculty." Melody's voice is turning now too. "He could ride up on his horse and kick your sorry butt all the way down the turnpike."

I let out a little yelp at the visual of Ram kicking *any-one's* you-know-what.

"Is that true?" Zen asks. "That Ram will kick my sorry butt to defend your honor?"

"No," I say simply, biting my lip to stop myself from giggling.

Ram is almost a foot taller than Zen and quite fit from farming, but he would never act in such a way. If

Ram were here right now, it would be customary for him to thank Zen for his approving appraisal of my physical appearance, then gently point out that it is inappropriate for any man to pay such compliments to another man's woman. But it's unlikely Ram would say this or much of anything else because it's against his nature to be confrontational. "Blessed are the peacemakers," says Ma about Ram. "For they shall be called sons of God."

"This has been fun," Zen says, his face suddenly straight and serious. "But I actually do have a reason for stalking you today. And it's kind of ironic too, considering what we were just talking about. . . ."

Melody squints. "Okay." She sounds skeptical.

Zen takes a piece of paper out of his back pocket, unfolds it, and holds it up for her inspection.

"Does *this* mean anything to you?"

Melody startles at the sight of it.

It clearly holds some significance for her.

And whatever it is, it's not good.

melody
harmony

FOUR YEARS AGO TODAY, MANDATORY BLOOD TESTS
confirmed that 75 percent of sixth through eighth graders
at Princeton Day Academy Junior School had been infected
with the Virus. Most parents hoped it was the unfunniest
prank ever. Mine anticipated the spread of the Virus all
along and had planned accordingly. Even though I'd heard
Ash and Ty talk about Human Progressive Sterility Virus
millions of times before, I never really understood what
the words meant.

Zen knew. He had done his research. Even then he
liked to be informed, even if such knowledge was the stuff
of nightmares.

He made me watch a video that explained what
had happened to us, or, more accurately, what *wouldn't*

happen: that we were among the roughly three-quarters of the planet who wouldn't be able to conceive or carry a full-term delivery in adulthood. Most of us would go irreversibly infertile sometime between our eighteenth and twentieth birthdays, and petri-pregging wouldn't be a viable option for us at any age. The video was called *The End of the World as We Know It* and it succeeded in making me so paranoid about what would happen to our depopulated nation—with a special emphasis on the inevitable takeover by the awesomely abundant Chinese—that I signed this letter of promise:

> *Zen Chen-Chavez and Melody Mayflower promise that if both of us have NOT made a delivery within the next four years, we will bump with each other. This agreement is voided if one of us (Zen!!!) says ANYTHING about it to ANYONE!!!*

To understand why I would sign such a document, you have to understand Zen.

See, Zen has always prided himself on being able to analyze and argue all sides of any issue. It's what makes him one of the top high school debaters in the state. I'm his best friend, so I know he doesn't believe half of what comes out of his mouth or across his MiNet profile. But he's so effortlessly persuasive that even I'm not always sure what half he believes and what half is bullshit. He knows what to say, when to say it, how to say it, and to whom.

These skills have served him well at Princeton Day Academy: Everyone loves him.

I think we became best friends because I was one of the very few kids who didn't do what he said.

"Why aren't you calling yourself Lem?" he asked on the day he made everyone refer to themselves by the backward spellings of their first names.

"Why should I call myself Lem just because you want me to," I replied. *"Nez."*

Zen loved that. He thought I was cool because I had a mind of my own. Only later, much later, did he discover the exact opposite was true and I wasn't a nonconformist by choice. No, Ash and Ty already had me on such an uncompromising regimen of self-improvement that there was simply no time in my life for Zen's ridiculous diversions.

Of course, my pact with Zen wasn't ridiculous. It was dead serious. And in my limited worldview at the time, it was the first time Zen's directives were totally worth following.

And yet, the letter was already a distant memory when I signed on with Lib at UGenXX Talent Agency a year later. Right away, I started getting major swag from the most affluential couples desperate for me to make a healthy delivery. At thirteen, I was boosting off the free merch and the surge in eyeballs on my MiNet profile but was in no way ready to settle down. By the time I was fourteen, my parents thought I was obsessed with famegaming and at risk of becoming terminally starcissistic if I didn't close a deal soon. Later that year I was matched with the Jaydens, who put in a very strong bid: full college tuition, a Volkswagen Plug, *and* a postpartum tummy trim. When Lib pushed—and got—a six-figure signing bonus, there was no question as to what I had to do.

It's hard to believe now, but this was a pretty radical decision at the time. Though popular in major cities on the coasts, going pro was still kind of a down-market thing to do in the suburbs, and at my school in particular. All preggers at Princeton Day Academy were amateurs, most of whom put deliveries up for nonprofit adoptions. I can count on one hand how many actually kept their deliveries, and those who did had them raised by the same nannies who had raised them.

Ash and Ty are—or *were*—Wall Streeters turned economics professors at the University who were way ahead of reproductive trends. They predicted sixteen years ago, almost before anyone else, that girls like me—prettier, smarter, healthier—would be the world's most valuable resource. And like any rare commodity in an unregulated marketplace, prices for our services would skyrocket. It wasn't about the money, really, not at first. It was about status. Who had it, and who didn't. And my parents did everything in their power to make sure I had it.

As for me, I figured, *Why not? I won't be using my uterus for anything else during those nine months!* So that's how I was the first girl in my class to go pro and sign on to be

a Surrogette. About a dozen girls at my school have followed my lead so far, with more trying to land contracts
every day. Now even amateurs who aren't quite upmarket
enough to go pro can make decent money at auction if
their deliveries earn high marks from Newborn Quality
Testing Service.

The point is, Ash and Ty knew that if anyone could
boost the image of commerical pregging in our community, it was me. It's what they groomed me for, after all.

And my life has been ectopic ever since.

Only Zen would try to legitimize a pact between two
twelve-year-old nubie-pubies who pretended to be more
familiar with the how-tos of pregging than we actually
were.

Only Zen would have any chance at succeeding.

harmony
melody

"WHAT IS IT?" I ASK.

"Nothing," Melody quickly replies, pinching the paper distastefully with her thumb and forefinger as she hands it back to Zen. He carefully smooths out the paper, refolds it along the original creases, and slides it into his back pocket before responding.

"I never pegged you for a renegger . . ."

The calmer Zen is, the more emotional my sister gets.

"I am NOT a renegger. You are beyond wanked if you think that piece of paper is binding. . . ."

I'm not following this at all.

Then, like the sun bursting through storm clouds, that grin.

"Dose down, Mel. I'm just scamming." Zen's cheeks

dimple even deeper. "I really came by just to say 'hey.'"

Melody eyes him warily. "So say it."

"Say what?"

Now it's Melody's turn to take a step forward, lean in, and get within a few inches of his face.

"Hey."

At first, Zen doesn't move. Then slowly, almost imperceptibly, he brings his face even closer to my sister's. I watch his lips part and I watch Melody's expression change to something expectant and—

Oh my grace! Stop watching!

I turn my head left. Newlywed Bliss Kits are on sale at Garden of Eden Sex Shop. . . .

Look away!

I turn my head right. The young trio from Babiez R U is immodestly strutting by us, flaunting their brand-new FunBumps. . . .

Close . . . your . . . eyes!

But I can't. I can't. I can't. *I can't stop watching.* I can't stop watching Melody and Zen as they hypnotically hover almost—*almost!*—mouth to mouth. . . .

"Hey," Zen whispers.

I'm startled by a sharp, high cry. Both by the sound and the fact that it came from me.

Melody and Zen lurch away from each other.

"YOU BLINKED FIRST!" they cry in unison.

Zen turns to me as if he wants me to vouch for him, but then his face darkens.

"Whoa. Are you feeling okay? You're breathing heavy. And your skin—what I can see of it—is all red and sweaty."

He's right. I'm feeling a little light-headed. "I'm f-f-f-fine," I stammer, fanning myself. "It gets hot under all these layers."

Melody is patting her hair, trying to look unconcerned. "Oh, it's nothing that a cold can of Coke '99 can't fix."

Zen seems genuinely worried. "You should really take off that veil. . . ."

"Enough about the mutherhumping veil," Melody says in a cold voice. *"She's not going to take it off."*

I don't want to take off my veil, but I can't catch my breath. I lift the netting from my face and flip it up and over my head so I can get some air. I shield my eyes until they adjust to the riot of light and color. I forget how much brighter the world looks without the veil. I avert my gaze from the Garden of Eden Sex Shop.

"Sweet Darwin's revenge," Zen says, eyes going wide at the sight of my bare face. "You're Melody!"

Oh my grace. If there's one thing I've already learned about my twin, it's that she does not like being seen as anything less than unique. I square my shoulders, ready for Melody to explode at Zen. Ma taught me to only raise my voice in praise, never in anger. Despite her musical name, my sister gives little thought to the sounds that come out of her mouth. She doesn't seem to understand that words can serve as a bomb *or* a balm and all too often Melody chooses to hurt instead of heal. This time she surprises me.

43

Her words come out not in a ferocious rush, but slowly, like ice.

"She . . . is . . . not . . . me."

I proceed very carefully. "She's right!" I say. "I have freckles!"

"You do?" Zen squints at my nose. "You do!"

Zen can't stop looking back and forth between us, comparing and contrasting and comparing and contrasting our faces. And he's not the only one. A small crowd has gathered around us, all winking, blinking, and rolling their eyeballs in our direction. I know that as I stand here contemplating my freckles, images of the identical-but-ideodemographically different twins are already streaming the MiNet. This must be what Melody means when she refers to a surge in optics—but I don't feel too good about it. It makes me squirmy, like a soilworm under observation in a terrarium. I pull my veil back over my face to put an end to it.

"I imagine this must be quite a change from your settlement," Zen says.

"Yes it is," I say. Then to provide an example of tolerance, I add, "I watched Melody try on FunBumps at Babiez R U."

Zen's enthusiasm wanes for the first time during this conversation. My sister takes in Zen's stricken face, and seems to find courage in it. She continues with a new gleam in her eye.

"I was, um . . ." She casts a quick glance in the direction

of Babiez R U for inspiration. "*Fertilicious*, wasn't I?"

Again, the word sounds false coming out of her mouth. And yet it still causes Zen to tug on his hairspikes. His obvious distress emboldens my sister even more.

"Wasn't I?"

I don't agree with what my sister is saying, but I want her to like me. She gives up when I take too long to corroborate.

"Oh well," she says with a shrug, "I'm done here. I'm taking the shuttle home."

No! This is going all wrong.

"But what about my veil?" I ask, trying to stay calm.

"If you need it so badly, why don't you go back to Goodside and get it?" She hesitates for a moment as if she knows she shouldn't say what she's about to say, but decides to say it anyway. "Maybe you should go back to Goodside, where you belong."

Where I belong. If she only knew.

"But . . ." I say, trying not to well up. "I hoped . . ."

"What? That I would give up everything I've got here and go back with you? That I would settle down and get married and make"—she spits out the last word—"*babies*?"

She's right. I had hoped—unrealistically so, I now see—that my blood sister would share Ma's and my housesisters' enthusiasm for marriage and motherhood. But Melody is nothing like the girls in Goodside. No, her reluctance to fulfill her feminine promise makes her so much more like . . .

45

Me.

I gasp at the similarity. "Sister!"

Melody looks like she's just been kicked in the chest. Oh my grace, I've said it again! She quickly rights herself, and without so much as even a careless farewell to me or Zen, spins around and speeds toward the nearest exit.

"Later!" Zen calls out, admirably unaffected.

I'm not ready to leave yet. There's too much more I need to learn about my sister, and Zen is the person who can teach me. I'm nervous, but the spirit moves me to put my mission before myself.

"Zen," I say before my tongue gets stuck. "Would you care to escort me to Plain & Simple?"

I've never been so bold with a boy—not even Ram. Church girls do *not* initiate. I know it's an innocent invitation, and yet my face burns hotter than you-know-what.

Zen rakes his fingers through his hair. "Are you sure your fiancé won't get jealous?"

"My fiancé? Oh, no. No! He won't mind at all!"

This is true. Ram would never get jealous because such expressions of envy go against our faith.

"'Let us behave decently as in the daytime,'" I say out loud. When I notice Zen is clenching his jaw, I keep the rest of the verse to myself.

"'*Not in sexual immorality,*'" I mouth silently, leading Zen down the causeway. "'*Not in debauchery.*'"

melody
harmony

"SO AFTER DELETING HIMSELF FROM MY LIFE FOR WEEKS, HE totally stalks me at the Mallplex just to let me know that he chauffeured a bunch of Cheerclones to one of their nasty masSEX parties. He's crazy if he thinks he can make me, like, *jealous* or something. . . ."

I'm home now, venting to my friend Shoko on the MiVu. She's totally couched, crunching her way through a bag of Folato Chips . . . *now with 250 percent more folic acid*!

"And then he busts out this bogus contract from when we were, like, *twelve* that says that if we haven't bumped anybody by now we're obligated to bump each other. . . ."

"Mmmm . . ." Shoko murmurs with her mouth full. Due to drop any day now, she looks like a Eurasian grass snake that swallowed the moon. When she shifts slightly in the pillows—no small task at her size—an invisible woman's voice bursts into the room.

"*AZUL* . . . BLUE . . . *ROJA* . . . RED . . ."

"Oy!" Shoko lifts up her shirt to reveal the HeadStart belly band straining against her midsection. "Where's the volume on this damn thing?!"

"*AMARILLO* . . . YELLOW . . ."

She scrambles to find the smartpod that slipped between her butt and the couch cushions and jabs at the volume until the invisible Spanish teacher fades away.

"*VERDE* . . . GREEN . . . *MORADO* . . . PUR-PLE . . ."

"Oy, I can't wait until Burrito and I part ways."

Burrito is the nickname for her pregg. This is Shoko's first go as a pro. She bumped as an amateur last time around, which meant *she* picked her partner—her boyfriend, Raimundo—a RePro Rep didn't do it for her. It also meant that she didn't get paid up front like I did, but had to wait and see what offers came in after her delivery was made. Unlike the Cheerclones and other amateurs who hit the masSEX party circuit hoping to be bumped, Shoko's first pregging wasn't *planned*, but it wasn't unexpected either because that's what happens when boyfriends and girlfriends do what they do as often as Shoko and Raimundo did.

Both bright, brown-eyed brunettes with pleasing if asymmetrical facial features, Shoko and Raimundo are above average across the board, but nothing that would inspire Lib or any other RePro Rep to make six-figure promises. Shoko had never been seriously wooed to go pro, so it was a bit of a surprise when there was unusually competitive postdelivery auction. The winning bidders were so thrilled with the outcome that they hired Shoko to bump with Raimundo again (they were broken up at this point, which made it waaaay awkward but business is business and pleasure is pleasure), so the second pregg she's carrying now is biosiblings with the first. She's signed an option agreement to try for a third pregg, though with her eighteenth birthday just a month away, it's not a sure thing. Even without number three, she's earning enough money to cover her first year at Rutgers, which makes her way better off than she was before she got the first plus sign on her pee stick.

She's ready to pop, so I need to get into maternity mode. I was honored when she asked me to be her peer birthcoach because she's two years older and the Pro/Am president. She could have asked *anyone* in the Alliance for support. Choosing me—the only prebump among us— was a bold statement. And sticking with me after what happened to Malia . . . Well, that was even bolder.

But that's Shoko. She's not afraid to say what she thinks, and she never worries whether what she says will affect her image. We met when I was the youngest player to make the Little Tigers elite travel soccer team, the only girl in sixth grade good enough to compete with eighth grad-ers. The older girls got pissy when I not only kept up, but kicked circles around them. They wanted to haze me hard and threatened to cut off my ponytail to serve as a warning to other upstart sixth graders, but Shoko wouldn't let them. She's the one who stood up for me.

"If she's kicking *our* asses," she pointed out, "imagine what she'll do to the other team."

Since that moment on the soccer field, I've looked up to her like the big sister I never had.

Not that I've told her about the sister I *do* have. Shoko doesn't need my DNA drama to distract her from her contractual obligations. Not that that's stopped me from ranting about Zen.

"Okay. So where was I?" I ask myself. "Oh, right. Zen . . ."

Shoko sighs and sets down her bag of chips.

"I don't get it," she says.

"Get what?"

"Why Zen isn't your everythingbut." She runs her tongue over her teeth. "I hear Zen gives *gooooood* everythingbut."

I feel my face burn. "Heard it from *who*?"

"Ooooh," Shoko says. "Burrito's squatting on my sciatic nerve, but that's nothing like the nerve I just struck in *you*."

"Seriously." I grit my teeth into a smile. "Who? One of the Cheerclones?"

The Cheerclones are the varsity cheerleaders who are impossible to tell apart by design. For high-scoring uniformity in competitions, they're all within one-half inch in height (five three) and two and half pounds in weight (105 pounds). They've all dyed their hair and skin to match the average hair color and skin tone for the squad as a whole. For serious, they are virtually identical from their ponytails to their pedicures—it would be easier to tell me apart from my twin. Unlike Harmony and me, however, they're as predictably identical in thought as they are in appearance. They think, speak, and handspring as a unit, so it's no surprise they tried to pregg as one last night.

I still can't believe Zen went out with them. Gah.

"Why does it matter who?" Shoko says. "Ash and Ty have made you totally paranoid about the perfect bump! You're afraid that if you let a guy so much as *kiss* you, you'll break your hymen, break your contract, and ruin everything you've worked for your whole life."

She's right. I hate that she's right. But she is.

"What's taking the Jaydens so long anyway?" Shoko says, licking green Folato Chip dust off her thumb. "I thought Lib said you'd be bumped by the end of your sophomore year for sure."

Lib assures me that I'm everything they want in an Egg. I look almost exactly like the Mrs. did at my age only I'm a little bit taller, which ups my value, of course. And they're so impressed with my IQ and EQ scores. The problem has always been with the Sperm. They haven't found a donor that is a perfect match for the Mr., only with less hair in his ears and more on his head.

"Lib says the Mrs. is trying to persuade her husband to go totally commercial," I say. "She wants to invest big money in a top man brand. . . ."

Shoko clutches the empty bag to her chest. "Like Fitch or Phoenix from the Tocin ads?"

These RePros have all become famous for popping up on the MiNet more naked than not, seductively cooing: *"Can't bump with me? Fake it with a dose of Tocin."* Tocin makes you feel like your best and most reproaesthetical self, and see everyone around you in the same artificially flattering way. Originally touted as "the Peacemaker" for its potential to end conflict in the Middle East, it's now the most popular medication prescribed by doctors for Surrogettes and Sperms. Taken as directed, it helps "exaggerate feelings of arousal and attachment" and "ease the awkwardness and anxiety" of bumping with a total stranger.

Don't get me wrong. The Tocin models are seriously reproaesthetical, but their famegaming turns me off.

"I don't know," I say cautiously. "Maybe."

"Or Jondoe!" Shoko falls back in the pillows in full swoon. "I'd pregg decatuplets with him!"

"Shoko!" She really is too much.

"Hey, if you're gonna get paid to pregg, it might as well be with the best man brand in the business!"

Shoko's getting far more excited by this prospect than I am. I mean, it's difficult to imagine what doing it will be like when I don't know who I'll be doing it with. After all this buildup, I can only assume that the Jaydens will finally pick someone who is—at the very least—as reproaesthetical as I am. In that case, doing it will be totally worth the wait.

At least I hope so.

"Well, they haven't made up their minds," I say, "And until they do . . ."

"Let Zen be your everythingbut!"

"Good*bye*, Shoko . . ."

"EVERYTHINGBUT!"

I shut her down before she can say another word.

I can't help but notice a new message from Malia. It's the seventh in as many days. This time I delete it without even watching. And though I know it's irresponsible—Shoko's water could break at any moment—I blind my MiNet for the rest of the night.

Honestly? I think Shoko might be better off in the delivery room without me.

I mean, in an emergency situation, what more can I do for her that I couldn't do for Malia?

harmony

melody

ZEN AND I ARE SEATED IN A BOOTH AT THE U.S. BUFF-A. A waitress has just delivered the cheesesteak I ordered in honor of my home state. I adjust the netting on my veil so I can eat. She stands to the side and stares.

"Why don't you just take it off?"

It's an honest question, really. One with a complicated answer.

"Because she doesn't want to," Zen says brightly before turning back to me. "Besides, white really works for you." His gaze lingers on me long enough to require a trip to the confessional.

I blush. I'm not used to such flatteries. I know it's unreasonable for me to expect Ram to behave like Zen or any other Othersider. It would be sacrilegious if he did. I'm about to thank Zen for the compliment when he blinks and squeezes his eyes as if a cloud of busy gnats has just flown right into them. As quick as it starts, it stops.

"So why get married now?" he asks. "I mean, from everything I've read on the quikiwiki, it seems that girls in the Church are usually married around thirteen. . . ."

Unlike the salesgirl, who was using this information to mock me, Zen seems genuinely curious. I decide to take a leap of faith.

"I was engaged for the first time at thirteen."

Zen nods, not a trace of condescension or scorn on his face.

"And what happened to the first fiancé?"

What happened was 1 Corinithians.

The wife's body does not belong to her alone but also to her husband. In the same way, the husband's body does not belong to him alone but also to his wife. Do not deprive each other.

When I was thirteen and newly betrothed, my house-sisters and I studied this verse in prayerclique. It was the last sentence that I didn't get, as "deprive" implied that doing without marital relations would be like doing without food or water or another life-sustaining necessity. I couldn't imagine feeling this way about Shep, my first fiancé. He was three years older and I secretly called him "Sheep" because of his woolly beard, bleating laugh, and fondness for chewing on long blades of grass. I didn't know much else about him than that, really. We'd certainly never kissed, never even held hands. And yet it would only be a matter of weeks before my body belonged to him and his belonged to me.

Inspired by 1 Corinthians, I asked my housesisters a question that I had wanted to ask for a very long time.

"Are any of you afraid of . . . *consummating* the marriage?"

My housesisters' cheeks caught ablaze like a wildfire in a windstorm.

"But children are God's best gift!" said Mary.

"The fruit of the womb is His greatest legacy!" said Lucy.

"I'm not talking about childbirth," I cut in. "I'm talking about the *marital act*, the *bodily sharing* that leads to childbirth. . . ."

They avoided my eyes and murmured prayers I couldn't make out.

"None of you are afraid of what it will *feel* like to become one flesh? The *pain*?"

And Annie, the only girl our age still waiting for a betrothal, the housesister so scared of being left behind, the one who had been conspicuously quiet throughout this conversation, finally spoke.

"In Genesis, God says, *'With pain you will give birth to children. Your desire will be for your husband, and he will rule over you.'*"

Mary and Lucy murmured amens to that.

I wanted to explain to Zen how my housesisters' reactions underscored the secret fears I'd been having since I began my Blooming. The Church promises that there's no greater way for young women to please God than to take the sacraments. But the closer I got to my own marriage and maternity, the more I felt like I was only as praiseworthy as my healthy womb.

Why was I the only one who seemed to see it this way?

Orders require us to put the Church before ourselves. It was this sacrificial argument that Ma repeated whenever I had expressed my doubts about marrying someone I didn't love. Both times.

"What does JOY stand for?" she'd ask. "Jesus first. Others next. Yourself last . . ."

"What happened?" Zen asks again.

I look at him through the haze of tulle. "He married someone else."

Less than two weeks after that conversation with my housesisters, Annie exchanged vows with Shep alongside Mary and Lucy. It was Annie who would share a marital bed in their household, Annie who would give Shep a son with golden red hair, Annie who would be pregnant now with his second child. Annie, and not me.

"Why?"

"The Church Council decided I wasn't ready."

It was another three years before the Church gave me my second—and last—chance to set things right. With Ram. Another boy I could only love in a brotherly way.

"And are you ready now?" Zen's got a penetrating

57

gaze, as if he's trying to see through the veil and straight into my eyes.

"I have to be," I say. "I *will* be."

And then I take a huge, messy bite of my sandwich to discourage Zen from asking any more questions. We chew in silence for a few moments before I muster the courage to ask him a question of my own.

"Do all Surrogettes and Sperms get along like you and Melody do?"

"*What?*"

Those are the terms Melody used in our MiChats. Right away I get the impression that I've used them incorrectly, and that I've just asked a question as unenlightened as those Zen had asked me earlier. I press on nonetheless.

"You have a conception contract, right?"

"You think *I've* been *hired* to bump with *Melody*?"

I nod.

"You think I'm a *professional*?"

I nod again with fire-branded cheeks.

"Oh, Harmony." Zen laughs ruefully. "I'm not upmarket enough to be a RePro."

"A RePro?" I ask.

"Reproductive professional," he says, looking down at the sloppy remains of his Texas BBQ brisket. "A stud-for-hire."

Zen is obviously smart, and he has a winning personality. He looks physically fit. He may not have the strength to split logs but he could certainly stack them after someone like Ram did it for him. And finally, at the risk of sound-ing inappropriate, his face is very nice to look at. Especially when his cheeks are dimpling just so. I don't understand how he would be considered not good enough. Not that I approve of any of this business, mind you.

"Insufficient verticality," Zen explains, holding his hand about six inches over his head. "No one pays to bump with a guy who's five foot seven and a half." He drops his hand and points it straight at me. "Now I know what you're thinking: *Why don't you dose some pharma-grade HGH?*"

"That's not what I was thinking at all," I interrupt. "And what's HGH?"

"Human Growth Hormone. Anyway, lots of shorties have pumped themselves up with HGH to make them-selves more sellable to RePro Reps. But you know what's happening? Users report that the increase in height is inversely proportional to a decrease in IQ! Ha! So these needle-happy juiceheads pass the test for verticality, but fail the minimum standards for intelligence!"

I'm able to understand approximately one in every five or so words that come out of Zen's mouth.

"And it also makes their stiffies shrink," he says, hold-ing up a pinkie.

That much I can understand. And I wish I hadn't!

"Unless someone develops HGH that pumps up brains *and* bodies, I'm only good enough for everythingbut. Doomed to be a Worm, never a Sperm."

"'I am a worm, not a man,'" I recite by memory. "'Scorned by man, despised by the people.'"

"Yes!" Zen says, his face alight. "That's how I feel sometimes!"

"Christ said it when he was under persecution," I explain.

"He did, did He?" Zen says bemusedly, shaking his head at me. "You make a really great witness for Goodside, Harmony."

I think this is a compliment, so I accept it. "Thank you."

"But you still have a lot to learn about life on this side of the gates."

Zen is right. I do have a lot to learn. Othersiders rumormonger about the willful unknowingness of the Church, but God has placed in the human heart a desire to know the Truth. The more I know about Melody's decision to turn pro, the easier it will be for me to show her that earthly riches can't compare to Heaven's rewards.

Then maybe, just maybe, we can take the right path together.

Zen searches through his pockets, then hands me what looks like a debit card.

"What's this?" I ask.

"It's a Lost-and-Found card, for emergencies. It works even if you're not on the MiNet. If you get lost, just finger-swipe right here," he says, pointing to a small *X* marking the spot, "and I get an alert to find you, wherever you are."

I clutch the card in my hand. "Why would you give this to me?"

"Oh, it's no big," Zen says. "My parents gave me a bunch of them after all the floods and earthquakes. I figure that you're new to Otherside and might wind up somewhere you didn't mean to go. . . ."

His kindness brings tears to my eyes.

"What I meant was, why would you want to help *me*?"

He shrugs. "Helping people is kind of my hobby."

I look down at the card once more. "But you don't even know me. . . ."

Zen shakes his head as if the answer is obvious.

"You're Melody's sister, Harmony. We'll know each other for the rest of our lives."

SECOND

A free society cannot force girls to have children, but a free market can richly reward those who do.

—Ashley and Tyler Mayflower, PhDs, Princeton University

harmony

I WAKE AT DAWN IN PANIC, NOT PRAYER.

Who am I? Where am I? Why am I here?

I'm on the floor, soaked with sweat, blankets twisted around my legs like invasive vines choking the tomato plants.

Why am I not in my bunk?

Where are Laura, Katie, and Emily?

I'm about to cry out when a lump on the bed next to me rolls over, smacks her lips together, and sighs. That's when I remember:

The sighing lump is Melody.

I'm on the floor of her room.

She's my sister.

She's my twin.

Melody mumbles a word I can't quite make out. And even if I could, I probably wouldn't understand what it means. She was studying her advanced biogenetics flexbook when I came in to say good night. She said her parents make her read her most challenging subjects before bedtime.

"Even my dreams are educational," she said. "I never get a rest, not even when I'm asleep."

I read the Scripture every evening. Is that why I dream of Jesus?

Almost immediately the guilt of being here instead of where I should be settles heavy upon me. I make up for the omission with a morning offering.

"'Let the morning bring me word of your unfailing love,'" I whisper, so as not to disturb Melody. "'For I have put my trust in you. Show me the way I should go, for to you I lift up my soul.'"

A good psalm usually sets me right. But I'm feeling particularly out of sorts this morning. I unwind the blankets from my legs, gather up my pillow, and tiptoe out of Melody's bedroom. I feel my way down the dim hall back into the guest room where I had started out the night.

When I got back to the house yesterday, my suitcase wasn't on the doorstep as I had feared. But Melody wasn't there to welcome me either, as I had hoped. The front door was locked but I didn't panic because I heard noises coming from the backyard, a *fwoop fwoop fwoop*ing that sounded mechanical but I could in no other way identify.

I made my way around back and found Melody in the backyard defending a soccer goal from a machine launching one ball (*fwoop*) after another (*fwoop fwoop*) at unpredictable angles and terrifying speed. I flinched with every *fwoop*. Melody jumped and lunged and caught each black-and-white blur with just enough time to toss it to the side before the next *fwoop* hurtled straight for her. She never stopped moving. Dozens of soccer balls rolled onto the grass, but not a single ball slipped past her fingertips and inside the goal.

Only after the final *fwoop* did Melody allow herself to bend over, rest her hands on her knees, and gulp for air.

"How long have you been standing there?"

"Just a few minutes," I replied. "How long have you been practicing?"

"Long enough so my parents won't get pissy about not practicing long enough."

I nervously patted the netting on my veil.

"Did Zen help you pick that out?" she asked.

"No," I replied. "This is the same one I was wearing earlier. I didn't buy one after all."

"Oh."

Then she picked up one of the balls and started bouncing it from one knee to the other. She seemed worried about something, but I was reluctant to ask what it was. I was afraid to say or do anything that might result in her asking me to leave and never come back.

"That's okay," I said, unclipping my veil from my scalp

and shaking out my hair. "It's a relief to take it off, to tell you the truth."

She let the ball drop to the ground and gestured for me to follow her inside.

"I moved your suitcase into the guest room so you can change into something more comfortable in there."

"Thank you."

Melody opened the door to the room in which I would be staying, and gestured up to the patchwork of pressed tin tiles in the ceiling, then down to a puzzle of dark and light, long and short wood planks in the floor.

"My parents recycled the whole house. It's totally green."

She paused, then waited for me to say something, so I did.

"That's interesting."

"I know it's not exactly the nature you're used to," Melody said, touching her hand to the brass doorknob. "But it's as all natural as you can get off the farm."

I realized then that she was trying her best to find common ground, to make me feel welcome in her home. I wanted to embrace her to thank her for her compassion before she closed the door behind her. But I didn't. I was afraid such a display might provoke a sudden change of heart.

This guest room is roughly the same size as the room I share with Laura, Katie, and Emily. But with just one bed in the middle of the room, it feels far more spacious than any room I've ever slept in. That's why I crept into Melody's room in the middle of the night and slept near her on the floor. I've never slept alone. I'm too used to falling asleep to the rise and fall of peaceful breathing. I knew I'd toss and turn all night in the silence.

"Melllooooooodeee? Hellooooooooo . . . ?"

Oh my grace! I jump at the sound of a voice coming from the front of the house. It sounds too low to be a woman, but too high to be a man. Who is it? How did he/she get in the house?

"Let me see yooooooooou."

I don't know who would be visiting Melody at this early hour, but I rush toward the front door to find out. I freeze when I reach the common room.

"I've got the BEST NEWS, Miss Melody Mayflower!"

The voice isn't coming from a visitor. It's coming from a man projected larger than life-size on the MiVu wall. It's almost impossible to notice anything about him other than his suit, which is illuminated with electrified stripes of red, orange, yellow, green, blue, indigo, and violet.

"I want to see the look on your face when I tell yooooooooou." He trills the last word, reminding me of a soprano who holds her notes just a beat longer than everyone else in the Church choir.

I timidly approach the screen. The first thing I do is lower the volume. This man's voice carries and I don't want him waking up Melody. There's a box lit up in the lower right-hand corner indicating that MiVu is in 1Vu mode right now. There are two more boxes that are blinking questions: 2Vu? 2Vu? 2Vu? Or: @Vu? @Vu? @Vu? We don't have MiVu in Goodside, so I'm not too familiar with the technology, but I believe "2Vu" means we can only see each other. And "@Vu" means that we can be seen by anyone who is plugged into the system right now who wants to see us. As I consider which box to press, the man on the screen keeps up his one-sided conversation.

"Whoopsie! What time is it there? It's nearly lunch-time here in Stockholm. This scouting trip has been UH. MAZE. ING. I was just saying to myself, *Lib. Have you ever seen so many blond, blue-eyed hunkaspunks in your WHOLE LIFE?* And myself replied, *No, Lib. I have not.*"

Lib. I rack my brains trying to remember who Lib is. I know Melody has mentioned him, but I can't remember. . . .

"There's one fine speci*man* I was all ready to introduce to the Jaydens. . . ."

Now I remember! Lib is Melody's Reproductive Representative! He's the one who recruited her to be a Surrogette! Melody said he was a colorful character, but I hadn't expected him to wear a suit that glows like an electric rainbow. Maybe I can tell him that Melody has had a change of heart. She doesn't want to be a Surrogette after all. Would he believe me? Of course then I would have to do some prayerful witnessing to make Melody believe it herself.

"GUESS WHAT?"

I press the 2Vu option.

70

"Hey gorgeous! You ARE there!" Lib crows when I come into his Vu. "Like the lumina suit?" he asks, stretching out to get a full view of the electric rainbow running up and down his arms. When I respond with a wince, he sighs, then presses a button on his wrist to make the lights go out. "It's a bit too much first thing in the morning, isn't it?"

Now that I get a better look, I see that Lib is bald, save for a silvery inch-wide strip of hair running front to back across his scalp. His skin is as brown as an acorn, and his face is stretched taut and unlined, as is often seen in older men of means in Otherside. Even the skin in his eye sockets is pulled tight, making them bulge in surprise at all times. Those lavender eyes are scrolling up down and all around as he takes in my appearance as carefully as I am taking in his. Usually this would make me feel uncomfortable, but something about Lib tells me that he's not looking at me with impure interest.

"You got some SUN! It gives you that FRESH, OUT-DOORSY look!"

It becomes clear that Lib uses his expressive voice to overcompensate for his frozen face. He drops it to a conspiratorial whisper, beckons for me to come closer to the screen.

"Just don't get too much. A little rosy glow is okay, you just don't want to get . . . ah, too dark. That's not what the Jaydens hired you for. They don't give a hoot about the multiculti trends! They are SO into Euro! That milky complexion is one of your greatest assets."

Oh! He thinks I'm Melody! She must not have told Lib that I'm staying with her for a while. I'm about to reveal myself as the twin sister, but he doesn't stop talking long enough to give me the chance.

"And while we're talking superficials, that . . . that . . . THING you're wearing is so TERMINAL and so FER-TILICIOUS at the same time."

I look down at my long white cotton nightdress.

"You are so smart to cover up as much skin as possi-ble," Lib continues with admiration in his voice. "I've been selling everyone since you signed with me: MELODY MAYFLOWER IS THE FULL PACKAGE. Beauty and brains. I wish all my clients were as bright as you."

I try to correct his mistake. "Actually, I'm not—"

"Oh, but you ARE. You must spend most your day fending off amateur offers from all the . . ." He screws up his mouth, just about the only part of his face he can move. "*Opportunistic humpers* at your high school."

"But—"

"Do you have ANY IDEA how many of my clients break their conception contracts? They have NO apprecia-tion for all the hard work I put in to making the perfect three-way match." He snorts. "TOO HORMONAL to think about how their choices affect their OWN futures."

"Mr. Lib, sir, I—"

"They all prooooooomise to keep it pure. They're all like"—his voice gets higher—"*Lib! I won't bump with him! He's my everythingbut!* Then they do a little too much TOCIN DOSIN' and the next thing I know these girls have forgotten the *but* in *everythingbut* and they're BUMP-ING with some unaccredited"—he turns his head and sticks out his tongue—"*WORM.*"

Worm. That's how Zen referred to himself yesterday.

"I'm sorry," Lib says with a sniff. "I'm just SO EMO-TIONAL today. Becaaaaaaaaause . . ." He makes a strange choking noise, then covers his mouth with his hands as if he's unsure whether he's capable of delivering his message after all. Then he opens up his hands to make a mega-phone. "YOU'RE GONNA GET BUMPED BY THE BEST MAN BRAND IN THE BUSINESS."

His words push me backward onto the couch, a sight that makes Lib cackle and clap with delight.

"W-w-what?"

"And you're not gonna BELIEVE who it is. I still can't believe it myself."

I can't believe any of this.

"I've got one word for you." He closes his eyes, takes a breath, then says with reverential solemnity, "Jondoe."

This word means nothing to me but it means every-thing to Lib.

"ARE YOU TERMINATED? BECAUSE I AM BEYOND TERMINATED."

I think I might be terminated and I don't even know what he is talking about.

"Jondoe," Lib keeps saying to himself. "Jondoe. When

the Mrs. finally convinced the Mr. to go commercial, I never dreamed their application would be approved by the all-time highest scorer on the Standards. Believe the hype! He's got the fastest, strongest swimmers ever recorded!" Lib mops the sweat off his forehead with his sleeve. "He's got a perfect five-star ranking among triple-platinum-level customers who have employed his services. Ash and Ty will TERMINATE when you tell them that!" Then Lib does his best to twist his frozen face into a look of exaggerated concern. "Oh, sweetie! You're IN SHOCK."

This, I understand. I *am* in shock. She's been waiting for this news for years. It certainly complicates my plans to get Melody to get married and live with me and Ram in faith and fellowship as all good and obedient Church girls should.

Lib leans in and cups his mouth with one hand to share a secret, and I instinctively come closer to hear it.

"I. EXIST. FOR. YOU," he says. "I live for *you* and I die for *you*."

I object to such Christlike claims coming from a sinner's mouth, but can't raise my voice in protest.

"You know to what *great lengths* I went to make sure your file was *flawless*," he says in an emphatic whisper. "I put my *reputation* on the line for you. I *pulled strings*. I called in *favors*. Let's just put it this way, Miss Melody Mayflower, I *earned* my fifteen percent!" He wipes his immobile brow, sits back, and raises the volume. "And it worked! It's a testament to all my hard work that Jondoe accepted the

74

Jaydens' bid. He's very selective, he takes only a fraction of the offers that come along. You can tell Ash and Ty that getting into the number one college in the WORLD will be a no-brainer after *Jondoe* gets into *you*!"

He cackles wildly.

"I cannot thank you enough for all your efforts in keeping your EYES on the PURITY PRIZE." He traces an imaginary line from my neck to my ankles. "Never in my wildest dreams did I think that you would have the opportunity to bump with Jondoe." His eyes are tearing up, the only visible sign on his face that he's overcome with emotion. "From what we've all seen and heard about Jondoe, he'll be WORTH EVERY MICROSECOND of frustrated restraint. . . ." He rubs his palms together with relish.

My sister is still chaste. It's not too late to protect that gift of purity, but I need to intervene right now, to tell Lib that I will endure fire raining down from Heaven before I will allow my sister to prostitute herself for procreation and profit. The best investment she can make is in God. If only Lib devoted as much time and energy into glorifying the Lord as he put into his immoral business, he too would be saved.

"I can see your heart pounding!"

I clutch my chest to feel what Lib can see. This is my chance to find my voice. To tell Lib I'm not who he thinks I am, nor is my sister. I must coax the words out of my throat. I can't let fear stop me. Being scared means that I trust my own feelings more than I trust God, and that's just disrespectful.

"Where are you in your cycle? Oh, WHO CARES? Let's get you two BUMPING right away. We don't want another trimester to go by with a FLAT TUMMY. And not to put any pressure on you or anything, but it would be just BREEDY if you could deliver the goods by next March. The Jaydens have an interest in zodiacology. Remember how I negotiated that bonus for delivering a Pisces? Another stroke of BRILLLLLLIANCE!"

I clear my throat. "Excuse me," I say more firmly, but he talks right over me.

"Let me put you in the mood! I've got his most recent Tocin ad right here! Prepare to be dazzled! Are you ready to be dazzled?"

"But I'm not Mel—"

"I mean it! You must prepare yourself right now!"

Lib disappears and in the very next moment . . .

"Behold the most BEAUTIFUL sight you have ever seen!"

"But—ohhhhh . . ."

This is a transcendent understatement.

"That flowing, golden hair . . ." Lib raves from a reduced screen in the corner. "Those soulful brown eyes . . ."

I am basking in the true light of the Alpha and Omega.

"No need for a dose of Tocin to OPEN YOU UP to this one! Look at him!"

I do.
And
I
am
reborn.

melody

I THINK HARMONY MISSES GOODSIDE ALREADY. SHE'S BEYOND wanked this morning. I mean, for *her*. Yesterday she couldn't wait to go out and faith hard in the face of non-believers at the Mallplex. But today she's content to stay in while I'm at school.

When Harmony first told me that she'd changed her mind about tagging along, I was for seriously relieved because I didn't know how I was going to break the news that she could in no way come with me to school today. We're all supposed to stop stressing about opposing belief systems because we're more, like, mature now and stuff. But guess what? The Churchies still freak everyone out. Not too long ago some Churchies from a local settlement took over Palmer Square and asked me, Malia, and Shoko if we had God when all we wanted to do was buy retro froyo. Then we all joked about how their godfreakiness could infect us and turn us from totally normal to totally not. And for days, even weeks afterward, the three of us laughed about it, like, "Ha. I'm going to burn in hell. Ha. Ha. Ha." But the jokes are never really all that funny.

Letting Harmony come to school with me on a regular day would be bad enough, but today it would be terminal. It's a big day for me with the Pro/Am vote and all. Ventura Vida poses enough of a challenge as it is. I don't need my secret identical twin stalking around the halls asking everyone if they have God.

Harmony was so calm and focused yesterday, remarkably so considering how jarring it must have been to leave Goodside behind. Since I found her on her knees in the common room this morning, however, she's been acting kind of blinky. It's possible she always wakes up like this. Maybe she's got undiagnosed ADHD and she needs to self-medicate by, like, milking a cow or something to calm down. But I have a feeling she's unnerved by something, or rather, someone else entirely.

"Hey. Did Zen say something . . . ?"

For all I know, he could've brought up our ridiculous "contract" and tried to persuade Harmony to proxy pregg on my behalf. When she doesn't answer I repeat the question, assuming she can't hear me over the cracklesnap of bubbling batter in a frying pan I didn't even know we owned.

"Who?" Harmony asks, without turning away from the stove.

"Zen."

"Zen?"

"Yes, Zen," I say, growing impatient, "The boy you met yesterday . . ."

She turns, a flicker of recognition crossing her face as she comes toward me with a steaming pancake balanced on a spatula. "Oh, *Zen*," she says in an airy, distracted way.

"Yes, *Zen*," I say in a tone that matches hers note for note. "Did he say or *do* something . . . um, *inappropriate* yesterday?"

"What?" Harmony clumsily flips the pancake half on, half off my plate. When she boosts it back onto the plate with the spatula, it breaks in half. "Oops. Sorry."

I'm trying not to lose it, but she is not making it easy. *"Did Zen say or do something inappropriate yesterday?"*

"Ohhhh . . ." she says, as if checking in to the conversation for the first time. "No."

When she doesn't elaborate, I do. "Because you're acting kind of . . ." I choose the next word carefully. "*Different* today."

"I am?" she asks, a note of worry in her voice. "I guess I'm worn out from yesterday. It's a lot to take in all at once."

I imagine that this is true. I barely know her, and yet I can't let go of the feeling that there's something *off* about her behavior this morning. But I don't think I'll get much out of her with repeated prodding.

"Well," I reply, deciding to keep it light. "You already make your way around this kitchen better than I do."

It's actually pretty funny seeing Harmony bustle around our kitchen. Ash and Ty know I'll never be bothered to nuke a freezerful of instant meals, so they provide me with a per diem for takeout whenever they're away. Watching Harmony put together a fine breakfast out of some eggs and left-behinds in our pantry, I get a glimpse of an alternate destiny. I see what I would've looked like if *I* were the one trained in the domestic arts to make a good wife at sixteen. (Or, as Harmony's starter engagement would have had it, thirteen.)

She brushes a strand of hair out of her clear blue eyes. *They're pretty,* I think, before remembering, *Oh, yeah. They're just like mine.*

"If you didn't buy a new veil, what did you and Zen do alone together for three hours?"

Funny how Zen has had zero time for me, and yet had all afternoon for Harmony.

"We went to Plain & Simple to shop for a new veil, but I didn't buy one," she says as she briskly mixes more batter. "They were all too expensive and . . ." Her voice trails off and her hand spins even more vigorously around the inside of the bowl.

"And what?" I ask.

"And then we got some dinner at the U.S. Buff-A. Have you been there?"

I try not to shoot her a condescending look. I remind myself that the U.S. Buff-A has yet to open a franchise in Goodside. I smile and nod instead.

"Zen warned me that the Maine lobster-roll appetizer wouldn't go well with the Pennsylvania cheesesteak," she says, clutching her stomach and sticking out her tongue. "But I didn't listen. . . ."

I take the final bite from my first pancake before reaching for my second. Harmony hasn't eaten a thing.

"Did you meet anyone else while you were there?"

Harmony doesn't stop stirring. "No. Zen blinded his MiNet so we could have some privacy."

Of course he did. How gentlemanly of him.

"So what did you talk about?"

"You." She stops mixing and levels her gaze at me. "Zen cares about you."

"Zen cares about everyone. It's, like, his thing."

It's almost pathological, really, his need to help people. This is why *he's* the go-to guy for driving home a bunch of wasted Cheerclones after their orgy. Gah.

"Maybe," Harmony says. "But he *really* cares about you. It's too bad about his insufficient verticality."

I choke on my pancake, coughing a puff of flour across the countertop.

"Then you wouldn't have to share yourself with someone you've never even met."

Then she picks up a sponge and cleans up the mess I just made.

I'm still thwacking my chest with the heel of my palm, trying to dislodge a wad of unchewed dough. I have no time to offer my rebuttal because I'm interrupted by an all-too-familiar annoyance coming from the MiVu.

"Wake up, Pell-Mel! Wakey-wakey!"

"Oh!" Harmony jumps, splattering a spoonful of batter across her nightgown.

"It's just Ash and Ty," I croak. "Right on time for their a.m. stalking."

Every school day at seven a.m., my parents shout at me until I turn on the 2Vu to confirm I'm keeping myself alive in their absence.

"PELL-MEL. PELL-MEL. PELL-MEL." So goes the chant in the other room.

"If I don't respond within two minutes, they call 911."

"It's nice that they care," Harmony says.

"Yeah," I snort. "That's one way of looking at it."

Between the wake-up calls, the 24/7 stalk app, and the GUARDIAN (Guaranteed Under-Age Remote Detection of Illegal Alcohol and Narcotics) monitor, my parents are far more oppressive when they're on the other side of the world than when they're right down the hall.

When Harmony makes a move with me toward the common room, I suggest that she stay in the kitchen instead.

"Don't you want them to meet me?" she asks, a wounded expression on her face.

"I do," I say. "Just not right now." This is true. I barely

have the time or energy to deal with the standard-issue Ash and Ty interrogation. I know I can't handle a grilling over the one girl in the world who could do *the* most damage to my uniqueness quotient.

"They know about me . . . right?" she asks in a fragile voice.

"*Of course* they know about you."

From the look of relief on her face, it's clear that she interprets the "of course" as proof of the value I place on our relationship.

I don't have the heart to tell her that "of course" has nothing to do with me and everything to do with my parents' "no secrets" policy, or that they came to find out about her as they discover most things: through high-tech surveillance. After they tracked my MiChat minutes and freaked out about all the incoming calls from Goodside, they jumped to ludicrous conclusions and confronted me with the "evidence" in their usual tag-teaming style.

"We won't stand back and let you run off with a Church boy!" warned Ash.

"We didn't prep you for all these years to lose you to a quiverfilling cult!" snapped Ty.

They were for seriously convinced that I'd fallen in with the evangelical crowd as an exercise in teen rebellion. Their accusations were so off-the-spring crazy that I hoped the truth—that I had been found by my identical twin sister raised by Churchies in Goodside—would strike them almost as anticlimactic by comparison. I was, of course, wrong. They didn't ask a single question as to the impact such an astounding discovery would have on me *emotionally*, but immediately started debating the impact Harmony could have on me *financially*.

"You're *certain* she's not on the market," Ash said.

"She's engaged to be married," I assured them.

"She could counterfeit and undercut you," Ty coldly pointed out.

"It's against her religion," I told them.

My parents made me promise to limit my contact with Harmony until after I bumped, which, you know, should be any day now. And I did. Or I tried to anyway. Until she showed up on my doorstep.

Harmony's very existence has the potential to raise too many questions about my family history, a mysterious mess that Lib has taken it upon himself, as my RePro Rep, to handle with the utmost skill. And only when absolutely necessary, *sketchiness*. Gah. If Lib knew Harmony was here he'd drop dead on the spot. And if he knew I'd taken her to the Meadowlands Mallplex yesterday and that she was flipping pancakes in my kitchen at this moment, he'd raise himself up from the grave just for the satisfaction of dropping dead again. He loves drama, but not when it gets in the way of business.

Meanwhile Harmony is unaware of the havoc she's wreaked, first by contacting me, and again by coming to stay. She seems pretty much oblivious to just about everything right now, as she smiles into space and dreamily traces her fingers along the sticky batter spiderwebbing across her nightshirt. Why didn't I blind her chats? Why didn't I make her go back yesterday?

Unfortunately, my parents already know more about her than I'd like them to. So as I stride toward the MiVu, I decide that all I can do is try to keep their meddling to a minimum at the moment, just long enough to get me through this day.

Ash and Ty are now arguing to themselves about whether they've given me enough time to respond or should they just dial 911 right now. For all the money my parents have shelled out on the latest in teen-tracking technologies, they don't seem to trust any of it.

"I'm alive," I announce to my parents as I sweep into their 2Vu. "Just like the stalk app says I am."

Ash and Ty are fit and attractive blue-eyed blonds, like me. From looks alone, I could totally pass as their own, but they've always gone out of their way to tell people I'm adopted. They knew the Virus would make this the likeliest parental model of the future, and have always held me up as the prime example of what could be achieved when nature's gifts are nurtured to perfection.

Not *too* much pressure, right?

Ash speaks first. She usually does.

"How *are* you?"

I clench. My parents never, ever begin a conversation by asking such a question. No, they begin all conversations by offering constructive criticism and pointing out all ways I'm not living up to my file. A more typical greeting would have been:

"You almost let two balls slip past you yesterday, sweetie."

"You didn't practice your guitar all week. You know the arts are the weakest part of your profile, and with a name like Melody . . ."

My parents were professors at the University until I signed my conception contract eighteen months ago. That's when they reminded me that they were both in their forties, which put them, statistically speaking, more than halfway to their deaths. This was just totally unacceptable because there was just so much of life they hadn't lived, so much stuff they had never gotten around to doing because they were too busy schooling, working, and, since they adopted me sixteen years earlier, prepping me to be the well-rounded and highly sought-after Surrogette they always knew I would become. Rarely were they themselves the ones instructing me in the fine art of gene splicing or eyeliner application, but all that expert outsourcing doesn't just happen by itself, does it?

Their investment in me paid off. Literally. Thanks to the generous six-figure signing bonus Lib got out of the Jaydens, they're now out there *living life*, which includes doing all that undone stuff like walking the Great Wall of China and learning the didgeridoo from Australian aborigines. They claim that it's all material for some great research project in progress, but I highly doubt it.

"Any word from Lib lately, honey?" they ask now in unison.

"Um, no. Why?" I ask.

My parents grin and grip each other's hands.

"Because we met an *awesome* couple on safari. They have a son your age," says Ash.

I don't like where this is headed.

"And they also have an older daughter who is *desperate* for a Surrogette," she continues.

"You should be that Surrogette," says Ty.

My parents are nothing if not direct. My mouth hangs open.

"Our friends are *loaded*, Melody," adds Ty. "We can cut out the middleman and save ourselves fifteen percent."

I'm beyond shocked. My deal with the Jaydens was their crowing achievement as parents. Why would they even consider messing it up?

"My contract . . ." I can barely speak.

"We're afraid you're wasting your reproductivity," says Ash.

"With all this waiting around," says Ty.

I've told them to lay off the Tocin. They are totally dosed. That's the only explanation.

"Hahahahaha. You got me, guys."

I'm the only one laughing. I can tell from their tight, downturned mouths that they are dead serious. They're starting to scare me.

"Here's the thing, Melody," Ash begins.

And that's when they tell me that it's not about the money that they spent and don't have anymore, it's the money they spent that they *never* had.

"We borrowed against the equity on your Eggs."

I cannot believe what I'm hearing.

"YOU *WHAT*?"

Harmony yelps quietly. I surprise even myself with the outburst.

I barely hear what they say next, but what I do hear is bad enough.

My parents had my reproductive potential appraised when I was eleven, before I even signed on with Lib. Then they took out a five-year Egg Equity loan, which basically means that they borrowed against my projected future earnings as a Surrogette. They put that capital toward the strategic development of my most marketable traits and talents.

"How do you think we could afford to send you to that soccer training clinic in Brazil?"

"Or guitar lessons with a Grammy winner?"

"You think the Global U. summer camp comes cheap?"

This strategic reinvestment in my brand, they believed, would up my market value and put me well over the original appraisal. And when the Jaydens' bid came in so strong, it looked like I would definitely earn back everything they had borrowed and more. There was just one problem with their plan.

"You should have delivered by now," says Ash.

"You should be finishing up your second contract and considering a third," says Ty.

They were banking that I'd deliver *three* times before my obsolescence?

"But you're not."

"And it's time to pay that money back."

How could they let this happen? How could they have turned their only daughter into a toxic asset in need of a quick bump bailout? I expected more from them. If not as parents, then as *economists*.

"You're still young!" says Ash with an edge to her voice.

"You can pregg with our new friends," says Ty, eerily matching her tone, "and *still* have time left to deliver for the Jaydens."

I can't listen for another microsecond. I wink and blink and make them vanish from the MiVu without a word.

Now I'm shaking from the inside out. I take a deep, calming breath and repeat the words my positive energist taught me to say when I've got a problem and don't know how to solve it.

I am smart.

I am stunning.

I am strong.

I am everything I need to be.

Hopefully the money they spent putting me *in* this crisis helped me develop the skills to get myself *out* of it.

"Do you want to talk about what just happened?"

Harmony has changed into a button-front dress that is plainer than the one she wore yesterday, tinged yellow, and slightly shorter too, a scandalous ankle length. Her gloves stop at the wrists. This must be the Church version of casual wear.

"No," I reply. "There's nothing to discuss."

"But—"

"Honor thy parents is one of *your* commandments. Honor thy contracts is one of mine." I try to say it like I mean it. "I'm *not* a renegger."

"So you're okay?"

I nod vigorously, afraid that my voice might betray my lack of confidence.

Harmony fusses with her gloves for a moment, then says, "Amen to that."

And if I were the praying kind, I just might have amened along with her.

harmony
melody

I'M SITTING ON THE FLOOR IN THE MIDDLE OF MELODY'S closet, averting my eyes as she models yet another outfit in front of the mirror.

"How does this look?" she asks, more to the mirror than to me.

Those second-skin jeans and Co-Ed Naked Human Evolution League T-shirt don't look any different from any of the other combinations of clothing she's put on and taken off in the past ten minutes: *sacrilegious*. But then I remind myself that here in Otherside, such provocative outfits aren't against the Orders. If I'm going to blend in here, I need to pay close attention to how such fashions are put together.

"Is this an outfit that says, *I'll be bumped any day now*?"

When she turns to look at me, I realize that she's waiting for my opinion.

"Y-y-yes?"

She slaps her hand to her forehead. "Look who I'm asking!" She gestures at my full-skirted day dress and matching gloves. "I bet you never worry about what to wear."

When I realize that she's being playful, not judgmental, I return her smile. "By dressing simply and humbly, we don't waste time worrying about our appearance. We have more time to serve God and our community."

"I wonder how much more I could accomplish," Melody says, throwing the T aside and reaching for a gauzy floral blouse, "if I didn't go through this every single day."

I think about my big housesisters, Mary, Lucy, and Annie, and it makes me giggle to imagine them agonizing over whether to wear the pink day dress or the *other* pink day dress, blue or blue. Even my little housesisters, Laura, Katie, and Emily, don't dither over which shade of white they'll wear today. They've been awake for two hours already, have already done their outdoor chores (gathering eggs, milking cows, collecting wood for the fire) and indoor chores (setting the table, serving the meal, clearing up) and are now gathering for the Monday-morning prayershare. This is the first one I've missed since I was struck down by mule flu last year. Forgive me for saying so, but I don't regret not being there.

Please don't think I'm disrespecting the power of

fellowship and group prayer. When we join together in worship, we gain one another's strength. However, we've been taught that we can only ask for things that bring glory to God and I don't see how it glorifies God when Laura asks Him to cure her bad breath. He's is all the way up in Heaven and not sharing the same loom. She's wasting God's time.

It pains me to say this, but Katie uses prayershare to shed embarrassing light on others' failings under the pretense of saving a soul. For example, a few weeks ago she said, "Please pray for my friend who has lust in her heart for her fiancé's brother." And nobody could pray hard for the rest of the session because we were too busy not so quietly speculating who in our prayerclique had lust in her heart for her future brother-in-law. Such gossip isn't praiseworthy. And it was doubly pointless because everyone already knows that Emily sobbed for a week after she was betrothed in her Blooming to the younger, bucktoothed Stoltzfus boy.

"Thanks for cleaning up."

Without even realizing it, I have gathered up all of Melody's T-shirts and folded them neatly in a stack. The one on top is printed with an image of a green pill on a wet pink tongue with the words OPEN UP WITH TOCIN. I instinctively turn it over to the blank side.

"So. What do you think?"

I look up to see that Melody has changed into a silky sleeveless T in a beautiful sky blue hue that I'm forbidden to wear unless—I mean, *until*—I give birth to a son.

"I like the flowery one better," I say, thinking quickly. "It's more . . . *maternal*."

"Maternal as in 'ready to bump.' Right?"

"Right," I reply, this time without a stammer.

Melody sighs as she puts the other blouse back on, assesses herself in the mirror once more. A look of triumph lights up her face. "Now, a last check on my hair and makeup!" she says as she runs out of the closet.

I don't follow her.

Instead, I pick up the blue shirt from the floor. The fabric is unlike anything I've ever felt before, virtually weightless, and so unlike the rough-hewn cotton and wool we use to make most of our clothing. I hold it up to marvel at the lack of discernible seams or stitches, clearly the product of neither spindle nor loom.

Melody bursts back into the closet. "Oh! I almost forgot!"

I yelp and drop the offensive shirt to the floor. Did she see me? No, she's too busy searching for something in her jewelry box. She holds what's she's looking for—a chain with a single, small bead—and regards it with a frown before putting it around her neck.

"So you'll be okay by yourself?" By the way she's blinking and rolling her eyes, I can tell that she's more focused on the MiNet than me.

I pray I won't be by myself for long.

"I don't have time to set up the touchpad for the MiNet

right now, so you won't be able to—"

"Oh, that's fine," I interrupt. "There's plenty in here"—I tap my Bible—"to keep me busy!"

"Um," she says distractedly, eyes racing in their sockets. "Right." Her eyes focus on the middle distance between us. "I'm leaving so . . . if you need . . ." More eye rolling. "Zen's *here*?" Without finishing her thought, she backs out of the closet in haste. A few moments later I hear the front door open and slam behind her. She doesn't say goodbye.

With fourteen housebrothers and housesisters, I'm rarely by myself. I like to go on long walks in the overgrown fields once cleared out for another never-built neighborhood. Ma still sees me as the sickly baby I once was and worries that I'll put too much stress on my delicate constitution. Going on those walks isn't against the Orders but is still a form of disobedience. I've always known my mother disapproves, but I've gone anyway. Not for the exercise, fresh air, or scenery. Just to be alone with my thoughts.

I pray I'll be forgiven for the worry I'm putting Ma through right now.

I shyly reclaim the blue T, then nervously hold it up to my own body, partly expecting to be discovered by several pairs of watching eyes all ready to chastise me for my transgressive ways. When it doesn't happen, I am emboldened to walk to the other side of the closet, where Melody's jeans are organized by color in tidy rows. I select silver.

The silence inside the closet is unnerving. I sing to

myself just to make some noise.

"*You're knocked up . . .*"

I bury my blushing face into my hands. Assimilating with the sinners is not going to be easy.

I have to remind myself that nothing I do here is against the Orders.

Cling to your faith in Christ, and keep your conscience clear.

I turn away from the mirror and unbutton my dress. Quickly, and still afraid of being scrutinized by invisible eyes, I pull on the jeans and slip on the T-shirt and . . . I still feel naked! The fabric is as light as air, no more than a whisper against my skin. It's indescribably strange to be covered up and yet, so . . . free. I cautiously look in the mirror, afraid that this is somehow a trick. . . .

That pretty girl in the mirror, openmouthed and pink in the cheeks, looks almost like an Othersider. There's just one minor adjustment.

The gloves come off.

Now she stands here in a T-shirt that brings out the blue in her eyes, and jeans that cling to every inch, two gloveless, ringless hands on her hips. This girl isn't Melody, though she looks exactly like Melody.

She is me.

melody

ZEN IS STRADDLING HIS BIKE IN MY DRIVEWAY.

"To what do I owe this great honor?" I ask, unlocking my own bike. "Are you here for me? Or are you and your new best friend shopping for chastity belts today?"

"I'm here to see *you*," he insists.

I wait for him to finish.

"To talk about *her*."

I knew it. I pull on my helmet and swing my leg over the crossbar.

"If you hadn't blinded your MiNet last night, you would know what I want to talk to you about."

"If *you* hadn't blinded your MiNet for the last *month*, you would know what I *don't* want to talk to you about."

"Look, I told you," he says, "I've got IAMs to study

for. Not everyone aces them the first time around."

A lot of good it's done me. My parents have already signed me up for another round because *near* perfect on the International Aptitude Measurements isn't perfect enough to get into Global U.

"I don't get why you're suddenly so obsessed with the IAMs anyway," I say, rolling my bike back and forth, crunching the gravel. "Weren't you the one telling me that brick-and-mortar institutions of higher learning are *so* last century? That my parents had the right idea, going out there and living life with the whole world as their classroom . . ."

I stop myself. My *awesome* parents are the last people I want to talk about right now. Gah. I change the subject.

"What did you say to Harmony yesterday?"

Zen looks relieved to return to this line of questioning.

"I said a lot of things," Zen says.

"You say whatever it takes to get everyone to like you."

He slumps over his handlebars and looks up at me with goo-gooey innocence. "Why do you think I'm always trying to get everyone to like me?"

"Zen! You *invented* the Like Me Algorithm!"

In ninth grade, Zen wrote an app that instantly cataloged the likes and dislikes of anyone who had ever created a MiNet profile and used that data to whatever ends he needed to get that person to like him.

"Not relevant," he says. "I never *used* it."

This is true. He destroyed the program immediately so it wouldn't be exploited by, in his words, "forces of evil."

"Your sister found me naturally charming. Just like you do."

I snort.

"In fact . . ." He throws his arms out in front of him as if presenting himself as a gift. "She might want me."

I make a big show out of laughing so hard I can hardly stand up.

"I'm serious!"

Still laughing, I push off down the hill.

"You're talking about a girl who thinks she'll go to hell if she shows a bit of ankle!" I yell into the breeze. "A person who wants me to marry one of her housebrothers at the end of the month."

"And why do you think that's so important to her?" he shouts from behind me.

"Maybe because she's been told her whole life that anyone who doesn't do things the Church way is going to burn in hell for all eternity? Because she's been brought up to believe that it's her mission in life to save as many of us sinners as possible? It would be a major failure if she couldn't even convince her own identical twin sister to have God."

"That's one way of seeing it," Zen says, struggling to keep up. He's got the better bike, but I've got longer, stronger legs. "I think *she's* the one who needs convincing, not you."

"And what did she say that makes you think that?"

"It wasn't what she said," Zen shouts. "It's what she *didn't* say. . . ."

Gah. Typical Zen.

"Promise me, Zen, you won't tell anyone at school about Harmony until I'm ready."

"Mel . . ."

"PROMISE OR I'LL TELL EVERYONE YOU STILL SLEEP WITH BOO BOO."

Boo Boo is Zen's girlbot. By sixteen years old, any self-respecting guy has replaced—or at least *supplemented*—his artificial lovin' with the real thing.

"We had good times together. I'm keeping her for sentimental reasons—"

"Oh, is *that* what they call it these days—"

"When you hit below the belt, you *really* hit below the belt—"

"JUST PROMISE."

"Okay." He rubs his helmet because he can't pull at the hair underneath. "I promise because I'm such a great friend, and *not* because I'm worried about anyone finding out about Boo Boo because guess what? It's common knowledge among dudes that we *all* hook up with our girlbots every now and again. . . ."

Gaaah. I pedal faster.

"Wait, Mel!" he says, panting harder now as I pick up the pace. "I'm being serious now. What if there's more than what Harmony is telling you . . . ?"

"I don't have time for your hypotheticals today!"

I zoom ahead, leaving him behind as if he's cemented to the sidewalk.

harmony
melody

NOW THAT MELODY IS GONE, ALL I HAVE TO DO IS WAIT.

"Do me a favor," Lib had said. "Skip school. Stay home today. Play NOOKY HOOKY. Because GUESS WHAT! It turns out our boy Jondoe was in New York City over the weekend to bump the mayor's daughter. She pregged on the first try! What a pro. Anyway, now he's got a few days free before he has to fly out to Los Angeles to promote his new fragrance. He can be there this AFTERNOON. Will you skip school so I can set up a one-on-one?"

I nodded mutely.

"THAT'S MY GIRL. I don't want another day to go by, Miss Melody Mayflower. Let's deliver what the Jaydens are SO WILLING to pay SO MUCH for. This is your FUTURE we're talking about." He stopped, assumed a more serious tone. "You do realize that your life is about to change."

My life already had.

"Once this news hits the MiNet, the optics are gonna go OFF THE SPRING. Your pregg will be famous. Morning sickness is NOTHING compared to how green with envy they'll be when they find out who's bumping you. . . ."

I didn't hear anything else Lib said. When he vanished from MiVu, taking my Morning Star with him, I fell to my knees, humbled by the task that God had put before me.

Lib believed that I was Melody—and it's his job to know everything about her. It shouldn't be too hard to lead a stranger into believing the same. I only have to pretend long enough to make him change his mind about . . . doing what he's supposed to do with my sister and, if possible, forsake his sinful profession altogether. If Jesus could spend His time preaching to the prostitutes, so can I.

Because I'm being challenged to serve a higher truth.

And saving Jondoe must be part of the plan now too.

melody

GAH. I HATE BIKING TO SCHOOL. BUT AS PRESIDENT OF THE
ECOmmunity Club, my parents say I have to serve as a
conscientious example.

I arrive at school all windswept and slightly sweaty, just
in time to see Shoko clamber down the steps from the bus
everyone calls the Bumpmobile. It provides rides to and
from school for all students with certified pregnancies, no
matter how close they live to campus. Malia, Shoko, and I
used to bike together every day and rant about the Cheerclones who can't walk one-tenth of a mile to school but
can still flip handsprings well into their third trimester.

"We're gonna rock big bellies on our bikes!" we used
to brag. "We won't be like those lazy breeders taking the
Bumpmobile."

Now Shoko sits next to those lazy breeders every morning swapping cures for stretch marks. Malia is in lockdown. And I bike to school alone.

I don't hold a grudge against Shoko. Really. She's been an awesome president. There's a lot of tension between amateurs and pros at school. Like, amateurs look down on pros for bumping with strangers, not boyfriends. Or they pity us for missing out on all the partner-swapping fun at the masSEX parties. And pros say amateurs are jealous because they aren't good enough to pregg for profit. And even if they were, they probably wouldn't have the willpower to keep their legs closed until it was time to fulfill their contractual obligations. That sort of cattiness threatened to end the Alliance before it even began. But as the rare amateur *turned* pro, Shoko has served as an inspiration and intermediary between both sides.

So that's the good news. The bad news is that this second pregg has given Shoko a major case of what experts call "adolescent amnio-amnesia." I swear she's dropped at least ten IQ points per trimester. She's at thirty-nine and a half weeks now and can't stay focused on anything. If she's carrying her third pregg in college, she'll fail out for serious. Like right now she waddles right past me without saying hello. As her peer birthcoach, the only nonrelative allowed in the delivery room, I'd be offended if I weren't so used to it.

I tap the bell to get her attention.

RING! RING! RING! "Shoko, hello!" *RING! RING! RING!*

"Oy!" she yelps, clutching her belly. "Don't break my water!"

She's joking. At least I think she's joking. Bounding off the bus right behind Shoko is none other than Ventura Vida. She and her adorable six-month bump believe otherwise.

"Oh, no!" she trills. "You rilly, rilly can't go into labor until after the vote!"

Ventura smiles with more gums than teeth. I guess she's figured out that she's prettier when she's meaner.

"Don't worry," Shoko says to Ventura and the group of variously pregnant girls surrounding her, many of whom I know from the Pro/Am. "I just know Burrito will take it to forty-two weeks, just like the first one."

"You've got a very *hospitable* womb," says Ventura, which makes everyone, including Shoko, laugh so hard that there must be more to it than what I'm hearing, the punch line for a joke that began on the bus.

"Ugh. I hope Sugar Booger doesn't go to forty-two weeks," groans Celine Lichtblau, who, in my opinion, needs to tell her OB to adjust the dose on her AntiTocin. Taken in the right amounts, AntiTocin counteracts the all-natural chemical bond between biomom and pregg. Too much AntiTocin makes you a cranky bitch for nine months straight.

Ventura hoists her cleavage to get attention. It works. Her bra started as an A minus and is currently a D plus. With her luck, by the time she pushes, she'll probably be a full F, the only time such a grade change can be considered progress.

"*My* donor has a flawless track record for making preggs that deliver within twenty-four hours of their due dates . . ."

If Ventura doesn't stop bragging about how her RePro scored in the highest percentile in every category measured by the Standards for Premium Ejaculated Reproductive Material, I will tie my tubes.

" . . . so I assume that Perfect will be no different."

Same goes for referring to her pregg as "Perfect."

Ventura picks up on my annoyance and runs with it as fast as a girl in her second trimester can run.

"All this bump talk must be soooooo booooring for you, Melody. . . ."

"Um, no," I lie. "It's fascinating. Braxton-Hicks and epidurals and Kegels and . . . stuff."

I know I should be fascinated. But I'm not. And my trip to Babiez R U to try on FunBumps certainly didn't help in this regard.

"I'm sure you do," Ventura says crisply as the group around her giggles. And before I can make an effort to sound more convincing, she adds, "Oh, by the way, we passed Zen on his bicycle. . . ."

Ventura is obsessed with my friendship with Zen. She never fails to bring him up in conversation. "He's so hot! I don't know why you two don't just bump and get it over with," she says. "You'd really make such a cute pregg."

Everyone knows why Zen hasn't bumped me or anyone else: He's a risky investment. It doesn't matter that mixmatchy rainbow families are so on trend right now. High IQ can't make up for his insufficient verticality. Apparently that hasn't stopped him from giving gooooood everythingbut.

I stay calm. "I'm already under contract. You know that."

"I bet he'll be amped when you finally do pregg," Ventura says, casting a look around at the crowd. "Then you and Zen can bump-hump all you want without worrying about breaking your contract. . . ."

On any other day, I could just let this go. But today isn't an ordinary day, what with Harmony in hiding at my house and my parents trying to pimp me out and everything. I swear, if it weren't a felony, I'd smack Ventura AND her adorable six-month bump.

Fortunately, if unintentionally, Shoko comes to my rescue.

"Hey, there's nothing wrong with humping when you're bumping. Raimundo and I went at it like crazy for the full forty-two and my first pregg didn't come out all cock-knocked in the head."

Doing it for *fun*. The one advantage to bumping as an amateur.

"Omigod, I was just *scamming*!" Ventura lies. "See you at the meeting!" Then she shoots me a departing smirk and leads the pregnancy parade into the school.

"Waddle with me," Shoko says, taking my arm to hold me back. With an extra thirty pounds on her barely five-foot frame, she's on pace with one of those giant prehistoric ground sloths. The journey from the parking lot to her locker is epic, like moving from one era of geologic time into the next.

I'm still seething. "She acts as if she's the first girl in this school to go pro."

"She's scored a sweet deal," Shoko says, adjusting her belly band. "Full college tuition, tummy tuck, a car . . . "

"A car! She doesn't even have a license! And what's the big humping deal anyway? I've got all that written into *my* contract!"

Shoko levels me with a look that is barely more sympathetic than pathetic.

"Well, yes," she says, patting my shoulder. "But you haven't . . ."

Her eyes drop to my flat tummy.

"It's not my fault!" I cry.

"I know it's not."

We inch our way up the steps before I say what I really want to say.

"You think Ventura is the future of the Pro/Am, don't you?"

Shoko sighs with every ounce of extra poundage. "It's not that I think she *should* be."

"But you think she *is*."

Shoko's four chins nod.

"Oh, this is just breedy," I mutter. "Not even my best friend thinks I'm qualified to take over."

I don't mention how I know Malia would feel about it: *Break your contract while you still can!*

"There is a question of your commitment," Shoko says.

"My *commitment*?"

No one shows more commitment to school activities than I do! I'm president of the ECOmmunity Club, cocaptain of the soccer team (though we had to forfeit half of our season because we'd already lost Shoko and Malia when our striker was diagnosed with gestational diabetes), coach for the Science Olympiad . . .

Shoko grimaces, rubs her lower back. "Commitment to the *cause*," she explains. "To bringing together amateurs and professionals in the promotion of positive pregging."

"*I* was the first girl to sign a contract at this school! *I* made it the cool thing to do! And *I'm* not committed to the cause?"

"Well, not to be painfully obvious or anything, but it's not like you can, like, *authentically* represent the Alliance when you're the only unbump—"

"*Pre*bump!"

"Prebump. Whatever. But you *did* just turn sixteen," Shoko says with a sympathetic shake of her head. "You don't have much time left. . . ."

For the second time today, I'm brutally reminded of the repercussions of my looming obsolescence.

This is all Lib's fault. As my RePro Rep, Lib needs

to man up and start earning his 15 percent. It's his job to put more pressure on the Jaydens to hurry up and hire the Sperm to my Egg because my biological clock is ticking away.

I must look pretty depressed because Shoko abruptly changes the subject. "Gossip!"

My breath catches in my throat. I blinded the MiNet last night because I was studying—as always—but also because I felt like being antisocial. I don't care if there are MiFotos of Melody Mayflower standing next to a veiled and anonymous Church girl at the Mallplex. I could easily claim that she came faithing hard at me as Churchies are known to do. But if the MiNet is surging with MiFotos of Melody Mayflower standing next to an unveiled Church girl who looks *exactly like her*, I wanted to avoid those pics as long as possible. Would anyone believe I was being foto-bombed?

"Did you hear the latest about Malia?"

I can't exhale yet.

If I take credit for making it cool for Shoko, Ventura, and everyone else to pregg for profit, am I also to blame for what happened to Malia?

harmony
melody

THE DOORBELL RINGS.

I take a quick glance in the mirror, relieved to see more of Melody than myself. I inhale deeply, unlock and open the door.

It's Him. I mean, him.

"Yes, it's really me," he says, removing his mirrored sunglasses and flashing a smile.

Haloed in a golden light of the late-afternoon sun, Jondoe is more glorious in person than he was on-screen. Or in my dreams.

"There's no spontaneity in these transactions, nothing left to chance," he says, with a wide, bright grin. "Lib said you'd be here, so I thought I'd just connect in your facespace instead of the MiNet. I know you don't like the traditional trappings of romance like flowers, which you are *so right* in saying is ironic because you're Miss Melody May*flower* and all. . . ."

I almost correct him. Then I remember. *I am Miss Melody Mayflower.*

"So I brought your favorite brand of GlycoGoGo Bars and a sixer of Coke '99 instead."

He presents me with a clutch of soda cans in one hand and a box in the other. Then he gives me a knowing look and says, "We might need these later, you know, to keep our energy up," and laughs in a way that is meant to encourage me to laugh along with him. But I can't laugh, I can't accept his gifts, I can't do anything.

"I'm Jondoe," he purrs. "But you know that."

He bypasses the handshake and extends his arms wide, waiting for me to give him a welcoming embrace that I am in no condition to give. When I don't respond, he makes a clowny frowny face.

"Oh, come on, I'm not *that* bad, am I?" He's smiling again, teasing me.

He must know that he is the very opposite of bad. He is the finest evidence of goodness on this earth that I have ever encountered.

"You're disappointed. You think I'm hotter in the ads," he groans. But the smile is still there, fully confident that he could be no such thing to me or anyone. He speaks with cozy familiarity, as if we have known each other forever. "Oh, there's not enough Tocin in the world to get you to bump with me. . . ."

"Oh my grace!" I gasp at this sudden reminder of Jondoe's intentions.

His face softens for a split second as it registers genuine surprise. "Ha ha ha!" He laughs beautifully, musically. "That's funny."

"I mean, um . . ."

My head fills with scrambled poetry from the Song of Songs, a book from the Old Testament that I've never cared much for before.

His mouth is sweetness itself; he is altogether lovely . . .

I cannot say such things! I will not! I swallow to clear my throat and try to speak.

"You look just like . . ."

Jesus.

He looks just like the Jesus in my dreams.

melody
harmony

I'M NOT PROUD TO SAY THAT I BLINDED MALIA AFTER HER LAST
MiNet rant.

*They told me if I loved myself, if I loved my country I would
give Angelina to her rightful parents and never think about her
again. Why did you let them say those things to me? Why didn't
you try to stop them? You were my birthcoach. You were supposed
to be there for me. . . .*

I just couldn't take the guilt anymore. I should have
known that wouldn't be the last I'd hear about her.

"Did she get out of the, um . . . you know, lockdown?"

"Over the weekend," Shoko says, leaning on my arm
for support. "Her parents are sending her to . . ." She looks
over her shoulders and whispers, "The Shields Center."

My intestines lurch. Only the worst cases get sent there,

mostly girls who go mad after misdelivering.

"She's totally lost it. Wackadoodledeedoo." Shoko crosses her eyes. "She was still wanking out and screaming to anyone who would listen that she's a victim of preggsploitation and that the deal was off and she was keeping her delivery for herself. She was even using the B word."

Where is my baby?

"Her parents are suing the RePro Rep for botching the whole transaction."

I don't blame them. Even before this postdelivery meltdown, we all talked about how Malia's broker was the worst. He totally lowballed her. True, she wasn't an easy sell. Malia is the nicest person I know, but niceness is not a quantifiable high-revenue quality. She's short and sorta thick in both meanings of the word—she struggled to keep up in her classes. But she was tough on the soccer field, a true team player who would sooner make an assist than go for the goal herself. So nice. Always so nice. I think she ran unopposed for vice president because we all felt like someone so nice deserved to excel at something. At least that's why *I* didn't run against her. (Ventura hadn't joined the Alliance yet. If she had, I doubt she would've had any such reservations because she's just that powertrippy.)

Malia was willing to deliver a pregg for someone who wanted one, either because she was really that nice or because the pressure to keep up with the rest of us— pressure that began the moment I signed my contract with Lib—was just too much. Or both. She didn't want to feel left out. And as the last prebump in the Alliance, I can hardly blame her.

Malia never disclosed the full terms of her contract but Shoko and I both have reason to believe that her Rep settled for something in the low four figures. When I told Lib about it, he told me it's quantity-over-quality brokers like that who give commercial surrogetting a bad name.

"It was *his* mistake for showing Malia the SimFant."

Surrogettes are never supposed to see 4-D because they supposedly come out really, really cute and we might get too attached. That's exactly what happened to Malia.

"You know they upped her dose of AntiTocin, right?"

"Right. And it wasn't enough?"

"Well, it *was* at first," Shoko says. "But it turns out that she stopped taking it for the last few months of pregging."

As I said, too much AntiTocin makes you a raving bitch for forty weeks straight. Too little and . . .

I want my baby.

"Malia can't remember to bring her flexbook to school every day; I should have known she'd forget to take her pill."

"Oh, she didn't forget," Shoko says brightly. "She confessed to her OB that she stopped taking her meds on purpose."

On purpose? I'm about to pop an outtie. "Why would she *ever* do that?"

"That's the best part." Shoko lights up. "She said it was making her fat!"

Shoko is laughing so hard that I'm surprised her delivery doesn't drop right here and now.

"It's not funny," I say.

"It is."

"It's not."

"She was pregging. She's *supposed* to get fat. How is that not funny?"

They took my baby.

"SHE'S OUR FRIEND AND SHE HAS POST-PARTUM PSYCHOSIS. HOW IS THAT FUNNY?"

"Oy." Shoko blanches, clutching her belly. "Keep your voice down. Burrito just kicked me in the kidneys."

"Sorry," I say without a trace of apology in my voice.

"It's just so Malia," Shoko says derisively. "Who else would stop taking AntiTocin on purpose?"

I could have prevented this. I should have done something as soon as she stopped calling her pregg Shrimpy and renamed it Angelina. I should have spoken up in the delivery room. I should have warned the doctors.

"I don't know how you can be so judgy about what's happened to her," I say, more to Shoko's stomach than to her. "You were pregg partners!"

For months I watched Shoko and Malia grow bigger by the day. I watched them swap MyTurnTees, share tubes of You Glow Girl! stretch-mark remover, and share bag after bag of Big Belly Jellies. I watched them bond with each other because they were forbidden to bond with their bumps. I watched them and thought I wanted to pregg right along with them.

Now I'm less excited to pregg than I am scared to be the only girl who hasn't.

"Oh please, I don't feel sorry for her at all," Shoko snaps, hands still rubbing her sides. "And if you had bumped already, you wouldn't either."

"What's *that* supposed to mean?"

"I know what it's like to look and feel like I've smuggled a watermelon up through my breedy bits, to need a half hour to waddle from the parking lot to my locker." She sighs heavily. "None of it is much fun, but pregging for the highest bidder was the best decision I could have ever made. If I had been traumatized by the experience, would I have agreed to do it again?"

I guessed that she would not.

"Reneggers like Malia make the rest of us look bad. If it keeps happening, it will be harder for Surrogettes to push for profit. Until you've walked a mile in my swollen feet, I doubt you'll be able to understand."

That's exactly why Malia picked me to be her birth-coach. As the only one who hadn't pregged yet, I was the only one who might listen to her pleas. She knew well before she was wheeled into the delivery room what she wanted to do. And if she had only trusted me enough to let me in on her secret, I might have tried to help her.

At least I'd like to think I would have.

By the time we reach Shoko's locker, I feel like I've walked a *million* miles in her swollen feet. This has been the longest, slowest trudge of my entire life.

"I'll see you at the meeting," I say.

"Uh-huh." She doesn't look at me.

I'm feeling for seriously sad as I press my way through the noisy, packed hallway to my own locker. The crowd doesn't part when they see *me* coming. . . .

Shoko and I never battled like this before she pregged. I've been blaming it on a combination of all-natural hormonal fluctuations plus synthetic ones brought on by AntiTocin. But maybe the tension between us has nothing to do with what's happening to her and everything to what's *not* happening to me.

A hand touches my shoulder from behind. Before I look, I know who it is.

"I'm sorry," Zen says.

I go for the hug, rest my chin on his shoulder, and hold on longer than necessary.

harmony
melody

I CAN'T SPEAK.

"So you were about to tell me how I look just like Jondoe from the Tocin ads," he says in a playful way. "I get that all the time."

I can't move.

He leans into the doorway trying to get a peek at the interior. "Are you going to let me in?"

"Oh my grace!" I jump to the side.

"Ha ha ha!" He laughs again. "That's funny. *You're* funny." He raises an eyebrow, as if we're sharing a secret. "The file didn't mention that you had a sense of humor."

He brushes past me and I breathe in his earthy-sweet scent.

"Whoa," he says, pausing at the two towers in the

common room. "This is an impressive collection of dead media."

He slips a square plastic case from the top of the stack and shows it to me. On it is a picture of a girl who looks to be around my own age, dressed in a tight red top and blasphemously short skirt. She's on her knees, but she's definitely not praying.

"You know the rappers Fed Double X?" Jondoe asks, without waiting for an answer. "This is their mom," he says, tapping the case. "She was a major bonermaker back in her prime." He glances up and gives me an appraising look. "You're way more reproaesthetical than she ever was." Jondoe carefully puts the case back where it came from.

I bite my lip to stop myself from yelping, but a squeal comes out just the same. He turns away from the rack and gives me a quizzical look, as though he's not certain whether the sound came from me or a small rodent.

"So. Your story," he says.

I wring my gloveless hands. "My story?"

"Yeah, your story," he says, stretching his arms above his head to touch the fleur-de-lis pattern in the pressed tin ceiling. "Why you decided to become a Surrogette . . ." His slim white T inches up, revealing too much.

"Oh my grace," I exclaim, again without thinking. I cover my mouth with my hands.

"Oh *my* grace!" he repeats for the second time, covering his mouth with his hands. Then he laughs the deep-in-the-belly laugh. "Ha ha ha ha ha! Your file didn't

say you'd be funny," he says again. "And you, Miss M̶
Mayflower, are funny."

I am Miss Melody Mayflower.

"You're a trailblazer," Jondoe says, running a hand along the irregular tree scraps jutting out of the walls. "I'm impressed. The first girl at your school to popularize reproductive empowerment."

"Right," I say, numbly nodding.

"All that, and smart too! So you're applying to Global U. I guess you're ready to expand your horizons?"

"Expand my horizons," I say truthfully. "Definitely."

We stop in front of a half-open door. He cranes his neck to take a peek.

"And this is your bedroom."

melody

NOT MUCH IN THE WAY OF VALUABLE EDUCATION HAPPENED today. If my parents had any idea, they would've made up for the wasted day by scheduling an after-school session with one of my academic drill instructors. Their cluelessness is by far the best thing about the schoolwide MiNet blind.

In first period, Luciana Holquist, Eiko Cooper, Dea Lan, and Brynn Mandelbaum interrupted the Mandarin lesson by requesting passes to the nurse's office. They're the Cheerclones who tried to synchro-bump with the select members of the varsity basketball team known as the Ballers at the masSEX party Zen chauffeured the other night. They just couldn't wait until the end of the day to see if they had succeeded. So it was all anyone could talk about for the rest of the class period because the biggest synchro-bump at our school so far happened last fall when three girls I coached on the Science Olympiad were tri-sperminated by Maxim, the only Olympian over five ten whose whole body wasn't armored by acne. This was a challenging conversation to have in Mandarin, however, because we haven't learned the words for "Cheerclones," "Ballers," "sperminated," or "masSEX parties."

It turned out that the Cheerclones were far less successful than the Science Olympians, who had the left-sided brainskills necessary for accurately calculating ovulation. When only Dea returned with a plus sign, the rest of first period and all of second period calculus was spent congratulating her and consoling the rest of the squad.

"You can always try again tomorrow!" Zen said encouragingly to Luciana, Eiko, and Brynn. "Why wait until tomorrow? How about right now? I've got five minutes!" He was determined to put the cheer back in Cheerclone. "Oh, I get it. You're in a rush! I'll do it in two!"

"Oh, Zen!" They giggled through their tears.

And then one of them—maybe Eiko, who can tell?—said something weird.

"You totally owe us for bailing the other night."

But before I could find out what she was talking about, the bell rang and Zen bolted out of the classroom for his favorite class, an elective on the Decline of Western Civilization.

My third period is Personal Health and Fitness. The girls in my class who were legitimately bent over with nausea in the bleachers were joined by so many others who were green with Sympathetic Morning Sickness that I had no choice but to join the boys in their soccer game, which was fine because after thousands of hours of drills and skills, I'm faster and have better footwork than half of them already and the other half had total-body hangovers from the weekend and could barely touch their toes to the ball without flinching in pain.

Periods four (North American Language Arts and Culture) and five (Biogenetics II) were spent reading and responding to all the notes Zen was passing me now that he had brought comic relief to the Cheerclones and was back to obsessing about my sister. Since our school went MiNet blind, it's for seriously more like 1836 than 2036.

I THINK YOUR SISTER'S MARRIAGE IS A MISTAKE.

I think you're a victim of your own false consciousness.

YOU HAVE MANY UPMARKET QUALITIES BUT A SENSE OF HUMOR IS NOT ONE OF THEM. FOR SERIOUS, THOUGH. DON'T YOU THINK IT'S STRANGE THAT SHE NEVER TALKS ABOUT HER FIANCÉ? OR HER WEDDING PLANS? WHEN MY SISTER WAS ENGAGED HER WEDDING WAS ALL SHE TALKED ABOUT. AND SHE WASN'T EVEN A VIRGIN. HARMONY HAS A LOT MORE TO LOOK FORWARD TO ON HER HONEYMOON. . . .

The Jaydens aren't paying me for my sense of humor. What are you being paid for? And I did notice. But most of what they do in Goodside is strange. Why should this be any different?

NO PRICE TAG CAN BE PUT ON MY SKILL SET. BUT DON'T GET
ME OFF TOPIC. WE SHOULD OFFER YOUR SISTER ASYLUM SO SHE CAN
STAY IN OTHERSIDE. FORCING MARRIAGE IS A VIOLATION OF HER
BASIC HUMAN RIGHTS.

What makes you think she wants to stay here?

I'VE DONE MY RESEARCH. MOST TRUBIES DON'T GET FIVE MILES
AWAY FROM THEIR SETTLEMENT BEFORE THEY GET SCARED, GO
BACK, AND MAKE A LIFELONG COMMITMENT TO THE CHURCH. THAT
SHE CAME HERE AT ALL PROVES THAT SHE WANTS TO STAY.

What if I don't want her to stay here?

IF YOU CHOOSE TO BE SO UNCOOL AND CAST OUT YOUR IDENTICAL
TWIN SISTER, THEN SHE CAN ALWAYS STAY WITH ME.

Won't the Cheerclones get jealous? And how exactly
did you bail on them Saturday night?

YOUR SISTER IS TOO IMPORTANT TO WASTE TIME GOSSIPING
ABOUT HOW I SPENT SATURDAY NIGHT. THIS IS A SERIOUS SITUATION,
MEL. YOU HAVE AN OPPORTUNITY TO DO SOMETHING HERE. TO
HELP.
THIS TIME DON'T WAIT UNTIL IT'S TOO LATE.

Wise enough not to mention Malia by name, Zen
made the most winning argument he possibly could.

harmony
melody

JONDOE PUSHES OPEN THE DOOR, SWEEPS INSIDE THE bedroom, then heads straight to the floor-to-ceiling windows. He taps the blinds so they raise up to reveal a view of the woodsy backyard. A creamy sunbeam fills the room. Without warning, he strips off his long-sleeved white shirt, under which he's wearing an even more formfitting sleeveless shirt. Across his chest spreads lettering I'm afraid to look at.

Despite my better instincts, I read them anyway:

OPEN UP WITH TOCIN.

I feel dizzy and my tongue tastes like rust.

"Come here," he says, still looking out the window. "What do you see out there?"

"Trees," I croak.

"Right," he replies with a wry smile. "Trees."

Then he turns, puts his arms around me, and pulls me toward the glass.

His left arm is under my head, and his right arm embraces me. . . .

"Smile, Miss Melody Mayflower," he whispers in my ear.

Then just as quickly he abandons me to examine the wall covered in Melody's MiFoto collage.

"This is your best friend, Zen," he says, picking him out from a group photo taken at the Science Olympiad. His face gets grim. "Insufficient verticality must be a major bonerkiller."

He points to a woman with her legs scissoring in mid-air, a ball floating on the flat of her shoelaces. "Ah yes, number fifteen, your favorite player on the U.S. national team."

He drags a soccer ball out of corner with his foot. "I play too. But you know that." He flips the ball in and out and up and around and over and through his two feet. It's all a blur.

"Ready? Your turn," he says, before passing the ball to me. But I'm not ready at all and it hits me in the knees and bounces back to the floor with a dull thud. Athleticism, apparently, is not something I share with my sister.

"Sorry," he says flatly. "I figured . . ." He stops midthought, starts again, lights up with another smile. He spots a guitar case in the corner. "I think it's cool that you play real guitar instead of guitarbot."

Melody plays guitar? I had no idea she had an interest in music! So do I! We have more in common than I thought.

"Play something for me."

"I don't know . . ." I say. I'm in the worship band back at home, but I don't know how to play any songs that are popular in Otherside.

"I've seen your file, I know you're talented. I'd like to hear you live."

Then he gets down on his knees in front of me and presses his hands together in prayer.

"Pleeeeeeeease?"

I nod yes, if only to get him up off the floor. A few more seconds and there would be nothing, and I mean nothing, I could do to stop myself from getting down on the floor with him. . . .

To pray!

He claps his hands, hops to his feet, and jumps back onto Melody's bed. He contentedly rolls among her pillows and blankets as if it's the most natural thing in the world.

I take the guitar and pluck some notes to see if it's in tune.

"Go on," he says, gazing up at me from his supine position.

Then, with my eyes closed, I sing a simple hymn to give me strength:

"Love on me
Love in me
Love through me
Jesus."

I sing it like I've never sung it before.

"Love on you
Love in you
Love through you
Jesus."

And as I do, I feel a tiny flame sparking deep inside me, the flicker of a single lit match in a place I'm not supposed to think about, and as I keep singing and strumming that light burns hotter and brighter and spreads its warmth up and out and throughout my entire body, and I sing and sing and sing until that tiny torch has set my entire body ablaze, an undousable conflagration of passion.

melody

WITH SO MUCH GOING ON TODAY I COULD BARELY FOCUS ON my flexbooks. The upside is that I've been too distracted to worry about what will happen once I catch up with Shoko for the Pro/Am meeting. I see her before she sees me, which isn't surprising because she's as wide as she is tall.

"Hey," I say.

"Hey," she says back. "I passed my mucus plug today! You know what that means! Burrito won't be far behind!"

Gaaaah. Why am I the only one who gets icked by talk like this? I've got to pull myself together.

"That's breedy! Get ready for payday!"

"Yeah," she says, rubbing the small of her back. "I'm just surprised. I thought Burrito would squat for a full forty-two weeks. . . ."

I catch Ventura and her adorable six-month bump making her way toward the classroom where the meeting is about take place.

"I'm sorry about this morning." This time I mean it.

"It's okay," says Shoko. "I've been thinking about it and, you know, I'd be wanky too if Malia was MiNetting me all the time about keeping my legs closed and not making the same mistake she did."

Malia isn't flaming me. She's warning me. Or trying to. Before it's too late . . .

"She's obviously not in her right mind right now. Hopefully she'll get whatever therapy she needs at the Shields Center, and by the time she gets back you'll already have delivered a pregg to prove that she was all wrong."

Ventura is almost within earshot. I don't want her making smirky contributions to this conversation. Thankfully, the conversation ends midsentence in a familiar way.

"Oy! I gotta pee."

"Wait," I say as she turns, "before you go!"

She smiles as I place both hands on her belly and rub it for luck.

harmony

WHEN I OPEN MY EYES, I SEE JONDOE GAPING AT ME IN UTTER wonder.

"That was . . ." He opens and closes his mouth a few times. For the first time since I met him at the door, he's at a loss for words. Our eyes are locked for a few seconds of silence, and I'm thinking that I could live the rest of my life like this, just gazing into his limitless eyes, when he breaks the connection with a word.

"Unexpected."

Jondoe pulls his knapsack onto his lap, reaches in and pulls out a thin white stick wrapped in plastic. He points it at me. I must look as thoroughly confused as I feel.

"You don't know what this is," he says, more of a comment than a question.

I shake my head.

"Whoa," he says with honest wonderment. "You're like a nubie. Innocent," he says in a quieter voice as he unwraps the plastic. "Surprising."

He opens his mouth, and gestures for me to do the same. I open my mouth and he laughs again.

"I can't do it from all the way over here!"

He beckons me to come away from the window and without hesitation I float over to him without my feet touching the ground. We are too close now. I'm feeling hot and swoony again, like I did in the Mallplex yesterday, as if I'm being smothered by a veil made of soaking-wet wool.

"Ahh," he says, presenting his open mouth to me with his tongue out.

"Ahh . . ."

Let him kiss me with the kisses of his mouth: for your love is more delightful than wine. . . .

He tenderly inserts the stick under my tongue, then pulls away and flops back onto the bed.

"Close and hold for ten seconds."

I do as he says, which isn't easy because my chin and the rest of my body are trembling. I realize now that the stick is a kind of thermometer. I watch as the white plastic turns bright green.

He swings into a sitting position on the edge of the bed, feet firmly planted on the floor. He pats the mattress, inviting me to sit down beside him. I shake my head, no.

I'm fine just where I am on the other side of the room, my back up against the wall.

He comes to me.

"Well," he says, pulling out the stick from between my lips, "it's a good thing I came today."

"It is?"

"Green means go!"

Green means go. I think of my green fertility gown hanging in my closet back in Goodside. Never worn.

"You're peaking." He tosses the stick into the recycling bin. "We can bump this out tonight."

Jondoe claps his hands and rubs them together, like he's warming himself up in front of a fire.

I gulp loud enough for God Himself to hear.

melody
harmony

VENTURA VIDA HAS THE PEE STICK.

"The Pro/Am has an image problem," she says. "We're just not *sexy* enough. I mean, rilly!"

We reviewed the fund-and-awareness-raising success of "Why Save Yourself When You Can Save the World?" T-shirt sale. We signed a petition to get caf services to offer more fertile, high-folate versions of pizza and french fries because we're gagging on the spinach and chickpeas in the salad bar. It's the last meeting of the year, so there's nothing else on the Pro/Am agenda except the vote for the next president. But this won't happen until Ventura surrenders the pee stick. And she's clutching the gold-plated positive pregnancy test like a talisman, unwilling to let it go and let someone else get a word in edgewise.

"Princeton Day Academy is already on track to rack up forty-two preggs this year. That's double last year's tally, but accounts for only twenty-five percent of our school's fertile female population! We shouldn't be satisfied until every Little Tiger is wearing one of these!"

She grasps the necklace that we all wear. Earlier in the meeting Ventura proudly added another bead to her chain during the Gestation Celebration, when all girls earn a bronze, silver, or gold bead for entering their first, second, and third trimesters, respectively. Everyone gets a glass bead just for joining, and births are commemorated with a diamond or rhinestone. Professionals usually have enough cash extra for the former, while amateurs have to settle for the latter—a good example of the type of thing that causes tension and called for the creation of the Alliance in the first place.

As if reading my mind, Ventura says, "We've gone so far in putting our petty differences as professionals and amateurs aside. We can come together as a united front to make girls do the right thing and bump like all of us." She makes a big show out of turning her head to look at me. "I mean, *almost all* of us."

Drawing attention to the embarrassingly blingless chain around my neck is totally uncalled for, even for Ventura.

"We owe it to our community, both locally and globally, to try even harder to do better."

"Maybe we should follow China's lead with mandatory

inseminations," I mutter to Shoko, hoping to get her attention.

Shoko's sitting right next to me, but she's too busy digging through a bag of Big Belly Jellies to acknowledge what I've said. Apparently Ventura did hear me because she holds up the pee stick and makes a slashing gesture across her throat. Gah, she has nerve for a new girl. I make a big show out of putting my hand in the air, a gesture that she just as elaborately ignores.

"The new man brands are getting way too much attention. You've all seen the Tocin ads. . . ."

The room explodes with everyone's favorite studs-for-hire.

"For serious. How hot is Phoenix?"

"I want me some Fitch!"

"Jondoe! Omigod! Jondoe!"

"Yes, they're all major stiffies," Ventura yells over the chatter. "But it shouldn't be about them! It should be about us!" She pops her belly out in a provocative bump-and-grind. "Can't PREGG without the . . ."

"EGG!" shout Tulie Peters (sophomore, amateur, eighteen weeks) and Dyanna Merrill (senior, professional, fourteen weeks) in unison. They obviously practiced this call-and-response before the meeting. I have to give Ventura credit for getting a professional and an amateur to chant together in the spirit of bipartisan pregging. I'd also like to point out that you also can't PREGG without the SPERM, but highlighting such contradictions in Ventura's logic would go over like a raging case of hemorrhoids.

Shoko's hazy expression suddenly snaps into focus as she holds a creamy yellow Big Belly Jelly between her swollen fingers.

"Lemon ginger!" she says to no one in particular. "Aids the digestion." She pops it into her mouth and then, as an aside, in between chews: "Burrito's got his foot stuck in my poop chute."

I snort with laughter.

"Excuse me," Ventura says sharply. "I'm the one with the pee stick. *I've* still got the floor."

"Sorry, Ventura," Shoko says. "Burrito is making me stoooopid. I can't stay focused for . . . um . . . you know . . . *shit*."

Heads all around the circle nod in sympathy.

"Well, that's all the more reason to vote before you go on birthleave," says Ventura, tossing her glossy black hair over her shoulder. Ventura for seriously lucked out on the hormonal draw because her hair is more lustrous now than ever before. Poor Celine Lichtblau (freshman, amateur, eleven weeks) is losing her hair by the handful and she's still got two trimesters left. By the time she reaches her due date, she'll be balder than the delivery she pushes out in the stirrups.

I'm now shaking my hand like a Cheerclone without her pom-poms. Shoko's face is back in the Big Belly Jellies. Ventura and her adorable six-month bump stand up and look over and beyond our little group, assuming a self-important posture as if she's about to address a crowd of thousands, not tens.

"If I'm so lucky to be voted our next president today," Ventura says, winking at the group, "I'll make it my mission to rilly overhaul our image. We need to get sexier to attract more girls to our cause."

She puts on her most life-or-death serious face.

"I know you're all aware of the unfortunate circumstances that led to the dismissal of our former vice president."

The whole room titters nervously. Ventura's tone is somber, and yet her heart-shaped face takes on an even rosier glow.

"We live in frightening times, girls, and we need to be role models, not reneggers."

Oh, no. I can already see where she's going with this.

"It's our duty to work together as professionals and amateurs to promote positive pregging for the sake of all the parental units who desperately want our deliveries. Do you appreciate how lucky we are to live in a true melting pot of races, ethnicities, and cultures? In the United States, deliveries of every color and creed are *valued*. Do you know that if we lived in the Middle East, or parts of Europe, we would be forced by law to pregg with our own kind to keep the gene pool pure?" A ripple of gasps moves through the group. "I know. It's shocking to think that the government would try to stick its nose in our ladyparts."

I'm hoping Shoko will break in with a joke about

Burrito sticking his nose in her ladyparts, but she's as hypnotized as the rest of them.

"Our mixmatchy preggs are the best way to promote peace around the world. Who are you going to hate if you have blood running through you from every continent?" She casts a sly glance in my direction. "That is, unless you're like Melody here, who's so pure that no swimmers are worthy of her womb. . . . *Just scamming!*"

Barely muffled laugher all around the room.

I hate Ventura Vida. I want to draw blood. And I'm *not* scamming.

"For the first time in history, teenage girls are *the most important people on the planet.*" She sings the last few words, of course. "We can't all be like Zorah Harding, who, as we all know, is due to make her ninth and tenth deliveries any moment now!"

The room breaks into applause for the most famously prolific eighteen-year-old in America.

"But we can all aspire to her greatness, can't we? Whether you're an amateur"—and she pauses to look meaningfully at Celine and Tulie—"or a professional Surrogette"—she stops again to lock eyes with Dyanna and a captivated Shoko—"our nation needs *all* our preggs, girls, if we have any chance of reclaiming our undisputed status as the most powerful country in the world well into the twenty-first century and beyond. If we hesitate"—and now she slowly turns her head in my direction again—"our multicultural American society, a shining beacon of tolerance and empathy around the world, will die. I mean, like, rilly *rilly* die."

Everyone is on their swollen feet. Everyone, including my best friend. Some are clapping, some are crying, all are rocking their huge bellies with patriotic pride. I imagine an army of unseen deliveries pumping tiny fists. "USA! USA! USA!"

Even before the votes are cast—all but two (thanks, Shoko) in Ventura's favor—there's no doubt in my mind that I am rilly, *rilly* humped.

harmony

melody

"TONIGHT?"

A look of disappointment crosses Jondoe face. "I know," he says apologetically. "I also wish we could get down to business right now," he says with a wolfish smile. "But you're my fourth call of the day. Even *I* need downtime to reload."

The fire deep in my belly shows no sign of fizzling out.

"On the upside, we've got a few hours to make some media."

He suddenly jumps up, heads to the windows, looks outside. He flexes his arms above his head, flashes a smile, holds completely still for a few beats, then drops his arms and the smile.

"What?" How is it possible to be so enthralled by

someone I can barely understand?

"You didn't get the itinerary?" His face contorts in something resembling anger for the first time. "My assistant should have messaged you earlier. This is totally unprofessional!" He sighs heavily. "We're going to all your favorite places. The Avatarcade, then the All-Sports Arena, followed by dinner at the U.S. Buff-A . . ."

This all sounds very exciting. "So it's a *date*?"

"A date? I've never been on a *date*."

"Me either," I say truthfully. We don't date in Goodside. We marry.

"I've had good hangs, but a date?" He can't stop smiling at me. "I don't think I've ever heard anyone under a hundred years old use that word. Though it *is* kind of cute . . ."

He starts walking out of the room before looking back behind him.

"Are you coming with me or not?"

Come, my darling, my beautiful one, come with me . . .

I nod yes before I can say no.

melody
harmony

I'M IGNORING MORE THAN 250 MESSAGES MINETTED WHILE I AM in school. I can wait until I get home to check them. I'm in no rush for 250 variations on SORRY U LOST.

The MiNet blind actually extends a hundred yards in all directions around our campus. About a dozen students are clustered on the first unblinded patch of sidewalk, too eager to catch up on eight technology-free hours to walk another step. The MiGamers are the most dangerous because they're too busy racing, blowing up, or otherwise challenging competitors in the virtual world to pay attention to people in the real world. Just last week a MiGamer was kickboxing a demonic gnome in Troll Troopers 4: Garden of Good and Evil and accidentally skulled a freshman mathlete with his foot. (The mathlete, of course, was too focused on his own chess match against a twelve-year-old Russian prodigy to get out of harm's way.) Those on MiTunes or MiChat don't jump around as much, but tend to sing or talk way out loud.

"It's human nay-cha . . ."

"And he was like, WHOO-HOO . . ."

"For me to sperminay-cha . . ."

"And I was like, NUH-UH."

"I wanna impregnay-cha . . ."

All of it contributes to the noisy muddle of nonsense that I can't get away from far or fast enough. One of the sidewalk MiChatters is Zen, wearing black shorts and a tiger-striped zip-front jacket. He must have had a match this afternoon.

"Dude, I'm telling you. If you're *serious* about the game, you've got to stop spreading your seed around. When I've got an important match, I store enough *hornergy* to power up every electricar on the eastern seaboard. . . ."

"Hornergy" is Zen's term for the indomitable athletic edge powered by sexual restraint. The basketball, baseball, and football teams haven't had a winning season in years. The table-tennis team, however, is undefeated.

I weave my bike in and out of the babbling crowd and don't even wait to see if he notices me. I'm about to pass right by him when he holds out his arm to stop me.

"Wait," he says. Then he unfocuses his attention and says, "Later, bro," to whomever he was MiChatting with, before winking, blinking, and shutting it off and fixing his attention back on me.

"I was just giving some advice to the captain of the lacrosse team," he says. "They lost again."

"Oh," I say.

"You lost too," he says, walking his bike alongside mine.

"Ventura sure didn't waste any time in alerting the MiNet, did she?"

Zen rakes his scalp. "I don't know why you even wanted to run in the first place," he says. "How does a virge on the verge represent the interests of the Pro/Am Alliance?"

I sigh. "Shoko said the same thing. Did you guys co-write your script? And don't call me that."

"What?"

"A virgin on the verge of obsolescence. It's offensive."

"Well, it's true, isn't it?"

I halt my bike. "It's *not* true. I have at least a year left to bump!" I hate having to defend myself to Zen of all people. "And unless you've got some cure for the Virus that you're keeping to yourself instead of sharing it with the world and going down in history as the hero who rescued humanity from its slow trudge toward mass extinction, then you're also on the clock. If I'm a virge on the verge, so are you."

"And so we are," he says in a satisfied voice. "Beep. Beep. Beep. *Boom*."

We climb onto our bikes and ride together in a tense

silence—him in front, me following behind. At a red light, Zen reaches out and—*RING! RING!*—triggers my bell. The he looks up at me with total seriousness.

"I know what would solve all our problems."

"What?"

"It's human nay-cha . . . For me to sperminay-cha. . . ."

I have to laugh. For serious, life would be so much easier if I could just take Zen up on his offer, make good on our secret pact, and get the whole thing over with already. Maybe it could even solve my parents' financial problems. I mean, if Shoko and Raimundo could make out so well in their postdelivery bidding . . .

Who am I kidding? No one who can pay serious money would be willing to take the risk on Zen.

Zen is humping his bicycle as he sings, *"Don't hesitay-cha . . . Or it will be too lay-cha. . . ."*

I punch him in the arm, then move forward at the sight of the green light.

"Hey, watch it, there," Zen says. "This arm belongs to the number one table-tennis player in the county."

"I'm sorry," I say. "I forgot to even ask about your match. Did you win?"

"No need to ask. Of course I won," he says. "Mel, my hornergy could end our country's use of fossil fuels once and for all. I was just telling the lacrosse guys that I can thank my virge-on-the-verge-ness for my total dominance over all my opponents."

I clutch a hand to my chest, pretending to swoon.

"And to think you would have given it all up just to cheer me up."

I *am* feeling better. Losing to Ventura doesn't seem like the omnicidal tragedy it was a half hour ago. Such is the power of Zen.

"I wasn't just offering to help you," he says grandly. "But all of humanity."

"Oh, *really*?"

He pauses for effect. "I'm starting to agree with the ranters who think the world is overpopulated with all the wrong people."

I choke as if I've just swallowed a soccer ball. Just when I'm about to accuse Zen of being the unlikeliest eugenicist, he explains himself.

"*Old* people," he explains. "There are too many old people with their old ideas and not enough new people with new ideas. We are in a state of cultural stagnation—I mean, the last great technological innovation was the MiNet, and that's been around for more than a decade. Did you ever stop to think about why we drink Coke '99? Because old people want the formula they drank when when they were young like us."

"But I like Coke '99. . . ."

"Of course you love it! Because all the old people who control all of mass media and commercial enterprises have manipulated the system to bend to their grampy whims! Old people control everything because there are so many more of them than there ever will be of us. Unless we want to wait until our parents' generation finally takes a dirtnap, it's up to thinking people like you and me to come together and create the next generation of innovators and game-changers. . . ."

I stop my bike and look Zen straight in the eye.

"Do you really believe this? Or are you still trying to have sex with me?"

Zen grins. "A skilled debater always knows how to win both sides of an argument."

harmony

I FOLLOW JONDOE OUT OF THE ROOM, DOWN THE HALL TOWARD the entrance to the house. He stops right before the front door, looks me up and down.

"Are you sure you want to wear your hair like that?"

I touch my braid.

"It's just that I always saw you with your hair down, except when you were on the soccer field."

Every girl in our settlement wears her hair in a single braid. It's one less distraction that can keep us focused on faith. I remove the elastic, and pull out the plaits, and let my hair loose. Something deeper and more fundamentally *me* is coming apart too. . . .

"Relax," Jondoe says. "Let the pro handle it. I'll do all the talking. Just remember to smile."

And before I get to ask him why, the mirrored sunglasses go on and his teeth come out. He opens the front door and I am blinded by intense beams of light shooting at me from all directions.

This is it! The end! The Rapture!

Lights flash all around us, and I falter on wobbly knees. Jondoe puts his arm around me protectively, pulls me to his car, opens the door, gently shoves me inside, and closes the door behind me. I want to tell him it's no use trying to get away in his car, the angels find us and carry us away no matter where or how well we hide. I'm screaming on the inside, I can't get any of the words out. He, however, is unshaken. Jondoe rushes around to the driver's side, opens the door, and slips in beside me.

Before he shuts the door he leans out and shouts, "Suck on this, scummers!"

Then he starts the engine, stomps the foot pedal, and we make our escape in a swirling dust bowl of gray earth and gravel.

melody
harmony

WE DON'T SAY ANYTHING UNTIL MY HOUSE IS IN SIGHT.

"So what's the plan?" Zen asks.

"What's *what* plan?"

"How are we going to get your sister to stay?"

"Not that again," I huff. "She's a person, not one of your causes."

"People *are* my cause."

Unlike Zen, I didn't think much about Harmony all day. After being alone in the house for hours, I imagine that Harmony is eager to see me. Did she *really* amuse herself all day by reading the Bible? I get to the front door and I notice that she's left it unlocked. I'll need to remind Harmony that even though we're not in a high-crime zone, we're not on the farm anymore either.

"Hey, Harmony," I call out. "I'm home."

No response.

Zen comes in behind me. "Where's my favorite Good-sider?"

No response. The silence makes me uneasy.

"Maybe she's taking a nap," I say unconvincingly. When I check the guest room I'm not surprised that it's empty.

"Maybe she went back home," Zen says, clearly disappointed.

"Her suitcase is still here." As is the dress she was wearing when I left this morning, which is folded neatly on her bed . . . next to her veil.

This isn't good.

Zen pulls on his hair. "I'll check to see if she left a note or something."

I head down the hall and peek inside my room, thinking she might have slept in there again, as she doesn't know I know she did last night. (I didn't say anything to her about it because I didn't want to make her feel more blinked than she very clearly already felt at breakfast this morning.) Though there are signs that she was definitely in here at some point during the day—my bedspread is messed up—she isn't there now.

"No note," Zen says.

I start to worry now. If I knew she was back in Good-side, I'd be fine. But all signs point to her being on the loose in Princeton, probably faithing hard in Palmer

Square, asking people I know if they have God . . .

"Zen! She went out without her veil! Everyone will think she's me!"

"So what?"

"What's to stop her from marching up to Ventura Vida and quoting—oh, I don't know—the book of Virgin Mary chapter whatever, which says, *'Thou art a dirty whore and thy pregg is a bastard and thou wilt burn in hell'*?"

Zen stops dead. "Does the Bible really say that?"

"YES!" I scream.

"Dose down," Zen says, his eyeballs flicking wildly in his sockets. "There's nothing new on the MiNet about you. Just the same stuff about getting humped by Ventura in the election. And if she does show up, you can always say it's a prank. . . ."

I scan the unread MiNet queue for the day, thinking maybe Harmony somehow tried to contact me while I was at school. There are few from my parents, a dozen nonsense messages from Lib asking random questions like RU TER-MIN8ED? HOW IZZE? and tons of scamspam claiming to be Jondoe of all people telling me how reproaesthetical I am and how special and surprising I am and how he's never met a girl like me before. Gah. Are there any girls out there who are gullible enough to believe that the hot-test RePro in the world wants to MiChat them up?

I know I should be focusing on my missing twin, but I can't stop thinking about the number of messages from Lib. He's in Stockholm right now scouting for Scandinavian talent. I haven't heard from him in weeks and to get so many in such a short amount of time must mean *something* even if I can't make any sense of what that something might be right now. My curiosity is about to get the better of me when the doorbell rings.

"Harmony!" Zen and I shout simultaneously.

I race to the front door. As annoyed as I am that she's still *here*, I'm relieved that she's not *out there* providing Ventura Vida and the rest of the Pro/Am with a new excuse to kick me out of the club entirely.

I fling open the door, amped to unleash a version of my own parents' favorite lectures about personal responsibility, when I'm confronted not with Harmony at all, but a hulking teenage boy I've never seen before in my life.

"It's you," he says simply.

This fair-haired, ruddy-faced stranger is wearing a straight-cut black suit and a white shirt buttoned to his thick neck, no tie. A black, broad-brimmed felt hat sits on his head, and muddy lace-up work boots are on his feet. Behind him is a beat-up suitcase very similar to the one Harmony brought with her yesterday.

"One guess where's he's from," Zen says, reading my mind.

He makes a move to hug me with massively muscled arms.

"Back off, farmboy!" I snap back. "I don't know who *you* are! But I'm not who you think *I* am."

He looks bashfully at his feet. I've embarrassed him.

"You're twin sisters." Then he mumbles something else that sounds like "shoulda known."

"Yes, I'm Melody," I say. "And you must be Ram."

"Ma'am," he stammers, eyes back on this boots.

"Ma'am!" Zen thinks this is hilarious.

"You look just like her." Ram's lips barely move when he talks. It's a wonder I can make out any words at all.

"Well, we *are* identical twins," I say. "That's usually how it works."

He looks at the ground and says nothing. He wears his suit uncomfortably, as if it's two sizes two small. His shoulders are hunched up around his ears but his arms hang heavy at his sides, like he's carrying burlap sacks of flour or cornmeal or whatever he carries in burlap sacks around Goodside.

"Unfortunately, your fiancée isn't here," Zen says.

"My *what*?" Ram asks, a genial if befuddled smile on his face.

I don't understand what's going on here, and it's not only because I need a translation app to decode Ram's mush-mouthed mangling of the English language.

"Har-mo-ny," Zen says, speaking very slowly and deliberately. *"Mel-o-dy's twin sis-ter."*

"Right," Ram says, now looking anywhere but at us. "Your twin."

Then he raises his left arm and holds up his left hand, revealing a solid-gold band on his fourth finger. Having remained impossibly still throughout this conversation

158

up to now, this modest gesture has the attention-stealing impact of Jondoe's half-naked humpdancing in the infamous Tocin commercial. But that's nothing compared to what he says next.

"And my wife."

THIRD

We shouldn't be using hardworking American tax-payer dollars to pay Americans to pregg because pregging is patriotic and America is the greatest nation under God, so God bless America and Americans!
—"Mission: Maternity," Fox and Freedom Party

melody
həɹɯouʎ

ZEN'S BOPPING HIS HIPS BACK AND FORTH, WAGGLING HIS finger in whole world's face, mimicking the famous moves that go along with Fed Double X's first hit, "Toldja (So)."

"I toldja toldja . . . Coulda bought and soldja soldja. . . ."

Zen is never happier than when finding out that one of his hypotheticals isn't so hypothetical after all.

"I toldja toldja toldja toldja soooooooo. . . ."

I grab a pillow and two-handed hurl it at Zen with all my might. It takes him out at the knees and he keels over.

"AAARGH. WATCH THE ARM. . . ."

Meanwhile Ram is lying on my couch with his eyes closed, wearing a cold-pack helmet that has saved my brain after countless soccer balls to the skull. Because Ram sure sounds like he suffered a major blow to the head, this helmet was my best attempt at trying to make him feel better.

"Harmony isn't here?" Ram asks for the dozenth time.

He clearly isn't the most communicative person on his best days, let alone after finding out that his wife has vanished off the grid.

"Where could she be?"

"We don't know. She didn't leave a message. Her suitcase is still here, though."

Zen speaks for both of us because I too have lost the ability to communicate intelligibly let alone intelligently.

"She can't go far," Ram says. "Her cabdriver told me she traded her ring to pay for her trip."

"Her wedding ring?" Zen asks.

Another nod.

"Oooh, that's cold."

I remember the edge in Harmony's voice when the Babiez R U salesgirl asked whether she was wearing a ring under her glove. No wonder she got so defensive!

"It wasn't worth much." Ram's voice sounds high and hysterical now, like it's being strangled in the back of this throat. "But it was the best I could do."

And then he presses his face into his hands to hide his tears.

I shoot Zen a panicked "Now what?" look. I'm really not good at stuff like this. Touchy-feely stuff. I mean, I aced the EQ exam, but that's only because my parents hired a tutor to drill me in all matters emotional.

Zen brings his arms together in a circle and panto-
mimes a way overdue pregg.

"What?" I mouth.

Zen now strokes his bodacious invisible bump.

"Why are you pretending to pregg?"

Ram opens his eyes to see this.

"I'm pretending to *hug*," Zens wails in exasperation.
"This man needs a hug."

When I don't go for it, he starts ripping his hair out.

"GIVE HIM A HUG."

Ram pushes his palm at me. "No, ma'am."

Zen chuckles again at "ma'am."

"That ain't right. I am a married man." This message is
as clear as it gets. Then his eyes well up again.

"Why don't YOU hug him, Zen?"

"Naw!" Ram recoils, horror-stricken. "That ain't right
either!"

Clearly, Ram is twitchy about man-to-man contact.

"We didn't know you were married," Zen says, slapping him on the shoulder in a very hetero way that still
makes Ram go rigid. "She told us she was engaged."

"Actually, Zen," I say, slowly hitting on the truth.
"She never *said* she was engaged. I just assumed that she
was engaged because of the way she was dressed when she
showed up here." I turn to Ram. "She made a big deal
about wearing the veil."

I didn't ask enough questions. Or any questions at all,
really. I was too busy thinking about myself, and how her

arrival in my life would mess it up.

"How did you know to find her here anyway?" I ask Ram as gently as possible.

He's quiet for at least a minute before he finally exhales a tremulous breath and says, "Until she found out about you, she didn't have anywhere else to go."

This is not the response I was expecting.

Zen suddenly hops up and says, "I have an idea to help this conversation along!" He bounces over to my parents' fully stocked bar, messes around for a few moments, then comes forward with a short glass of dark liquid. Gah. Somewhere in the African savannah, Ash and Ty's GUARDIAN alarm is going off.

"Take this," Zen says to Ram.

"What is it?" Ram hiccups.

"This," Zen says, holding out the glass, "is a shot of premium aged whiskey. It will help open up your mind." He turns to me and whispers, "And your mouth."

Zen might be a bit of a genius. A light buzz might actually make Ram less self-conscious and more communicative—I mean, I know I'm far more fluent in Mandarin after I've knocked back a few. But the manboy isn't having it.

"Nononono." Ram pinches his mouth and shakes his head.

"Okaaay," Zen says in resignation. "I didn't want to have to give up my stash but . . ." He reaches into his back pocket, pinches a tiny baggie containing a small green pill.

"How about this . . . *vitamin*. A vitamin that will make everything feel better!"

That's no vitamin. That's a 10 mg of Tocin!

"I want to feel better," Ram says in a small voice.

Without another word, I yank Zen out of the common room.

"WATCH THE ARM. That arm belongs to the number-one-ranked—"

"Pause it!" I hiss. "Have you gone terminal? What are *you* of all people doing with that stuff anyway? I thought you were all against the, um, chemical manipulation of our most basic animalian instincts or, um, whatever."

Zen talks so much that it's difficult to remember anything that he actually says.

"You're overreacting," he says.

"For serious? *You* were the one to go manifesto on Shoko when *she* was dosing. About how it's totally illegal to hold without a scrip."

Up until now, I thought Zen and I were the only two sophomores at Princeton Day Academy who *hadn't* dosed. It's a popular party drug, way easier to score than beer, weed, or even Oxy. Lib always warned me to stay away from illicit recreational use because he'd seen too many clients breach contracts with amateur bumpings that would have never happened without it.

"If *you* want to get all high and humpy, that's your choice. But who knows how *he'll* react?"

"Have you looked at him?" Zen asks incredulously.

"He's a two-hundred-and-twenty-pound mountain of muscle. That's a tiny dose for a Goliath like him. It'll be enough to make him feel good, but not *too* good."

"I want to feel good," Ram says from the other room.

"Good enough to tell us the truth about that mysterious sister of yours," Zen says. "The one who is out there impersonating you as we sit here and have this debate."

I sigh, knowing this is really our best option for getting any answers out of Ram that will make any sense. Plus, if he gives the Tocin to Ram, he can't take it himself and use it with . . .

Whomever Zen planned to use it with.

"Zen?"

"Yeah?"

"If he tries to impregnate my couch, *you're* cleaning it up."

"You can't be the designated driver as many times as I have and not know how to clean up such messes," Zen replies affably, as if none of this is out of the ordinary. "Besides, that only happens when you crush and snort it."

I don't even want to know how he knows that.

harmony

melody

HIS VOICE—RESONANT AND REASSURING—IS THE FIRST
sound I hear.

"We're here."

I've had my senses shut off for the whole wild ride.
How long we've been chased, I can't say. It might have
been an instant or an eternity.

"Don't worry," he says in his smooth, soothing voice.
"You're with me. I'm a pro."

I'm with Him. That's all I need to hear. There's nothing to fear as long as he's beside me. Ready to know the
unknowable, I slowly open my eyes to see . . .

A parking lot?

"We're at the Avatarcade," he says. "You're into 4-D,
right?"

I shake my head no.

"Really? I thought I read in your file. . . ." He stops himself again. "I went to the first Avatarcade when it opened in Tokyo a few years ago. I'm not so into facespace role-play but it was all the surge on the MiNet and I wanted to see what all the yawping was about. So I go there and guess what? The Jondoe avatar was their top seller! Japan loves me! I had no idea! I've been making major yen off my simulation rights but I didn't even know it. Anyway, I wanted to try out the Jondoe avatar, you know, to see how others experience being me, but they wouldn't let me because there's risk of a permanent schizophrenic split."

I don't even pretend to know what he's saying.

"It's go time," Jondoe says. He hands me a smaller pair of mirrored sunglasses that are otherwise identical to his own. "There will be more of what we had before, so wear these."

I put them on only because he seems to know what's going on and I don't.

"I'll get out and say my lines to the paps. All you have to do is look at me adoringly and smile. Then we'll slip back into the car without going inside. The whole scene will take about a minute, then we'll move on to the next location. The paps all know the deal, we worked it all out in advance. It's all been awesomely staged."

And just when I'm about to beg God for his forgiveness, that I never wanted to be deceitful about my true identity, Jondoe gets out the car and shouts, "Get out of our facespace! We only want to role-play in peace!"

And then he comes around to my side and throws open the door and I'm again bombarded with flashing lights as I was at Melody's house. Only now, through the filtered lenses of the glasses, I can see the truth behind where they're coming from.

"If you scummers don't leave us alone, I'll have to put an end to my charity work!"

I'm not being chased by angels . . .

"Miss Melody Mayflower is just a regular girl! She deserves her privacy!"

I'm being chased by the press.

Jondoe rushes to my side and wraps his arms around me. He whispers in my ear, "Give 'em what they want! That's the deal! Or they'll never leave us alone."

Too stunned to think for myself, I look up at him in adoration, smile for the cameras.

I'm blinded by the explosion of flashes. Dazed, I slip back into the car.

Moments later, Jondoe is beside me once again.

"I knew you were a natural," he says, tearing out of the parking lot.

melody
harmony

"I FEEL GOOD," RAM SAYS. "I FEEL BETTER."

Zen nudges me in the shoulder. He's mouthing *toldja toldja* and doing a downscaled version of the dance. He's not taking any of this seriously. I reach for another pillow and threaten him with a penalty kick to the manparts. He stops the dance.

"Do you feel like telling us about Harmony?" I ask Ram trepidatiously, pulling the pillow in front of my chest. I don't want him getting any amorous ideas.

He tilts his head to the side. "Sure," he says loosely.

He's already unbuttoned the top button of his shirt, removed the ice helmet and muddy boots. He's now nestling his large frame into the oversize couch cushions, his whole body totally at ease.

"You can start talking now."

He looks genuinely surprised. "Oh, you mean *now*?"

I'm trying my best to be patient, to remind myself that it isn't his fault he's one haybale short of whatever haybales are used for.

"Yes, now."

"All right," he says seemingly unaware of my agitation. "Well, we were all shocked when Harmony told us that she had found an identical twin sister." He stops and dips his head in my direction. "That's you."

I'm smiling so hard my teeth might fall out.

"You look just like her," he says. "Are you *sure* you aren't her?"

I roll my eyes. "Just keep talking."

"Sure," he says genially. "And by the next prayer service, she had the whole settlement praying on you. How thrilling it must have been for you to feel our prayers filling up that God-shaped hole in your soul!"

Unless prayer can be mistaken for the indigestion brought on by too many instant chimichangas, I haven't felt a thing.

"Harmony really, really wanted to witness to you. She felt awful guilty that she had been chosen to live with the Church and that you had been forced to live in sin through no fault of your own. It didn't seem just, especially when it could have just as easily gone the other way round. And the more she talked to you and got to know you, the more she was worried about you living without the Bible out here in

Otherside and not having God and suffering in a Jesus-free eternity and all that bad stuff. She became convinced that it was her mission in life to save you from wickedness in this life and the next. Especially when she found out that you were selling your babies."

He says all this without a trace of judginess in his voice. He's simply stating the truth as he sees it.

"Harmony believed that once you met her you would want to move to Goodside, get married, and join our household."

"She really believed that?" Zen asks. "She clearly doesn't know Melody."

"And I certainly don't know Harmony, do I?" I retort.

Ram keeps talking. "That's Harmony, for you. Dedicated to ministering to the unchurched, more than any other girl in our settlement. Especially after the bust-up of her first engagement."

Ooooh. Now we're getting somewhere.

"What happened to the first fiancé anyway?" I ask.

Ram stiffens. "Well, he up and married someone else, one of her other housesisters, actually. The Council prayed on it and decided she wasn't ready. They said Harmony asked too many questions. Too hardheaded and rebellious to husband to. I thought that was a load of goose poop." He pauses. "Until . . ."

Until she ran off without him.

Ram is clearly hurting, and yet he's reluctant to say anything neggy about his wife.

174

"She had hoped you would come out to see her, but you didn't. When she went missing I knew right away that she had disobeyed the Orders and gone Wayward to see you. I just don't understand why she wanted you to believe she was engaged and not . . ."

The unsaid "married" just hangs there, suspended by the palpable tension. It's what we all want to know, but none of us can answer. Ram's eyes are getting all watery again, which makes me nervous that maybe the Tocin isn't as powerful as we thought it would be.

"Why would she leave without me?" He tries to smile again. And fails.

I make my best guess. "You're telling us it's against the rules to leave the settlement, right?"

Ram nods. "Except for approved missionary trips or trade, yep. She's Wayward right now for sure. She'll have to wear a red dress when she returns."

"A red dress?" Zen and I ask.

"Red's the color for shunning," Ram says grimly, twisting at his wedding ring.

Shunning? "How long will she be shunned?" This is alarming, to say the least.

"We won't know until the Council prays on it," Ram says. "I got three months when I got caught—" He thrusts a clenched fist to his mouth and squeezes his eyes tight.

Zen and I gape at each other.

Caught doing *what*? What could be so bad to deserve being ignored by your family and friends and everyone you know for three months? It's clear from the panic-stricken expression stretching across Ram's face that there's no way he'll tell us what he got caught doing.

Zen handles this tricky situation with ease.

"If you had gotten in trouble before," Zen says in a very leading way, "I bet Harmony didn't tell you so you wouldn't get in trouble again."

"But I'm her husband, she should have trusted me," he says softly. "It's *my* fault that she couldn't trust me. Something's wrong with *me* . . ."

Maybe Ram was caught with another girl? That would help explain why Harmony was unhappy to marry him.

"How long have you and Harmony been married?" I ask.

He counts off on his fingers. "Three days."

Zen and I both reel back in surprise. "Three days!"

"Three days," he repeats. "Counting today."

"What?" I'm sure I've misunderstood him. "She ran away the day after you got married?"

He nods solemnly, sniffs. "The morning after."

Zen and I exchange the same look, asking the same question: *What happened on the honeymoon?* Only Zen has the nerve to actually ask it out loud.

"What happened?"

The point-blank shot to the heart is too much for Ram to take, even under the cheer-uppy influence of Tocin. He buries his tear-stained face in his hands again.

I look to Zen for help but this time he just shrugs.

After what seems like a full trimester, Ram finally gets himself together. He leans in very close and lowers his voice to a whisper.

"If I tell you something, you promise you can't tell anyone."

"Promise," Zen and I say.

"The truth is, we may not be really married in the eyes of God."

harmony
melody

AFTER WE LEFT THE AVATARCADE, WE SPED THROUGH THE
darkness once again and headed to the Underground
All-Sports Arena, where an even thicker "scrum of scummers," as Jondoe put it, followed, fotoed, and filmed us
as we kicked around a soccer ball for a few minutes. Or
rather, Jondoe kicked around a soccer ball and I took a ball
to the head, shins, and—at least once, to the shock of the
crowd—belly.

Jondoe joked with the paps. "No more of *that* after
tonight!"

And now, sitting across from Jondoe while he peruses
the menu at the U.S. Buff-A, I'm embarrassed to admit—
even to myself—that I had thought—if only briefly—the
Rapture had arrived. I know Jondoe would mock me

mistaking camera flashes for the Apocalypse. But that's only because Othersiders like him don't fret nearly as much about End Times as Goodsiders like me do.

Or did.

"She'll have the West Virginia pepperoni-roll appetizer and the New Mexican Tacos Supremos as her entrée," Jondoe says to the waitress. Then to me, "I know it's your favorite."

I manage a feeble smile. I don't know how he can act so normal with so many eyes on us.

"And I'll have the eastern seaboard seafood special. Grilled, not fried," he says, patting his abdominals. "Gotta stay fit, you know." Then he hands the menus over to the waitress, who takes them as if she were Moses receiving the Ten Commandments.

There are dozens of eyes on us in the restaurant. And thousands, maybe even millions, more watching live on the MiNet. The small crowd has kept a respectful distance so far, until two girls break rank and flutter over to our table. With their reddish blond hair, full-moon faces, and slightly slanted eyes, they remind me of my housesister Annie, whose unusual beauty always caused her so much worry until she married Shep.

"I'm your biggest fan," says the older sister, who is wearing a Princeton University sweatshirt.

"My sister wants me to bump with you," says the younger girl, fiddling with the strap on her First Curse Purse.

The older sister steps directly in front of her. "I think you two would make me the most beautiful mixmatchy pregg. It's never too early to plan these things, is it?"

Jondoe smiles weakly, reaches into his front pocket, hands her a business card. "Contact my agent." Then he tugs on his ear. Within seconds, two bear-size men in black drag the two girls away.

"Oh my grace!" I cry as the girls struggle to free themselves. "Are they going to be okay?"

"Don't worry," Jondoe says. "They're on my security detail. It always gets a little mobby whenever I'm paired up for a new pregg."

Roughly twenty-five yards away, his security team has cordoned off the opposite corner of the restaurant for the gathering crowd of curious onlookers. We're sitting at a booth in Hawaii. They're kept all the way across the floor map in Maine.

"So." Jondoe returns his attention to me as if none of this has just happened. "What were we talking about?"

Nothing. And that's because I've barely uttered a word since we left Melody's house.

"You're upset about those two humpers, aren't you?" he says.

I nod.

"I'm not here to make any side deals," he says reassuringly. "When my agent found out I was coming to town, she tried to hook me into being a ringer at a University Bump-a-thon being held tonight at one of the campus eating clubs." He gives me a reassuring look. "I told her to delete herself. That kind of mass insemination is something you do at the start of your career, or at the end, not in your prime. So she put Phoenix on booty duty, not me. He's a good guy, but he just turned eighteen, which is a major bonerkiller, right? I mean, none of us know *exactly* when our systems will shut down, but he's lucky if he's got another year in him before he's forced to retire."

The waitress returns. She carelessly plunks my soda down, the drink spilling over the side and into my lap. Then with no small measure of ceremony, she very deliberately leans over the table as she sets down Jondoe's bottle, providing us both with a clear view of that which we should not be able to see. "I'm peaking," she whispers before walking away.

Jondoe keeps talking, seemingly unaware of our waitress's flirtations.

"This town is full of girls who put their virginity on lockdown because they think they're better than everyone else. Why settle when there's always a better deal right around the corner? These Eggs are priceless, right? So they pass and pass and pass and then they're eighteen-year-old freshgirls and suddenly find themselves with no prospects for continuing their precious bloodline because all the smart Sperm have already hedged their bets on less discerning fourteen-year-olds. So their parents are losing their minds because they don't want this to be the end of the family line, so these prissy freshgirls get so failful that they end up bumping with the first loser splooger that comes—ha, *comes*—their way. Or, in the case of the girls at the Bump-a-thon, they end up spending money to *hire* a professional when they should have been making money *as* a professional. Either way is a poor investment strategy. Surrogettes like you have gamed the system, and for that I raise my bottle."

Jondoe holds up his bottle of Potent Pale Ale for the press to see before taking a long draft. "Making great nights last even longer!" He delivers the line with hearty cheer.

I fold my hands and say a silent prayer over my soda. *Bless this beverage, Lord. And please let it not be tampered with by demonic forces of envy and evil. Amen.*

I sip my glass of Coke '99 quietly. It's too sweet and the bubbles tickle the inside of my nose, but I don't want to trouble the devilish waitress by asking for a drink of water any more than my mere presence with Jondoe in this booth already has.

"With your reproaesthetical looks, you'll cash in on endorsements," he says, winking left, winking right, then blinking a few quick times in succession before winking once more. "It's a major revenue stream. . . ."

"Mmm."

It's the only thing I can say.

Then, without a word, Jondoe holds his bottle out to me. A trickle drips down the side of the bottle, like the sweat I can feel tickling against my own skin.

He knows what I need without even asking

Jondoe presses the bottle up to my parted lips and I drink greedily, as hundreds, thousands, millions of eyes watch.

melody
harmony

NOW, THIS IS TOO MUCH FOR ME TO TAKE.

"What do you mean you may not really be married? Did you say your vows or not?"

"We did! But . . ."

"BUT WHAT?"

"We didn't, you know." Ram looks away shyly. *"Consummate."*

I let this sink in for a moment. Zen makes an immature simulation of coitus with his fingers.

"You mean you never . . ."

"NO!" Ram shouts, eyes squeezed tight, face burning red. "Or. Yes. I mean, sort of."

"Let me guess," Zen says. "Misplaced payload."

Ram hangs his head, neither confirming nor denying Zen's accusation.

"What does the Pro/Am call it when a guy finishes before he begins? Ejaculatory genocide?"

DELETE MY BRAIN CACHE, PLEASE.

I know they're married and naked activities are a natural part of honeymooning and all, but hearing this about Ram and my sister is making me gag. This doesn't escape Zen's notice.

"For a Surrogette, you are for seriously repressed about sex."

"Am not."

"You do realize that *this*"—Zen makes the porny gesture again—"is how preggs are made, right? Or are you hoping that science comes up with a viable form of Artificial Biological Conception just in time for you to bump?"

The physical act of pregging is not something I spend a lot of time thinking about. But that doesn't mean I'm repressed. It just means that my parents have seen to it that I'm too overscheduled to think about such things.

"I think I need to get right with myself," Ram says out of nowhere.

"Okay," we say.

Ram fills his chest with air, opens his mouth—and two hysterical voices fill the room instead.

"WHAT IS GOING ON, PELL-MEL?"

harmony
melody

JONDOE WAVES HIS HANDS IN FRONT OF MY FACE. "WHERE ARE you, Miss Melody Mayflower?"

I startle at the sound of his voice. I look up and catch a glimpse of her face—my face—in the mirror on the wall directly in front of our booth.

I am Miss Melody Mayflower.

A cheese-covered lump is getting cold sitting on the platter in front of me, untouched. I hadn't even noticed the arrival of my entrée.

"I'm here," I say, feeling not very here at all.

"*You* were hypnotized by something unlookawayable, that's for sure. Maybe a few dozen messages from a certain top-five trender on the MiNet?"

"I'm not on the MiNet," I reply. The words come out

easily. A few sips from his bottle have loosened my tongue. The longer I'm with him, the more myself I feel. Even as I pretend to be someone I'm not. I'd be confused by this if I weren't so . . . content.

"Why haven't you replied to any of the links I sent you?" he asks, squeezing lemon onto his fillet.

"I wasn't on the MiNet."

He can't stop smiling. "I wanted to be the one to warn you that there's a lot of scum out there about me."

He turns in the booth and makes a point of staring down the paparazzi still "respecting our privacy" from across the restaurant. The crowd is getting rowdier now, with the press being outnumbered by girls waving hand-made signs that say things like: PICK ME! I'M PEAKING! Or: MAKE MY PREGG! They're held back by a half-dozen senti-nels on Jondoe's security team, all of whom look like they could easily tote a cow under each arm. I wonder if they've taken that HGH that Zen told me about. If so, they must have very small brains. The Bible says that a wise man is better than a strong man, but an army of wise men would not be able to keep these peaking, shrieking girls away from what they want.

And what they want is Jondoe.

"I'm not on the MiNet," I repeat, before remembering who I'm supposed to be and quickly adding, "right now."

"Really?" he asks, slightly deflated. "It's fine if you don't want to follow me. But aren't you the least bit curi-ous about public opinion? Don't you want to know what the MiNet is saying about you?"

"About me?"

"Yes, you," he says with a laugh. "There are a lot of eyeballs on you right now. You're trending in the top ten. Everyone wants to know all about Melody Mayflower, the 'regular girl' bumping with the hottest RePro. . . ."

"I LOVE YOU, JONDOE!" shouts a voice in the crowd.

"ME TOO!" screams another.

I suddenly feel very queasy. My West Virginia pepperoni-roll appetizer is spinning in my stomach.

Jondoe acts as if he can't hear the commotion we're causing. "More than ninety percent of my followers think that we'll create the hottest pregg since I bumped with Miss Teen Venezuela. . . ."

"PREGG ME!"

"You might want to watch your language, though," he says. "When you said, 'Oh my grace!' your poll numbers shot up in the Bible Belt, but dipped on both coasts. . . ."

"You were reading about me?" I shiver involuntarily. "This whole time?"

"Hell yeah," he says. He reaches out to touch my braid. "Girls in the six-to-twelve demo really like your hair that way."

At some point I had twisted the plait back together again. A nervous habit.

"And I'm not just reading, but watching the live streams as they happen, so I can see us as they do," he says. "And we look like we'll make one hot bump."

Hysterical screams now. It reminds me of the primal panic of livestock on the way to the slaughterhouse. Only I feel like the doomed animal.

Jondoe and I lock eyes and express the same thought at the same time.

"We need to get out of here."

Our voices coming together make the sweetest music in my soul, a respite amid the chaos.

He tugs on his ear and two out of six bodyguards leave their posts to escort us out of the restaurant. I fear for the safety of the four bodyguards left behind.

"NO! DON'T GO!"

And then it happens: The adoring throng has turned into an angry mob. The girls push forward in a frenzied stampede that will trample anyone that stands in its way.

"JONDOE!"

I am the obstacle between what they want, and what they cannot have.

Jondoe assertively wraps his body around me, a human shield against this animal crush. And right then, in the middle of the desperate scuttle out the emergency exit to safety, he whispers soothingly and so quietly that I shouldn't be able to hear it over the delirious din but I do.

"Melody . . . Melody . . . Melody . . ."

And even though it's me who Jondoe is protecting and not her, not my own twin, the one who has been waiting for him for years, I am overtaken by the raging sin of jealousy. I am the sisters. I am the waitress. I am the girls who are now punching and kicking and raging at the locks on the opposite side of the emergency exit, because I hate hearing him say so tenderly, so lovingly, the name of this girl Melody who is not me.

I need to tell Jondoe the truth about who I am.

I need to hear him say *my* name.

melody

"WHAT IS GOING ON HERE?"

Ash and Ty are more ectopic than usual because they think *I'm* the one boozing from their liquor cabinet.

"GET IN THE 2VU WHERE WE CAN SEE YOU RIGHT NOW."

"Don't move," I say, before checking to make sure that the couch is just out of view. One look at Ram and my parents would be convinced that I'm up for Churchy indoctrination. "You stay out of view too," I warn Zen, just for good measure. My parents don't have anything against Zen personally. They simply regard him with the same wary suspicion that they regard every other male between the ages of twelve and obsolescence, as a threat against everything they've worked toward for the past sixteen years.

My parents are still screaming at each other, their eyes practically popping off their faces. "SHE HACKED THE SYSTEM!"

I press the 2Vu. "Who hacked what system?"

My parents quiet at the sight of me.

"You're home," Ash says.

"Just like the stalk app said you were," Ty says.

"The whole time . . ."

"Right," I say. "I came home straight after my Pro/Am meeting today and haven't left the house since. Look, I'm sorry about the—"

"But you're all over the MiNet!" Ash says, not letting me finish my bogus apology about the missing booze. "At the Underground All-Sports Arena, the Avatarcade—"

"You caused a riot at the U.S. Buff-A on Route One," Ty breaks in. "A dozen girls got stungunned!"

I hear a curious "Huh?" coming from direction of the couch. I glance over to see Zen's eyes winking and blinking furiously.

"Why didn't you tell us you were bumping with the highest-ranked RePro in the history of the Standards?"

"Why didn't you tell us all our financial problems are solved?"

Wow. And I thought my parents were dosed when I talked to them this morning. I *told* them to lay off the Tocin brownies.

"You're getting very high approval ratings, Melody, just as we always knew you would!"

"But you could try harder to win over the thirteen-to-seventeen demo, who are jealous that you're bumping with Jondoe and they're not—"

"Who?" I ask. "What?"

"Jondoe," says Zen, coming toward me, a stunned expression on his face.

"And to think that we were *this close* to going off contract and setting up a sub-rosa spermination . . ."

Zen steps between me and my parents on the MiVu.

"Hey, Ash!" He waves spastically at the screen. "Hi, Ty!"

Oh, no. He's put on the synthetically chipper voice that he uses whenever he's in major neg, which doesn't happen all that often and is doubly worrisome when it does.

"Congratulations! You've waited so long and worked so hard to see Melody reach the tip-top of her profession, and must be so proud of yourselves. You deserve a reward! Now go out and party your parental asses off! Starting right now!"

He blinks off the MiVu and then, on second thought, removes the whole system from the powergrid.

"What was *that* all about?"

He turns back to me, puts both hands on my shoulders, and gives me a sobering look.

"You need to MiNet yourself right now."

"Why? What's going on?"

"Just do it."

My eyes can't move fast enough. When I log on to the

MiNet, I see that I've got thousands of new followers sending me thousands of new messages. They're easy to read, though, because most of them ask variations of the same question:

JONDOE WTF?

At this point, I'm wondering the same thing myself.

"Why am I getting spamslammed about Jondoe?"

"Look at the links I just sent you!"

I open Zen's links. And there, before my very eyes, is foto after foto of me with the hottest RePro on the MiNet.

There's me and Jondoe splitting a West Virginia pepperoni roll at the U.S. Buff-A. There's me and Jondoe kicking the ball around at the Underground All-Sports Arena. There's me and Jondoe standing beside a car in the parking lot of the Avatarcade. Finally, a grainy shot of me and Jondoe standing in front of the window in my bedroom . . .

"Who would go to such trouble to fotobomb me?" I ask.

"No one fotobombed you, Mel."

Zen sends a video. I recognize the setting right away as the parking lot to the U.S. Buff-A on Route 1. Jondoe has an arm around my (my!) waist and is addressing the crowd of gawkers. The audio quality is pretty pissy, even after I adjust the volume on my earbuds.

"Melody and I both just want to thank our Repro Reps—Lib from UGenXX Talent Agency, and Stella from Exceptional Conceptional Management—for making the deal," he says. "We can't wait to start working together."

I blink it off. I can't watch any more, now that I've finally grasped what was so obvious to Zen.

I wasn't fotobombed. The footage is real, but it's not me posing next to Jondoe. . . .

"She counterfeited me."

harmony
melody

WE'RE HURTLING OVER THE HILLS AT A HUNDRED MILES PER
hour.

"Whoa," he says. "That was pretty intense. But it was
worth it, right?"

I don't think I've exhaled since we got in the car.

"We're done with promo for the night. The paps got
more than they needed, so they'll leave us alone now," he
says. "It doesn't help any of us to get too overexposed too
soon. The asking price of their footage goes down. And
our value is subject to backlash fluctuations. . . ."

None of this means anything to me. "Where are we?"

"Not too far from the last stop on our . . . *date*."

He wants me to ask where we're going so he can refuse
to tell me. Don't ask me how I know this. I just do. I *know*

him. I know him better than I know my own husband, and we were in diapers together. Jondoe is totally focused on me, which would be glorious if it didn't mean he wasn't paying any attention at all to the road. The car directly in front of us is flashing its brake lights.

"Watch out!"

He jumps, looks behind him. "For what?"

"The car!" But before I've even said it, our car slows down to avoid a collision.

He gives me a curious look. "I've got it on Autodrive," he says slowly, cautiously, the equivalent to tiptoeing around a field to avoid cow patties.

"Autodrive," I say. "Right. Of course."

Our settlement shares a garage of cars and trucks, all of which are at least thirty years old and don't have the modern amenities commonly found in Othersiders' personal transport. Gas-powered putterers are just fine when your whole world exists within a few square miles. No one is ever in a real hurry to go anywhere when there's nowhere to go.

"I don't have a car like this," I say, hoping this might provide a logical opening for me to tell him the truth. "Because . . . well . . . you see . . ."

He nods in acknowledgment. "You ride a bike to school because you're the president of the ECOmmunity Club. I read that."

Melody's file.

I am fascinated by Melody's file. As much as I want

Jondoe to know who I am, I want to know who my twin is even more.

"What else does my file say about me?"

"It's your file." He gives me a blank look. "You already know it."

I think fast. "I want to hear it from you."

"You want to hear about the file that told me that you don't like flowers but love Coke '99 and GlycoGoGo Bars."

Yes. I nod for him to keep going.

"And told me you were a varsity soccer star and didn't allow a single goal before your team had to forfeit the rest of the season. Your favorite player on the National Team is number fifteen. You play real guitar, not guitarbot, are far above average in intelligence, and plan to apply to the Global University, where you will pursue a career in epidemiology. Your personal heroes are the international team of scientists who found a cure for HIV and you'd like to be on the team that either finds a cure for the Virus or develops a viable form of petri-pregging, maybe through, um, embryonic stem-cell research or something called partial reproductive organ transplantation—whatever any of that even means." He raises an eyebrow. "You're aware that all of this would put us out of business, right?"

I'm learning more about my sister from this file than I've heard from her. I get so caught up in my silent prayers of gratitude that I almost miss what he says next.

"Your birthparents are unknown, you were abandoned

at a hospital when you were just a few hours old and adopted a few weeks later."

I can barely eke out a whisper. "You know that?"

"If it's in your file, I know it," he says. "You're lucky you didn't try to become a Surrogette twenty years ago before the YDNA tests could prove your Northern European ancestry within one one-hundred-thousandth of a percentage point. The Jaydens would've never signed a contract without it. Anyone willing to take a chance on a total unknown might as well save money and make a postdelivery bid on an amateur." He pauses, puts on a meditative face. "Then again, it wasn't legal to pay teens to bump back then. But I guess that's because there wasn't the supply-and-demand issue that there is now, you know, until a bunch of brains like you find a cure for the Virus—"

Then car slams the brakes so suddenly that I'm thrown toward the dashboard. I'm wearing my seat belt, but Jondoe throws a protective arm over me anyway.

"HEY, JACK-OFF. TRY AUTODRIVE," Jondoe yells to the driver of the car that cut into our lane. "Sorry about that," he says, though he doesn't seem sorry at all to have a reason to keep his hand resting across my lap.

We blur past a few dozen streetlights before I finally will myself to speak. "The file."

"Right," Jondoe says as the car slows down and turns onto a narrow path. "It said that you wanted to book a room at the only MiNet-blinded accommodations in the county."

He points out the window toward a sign: WELCOME TO THE INN IN THE WOODS: DISCONNECT TO RECONNECT.

"Surprise! I didn't put that on the itinerary because I didn't want it to get leaked to the press," he says. "I know you don't want any distractions when we get down to business."

Get down to business?

"It's your first time," he says. "You're nervous. I understand." He reaches into his knapsack, takes out a small bottle of pills, shakes it. "Tocin will help you open up."

Open up?

"And I'm not just saying that because I'm a paid spokesperson," he says. "It will be fun. Satisfaction guaranteed."

Satisfaction? Guaranteed?

"I know it's hard for you to believe, but I was a virgin once."

I back myself up against the car door and blurt, "What's *your* story?"

At first he looks alarmed, but then his features soften into something else. Amusement maybe.

"My story?"

"Why do you do . . . *this*?"

He closes his eyes, rubs the golden hairs on his chin. When he finally speaks, it's in a voice much quieter, yet even more commanding than before.

"The answer isn't in my file, is it?"

Of course I haven't the faintest idea what's in Jondoe's file, but I don't let on.

"I've been subjected to more physical and mental evaluations than I ever thought possible. I've done the YDNA, of course. VO$_2$ max, flexibility, and isoinertial strength assessments. Myers-Briggs, Winfrey-McGraw . . ."

He smiles ruefully.

"And?"

He looks up, right into my eyes. "And no one has ever asked me that question. Not once. They just . . . assume."

"Who assumes what?"

"Everyone assumes I do it to *do it*." He rolls his eyes, laughs. "For the sex."

I feel my cheeks burning. "Y-y-you don't?"

"No," he says dismissively. "With so many girls waiting to be bumped, just about any guy can get some ass anytime."

I flinch at his coarse language, then think of Melody's friend Zen, who would offer an altogether different opinion on the subject.

"It's not the money either. Though it definitely doesn't suck getting paid to do something I would do for free." His eyes dart toward the window. "And I know you won't believe me, but it's not about the famegaming."

"Then why *do* you do it?"

"It's really not about me at all. It's about . . ." He falls back onto the headrest and looks up through the moonroof. "I'm providing a valuable service." Unhappy with his explanation, he screws up his perfect face and tries again.

"No. It's more like . . ." He stops himself once more. "I want to do good. That's why I accepted the Jaydens' application."

"I don't understand."

"Oh, come on," he says. "The Jaydens do okay for themselves, but they weren't anywhere near affluential enough to meet my minimum bid. It just so happens that I am very passionate about helping aspirational couples who want an upmarket pregg. So once a year I do some pro boner work and the Jaydens are this year's pick."

"That's very generous of you."

"If you had something that could change people's lives for the better, wouldn't you want them to have it?"

I suppose I would.

"Such an extraordinary gift is meant to be shared."

It is, isn't it?

"I figure that if I was put on this earth to do this one thing, I should do it to the very best of my ability for however long as I'm equipped to do so."

Yes!

"I feel exactly the same way!" I say.

"About delivering a pregg?"

"No!" I cry, my heart beating madly. "About spreading the Word of God!"

Oh my grace! I just couldn't stop myself! The spirit moved me to tell the Truth. I'm ready for Jondoe to call me a freak, kick me out of the car, and dash away faster than an unbroken pony.

But he doesn't.

"You're a surprising girl, Miss Melody Mayflower," he says. "So encrypted."

My cheeks are roaring now, I can feel it.

"I've been in the business for three years now," he says. "I showed up here today thinking I knew everything I needed to know about you to make this transaction go as smoothly as possible. But . . ."

He leans back, looks me over. If I could show him all of me, my soul, my everything, I would. I *will*. It's time to make my confession.

"I'm not the girl in the file!"

Jondoe doesn't hesitate. "I'm not who I am in my file either."

"You're not?"

Even though there's just the two of us together in his car, he motions for me to come closer. My flesh goose bumps at the warmth of his whisper on my neck.

"Jondoe obviously isn't my real name. That's just the name my agent at ECM gave me because she thought it would be better for my man brand. I've never told a Surrogette my real name. But you, Miss Melody Mayflower, are no ordinary Surrogette. You're special. Do you want to know my real name?"

"I want to know everything."

And not just in the spiritual sense of knowing him in my heart, but the physical, tangible sense of knowing him, a knowing that lets me reach out and touch his hands, as he touched me moments ago.

"Then let me take you somewhere else that isn't on the itinerary," he says.

I tell him I'm ready to be taken.

REBIRTH

Push it out or pull it out
Ain't nuttin' to worry 'bout.

—Fed Double X, "Bumpin"

harmony
melody

I OPEN MY EYES TO SEE THE MAN WHO HAS WALKED BESIDE
me in my dreams for as long as I can remember dreaming.

"Wake up," Jondoe says.

I unstick my cheek from the window, dislodge my
tongue from the roof of my mouth, wipe the sleep out of
my eyes.

"How long was I asleep?"

"Not long." Then he looks as if he's about to add something, then reconsiders.

"What?" I ask.

"What *what*?"

"You looked like you were about to say something. . . ."
He lowers his chin, looks up at me through his lashes.

"You talk in your sleep."

My cheeks burn. How shameful for him to know this about me.

"Now, now," he says, patting me on the back, "Don't be embarrassed. You didn't say anything too incriminating. . . ."

"No man has ever heard me talking in my sleep!" I say. "Not even my h—"

I should have just come out and said it. Husband. Not even my husband.

"Who?" Jondoe asks.

"No one," I reply.

I think about Ram. I hope he hasn't come looking for me. I pray he uses this time apart to recognize that he'll never be able to hold up his side of the marital quadrangle: God, man, woman, child(ren). I know this, our parents know this, and the Church Council knew it when they put us—two unteachable spirits—together. If he finally accepts the truth about himself, then I'll know I did him a favor by leaving. I only wish I'd had the courage to do it before the wedding.

Ma remembers the last horse-and-buggy days and the arrival of the first truck. "A Dodge *Ram*," she likes to remind me, as if this alone would make him the ideal husband. Ma has seen how Orders are made and Orders are unmade as mere men interpret God's Word one way and then change their interpretations to see it another, altogether different way. Maybe one day I'll tell my daughter about how I had to wear veils and dresses that fell to my ankles and she, in her T-shirts and jeans, won't believe me. Maybe I'll tell my daughter about having to marry a man I didn't love, and how lucky she is that she grew up in a different time.

If I have a daughter.

If I ever go back.

"Let's do this," Jondoe says, opening the car door.

I get out of the car and make note of our surroundings for the first time. We're parked in the circular driveway of a two-story house that sits on the wide corner lot of a block lined up with near-identical homes. The large, boxy structure doesn't look all that different from our houses in Goodside. True, the front and side yards aren't cultivated with any plants worth growing—it's three-quarters of an acre of wasted greenspace. And there's a detached garage where a barn should be. Otherwise, this vinyl-sided house with the stone facade is in keeping with the outsize suburban fashion of the early to mid '00s. Just like ours—only we fill our houses with four families instead of just one.

A lamp turns on in the downstairs window. Someone knows we're here.

"I haven't been back here in almost a year," Jondoe says.

"Where is here?" I ask.

"Where Gabriel spent the first fourteen years of his life."

Gabriel. Like the angelic messenger sent by Jesus to work on His behalf.

The front door swings open and a man and a woman step out onto the front porch. They're both wearing robes over pajamas, bedroom slippers, and big, toothy grins.

"Gabriel!" they cry out, arms outstretched.

"Who are they?" I ask.

"Gabriel's parents," Jondoe says as he takes the first steps toward them.

I point at him. "Gabriel?"

He says nothing, answering instead with a smile brighter than all the shining lights in the heavens.

melody

harmony

I AM QUITE LITERALLY FLOORED, PARALYZED BY THE NEWS that my married, trubie twin sister spermjacked my RePro, not just any RePro, but the hottest on the MiNet. Which meant that if she *hadn't* showed up on my doorstep, *I* might have already bumped with the hottest RePro on the MiNet.

If that's not enough to floor a girl, I don't know what is.

I have stared at his fotos for . . . I don't know? Hours? Weeks? Aeons? His is an unlookawayable face. Jondoe's face defies any improvements made by the attractiveness app. No tweaking of the distance between his chin and lips, forehead and the bridge of his nose, or between the eyes. The geometry of his face is scientifically perfect. And don't even get me started on his abdominal muscles, which are a study in anatomical symmetry.

I'm supposed to bump with *him*?

Or *was*.

Finally, after whatever amount of time it was, Zen speaks up.

"If Jondoe thinks he's with you," Zen says, "he's probably been messaging you this whole time."

I gasp, knowing that Jondoe *has* been messaging me this whole time . . . only I thought it was spam! I double-blink-wink-left-right-left-blink to read the rest of Jondoe's messages.

Amid all the flattering messages about how reproaesthetical I am, I got an itinerary that matches up with what I saw in the fotos:

Avatarcade

Underground All-Sports Arena

U.S. Buff-A

Surprise!

Then Jondoe spammed me with a bunch of flattering feeds about . . . himself.

But it's the last few messages that made no sense at all:

PSALM 127:3

PSALM 128:3

PSALM 37:5

If Harmony told him that *I* have God, why would *Jondoe* send *me* psalms? Unless, maybe, he was trying to impress her . . .

"Ram! What are the Psalms?"

He thinks for a moment, scratching his head. "Bible verses."

I am dangerously close to throwing a clot.

"Even *I* know that!" I snap. "But what *are* they?"

I don't even wait for Ram to say "don't know" or Zen to look up the passages before messaging Jondoe back. The whole time he's been with Harmony, he thought he was with me. And now he thinks *I* have God! She converted me behind my back. I waste no time in updating my status.

THIS IS THE REAL MELODY

"Psalm one hundred twenty-seven, verse three," Zen reads from the quikiwiki. "'Don't you see that children are God's best gift? The fruit of the womb his greatest legacy?'"

U R WITH MY GODFREAKY TWIN SISTER

"Psalm one hundred twenty-eight, verse three," Zen continues. "'You will bear children as a vine bears grapes.'"

ASK WHAT HER REAL NAME IS

"Psalm thirty-seven, verse five. 'Open up before God, keep nothing back; He'll do whatever needs to be done.'"

TELL HER I'M FOR SERIOUSLY PISSED

A second goes by. Five. Ten.

"That's some righteous versin' right there," Ram says.

Nothing.

"It looks like Jondoe changed his strategy," Zen says, trying to lighten the mood, "from humpy to thumpy."

I. Am. Beyond.

"TERMINATE! NOW! SERIOUSLY!"

I don't need to say it twice. Zen and Ram disappear into the kitchen.

WTF?

Another second goes by. Five. Ten.

I check his location on the MiStalk but he's nowhere to be found. No surprise. He's either blinded himself or has gone off the grid.

WHERE R U?

WHERE R U?

WHERE R U?

harmony
melody

THE SOBBING, HEAVING COUPLE IS HUGGING JONDOE (GABRIEL!)
with no signs of ever letting go. The emotional embrace
that began outside on the front porch has danced itself
inside to the entrance hall.

"It's been so long!"

"Too long!"

I'm uncomfortable watching this reunion.

I've never shared a group hug with my parents. It's just
not appropriate. Church folk don't glorify displays of affections, choosing to support each other through shared labor
rather than shared embraces. My father was remote even
by Church standards and was always far more interested in
my housebrothers than me. Occasionally he gave me pats
on the head, but only when I was much younger and after

I had made myself useful by cleaning the chicken coops. I'm not sad that he never hugged me because that's just the way it was.

My most intimate moments with my mother were also when I was much younger, when I sat in her lap as she braided my hair. Those mornings are the only times I can say her affections were fully focused on me and me alone. She would hum hymns to herself as she smoothed and straightened and plaited my hair, but her fingers were too deft for my liking. Her one-on-one attention never lasted more than a few short minutes before my next housesister was in her lap. I know it's wicked, but I often tied knots into my hair just so Ma would need extra time to comb them out. I don't remember the pain of having my hair pulled into submission, just happiness that I would get to hear Ma hum a whole hymn.

Jondoe's parents haven't noticed my presence, or likelier, they don't care. Even though it's the middle of the night, they are overjoyed beyond words by Jondoe's surprise arrival, barely communicating through undecipherable keening punctuated by the occasional semicomprehensible word burst.

"Gabey! It's you! It's really you!"

"My boy! I can't believe it!"

Jondoe is more object than participant, at one point going out of his way to wink at me over his mother's fluffy pink shoulder, to let me know that he at least remembers that I'm still here.

Motivated more by a need for a distraction than genuine curiosity, my eyes are drawn to one of several small wooden signs mounted by the front door.

GET AN AFTERLIFE!

I quickly read some the other plaques adorning the walls.

THIS HOUSE IS PRAYER–CONDITIONED!

AMERICA NEEDS A FAITH LIFT!

I've never seen so many forms of idolatry in one place! And we've barely gotten through the front door! As a contrast to the humorous exclamatory plaques, there are other more serious displays of faith: A foot-long wooden cross, a large mirror etched with an image of the Last Supper, an ichthus symbol. The Church and other plain sects strictly prohibit any such objects of worship. Crosses and other symbols or artistic representations of passages from the Bible are all too showy. I know these things exist, and that many devout Christians consider such displays a way of being bold for God. But I never, ever expected to see such things in *this* house. . . .

Oh my grace! Could it be?

"Praise the Lord!" chorus his father and mother.

Jondoe's parents have God!

melody

FOR ALMOST TWO YEARS I WAITED.

I kept my eye on the purity prize. I said no to Tocin.
I stayed on the sidelines during group gropes, or stayed
home and missed the masSEX parties altogether. I turned
down offers from unaccredited worms and free-agent
Sperms until they stopped asking. I watched amateurs turn
into pros, accidents into possibilities. I watched my MiNet
status fall from the "six-figure Surrogette" to a "virge on
the verge." I resisted the pressure to get an everythingbut. I
strenuously avoided touching any member of the opposite
sex, refusing so much as even a first kiss in the fear that any
accidental skin-to-skin contact could—

A warm hand brushes my waist and I nearly leap across
the room.

"AHHHH!"

"Dose down," Zen says. "Get Lib on the MiVu! He's got too much at stake in this to just let the whole deal fall apart, right?"

I nod mutely.

Zen is in his element now. This is where he excels: crisis management.

"Only Lib can tell you when Jondoe signed up with the Jaydens," he says. "Only he can explain why you didn't get the news and how Harmony wound up being your doppelbanger."

I call up Lib on the MiVu.

"LIIIIIIIIIIB," I shout. "WHEREVER YOU ARE. GET IN VIEW RIGHT NOW."

I stare at his icon, willing it to animate already.

"LIIIIIIIIIIB," I call out, yanking Zen in front of me. "I'M IN CRISIS. I'M ABOUT TO BUMP WITH A FIVE-FOOT CHINO-CHICANO."

Zen doesn't know whether to be flattered or insulted. "Five foot *eight*."

I shoot him a look.

"Five foot seven and *a half*," he huffs.

I drag Ram into view. "FOR SERIOUS, LIB. I'M GONNA ORGY WITH AN ILLITERATE AGRI-CULTY UNLESS YOU TRY TO STOP ME. . . ."

In an instant, Lib's frozen icon comes to life, or as much life is possible when 95 percent of your face is made from synthetic skinfeel. He starts raving and doesn't stop.

"WHY are you threatening the man who made you the hottest Surrogette on the MiNet? WHY haven't you responded to any of my messages, gorgeous? I've been TERMINAL over here. How many hours has it been since insemination? Is it time to piss on the stick? I've already written the press release. It's fertilicious. Knowing Jondoe, I bet you bumped it out on the first try! Though I certainly wouldn't blame you, Miss Melody Mayflower, if you wanted a few do-overs."

It's only when he notices that I've got my arms around Zen and Ram that he breaks from his tirade. His eyes narrow as narrowly as his surgeries will allow.

"Who are these two . . . wor—?" He stops short of calling them "worms."

"Oh, these two?" I say with feigned casualness. "They're my top prospects for going amateur."

Zen and Ram tense up on either side of me.

"WHAT?" Lib mops his sweaty brow with the back of his hand. "Where is JONDOE?"

"I have no idea where Jondoe is," I say. "I never met Jondoe, Lib. I didn't know he had signed with the Jaydens until I saw the news."

Lib laughs high and hysterically. "You're scamming me."

"No, I'm not," I say.

And that's when Lib loses it.

"I SET IT ALL UP WITH YOU THIS MORN-ING," he yells. "I SAW THE FOOTAGE. YOU AND

220

JONDOE AT THE HOUSE, THE AVATARCADE, THE ALL-SPORTS ARENA, THE U.S. BUFF-A. *EVERYONE HAS!*"

"It wasn't *me*, Lib," I say, leaving it to him to figure out the rest.

His perma-tan pales as much as such artificially tinted synthetic skinfeel can pale, as he suddenly grasps the truth.

"I spoke to *her* this morning?" His voice is barely audible.

"My twin," I whisper. "The only flaw in my file."

harmony
melody

THE THREESOME BREAKS APART. HIS PARENTS' FACES ARE
wet and shining with tears of joy. Jondoe is smiling but his
eyes are dry.

"It's okay that I came home without telling you first?"
Jondoe says, knowing the answer already.

His father looks up at him with adoration and says, "'My
son, you are always with me, and everything I have is yours.'"

He couldn't have chosen a more appropriate passage.

"The parable of the lost son," I say in appreciation.

And for the first time, Jondoe's parents have pulled
their attention away from Jondoe and are gazing upon me
with more than mere interest. Awe.

"Mom and Dad, this is Melody," Jondoe says.

His parents pull me into their group hug with no time

to make room for the Holy Spirit between us. My mouth smashes up against Jondoe's collarbone, my bosom presses against his torso. I let lose a little squeak of shock.

"We're crushing the poor girl!" his mother exclaims as she loosens her grip on me without letting go entirely.

"I'm fine." I realize that I don't know Jondoe's last name. "Mrs. . . . ?"

This question inspires orchestral laughter from parents and son.

"Mrs.?" His mother whoops when she finally catches her breath. "No need for such formalities! Please call me Shelby!"

Shelby has her son's fair hair and skin. Or *he* has *hers*, I suppose. Despite it being the middle of the night, her pretty features pop with more makeup than all the women of Goodside will ever use in their entire lives: slick pink lips to match her bathrobe, thick black lashes, a golden shimmer across her cheekbones.

"And I'm Jake."

His father is a faded version of Jondoe, which is to say that there is a handsome paternal resemblance—warm brown eyes, elastic expressive mouth, strong jaw—and yet he still lacks that mesmerizing quality that makes Jondoe so . . . How did he put it? *Unlookawayable.*

"Thank you," I say, then to be polite, "I was admiring your . . ." I stop myself from saying "idolatry." "Decor."

"We truly believe that a joyful heart is good medicine," says Jake.

I identify the passage automatically. "Proverbs."

His parents gape at each other, then Jondoe.

"She's quite special, isn't she?" Jondoe says.

"*You're* special!" Shelby cheers, fresh tears springing to her eyes.

"You'll have to forgive us, Melody," Jake says. "We are the proudest parents you are ever likely to meet!"

Proud?

"And we don't get to see too much of our boy these days. Not since he got the call!"

The *call*?

"He has given so much of himself over to his mission." Jake honks into a tissue and tries to get ahold of himself. "Well, we don't have to preach to *you* about the joy of doing the Lord's work. I'm sure your parents are just as proud!"

"I'll tell you *all* about it," Jondoe says to his dad before turning to his mother and asking, "but any chance that a prodigal son can get a home-cooked meal around here first?"

And despite the late hour—it's well past midnight— his mother is all too happy to comply. Of all the grown women and young girls I've watched fall helpless to Jondoe's charms, there is none who is more at his mercy than the one who carried him for nine months in her womb. And his father is equally enthralled by his presence, stopping to turn back and look at him *three times* on the short trip down the hall to the kitchen.

I don't know what to make of all this. There is no way his God-having parents would so happily welcome their son home if they had any idea he was getting rich from premarital sex and sin! If Jondoe is so famous, how has his devilish vocation remained a mystery to his parents? I have to ask.

"Your parents don't know about your . . ." I search for the right word.

"*Job?* Of course they know about my job. That's not a secret. Why do you think they're so happy to see me?"

"They think you're a missionary?" I ask.

"I *am* a missionary." His eyes are twinkling with irrepressible mischief, like one of my housebrothers when he's rigged a bucket of water to fall onto an unsuspecting head. "Surely by now you've guessed my secret?"

I shake my head no, even though I mean yes. I want to hear him say it.

"Gabriel has God too." He taps his fingertip on my nose. "Just." *Tap.* "Like." *Tap.* "You."

This confession should shock me. But it doesn't. And not just because of his parents' showy faithing. His revelation is confirmation of the knowledge I held in my heart all along. Faith is accepting what makes no sense, what we cannot prove, but know down deep in our souls is real.

Now that I've heard it from his lips, that he too has God, everything that has happened to me since leaving Goodside—even my decision *to* leave Goodside—now makes perfect sense of the sort that could never stand up to the scrutiny of the logic and reason revered by Melody and Zen. I know I've done the right thing in leaving Ram behind, even leaving Melody behind, even if my actions have unfortunate unasked-for consequences.

"Come," Jondoe says. "My mom's mac-and-cheese is a taste of Heaven here on earth."

melody

I KNEW ABOUT HARMONY WAY BEFORE SHE KNEW ABOUT ME.

I knew about her because Lib is very good at what he does. The best. So Lib did what any high-stakes broker does: He did a beyond-thorough genetic background check on me, a process made more complicated—and necessary—because of my unknown bioparents.

You know what great lengths I went to to make sure your file was flawless. He'd remind me at least once during every conversation we've ever had. *I put my reputation on the line for you. I pulled strings. I called in favors. I earned my 15 percent.*

I don't know who he paid off or how much he paid out, but Lib gained access to my Good Shepherd Family Placement Services records two years before I was legally allowed to do so myself. And that's how he—we—found out I was, in fact, a monozygotic twin.

At first this was thrilling news. Imagine! A sister! An identical twin! With no genetic connection to my parents, I was fascinated by the possibility of seeing myself in another person. Even though she was a Churchy, I desperately wanted to meet her. There's no closer biological relationship between two people and I just knew that this sister would understand me the way no other person ever had.

"You CANNOT meet her," Lib said. "You CANNOT TELL ANYONE SHE EXISTS."

"Why not?"

"It's very bad for business."

Years later, I'd hear this same line from my parents when they got the news.

"My job is to talk up your unique quotient," Lib explained. "When I make my pitch to affluential parental units, I must convince them that you are the ONLY GIRL ON EARTH whose DNA is designed so deliciously. ONLY YOU can make the DELIVERY of their DREAMS. I can't very well do that if there is someone else who is EXACTLY LIKE YOU and can do the job just as well as you can."

I told him it was unlikely that a Churchy would ever agree to be a Surrogette.

"Helllllooooooo? There are Surrogettes in the Bible," Lib says. "Genesis, chapter sixteen. Sarah gives her maid Hagar to bump with her husband, Abraham."

I had no idea that there was anything in the Bible like that. But I was even more stupidified by the fact that Lib knew so much about it.

"It's my JOB to know things like that, gorgeous. To have the inside angle on any and all competition for my clients. It's what makes me the best." Lib tipped his head back and laughed. "If she was convinced that Surrogetting was a way to serve God, she most certainly would COUNTERFEIT YOU in a THUMPY HEARTBEAT. And because her religion rejects material riches, she'd do it for FREE. Now I ask you: How can YOU compete with THAT? I'll answer: You CAN'T. And that's why SHE is bad for OUR business."

My parents had been prepping me—*pushing* me—toward platinum-level Surrogetting my entire life, even before such arrangements were legal. Ash and Ty predicted that market demands would eventually call for the decriminalization of commercial pregging, and who better than their only daughter to put their theories to the test?

Of course, I didn't think about this when I was fourteen. All I knew then was that I owed my parents for saving me when I was an infant. I couldn't let them down just because the identical twin they *didn't* pick underbid me.

"She isn't your sister," Lib said. "She is the COMPETITION. The ENEMY."

I tried to repeat this out loud to prove how committed I was to our commercial venture. And yet I couldn't bring myself to say the words, to betray this person who was quite possibly my only living blood relative. . . .

"I will never speak of this twin again," Lib said. "And if we are to continue our professional relationship, neither will you."

So I didn't tell my parents—they found out for themselves when Harmony contacted me two years later. I only confided in Zen, who knew this was the one topic for which no questions were allowed. He kept his promise and didn't tell anyone.

Lib, also true to his word, never brought it up again. There was just one hitch: Lib could pay someone off from the Good Shepherd Family Placement Services to expunge Harmony from *my* file, but was powerless to remove me from *hers*.

"It won't matter," he said blithely at the time, the last time we talked about her. "By the time she's old enough to take a looky look, you'll have bumped twice already!"

Well, it didn't quite turn out that way. And now that my secret twin has taken off with my RePro, laying waste to two years of string-pulling and favor-calling and reputation-risking, I'm waiting for Lib's face to combust in a toxic conflagration of synthetic skin.

"So it's your identical *twin*, the Churchy who has God who's bumped pretties with Jondoe."

Ram suddenly comes to.

"Hey, that's my wife you're dishonoring like that!"

The outburst takes me by surprise, and him too, I think. He just as suddenly thuds backward onto the couch as if he's expended his last milligram of energy. Tocin drop.

Lib cackles and claps with delight. "She's *married*?"

"My wife is *not* an adulteress," Ram moans.

Lib is smiling in an unpleasant way. "You all HIGHLY misunderestimate Jondoe's gifts. . . ."

Lib's whatever attitude about this fiasco is giving me a squelchy feeling in my stomach. And it doesn't help that word has gotten out that I'm on the MiVu right now. The screen is filling with 1Vu pop-ups on mute: Celine Lichtblau, Tulie Peters, even Ventura Vida herself mouthing away with her abundant gums. All these bubbleheads think I'm still with Jondoe and hope I'll go into @Vu mode so they can all get a glimpse of the world's hottest RePro for themselves.

"I had NO IDEA I was talking to HER this morning," Lib says.

"You *talked* to her this morning?"

I woke up to what I thought were the sounds of Harmony talking to someone on the MiVu and she denied it. She was on her knees and claimed she was praying. My reproaesthetical ass, she was praying. She was plotting to counterfeit me. Is that really why she came all the way out to Goodside? I assumed that she had wanted to thump me into becoming like her. Is it possible that she really wanted to become more like me?

Lib is still chucking to himself. "It all makes SO MUCH SENSE now. Why she was wearing that TERMINAL nightdress . . . And the freckles!" He leans into the

231

screen to get a closer look at me. "YOU DON'T HAVE FRECKLES AND SHE DOES!" He goes into a whole new fit of giggles.

I'm trembling with fury. And the happier Lib gets, the more off-the-spring crazy I feel. Zen has tightened his grip around my waist, as if to hold me together, to keep me from disintegrating on the spot.

"Where are they now?" Zen asks Lib.

Lib sucks on his polymer veneers.

"WHERE ARE THEY NOW?"

Lib is annoyed that someone as lowly as Zen thinks he can speak to him like that.

"We don't know," he says casually.

"What do you mean you don't know?"

"No one knows. They've gone off grid. I'm SURE they'll turn up after she tests positive."

Holy piss on a stick.

He pauses and quickly shifts to business mode. "So you and . . . what's her name?"

"Harmony," I say.

"Harmony," Lib says, almost as if he's having a private conversation with himself. "She has the same DNA as you? So there's really no difference between you and her? She could be you." Another high-pitched hoot. "Right now she *is* you! Only frecklier!"

It's exactly what Lib had warned me about. We are the same. Interchangeable. Which makes me utterly expendable. And before Lib even gets around to asking if she has representation, I know that he has already given up on me. I am bad business. A worthless investment. But if he plays this right, there's still a chance that he could recoup his losses with the product of Harmony and Jondoe's union. He's already winking and blinking and eye rolling his way to finding my twin before I do. If he has any clue as to where they might be, there's no way he'll let me get to her before he does.

I cannot for another second look at his fake approximation of a face.

"Fuck you, Lib," I say, blinking him out of my view. "And this whole business."

There's a moment of stunned silence before Zen explodes with excitement.

"I always knew you had it in you!"

Zen is still carrying on, clapping and congratulating me for finally standing up for myself, when one of the 1Vu bubbleheads catches my eye. It's Shoko, the only one smart enough to know that I've probably turned off the volume. She's waving a handwritten sign to get my attention. I tap her pop-up to enlarge. It reads:

WATER BROKE! BIRTH CENTER! NOW!

harmony

melody

WE'RE SITTING AROUND THE KITCHEN TABLE, OUR HEADS BENT over four bowls of orange noodles. My right hand is holding Jondoe's left, my left hand is holding his mother's right, as his father leads us in prayer.

"Father God, when more than two of us come together we know that You are with us, and we just come to You to give up our thanks for all the blessings You have seen fit to deliver. . . ."

Only my right hand is sweating.

"We just want to thank You, O Lord, for watching over the hands that made these bowls of macaroni and cheese. And we also offer our thanks for bringing the beautiful Melody into our home because her beauty is a gift from You, O Heavenly Creator. . . ."

Jondoe squeezes my slippery hand.

"And we just want to give our thanks once more for returning our potent son home to us, even if it's just a short while. Because as much as we would like to delight in his company, O Lord, we can't be selfish, we must let him do the work that You have called him to do and we hope that You will continue to protect and bless these two soldiers in Christ's army so they can carry on in their mission to glorify God's kingdom and sow the seeds of faith in His blessed name. Amen."

"Amen," says Shelby.

"A-men to that," says Jondoe.

Everyone's eyes are on me. I am bewildered.

"Amen?"

The prayer finished, the three begin to dig into their bowls.

"Gabriel," his mother says, "please tell us about your mission with Miss Teen Venezuela."

"You read up on that?"

"Oh, Gabey!" his mom says, tousling his hair. "We follow everything you do!"

The tabletop is gray stone tile, and every fourth square is engraved with a different inspirational passage. I look to the wisdom of the Scripture to ground me.

Whether, then, you eat or drink or whatever you do, do all to the glory of God.

I imagine that this is what our kitchen would look like in Goodside if we were allowed to use more than a wood-burning stove, a small propane-fueled refrigerator. My housesisters will be rising with the sun soon enough, gathering wood for the fire in the stove, scrubbing the cows clean for the milking. The Church rejects most modern technologies because an idle life would give us too many free hours to make trouble out of nothing. Melody can't even bring herself to press a button to warm up a meal that was made in a factory on the other side of the world. Too much idle time! It's no wonder her parents try to fill it up for her.

I hope she'll believe me when I say that I never meant to hurt her.

If she ever speaks to me again.

I read another tile.

The soul of the sluggard craves, and gets nothing: but the soul of the diligent is made fat.

Shelby catches me staring.

"You like that verse?" she asks.

"My sisters do," I say. "Work hard at being a good wife and God will reward you with a husband and a big, blessed belly. . . . "

Shelby's eyes light up. I see more of her in Jondoe—and Jondoe in her—when she gets excited.

"How many sisters do you have?"

"Seven."

"Seven!"

Jondoe raises an eyebrow. "Seven?"

"Three have already moved out to start families of

236

their own," I explain.

"Any brothers?" his mother asks.

"About the same. Six or seven."

The three of them laugh. "You're not sure?" Shelby asks.

Does Ram count as my housebrother now that he's also my husband?

"It's complicated," I say.

"She was adopted," Jondoe explains. "And wants to do for others what her birthmother did for her parental unit. She wants to make a family."

Shelby and Jake have tears in their eyes. "Praise the Lord."

I wonder how many times Jondoe's mother has grown fat from God's rewards.

"Do you have any siblings?" I ask Jondoe.

"You haven't told her about Joshua?" Jake asks.

"No," Jondoe says, examining his reflection in a spoon. He turns it back and forth, concave and convex, his face flipping upside down, right side up, upside down, right side up.

"He's being too modest again," Shelby says in a teasing voice.

"Is Joshua your brother?" I ask.

"Yes," he says. Then he looks away from his own face and says, "He was also my first client."

melody

GETTING TO THE BIRTH CENTER ISN'T AS EASY AS IT SOUNDS. It's only a few miles away, totally doable by bike, but I need to get myself on the pedal, like, *right now* and Zen is for seriously roadblocking me.

"You can't go alone," he says, placing himself between me and the front door. "You've been through too much already today. . . ."

"You *can't* come with me," I remind him. "You won't be allowed anywhere near the place."

It's totally true. Too many deliveries were getting stolen by black-market traders sneaking into the centers by claiming to be friends and relatives of the birthers. Now access is restricted to a list of vetted guests submitted at least sixty days prior to the due date.

"So what are we supposed to do while you're there?"
Zen asks.

A snort rips through the house and shakes the rafters.
I refer Zen to the common room, where Ram is in full
snore on the couch.

"*You* are going to nanny *him* through his narcoleptic
Tocin nap," I say. "Now step aside so I can fulfill my duties
as a peer birthcoach."

And Zen does the surprising thing by actually step-
ping aside the first time I ask. And he continues to do the
surprising thing by not saying a word as I unlock my bike.
By the time I've turned on all my night-lights, put on
my helmet, and am ready to kick off down the gravel, his
silence has become more oppressively judgy than anything
he could possibly say. I can't take it.

"WHAT?!" I shriek.

He shifts uneasily in his thick-soled sneakers. Five foot
seven and a half. Ish. If that.

"I hope it goes better than last time."

I take off toward the birth center without a thank-you
or a goodbye.

I put all my energy into pedaling as fast as I can.

Into forgetting about what happened the last time I
took this same trip.

I was there when Malia awoke from her Obliterall nap
and asked to hold her baby. The nurses told her the delivery had already crossed state lines. She started screaming,
"Where is my baby? I want my baby! They took my baby!"

A half-dozen medical professionals put her in the restraints and gave her enough Obliterall to keep her under for the rest of the day.

I was there eight hours later when she came to. She started right up again with, "Where is my baby? I want my baby! They took my baby!" as if she had never stopped. They knocked her out again.

I was there when she woke up for the third time. She apologized for her hormonal overreaction and convinced everyone that she was back to her nice and normal self. She waited for all the doctors and nurses to leave, looked me dead in the eyes, and said, "*You* let them take my baby." Then she smashed a vase on the floor and slashed both wrists with a jagged triangle of broken glass.

I can't say any more.

Not because I'm not allowed to, but because it hurts too much to remember.

harmony

JONDOE'S FATHER BEGINS THE STORY.

"Joshua is eight years older than Gabriel. He never dated much in high school. In his sophomore year at Somerset Christian College, he fell in love with a sweet girl named Hannah."

"They were both twenty years old," says his mother in a whisper.

I hear the unspoken: God had already closed her womb.

"They got married after graduation . . ."

"It was the most beautiful wedding! What a blessed day!"

"And right away looked into their options for starting a family. They didn't have a lot of money—Joshua works as a youth pastor—not enough to hire professionals anyway.

But Gabey was fourteen at the time, and Hannah's sister, Diana, was sixteen years old and they were both looking to find a way to put their faith into action. . . ."

Jake lets me connect his unfinished sentence to what Shelby says next.

"And now we have one beautiful grandchild with a second on the way!"

Like my housesisters, Jondoe's parents are ignoring the *act*. I guess they'd like to believe that all these births are virgin births, like Mary herself. That is, if it weren't blasphemous to think so. I, however, can't hold my tongue.

"But it's a *sin*!" Then I stop myself because I've forgotten who I'm supposed to be right now. Am I Melody? Or am I me?

Jondoe's parents exchange looks.

"There's nothing wrong with sex," Shelby says. "God invented it, after all. If He didn't want us to do it, He would have designed another way!"

"We're procreationists," Jake tells me.

"Amen to that," Jondoe says.

I'm so confused. The Bible has a *lot* to say on the subject of premarital immorality. Did they somehow miss Paul's letters to the Corinthians?

"But Jondoe and Diana weren't married! Aren't you supposed to believe that bodily sharing is for the marriage bed?"

I say this, but I don't quite believe it myself.

I think about the first—and only—time I lay down with

242

Ram. Or tried to. He was patient and kind and, thinking about the way he shook under the sheets, as petrified as I was. The kiss on the cheek that sealed our marriage was our first brush with intimacy. How could we expose ourselves to each other physically and emotionally just a few hours later? We weren't ready for this—at least not with each other. We put on our clothes, and slept fully dressed and back-to-back until I snuck out.

I never understood how my housesisters were able to give themselves over to their new husbands on their wedding nights.

Then I met Jondoe.

"Sex *is* biblical," Shelby says matter-of-factly. "If you choose to read it that way."

Jondoe is nodding with studied seriousness, the way my housebrothers do during Sunday services when they're only pretending to pay attention.

"The way we see it, Jondoe and Diana were bodily stand-ins for Joshua and Hannah," Jake says. "It was a spiritual marriage, not for pleasure, but for procreation."

Jondoe is biting his lip.

"Look to the Bible," Shelby says.

Here's what I find troublesome about that advice: I know the Bible. Very well. I know it as a curious reader who loves words with little to no access to any other reading material. The Bible contains some of the most inspirational and miraculous stories ever put to paper, but also some of the most vicious and vile acts imaginable. Mass murder!

Human sacrifice! Inappropriate affections with livestock! I know the verses that the preachers don't like to talk about on Sundays. I also know that you can find a verse to support just about any argument, and another verse to shut it down. If it's all the Word of God, how can we simply ignore the parts that don't fit our beliefs?

I was twelve when I asked Ma these questions; she said, "You better not let your husband hear you ask questions like that."

I was told to put my faith in the Council, who knew more about the Scriptures than I did. They would tell me what verses to read. And they would tell me what to think.

And now, four years later, I don't know what to think about anything.

Which, as I'm finally realizing, is exactly the way the Church wants it.

Jondoe clears his throat. All eyes are on him.

"Humans are sexual beings," Jondoe says. "Instead of fighting our natural, God-given urges, we should find the best way to use them to glorify His kingdom."

When he speaks, it's like I can't *not* listen. And believe.

"I've got this great gift," Jondoe says, speaking for himself for the first time. "A gift that can really help people and bring them happiness and fulfillment in their lives. I'm giving people what they want more than anything else on this earth, but can't get without my help." His eyes are brighter, his face flushed. "You know, before the Virus, people created life in a petri dish. No intimacy! I think it's deep that two souls come together as one body and create a new life."

A one-flesh union, I think to myself.

"To me, it's even deeper when *four* souls come together and create a new life."

When he puts it like that, it does sound divine.

"Our granddaughter, Ruthie, is truly the most precious angel that you will ever lay eyes on," Shelby says.

She shows me a picture of a cherubic toddler who looks like a tiny version of . . . herself! It's no wonder that she's so taken with her granddaughter. This is a possibility I had never considered before: I might see my unknown birth-mother's face reflected in that of my own child.

"Ruthie has brought so much joy into all our lives," Shelby says, before turning to Jondoe. "*You* have brought so much joy into our lives and the lives of so many others!"

Jondoe lowers his head, closes his eyes. A humbled pose.

"He got the call," Jake says, clapping his son on the shoulder. "To do the Lord's work in his own unique way."

"Not everyone gets the call," Shelby says wistfully. "But my son did and answered it!"

Jondoe pushes his bowl away and stands up.

"Speaking of," he says. "It's about time we got down to ministrations."

His parents hold out their hands for us to take.

"'Behold, children are a heritage from the LORD, the fruit of the womb a reward,'" Jake prays. "'Like arrows in the hand of a warrior are the children of one's youth. How blessed is the man whose quiver is full of them! He shall not be ashamed.' Amen."

His parents look at me eagerly, hoping that I'll be able identify the verse. But I don't. I can't. I'm speechless.

His parents know exactly why I'm here and what Jondoe's intentions are.

And they couldn't be happier about it.

melody

harmony

A LARGE SIGN AT THE ENTRANCE TO IVY OBSTETRICS AND Birthing Center reads:

> NO INFANTS ON PREMISES
> All deliveries are brought to separate processing
> facilities immediately following postpartum approval
> screenings by the Newborn Quality Testing Service

I reluctantly approach the security kiosk.

"I'm here for Shoko Weiss."

The guard slouches over her screen and starts finger-swiping. Like many obsolescents, she's obliterated any signs of her ancestry with a total body overhaul. This is fresh work. Everything from the slant of her green eyes and the delicate slope of her nose to her toasty brown skin and white-blond Afro is all right on trend for the season. She could be from all continents, or none at all. She could be from another galaxy.

"Name?" she asks, without looking at me.

"Melody Mayflower."

Her head jolts up.

"Melody Mayflower?" Her squinty eyes are bulging beyond capacity. "Omigod."

Uh-oh. I was afraid of this. That they would remember me from last time. That I was the one with the girl who went all Postpartum Psychotic on them. They don't want to take any chances this time around.

The guard is fumbling with the pen. "Um, could you sign this?"

I do.

With a shaking hand, she taps to clear the screen.

"Can you? I mean, do you think you could? Would it be possible for you to . . . ?" She holds out the pen once more.

I don't remember having to sign in more than once last time, but I'm not going to argue unnecessarily.

She taps a few more times.

"And just one more time?" she asks. "Only this time, write something like, 'To Poe: Be breedy! Love, Melody Mayflower.'"

I drop the pen. "WHAT?"

"It's for my little sister," she explains. "She's, like, your biggest fan."

I have *fans*?

I sign the autograph anyway because it seems easier than *not* signing the autograph and having this girl put out on the MiNet that I'm a for seriously starcissistic bitch who won't sign autographs.

I race right up to the front doors, not even bothering to lock my bike before ditching it in the bushes and rushing through to the second security checkpoint. When I get there, I'm greeted by a second guard who must have gone to the same surgeon because she looks almost identical to the first.

She too has a pen in hand.

Before I can ask to whom I should sign the autograph, my hand is seized by one of the wrinkliest ladies I've seen in a long time. For serious, she's old enough to have biological children *and* grandchildren. I know she works here because she's wearing the scrubs worn by all staff members: pink and blue stripes entwined with embroidered ivy leaves.

"I'm Madison Lutz-Lewis! Branch manager!"

She's got a shockingly firm grip.

"I'm Melody May—"

"I know who you are! *Everyone* knows who you are!" I try to shake her off, but she will not let go of my hand. "We're beyond excited to host a celebrity! We're aware that you could choose to deliver anywhere in the world, but we do hope that when it's your time to deliver your precious pregg, you will at least consider Ivy Obstetrics and Birthing Center."

I pry her mottled claw from my flesh. "I'm not here for a tour. I'm here to help my friend."

"Yes!" she yips. "Miss Weiss!"

Ms. Lutz-Lewis has only one mode: POSITIVE! But it's a relief to talk to someone who seems like she might know something worth knowing.

"You can't see her!"

"I can't? Why not?" I'm about to go diva on her ass. If I'm such a celebrity, I might as well start abusing all the privileges that come with it.

"Miss Weiss is in the OR."

"The OR? So she's having a cesarean?"

Part of me actually smiles at this, thinking it's *so* Shoko to get exactly what she wanted with this second pregg. She swore after the first one turned her breedy bits into a U.S. Buff-A burger (her words) that she was going to let them go in through the belly the second time around.

"No more pushing," she had insisted. "This time they can pull the sucker out."

"I can't comment on births in progress." Ms. Lutz–Lewis is still smiling, but the tiniest deflation in tone tells me that Shoko is not having a routine C-section.

"Please," I whisper. "She's my best friend."

Ms. Lutz-Lewis puts her hand on my back and gives a gentle push.

"Take a seat in our waiting area and one of our highly trained medical professionals will come talk to you shortly. In the meantime we will do everything we can to

250

accommodate your every need! We have fresh linens for guests pulling all-nighters."

It's way past midnight and I'm too exhausted to argue anyway. I trudge to the waiting room, which is also decorated in the infantile pastels and twining ivy motif. The room is empty except for a brittle blond piece of plastic I instantly recognize as Destinee, Shoko's RePro Rep. She's a ruthless cradlegrabber who used to work in corporate real estate before shifting her focus to human property. I know her well because she has repeatedly tried to woo me away from Lib.

"I recall that your last experience at our center was not optimal. . . ." Ms. Lutz-Lewis is in full pitch mode. "And I hope that we can prove to you that we may not be the fanciest, but we do run a top-notch facility."

I ditch Ms. Lutz-Lewis to interrupt Destinee's MiChat. "Destinee!" I cry out. "What's happening to Shoko?"

Destinee pretends she's thrilled to see me and apologizes to whomever she's speaking to.

"The delivery is one hundred percent perfect," Destinee says to me in a voice as tight as her face.

"That's not what I asked!" I say. "How is Shoko?"

Every time I say Shoko's name, Destinee twitches inside her shimmery suit. This only makes me want to push more. *"WHERE IS SHOKO? I NEED TO SEE SHOKO."*

"Let's finish this conversation in facespace tomorrow when you pick up your delivery," she MiChats. "Congratulations, again!"

Then she blinks off, rips out her earbud, and collapses into a chair right next to latest ad from the Save America Society. It presents real girls and their awesome thoughts on pregging. Every five seconds, a new girl. A new reason to pregg.

PREGGING IS . . . PRETTY!

"I was MiChatting with Shoko's *investors*, the Ruiz-Lees," she says. "And they're already worried about their delivery and don't need you getting all shouty in the background."

PREGGING IS . . . PROUD!

"*What* happened? What's going on?"

Destinee takes a pack of smokeless cigs out of her bag, removes one from the box, and takes a long, hard pull before answering.

PREGGING IS . . . POWERFUL!

"The delivery is one hundred percent perfect," she repeats. And before I can remind her that she's said this already, she adds, "But it will be the last one Shoko ever makes."

harmony

WE STAND IN FRONT OF A CLOSED DOOR ON THE SECOND
floor. I don't wait for him to invite me in before opening
it myself.

I'm initiating.

And I like it.

"This is my room," Jondoe says. "Or *was*."

The room comes as bit of a surprise.

"My parents have kept it just as I left it," he explains.
"They don't seem to realize that I'm not fourteen years old
anymore. I'm not the same person I was when I left."

This room certainly does not look like it was ever
inhabited by a world-famous sophisticate. It's more like
a child's playroom, with half the space taken up by a
messy assemblage of knee pads, shin guards, and helmets,

surfboards, snowboards, and other sporting equipment I don't recognize.

"Go ahead," he says softly. "Take a look around."

One wall collage is covered in images of a younger Jondoe flipping in midair and otherwise defying gravity with or without one of his boards.

A second wall collage brings him closer to earth. He's licking a vanilla ice-cream cone, holding a trophy over his head, getting hugged by his parents.

It's the third wall that really gets my attention. There's a line drawing of Christ riding on a skateboard. Underneath the words:

SERVE THE LORD ON THE BOARD
X-TREME YOUTH MINISTRIES

"That was my passion," Jondoe says, his voice right in my ear. "Before I found my true calling."

He places his hand on the small of my back. I know I should inch away but it feels like his hand should have been there all along.

"Don't you think it's disrespectful to show our Savior in that way?"

"Jesus was as extreme as it gets!" exclaims Jondoe. "I mean, think of all the cool shit He does in the New Testament. He rocks all those miracles and then He goes out of His way to be a friend to all, the freaks and whores, everyone. He's got major rebel cred, right? That's how I see myself."

His hand moves in a slow circular motion.

"But Jesus never tried to deny who He was," I reply. "How are you serving Him through your work if no one knows the truth about you?"

A warmth spreads across my lower back, around, and down.

"My partners see the Truth with a capital *T*," Jondoe says. "Maybe not before or after, but definitely *during*."

I'm afraid to ask what he means by this.

"I make them see God. Or rather, God, working through me, helps them see God. He gets all the credit. Only our Creator has the power to stir such feelings of ecstasy. Each and every one of my preggs has been touched by His divine hand."

His hand . . .

His hand is under my shirt!

"The more I give to God, the more blessings I'll receive in return," he whispers into my ear. "I'll never be able to outgive Him, but I'm having fun trying."

His hand is not one or two—it feels like thousands of hands roaming all over my body, even in the hidden places he hasn't dared to touch. He is leaning into me and I feel as if I'm hyptonized. I should move away, I should . . .

"Oh!"

He's pressing his mouth against mine.

I'm receiving him and he's receiving me.

I'm losing myself and finding myself.

Through the sublime transcendence of this kiss.

melody

POSTPARTUM HEMORRHAGING IS SOMETHING WE LEARN ABOUT in birthing class. Not even a whole class. Half a class— fifteen minutes—devoted to "Bad Things That Could Happen But Totally Won't So Don't Worry About It." We're told that teenage girls just like us have been the most prolific breeders throughout human history and advances in modern medicine have eliminated nearly all the risks. "Placenta accreta," "preeclampsia," "uterine atony," "hypovolemic shock," "diminished myometrial contracta- bility" are nothing more than multiple-choice responses on a exam. "Postpartum psychosis" is also something that we learned about. It too had (A), (B), (C), (D) answers to choose from, but never happens in real life. Or if it does, not to anyone we actually know.

So we are told.

Shoko nearly bled to death when her uterus failed to contract after it afterbirthed. And she might have too, if the on-site surgeon hadn't rushed her into the OR and removed her uterus with a million-dollar laser.

I cannot believe this is happening. First Malia. Now Shoko. Who's next?

"She's recovering fine now," Destinee insists in between drags. "But this is definitely a deal breaker for pregg number three."

I want to strangle this horrible woman with her hair extensions but she's my only source of information.

"Where are Shoko's parents?" I ask. "Raimundo?"

A lung-rattling sigh. "They annoyed her too much last time, so she didn't put them on the guest list for delivery this time. They'll probably stop by tomorrow."

"So we're the only ones here for Shoko?" I'm afraid to hear the truth.

"You are," she says pointedly. "Because I'm beyond tired and need to get some sleep before I face the Ruiz-Lees tomorrow and have to explain why a hysterectomy is not a violation of their option agreement."

She click-clacks toward the exit but stops before going through it.

"And by the way," she says with acid condescension. "If *I* were your Rep, *I* would've sealed the deal with Jondoe two years ago."

I'm beyond terminated at this point. Even if I had the

energy to make the ride home, I wouldn't.

I take a pillow and blanket left behind by Ms. Lutz-Lewis and curl into the couch, committed to staying the night. Someone needs to be here for Shoko when she wakes up. As her birthcoach, that's the very least I can do. But this time, I won't just be there, I'll be there for *her*.

More than I was for Malia.

harmony
melody

I AWAKE NOT IN PANIC, NOR IN PRAYER.

At peace.

Jondoe is still sleeping beside me, warm and sweet.

I arose to open for my lover

I am my lover's

And my lover is mine. . . .

It wasn't a dream.

We are still naked.

I am still unashamed.

Eyes still closed, Jondoe nuzzles his beard into my bare shoulder.

"Melody," he says. "Now, *that* was something."

He knew me last night. But he still doesn't *know* me.

Before this goes any further, I have to tell the truth. Not because the Church has taught me that to do otherwise is a sin, but because I know I must.

"I have a confession to make. And after I make it, I will understand if you hate me."

"I already know that I could never hate anyone who is capable of making me feel the way I'm feeling right now."

His is the kindest, gentlest voice I've ever heard.

"You might."

"I promise you," he says, "I won't."

I take a deep breath to brace myself. When I exhale, the words come out all in a rush. "Because I'm not who you think I am. I'm not the girl in the file."

My chest tightens, my throat clamps shut, and my eyes fill with tears. And before I can explain further, a look of relief falls over Jondoe's beautiful face. He takes my hands in his, squeezes them gently.

"And I'm not the man in my file either!" Jondoe replies cheerfully. "We know this already."

I'm ready to give my confession, but Jondoe isn't willing to receive it. I try again.

"What I mean is, I'm not Melody. I'm not the girl you're being paid to . . ." I can't say it.

"Shhhhhhhh," he says, pressing a finger to his own lips, which only makes me wish he were pressing it against mine. "Let's not talk business right now."

He rolls on top of me and—oh my grace—there it is again!

"Not when there's still time for pleasure."

The bone of his bones . . . The flesh of his flesh . . .

"I have a twin!" I cry out.

melody ʎuowɹɒʜ

I'M YANKED OUT OF SLEEP BUT NOT QUITE INTO FULL
consciousness. My eyeballs are vibrating and my ears are
crackling. Someone has a hand on my shoulder.

"Are you okay?" a voice asks.

No, I'm not okay. I'm for seriously janked. I blindly
grab around inside my shoulder bag to find the carrying
case for my MiNet contacts and earbuds. I always have
the mindhumpiest dreams when I forget to remove them
before I fall asleep.

Ventura Vida was the first Southeast Asian–American
woman president of the United States. She was giving a
speech.

"Only you can choose how and when you want to
pregg. The power is yours!"

And then I charged the stage.

"Power? We don't have any power! Not until we can make the choice to have un-preggy sex!"

And President Vida was all like, "There's a delivery deficit of epic proportions! You have the rest of your life to hump around!"

And I didn't get the chance for a comeback because that's when I woke up. I must have been picking up on someone's MiNet newsfeed or something. But, whoa, it felt more real than any 4-D role-play at the Avatarcade.

I rub out my MiNet contacts, pry away my earbuds, and put them away. It takes a few seconds to adjust to reality.

"I'm Freya," chirps the pigtailed pre-pubie whose hand still rests on my shoulder.

She's looks even younger than the girls I saw in Babiez R U over the weekend. She's wearing one of those horrible "Born to Breed" Ts that must be so on trend at the elementary school right now, only the lettering on her shirt is nearly stretched beyond legibility because she was talked into buying a FunBump way too big for her tiny frame. She looks like she could topple over and faceplant any second now.

I push myself up into a sitting position, still trying to reorient myself to my surroundings. It's a little after nine a.m. No wonder my whole body hurts. I slept in a twisted ball on this uncompromising couch for six hours.

Freya is still standing there, staring at me with these

huge anime eyes. Without saying anything, she hands me a cold can of Coke '99 and a Chocolate Chip GlycoGoGo Bar. It's my favorite flavor and I don't hesitate to tear open the wrapper. Oh, sweet chemical fortification! I pop open the can and take a big swig of soda. I can feel myself returning to this waking world as the vitamins and minerals do their job.

This pre-pubie is obviously obsessed with pregging because she's gawking at my flat tummy as if it's the most unlookawayable site she's ever seen. I know she's young, but she's old enough to know that such blatant bumpwatching is just about the rudest thing you can do to someone in my concave condition.

"Thanks," I say, holding up the remainder of the bar and soda.

"Your favorite flavors? Right?" She claps her hands eagerly. "Right?"

"Ummmm, right."

And just as it strikes me as odd for this girl to have any knowledge of my favorite snack foods, she rushes forward to press her palms to my navel.

"Hey!" I scold, gently slapping her away. "Hands off!"

"Sorry!" she says, sounding more apoplectic than apologetic. "I just can't believe I'm this close to *Jondoe's pregg*!"

I poke a finger in my empty ear, just to make sure I'm not having another aural hallucination.

"What's Jondoe *really* like?"

Just hump me now. How could I have forgotten that

my most bizarre nightmare is still a reality?

"Good morning!"

It's Ms. Lutz-Lewis, relentlessly chipper for a grammy who was up as late as I was. Did she even go home last night? Does she live here? I'm about to ask when I remember something important: I don't give a damn.

"Pleeeeeeease! Just tell me!" The arrival of Ms. Lutz-Lewis has made Freya more desperate for answers. "Is Jondoe *really* erection perfection like it says on the MiNet?" She for seriously looks like she's going to pee herself.

I open my mouth to tell her that she's too young to be asking such pervy questions when Ms. Lutz-Lewis for seriously loses it.

"*MISS FREYA ALEXANDER. What are you doing out of your room?*"

"I got bored."

"You're not here to make friends!" She swoops in on the little girl. "You're here to make a delivery!"

Waaaait. That's *not* a FunBump she's wearing? Freya is not a day older than eleven. Has she even lost all her first teeth? She can't fill a training bra! And anyone with eyes can see that she doesn't have adequate hip width. There's no way she's pushing it out. They'll have to cut and pull.

"Wah," whines the girl, acting every bit the kid she is.

Ms. Lutz-Lewis has her by a bony elbow and tries to guide her back to her room.

"When's this thing gonna be borned?" Freya hollers. "Borning is soooooo boring!"

"Now, now. With an attitude like that, you'll *never* win the FedEx 'We Live to Deliver' Scholarship. . . . "

GAAAAAH! She hasn't graduated from elementary school yet! She shouldn't be worrying about college scholarships! Especially one that requires her to pregg every calendar year between now and obsolescence! I don't even need to ask who put her up to it because I know the answer all too well: her parents.

There are reasons why commercial pregging is illegal under the age of thirteen. Who *did* this girl bump with? Her *boyfriend*? I've read about so-called preemie pregging in the third world, but it's not something you see in suburbs like Princeton, where it's a very, *very* down-market thing to do.

As it was once down-market at my school for anyone at any age to pregg for profit.

Until I signed on with Lib.

And everyone tried to follow. And if they couldn't get a deal like mine, they hoped to go from amateur to pro. Just like Shoko.

Is Freya the future? Will there be a time where there will be no such thing as too young to pregg? Zen swears that the Chinese are plumping their newborns with the same hypergrowth hormones that can turn an egg into a bucket of fried chicken in fourteen days (growth hormones being a subject of great interest to him, for obvious reasons).

"I'm so bored," the girl whines. "And my tummy hurts."

I'm sick to my stomach. And it's not sympathetic labor pains.

"Oh! In all this commotion I nearly forgot to tell you!" Ms. Lutz–Lewis calls out. "Miss Weiss is ready for visitors now!"

I'm not ready for her.

harmony

melody

"A TWIN."

Jondoe laughs uneasily, searching my face to find a trace of humor or anything else that will explain why I just said what I said.

"*She's* Melody and—"

He puts a finger to my lips to hush me up.

"Shhhh. We are so alike. It's like you're the girl version of me."

"I am?"

"I'm vibing on everything you're saying right now," he says. "I've spent a lot of time on the therapist's couch, so I get it, the whole twin thing. You woke up this morning feeling guilty about everything we did last night."

An angelic smile takes wing across his lips.

"Actually, I don't feel guil—"

He keeps talking. "You created a twin self to represent the contradictory parts of your psyche, your soul—"

"What?" I honestly have no idea what he's talking about. By the unguarded look in his eyes, I know he is thoroughly convinced that what he is saying is the irrefutable truth.

"You have trouble reconciling the dual parts of your personality." He brushes his lips against my neck. "The part that wants to be prayerful and pure, and the other part that wants to experience more . . ." He nibbles on my earlobe. "Earthly delights."

I push him off me. "Nonononono," I protest, flaming from the inside out. "I'm *really* Melody's twin."

His eyes light up. He smiles more broadly than ever before.

"Oooh, you *are* a fun one. You're taking it to a whole new level!" He looks at me with admiration. "You're even more complex than I could have ever imagined. More than any girl I've been paired with before."

"Really?"

"Um-hm." He dances a fingertip across my lips, down my chin, and across my collarbone. "You're my perfect match."

"But you don't even know who I am! My real name is Harmony."

Jondoe doesn't react with anything resembling surprise. He seems completely unfazed by this revelation.

"You can be whoever you want to be."

"I barely know *who* I am! I'm not ready for all of this!"

Jondoe attempts a serious face, but he's still grinning in his eyes.

"God will never tempt you with more than you can withstand. . . ."

I groan. "I don't need Corinthians right now."

"Okay, then. How about this?" Jondoe pauses. "Nothing about you is a surprise to God. He knew I would become part of you. Your life."

"Speak from your own heart!"

"I'm sorry," he says. "I'm kinda off script right now."

"Off Scripture?"

"No," he says. "Off *script*. I mean, just when I get into the whole godfreaky thing, you want to change it up on me again with this twin thing."

I bristle at the word "godfreaky." Why would he put it that way? Maybe the word isn't as harsh or hateful out here as it is where I come from. . . .

"I like Harmony," he says.

"You do?"

"I do," he says decisively.

"And it really doesn't matter that I'm not Melody?"

Jondoe kisses the freckles on my nose.

"I promise this is just the beginning for you and me. But right now, we must complete our mission," he says, rolling back on top of me. "So let's assume the position. . . ."

melody
harmony

I DON'T KNOW WHAT I'M EXPECTING TO SEE WHEN I GET TO Shoko's room. But I certainly don't expect to find her healthy enough to be sitting upright in her bed wolfing down on a double U.S. Buff-A burger and grooving along to Fed Double X on MiTunes.

> "Ima bump-bump-da-bump-da-bump-bump N grind. Gots 2 hump-hump-da-hump-da-hump-hump U so fine. . . ."

"Hey Shoko," I say tentatively. "I'm so sorry—"

"M-M-M-Mel!" mumbles Shoko between mouthfuls of meat. "You *should* be sorry!" She sets down her burger on the tray, wipes the ketchup off her hands with a paper napkin, then huffily folds her arms across her chest.

When they drop awkwardly into her lap she looks down and laughs. "Oops. I forgot I don't have my built-in belly shelf anymore."

"I'm really sorry, Shoko," I say quickly. "I'm sorry I wasn't here in time to coach you through the delivery."

"You're sorry about *that*?" She looks genuinely surprised. "Oh, don't be sorry about that. There was no way I could hold in the Burrito until you got here. The nurse says they had just enough time to hit me with Obliterall before it just kinda shot out!" She thwacks her palm over her open mouth. *POP!*

"So what am I sorry for?"

"For not telling your *best friend* that you're bumping with Jondoe! I mean, we were just talking about him yesterday! I don't know whether I should scream *at* you or squee *with* you!"

I press my face into my hands. Where do I even go with this?

"TELL ME EVERYTHING," Shoko demands, bouncing up and down in her bed. "Is Jondoe as reproaesthetical in person as he is in 4-D?"

"Um . . . about that," I say, taking a deep breath.

"Does he smell like a heady and penetrating combination of cinnamon, black pepper, amber, and tobacco?"

"*What?*"

"Does he smell like Jondoe: the Fragrance?"

"I don't know," I say, trying to hide my irritation. "Because it wasn't me with him last night. I've got an identical twin sister."

And before I lose my nerve, I go on to tell her the whole crazy story.

That my twin's name is Harmony and we were separated at birth and she grew up in a Churchy settlement with the thumpiest trubies and she showed up in my facespace for the very first time two? three? whatever days ago and *she's* the one who was with Jondoe last night, not me, *she's* the one who has probably bumped with him by now, not me, because I've never met him and so I have no idea if he smells like cinnamon or recycled grease or what.

Shoko stabs a fry into a bloody splurt of ketchup. She says nothing.

"You don't believe me, do you?"

And why should she? I don't believe it and it's happening to me.

"If you have a special confidentiality clause in your contract," Shoko says darkly, "you could have just said so. You didn't have to make up some bullshitty story."

She stuffs the uneaten half of her hamburger into the crinkly plastic bag and pushes away the tray.

It's pointless to tell the truth. I could present a 4-D of my unbroken hymen and Shoko would still insist that the ability to pregg without full penetration is proof of Jondoe's unrivaled artistry and expertise. Until Shoko sees me standing side by side with my identical twin in her facespace, she's never going to believe that Harmony isn't me.

"I'm sorry, Shoko, you know how these deals are," I

say cagily. "But I promise to tell you everything as soon as I'm allowed to."

She leans forward in the bed. "Just tell me." She raises a very serious eyebrow. "Cinnamon?"

I nod because why the hell not? Shoko swoons. But if she starts asking if Jondoe sounds like sunshine and tastes like sprinkle-dipped rainbows, I'm done.

"Oooh! It's nine thirty! Time for more Humerall!"

Humerall, the less amorous pharmacological cousin to Tocin. She presses a button at her bedside and within seconds I can see all tension release itself from her face and shoulders. She oozes into her pillows, her eyes soft and her lips spread into a dreamy smile.

"Cinnamon . . . cinnamon . . . cinnamon," she mutters happily to herself. Then she snaps into focus. "We should make a cinnamon-flavored snack fortified with Tocin. And you know what we should call it?"

I hazard a guess. "Tocinnamon somethings?"

"YES!" she says, slapping the mattress. "Tocinnamon somethings. We should for seriously invent that."

If Shoko was ragey a minute ago, she isn't now.

"Sooooooo . . ." I venture. "Do you remember anything about your delivery?"

She gives me the side eye. "Ummmmm, hello? Obliterall!"

"Um." I broach the subject as gently as possible. "You almost, like, *died*, Shoko. Did anyone mention that?"

"Sorta," she says, her head slithering like an intoxicated snake. "I got all bleedy or whatever and they had to suck out most of my breedy bits." She makes a nauseating slurpy sound and twists into the pillows in a fit of giggles. "So no more preggs for me." Her face clouds for a moment. "You know what makes me sad?"

"That you almost died?"

She ignores me. "I have to wait eight weeks to recover from my hystericalectomy,"

"Hysterectomy."

"Whatever," she says. "I'll have to wear a one-piece all summer. Because by the time I get my tummy trim, swimsuit season will be over!"

I can't believe this conversation.

"You almost died."

"But I didn't," she says, grinning. "I'm still here. And I don't remember a thing."

"I know you don't remember, which is why I'm reminding you."

"If you don't stop being so dramatic, I'm gonna have to ask the nurse to give me more Humerall."

And then she turns up the music.

"Investin' like da stock mockey
Get yoself a cock jockey
Partyin' at MasSEX
Deliverin' Fed Double X. . . ."

Shoko's blankets pop up and down with every attempt at a hip thrust.

"I don't think grinding is a good idea right now," I say. "Um, considering you almost died yesterday."

Shoko sucks in her cheeks. "Oy vey. I am for seriously regretting approving you for my guest list. You are being so neggy right now."

I sit down beside her. Time to get tough. "Shoko. You're my best friend and you almost died. And for what?"

She looks stunned. "For *what*? Are you listening?"

"No."

She rewinds the music, turns it up, then raps along:

"Take yo pillz 2 get no illz
Bump yo skillz 2 pay da billz. . . ."

Gaaaaah. I have to say it: If I could abort Fed Double X, I would.

"So 'for what?'" Shoko repeats. "For my *future*. So I can pay for a decent college without having to take out a quarter-million dollars in loans. So I can get a decent job and make decent money. So when I'm old I can afford to pay a high school girl like me to push out a pregg of my own someday."

She's totally overlooking that she just pushed out a pregg of her own and gave it away to a couple she's never met without even looking at him. Or her. Or whatever it was. I can't blame her for thinking this way. Because until very recently, I had bought into it all too.

"Don't get all judgy, Mel," she says. "Just because I

276

haven't bumped with a billion-dollar spermbank doesn't make me, you know, down-market."

That is a misconception in every sense of the word. I attempt the truth once more.

"But I haven't bumped with Jondoe!"

"Remind me to resume this conversation with you whenever that confidentiality clause runs out." With that, she rings the nurse for more Humerall.

I take that as a sign to make my exit from Ivy Obstetrics and Birthing Center. Unfortunately, Ms. Lutz-Lewis won't let me go quietly.

"I've taken the liberty of MiNetting you the most up-to-the-moment information about our staff and services!" she exclamates. "We hope you'll think local when choosing your birth facility."

With those words, it hits me. I know exactly what to do to put an end to this crazy charade.

"Oh," I say casually, "I won't be needing your birthing services."

Every wrinkle droops with disappointment.

"Don't take it personally," I say. "It's just that I won't be needing *any* birthing services. From anyone."

Ms. Lutz-Lewis is confounded. "But . . . you . . . and Jondoe . . ."

We have gathered a little crowd of winking blinking onlookers. Freya, of course, and several others, even Shoko has gotten out of bed to gawk. Great. The more MiNet footage, the better.

"Jondoe and I had un-preggy sex!" I declare, getting flushed just by the thought of it. "For pleasure. Because we are in looooooooove."

"What?!" The whole group is scandalized, but none more than Ms. Lutz-Lewis. "Making love? At *your* age?"

"Yes!" I say proudly, making deliberate eye contact with every set of eyes. "With CONDOMS!"

If that sound bite doesn't coax Jondoe and Harmony out of hiding for a damage-control rebuttal, nothing will.

The devastating impact of this word is stunning and immediate. Ms. Lutz-Lewis looks like she's about to faint into the arms of a nervous nurse. Freya and the rest of the girls don't see her, don't see me, don't see anything at all except the MiNet and who can be the first to launch this footage and exploit its famegaming potential.

Only Shoko is nervy enough to address me directly.

"You were telling the truth before, weren't you?" she whispers. "About the twin?"

"Yes," I say quickly. "Why do you believe me now?"

"Because even *that* makes more sense than *this*."

Ms. Lutz-Lewis is muttering something about condoms, starting to come to her senses.

"You better get out of here before they diagnose you with *pre*-partum psychosis," Shoko urges.

She's right. I've got no time to waste. There's no way I can go home. By the time I get there, it'll be surging with paps hoping to catch me screaming about rubbers . . . if they aren't already.

I message Zen.

911. GET OUT.

Two seconds later, he responds.

OK. OUR SPOT?

Not even a second passes after I say YES before Zen has the same response as a billion other MiNet commenters following Jondoe and Melody Mayflower's newsfeed.

CONDOMS?!??!

harmony
melody

MY SECOND AWAKENING IS SO MUCH WORSE THAN THE FIRST.

I'm alone.

The sheets are damp and clammy against my bare skin.

And I hear voices raised in anger right below me.

"PLEASE tell me that you were SCAMMING."

I recognize the voice from the MiVu. It's Lib. And he does not sound happy.

"Now you're some kind of GODFREAK."

That word again. I shiver.

"Dose down," I hear Jondoe say. "I did what I had to do to get the job done. . . ."

"What EXACTLY were you THINKING bringing HER here?!"

Guilt drops a stone in my gut. I know that I'm the

HER. This argument is about me.

And what I've done.

"You're not even my agent—why do you care about my business?" Jondoe is asking. "Anyway, all traces of Gabriel have been trashed from my file. . . ."

I hear cruel laughter. "Your business is Melody's business and her business is my business. It's my JOB to rewrite files like yours. To keep all those dirty little secrets *secret*. I'm the one who found out that my client even *had* a twin. . . ."

"Are you *sure* I've got the wrong one upstairs?"

Wrong one? If I'm the wrong one, does that make Melody the right one?

Lib cackles again. "You didn't think it was at all weird when she started calling herself by a different name and got all THUMPY on you?"

I told him I wasn't Melody!

"I thought that was her *avatar*," Jondoe says.

He didn't believe me.

"Her AVATAR? We're not playing GAMES here, Jondoe."

He thought I was Melody the entire time . . . ?

"A lot of these Surrogettes are into the whole 4-D role-playing thing. It's a technique their positive energists recommend to help distance themselves from the whole experience, another layer of detachment between the Surrogette and the delivery. So it's, like, you know, another coping mechanism."

The love he gave wasn't meant for me, but for my sister?

"Myyyyyy. SUCH BIG WORDS YOU HAVE. SOMEONE has spent a lot of time getting SHRINKY."

"I was just playing along. I spent the first fourteen years of my life pretending to be as perfect as my brother. I figured a few hours wouldn't be a problem."

Wait . . . Jondoe doesn't have God?

And Gabriel *never* did?

Why would he lie?

"I just wanted to get down to business. But then—"

"Did you?" Lib interrupts.

"What kind of limpdick do you take me for?" Jondoe asks, anger rising in his voice. "You think I don't know when I've hit my target?"

Lib laughs. It's a hard, hateful sound and it makes me physically ill. Sickness comes on like a stampede inside my stomach. I have just enough time to grab one of Jondoe's helmets into which I spew the toxic contents of my gut.

"Her egg was blasted by the fastest sperm ever recorded! Of COURSE you did your job."

I'm gasping for air, grasping the ugly truth.

Jondoe doesn't love God.

He doesn't love me.

I was just another job.

This insight brings on a second wave of violent nausea. But this time nothing comes up. There's nothing left.

I've never felt so used up in my entire life.

"The deal is done," Jondoe says in a low growl. "Anything less would do major damage to my brand at this phase of my career."

"But you should make her piss on a stick just to be sure it's in there."

It's in there.

In *where*? In here?

I knock on my emptied belly as if expecting a tiny fist to knock back from the inside.

In *here*.

Do I feel any different?

No.

And yet . . .

I know in my soul that Jondoe is right.

A life is starting inside me.

melody

I'M WAITING FOR ZEN IN OUR SPOT. THE TREE HOUSE.

The tree house isn't a real tree house. It's a plastic tree house in the children's library on the University campus. It's a library as in ink-on-paper books with *pages*, so the whole place kind of smells weird, like mildew and rotting logs. Needless to say it's beyond boring and retro and there are never any kids here. Every few years someone petitions the University in the attempt to demo the whole place and build a Kiddie Avatarcade or something in its place, but it's protected by some historic preservation act through the next decade.

One of my many babysitters or nannies or tutors loved every MiNet-blinded inch of the place. He or she—I can't remember, there were so many of these educators and caregivers over the years—brought me here all the time when I was little, even after he or she discovered the hard way that I'm for seriously allergic to ink on paper. I might get a little sniffly and sneezy, but I won't have a massive allergic reaction as long as I don't attempt to turn any pages. Just cracking the binding of *The Cat in the Hat* almost put me in anaphylactic shock when I was three.

Despite the risks—or perhaps because of them—the tree house became my go-to for secret-giving-and-taking. It's the only place in town we could guarantee we wouldn't be watched by electronic or fleshy eyeballs. The tree house, in fact, is where Zen wrote and I signed the secret pact four years ago.

His face is sticking out the plastic window when I arrive.

"We could have met at the house because most of the paps already left," he says. "You're only trending in the top twenty. Zanadu and Zissou are making all the media right now."

"Who?"

"Babies nine and ten."

Zorah Harding. An inspiration to us all . . .

"No Zen?"

I thought for sure that Zen would be used for one of her latest deliveries. All Zorah's deliveries start with *Z*: Zahara, Zoe, Zachary, Zayd, Zsa Zsa, Zeus, Zelda, Zane . . .

He holds up two sets of crossed fingers. "Number eleven!"

With leaden feet, I trudge up the hill of stairs to the hole at the top of the tree. I squeeze myself through the small opening and plop myself down on a pillow. The tree house is meant for toddlers, not teenagers, so we can't both sit inside without part of me touching part of him. I hunch and scrunch myself in such a way that only the soles of our sneakered feet make contact.

"So," Zen says.

"So," I say.

"How's Shoko?"

It's such a simple question. And yet it was one that no one at the birth center seemed to trouble themselves with. My eyes start to water, and not because of Dr. Seuss.

"She'll be out of the hospital in a day or two and go on with her life as if nothing ever happened," I say. "As if she almost didn't die . . ."

And that's when I totally lose it.

I'm sobbing because Shoko almost lost her life and because Malia lost her mind. I'm sobbing for Zorah, who's already given a thumbs-up for her eleventh delivery and little Freya, who aspires to be just like her. I'm weeping for bald and cranky Celine Lichtblau and also for glossy-haired and glowing Ventura Vida, even though I still for seriously hate her and her adorable six-month bump, and for all the other pregging Pro/Ammers and the Cheerclones who'll try again with the Ballers at the next masSEX party and all girls everywhere who are valued far more for what's between their legs than what's between their ears.

I'm crying hardest of all for my twin.

My sister.

Pregging with a stranger is degrading enough. But how would I feel if I were forced to *marry* someone I barely know, let alone love? Is it any wonder that she ran off with Jondoe?

Zen strokes my hair.

And now I'm crying for him too.

Because when he's holding me like this, letting me wipe my tears, my snot, and slobber all over his sleeve, size doesn't matter. Forget insufficient verticality. To me, my best friend is bigger and stronger and more capable than any cock jockey on the market. I'm feeling closer to him that I ever have.

"Melody?"

I feel each syllable, his chest buzzing against mine. I can't seem to catch my breath.

"When you said what you said about you and Jondoe, I got jealous."

I want to ask, *As jealous as I get whenever I hear rumors about you taking up with another everythingbut?* But I can't.

Instead, I ask, "Why? You knew I was making it up."

"I know," he says, "But . . ."

"What?"

He loosens his grip on me just enough to reach into his knapsack.

"I have something I want to show you," Zen says.

How many times have I heard Zen say this before

producing an impossible-to-find something or other—
World Cup tickets, limited-edition couture denim in my
size, whatever—that wasn't impossible for him to find at
all. Something he had access to that no one else did.

"Something . . ." He pokes his head out the hole in
the tree, surveys the library, then pops his head back in.
"Illegal."

This isn't unusual. Zen has made many friends by
distributing all sorts of contraband MiPlay games from
Russia.

"What is it?" I ask, playing along, my voice dropping
to a whisper.

Zen reaches deep into his bag and pulls out a tiny lock-
box that fits into the palm of his hand. He taps the code
and it springs open to reveal a small, square piece of foil.

I don't know what it is, but that's not unusual either.
Zen answers before I even ask.

"It's a condom."

harmony

AS HEART- AND STOMACH-WRENCHING AS JONDOE'S CONFESSIONS are to hear, I can't stop myself from listening.

"Now, about your career," Lib says. "I've got some media for you."

"Have I gone down in the polls?" Jondoe asks, a note of panic in his voice.

"Just watch."

Then I hear Melody's voice.

"Jondoe and I had un-preggy sex. For pleasure. Because we are in loooooove."

Oh my grace! Melody and Jondoe?! Did what *we* did?!

"Yes! With CONDOMS!"

"She's LYING! That's SLANDER!" Jondoe splutters. "I mean. That could kill my career. . . ."

"You're lucky Zorah Harding pushed out numbers nine and ten fifteen minutes ago," Lib says. "Otherwise, Melody going all LOVEMAKEY would be the number one clip on the MiNet. As it is, it's only trending in the top twenty. But don't think that won't do major damage to your man brand. . . ."

There's a pause.

"What are we going to do about this?" Jondoe asks in an uncertain voice.

"I was WAITING for you to ask me that!" Lib claps his hands and lets loose a barky guffaw. "Do you think I would come here without a PLAN?"

Jondoe mumbles incoherently.

"I EXIST for this pregg, Jondoe. I LIVE and I DIE for this pregg. . . ."

I didn't like his messianic talk before, and I certainly don't like it now that he's talking about my baby!

"The way I see it, there are two options," Lib says. "Option number one: We tell the Jaydens the truth, that you bumped with the wrong twin but explain that it hardly makes a difference because Melody and Harmony are the same exact girl who'd make the same exact preggs with you."

No, we're not! And, no, we would not.

"But isn't that a breach of contract?" Jondoe asks.

"No," Lib says. "That's the beauty of it. Because as soon as I found out that Melody had a twin, I wrote a twin proxy pregging clause in the contract that was so brilliantly obscured by legal-sounding bullshit that the Jaydens didn't even notice it was in there. But that might not stop them from suing me for fraud. If they sued, they would lose. But the attorneys' fees would eat up all my profits, and quite frankly I don't feel like going through all the muther-humping hassle."

"So what's the second option?" Jondoe asks calmly.

"Option number two: We convince the one upstairs . . ."

"Harmony," Jondoe says.

"WHATEVER her name is. We'll have her pretend she's Melody for the duration of the pregnancy. We can send her away, somewhere far and safe. We can say that she's got some high-risk condition and needs bed rest and . . ."

No. I will *not* be treated like property! Not here! Not in Goodside! Not anywhere, ever again!

"We can send the real Melody away somewhere too," Lib continues. "She likes role-playing. Maybe she'd have fun pretending to be her Goodside sister for nine months."

Oh, no. I cannot—I will not—let them do this to Melody. Not when this mess is all my fault.

I've got a new mission now.

I gather up my clothes off the floor and get dressed as quickly and quietly as possible.

"If I bump Melody as planned," Jondoe says slowly, "can't we just let Harmony go back to Goodside and leave her out of this whole mess?"

I don't need to hear any more to know that I've got to

get out of this house. And fast.

"How do you expect her to keep quiet with no incentives to do so?" Lib asks. "If she pretends to be Melody, she will—thanks to that twin proxy pregging clause that I so cleverly inserted into the contract—be entitled to all the financial rewards that would have been earned by her sister."

Fortunately for me, I've got practice in making hasty escapes.

"I didn't have to write it that way, you know. I could have humped her out of all the money, especially when she's probably just gonna go and tithe it to her Church or whatever. But I didn't. And that"—Lib pauses and takes a deep, loud breath—"is why I am a great man."

I open the window and the screen. I get a firm grip of the frame, then swing my body out and down into a vertical hang. There's a clear ten-foot drop between the soles of my sneakers and the ground, and I land gracefully on two feet. I've barely touched down before I take off in a full sprint down the block. This is all a lot easier to do when one is not wearing an ankle-length engagement gown and veil, although without such concealment I'll be easily discovered. Without breaking my stride, I reach into my back pocket and pull out the Lost-and-Found card Zen gave me at the Mallplex.

How could he have known I'd find myself in such a state of emergency?

I fingerswipe the card and pray Zen will make good

on his promise. I pray that he will find me.

Until then, I run and keep on running, trying to put as much distance between me and Lib as possible before he realizes that I—that *we*, this baby and me—are missing.

Even though I'm hurt, betrayed, and have been played for a fool, I regret not being able to give Jondoe a proper goodbye. Maybe it's because I know it's not really a goodbye. He's a part of me forever now, a sacrament that can't be taken back.

Even if it wasn't intended to be mine.

melody
harmony

"A CONDOM!" I SHRIEK, MY VOICE ECHOING AROUND THE ROOM.

Zen clamps his hand over my mouth. "Are you trying to get me arrested?"

"Where did you get that thing?" I mumble into his palm.

"Let's just say that it's an antique," he says, holding it up for me to see the expiration date: MARCH 2025. "The last batch before the ban." He regards it with a look of awe. "It should really be in a museum."

"I didn't think it would look like *that*," I say. "How are you supposed to put *that* on your . . ."

He points helpfully to his crotch. *"This?"*

Even in crisis, Zen can't help but perv for a laugh. Only I'm too tired to laugh.

"Um, yeah."

He looks at the small, square piece of foil, then me.

"The rubber is *inside* the wrapper."

"Oh." He didn't say it in a snarky way, but I feel my face flush with dumb embarrassment nonetheless. I pick it up gingerly by its corner and examine it closely.

"Where did you even get that thing?" Even for Zen, this is quite a coup.

He closes his eyes, inhales deeply.

"How isn't important. It's the why that's important."

"Go on."

"You've noticed that I haven't been around as much lately."

I pinch my lips to stop myself from saying something judgy.

"I wanted you to think that I was cramming for my IAMs, or everythingbutting with random Cheerclones. . . ."

I sit up in the pillows. "You weren't?"

He tugs on his hair. "Most of the time, no."

Of course, the hysterical girl in me is, like, *But that means some of the time, yes.*

"The truth is," he says, nervously running his thumb along his lips, "I just couldn't do it anymore."

"Do what?"

I can't take my eyes off his thumb. His lips.

"I couldn't be so close to you all the time and not . . ."

He presses the thumb into his lips, as if to stop himself from saying the unsayable. Then he reaches across the inches between us and now that same thumb is delicately tracing the outline of my own mouth and I'm afraid to even breathe.

"I . . ."

He stops himself again. The dimples vanish. Gone is the boyish exuberance that wins everyone over. I know Zen's face so well, and yet I've never, in all our years of friendship, seen this expression before. He is transformed and I am transfixed by the way he's looking at me right now, with a mix of longing and hope and . . . fear.

"You *what*?" I'm surprised by my own desperate need to hear what comes next.

But just like that, he withdraws his touch. His eyes go blank for a second before he starts winking and blinking. It's too late. Zen's already caught up in someone else's drama. In two seconds he'll take off to tackle someone else's problem. Typical, only this time, I'm furious. What could possibly be more important than this?

"How are you even on the MiNet?" I mutter. "This whole place is blinded. . . ."

He pauses long enough to raise an eyebrow.

"Right, right," I say. "Their MiNet blind is an insult to hackers everywhere."

After a few more seconds he shuts his eyes with a sense of finality.

"So who needs saving now?" I snap.

He slowly opens his eyes and says simply:

"Your sister."

harmony
melody

I DON'T KNOW HOW LONG I'VE BEEN RUNNING, DARTING DOWN empty side streets and avoiding busy roads, hoping that Zen will reach me before Lib does.

I have to protect myself. I have to protect this baby.

I've found myself on a gravel path cutting through a short stretch of woods. It opens up to a parking lot that abuts a rectangle of red and white grass. A gaming field, obviously, but for what sport I don't know. I hear commotion on the other side of a muddy hill, almost as if all the sheep and cows, goats and horses had been set free simultaneously. I crest a small incline and see that there *are* animals running wild, but of the human variety.

Hundreds, maybe thousands of students are swarming the squat but sprawling brick building. Boys and girls dozing on benches and bounding across car hoods. Boys and girls bouncing on the grass and sulking curbside. Boys and girls, still and silent amid the chaos. More boys and girls and boys and girls and boys and girls than I've ever seen together before in my entire life.

Like everyone in my settlement, I was homeschooled with my housesisters until the Blooming. I've never seen a real school like this before, the kind Melody attends. I want to be normal like them. I want to lose myself in that crowd. But then I remember: I'm not anonymous anymore. I quake at the memory of the riot that broke out at the U.S. Buff-A. If this crowd of thousands found out that I was here . . . Oh my grace. They'd string me up for sure.

I'm starting to worry for my safety when I spot a car approaching the parking lot. The window rolls down and I see . . .

Zen!

The car stops a few feet away from me and I run to greet it. Zen gets out on the driver's side . . . and my sister gets out on the other.

My sister!

I have never, not ever, been happier to see two people in my entire life.

And before I even know it, I'm hugging them and they're hugging me and I'm not lost anymore.

I'm found.

"Thank you, God," I say.

melody
harmony

HARMONY IS BEYOND EMOTIONAL.

She's laughing and crying and having a hard time staying on her feet. Zen and I walk her all wobbly-legged over to a patch of grass and sit her down. Zen respects our privacy and returns to the car. I settle down beside her.

I keep hoping a psychic twin connection will kick in, so each of us would instantly and intuitively know and understand what the other is thinking and feeling. We could just look at each other and be, like, "Ohhhh, okaaay. I get it," and be done with it. But without the benefit of a monozygotic mindbond, the only way we're going to work through our issues is to talk about them. I put in some practice with Ram, but I'm not so good with feelings. Where to begin?

Harmony decides for me.

"I'm so sorry," she says, fresh tears still falling. "I hope you can forgive me."

"I already have." I mean it.

"For *everything*," she says, sniffling. "For . . ." She buries her face in her hands, unable to catalog her mistakes out loud. Which is fine by me because the less I hear about her and Jondoe, the better.

"I know. I forgive you. For *everything*."

Harmony exhales with a shudder. I put an arm around her shoulder to comfort her.

"It's not my forgiveness you need to ask for," I say. "But Ram's . . ."

Harmony startles. "You know about Ram?"

"He came to find you," I reply. "He's a mess without you."

Harmony sighs heavily.

"I understand that you bolted on your honeymoon because you don't love Ram," I say. "But what I don't get is why you were trying to get me to come back with you."

"I *thought* I wanted you to return with me," she says, keeping her eyes on the ground. "Goodside is all I know. As much as I couldn't see myself living there for the rest of my life, I couldn't imagine living anywhere else either. I thought that if we made our own household together, I would feel less alone. I could repent and stay married to Ram, even if he could never love me in that way. . . ."

300

She doesn't give me time to ask what she means by this. Is Ram in love with someone else?

"I now know how unrealistic it was for me to think you'd join the Church with me," she says matter-of-factly. "It's the only way I've been brought up to be and believe and *I* can't make the commitment myself!" She looks up at me now. "Does that make any sense?"

Yes.

Yes, it does.

"I don't want to be a Surrogette." It's a relief to finally say this out loud for the first time. "I never got to make that choice, and neither did you. Our parents chose for us."

Our eyes meet in commiseration, but I don't turn away. Harmony looks just as intently at me and we don't break the gaze, not even when our shared stare approaches awkwardness. Then a strange sensation comes over me. I don't know how to describe it really, but in this moment, I feel like I'm discovering part of myself through her, and she through me. Something lost, now found.

All at once, we ask the same question at the same time.

"What now?"

It's not funny. Not in the least. And yet, for some inexplicable reason, we both giggle, then laugh, then all-out snort and roll on the grass.

When we finally calm down, I mouth the words to help me. Help *us*.

We are smart.

We are stunning.
We are strong.
We are everything we need to be.
I just hope it's enough.

harmony
melody

I LOOK OUT THE WINDOW, THE SCENERY WHIZZING BY TOO quickly to make sense of anything I'm seeing. None of us speak, though Melody's lips are moving. She seems to be praying, even though she's not the praying kind. I want to follow her example but all the verses ring hollow in my heart. And my own prayers in my own words—*please, Lord, let Jondoe come back for me, please*—rival my little house-sisters' pleas in their petty selfishness. I've given God enough hassle already.

Then, without any obvious provocation or warning, Zen taps the steering wheel with his palm to get my attention.

"You're not the only Church girl who has doubts."

A flinty flicker of hope sparks in my chest.

"I'm *not*?"

I can tell that this remark has taken Melody by surprise.

"How do you know?" she asks.

"I *know*," he says resolutely. "There are girls like you in every settlement in the tristate! It's hard for you to wrap your head around, but you can turn away from the Church Orders without turning away from faith."

"I *can*?"

"You can," Zen says, with a pointed look in Melody's direction that implies that there's far more than what he's actually saying. "You're not a blind believer, Harmony; otherwise you would've married that first guy when you were thirteen. You're a thinker. And thinking and following the Church Orders is like trying to take a sip from a shaken-up can of Coke '99."

He's right.

"I was tired of the Church always telling me *what* to believe without explaining why."

Melody finishes my thoughts for me. "But you can't get any answers if you don't ask any questions."

Zen nods appreciatively. He locks eyes with me in the rearview. "You have *choices*, Harmony."

"You do," Melody concurs. "We both do."

I suddenly understand what Melody and Zen are offering me.

They want to help me take permanent leave of Goodside.

Who would miss me if I never came back? Ma? She

already said goodbye—twice—when she tried to marry me off—twice—to someone I didn't—I don't—love. And there are my housesisters, more compliant than I will ever be, who will—who surely already have—taken my place in service of the Church community. My chores have not gone uncompleted in my absence, that's for sure.

The spread of the Virus all around the world has given Church elders good reason to put even stricter prohibitions on our contact with the outside world. By forbidding us to go beyond the gates for all but missionary or agricultural business, we're quarantined from contagions that cause sickness in the body *and* soul. I knew when I left Ram that the red dress—my punishment for going Wayward—would await my return. I hoped that the Council would go easier on me if I saved Melody's soul; a short-term shunning was a small price to pay for her salvation after all. I should have realized much sooner that Melody would never trade her world for mine. I see that now, and my naïveté almost makes me want to cry.

Did I *really* come here to bring Melody to Goodside?

Or did I come here to bring out the Otherside in me?

"We're here," Zen says as he pulls into and up the gravel driveway. "Melody's going to drop me off at school to do some damage control, but she'll be back soon to help you sort this all out. Won't you, Mel?"

"Of course I will," she says. "Ram's waiting for you."

As I get out and take the first uneasy steps toward the house, Melody sticks her head out the car window and gives me a thumbs-up.

"You can do this, sister!"

Sister! Her acceptance uplifts me. I feel as free as the veil that caught the wind and flew away. . . .

I dream of a life where girls don't hide behind veils. And they can dress as they want to and cut their hair or keep it long if that's what they like. And they can study the Bible, really study it by asking questions and having them answered, and also read other, unbiblical books too. Where red is the color of strawberries, cardinals, and morning glories, not shame, shunning, and sin.

A life where girls are free to fall in love . . .

Even if that love proves to be something else entirely.

I want all these things, not just for me, but for the baby growing inside me.

melody
harmony

ZEN INSISTS THAT SCHOOL IS THE BEST PLACE FOR HIM TO do damage control. Apparently Ventura Vida is making major media by spilling all the insidery gossip about me that only a best friend like her would know. But I couldn't care less about her or my image right now. All I can think about is Harmony.

"You think we can help her?"

"I hope so," he says. "Her situation is . . ."

I finish for him. "Complicated."

"To say the least," he says. "But she'll have options out here that she wouldn't have if she went back to Goodside."

And for the first time since I met her, I'm awed by Harmony's bravery. She's rejecting the only life she's ever known in the hopes of building a better future for herself. I'm proud to call her my sister. I can't wait to tell her so.

"You have options too, Mel," Zen says. "You never wanted to be a Surrogette and now, because of Harmony, you may not have to."

"What do you mean?"

"Don't be surprised if she offers to make the delivery to the Jaydens for you," he says frankly.

"I would never ask her to do that!"

"She might do it as a form of penance," he says. "Church guilt runs deep."

I shake my head firmly. "No way."

Mark my words: If it were up to me, no girl would ever sign on to be a Surrogette again.

We pull up in front of the school.

"I'll stick with what Jondoe's Reps are spinning," he says. "That yours is a professional working relationship and you never, ever had lovemakey sex."

I really don't care what anyone thinks about me and Jondoe anymore. Now that I know that there's hope for Harmony, there's only one unresolved issue that needs resolving and it's between me and Zen.

" . . . I'll say you were fotobombed and—"

"Zen?"

I have his undivided attention. "Yes?"

"That Tocin you gave Ram last night," I say. "It was for me."

His mouth falls open.

"You were going to dose me," I say quickly. "Then talk me into using the, um . . . condom. With you."

He jumps up in his seat and smacks his head on the car roof.

"No! I'd—never! No!"

"It's okay. I'm not mad," I insist. "I mean, it was a compromise, right? We could make good on our pact, without jeopardizing my contract with the Jaydens."

Zen is shaking his head, both hands pulling at the hair right above his ears.

"I'd never try to trick you into doing anything like that. With me. Never."

I'm trying not to let this hurt my feelings. "Then who was it for?"

"Me . . ."

His voice trails off and his eyes keep flitting away from mine. It's not that he's on the MiNet. He just can't bring himself to look at me. And I can't bring myself to ask him to.

"You've never been anything but up front about where you stand, Mel. Your contract has always come first. I'm just an optimistic idiot for letting myself believe otherwise. I guess it wasn't until after I confronted you at the Mallplex the other day that I finally said, 'Fuck it.' Literally. Fuck. It. I decided I'd get dosed enough to do it with one of the Cheerclones. It didn't matter which one because none of them were you."

He laughs in a hollow way that makes my chest ache.

"That's when I finally let go of the dream that *my* first time," he says, "would be *our* first time."

harmony
melody

I'VE MEMORIZED PLENTY OF VERSES, BUT PRAYING ON THEM
hasn't brought me any closer to understanding what they
really mean. Knowing the words doesn't equal knowing
the *Word*. When it comes to the Scripture, I'm as superfi-
cial as my little housesisters. Maybe I should go back to the
basics, the first prayer I ever memorized.

"Forgive us our trespasses as we forgive those who tres-
pass against us," I say to myself, hoping it's not an insult to
skip ahead to the part I really need right now. "Lead us not
into temptation and deliver us from evil. . . ."

I'm standing in the spot where Jondoe once stood. My
finger touches the buzzer Jondoe's finger once pressed.
The same finger that traced the curve of my hips . . .

The door opens.

"HARMONY!"

And in an instant I am swept up in an all-encompassing crush of grass and manure, sweat and oatmeal soap.

"Oh, Harmony."

Oh, Ram.

The only person in Goodside who is more lost than I am.

melody
harmony

ZEN IS STRUGGLING. I HAVE NEVER, EVER SEEN HIM AT SUCH A loss for words.

"You have to understand, Mel. You're the only girl I've ever wanted to be with."

"In that way?" I ask.

"In *every* way."

I do understand. More than he can possibly know.

But I can't . . .

Can I?

After sitting in silence for more than a minute, waiting for me to respond to his confession, Zen finally opens his mouth.

"Well." Pause. "I guess I better get." Pause. "Going."

He gets out of the car swiftly, but hesitates before

taking the front steps leading up to the school. I watch him through the window, and something—a biological drive, a human instinct, an evolutionary pull that I'm powerless to resist—takes over. Head to toe. Limb to limb. Top to bottom. Inside and out.

"Wait!"

He runs back over to the car and crouches down in front of the window so my mouth is just inches from his. "What?" he asks.

"Nez."

He slowly breaks into a smile.

"Lem."

And before I can stop myself, I cradle his cheeks in my hands, pull him close, part my lips, and . . .

My first kiss.

Ours.

All of us.

All of our ancestors, and all of our descendants, are coming together to celebrate this kiss, to clap and fist-pump and foot-stomp and shout out loud to the universe YES! YES! A million billion years of YESSSS!

We break apart, stunned and breathless.

And for a moment, I'm afraid that Zen will launch into a quikiwiki spiel about how kissing is a sort of evolutionary taste test, that healthier offspring are produced by partners with different immune proteins, and those differences can be detected in the sloppy swap of genetic information encoded in our spit.

But he doesn't say any such thing. Instead, I find out what he started to say in the tree house.

"I love you."

And then he breaks into the most deranged grin I've ever seen on anyone, anywhere, except maybe my own crazyface in the rearview mirror.

harmony
melody

WHEN I LAY DOWN WITH JONDOE, HE PROMISED TO SHOW ME
the Truth.

I just wish it hadn't taken me until right now to see it
clearly.

"Ram . . ." I begin. "I'm . . ."

"I forgive you," Ram says automatically.

I need to be punished. How can I expect to be punished by a sweet soul whose transgressions are far worse
than my own?

"When Melody found out I was with—" My throat
closes on his name.

"With *him*?" Ram asks.

I nod. "How did she react?"

Like a little kid avoiding trouble, Ram looks everywhere—his feet, the ceiling, out the window, down the hall—but at me.

"What did she say, Ram? I have to know."

He speaks quickly, hoping to get this unpleasantness over with. I brace myself for the worst.

"She said she wished you had never come into her life." He gulps down more air. "She wished you had never been born."

It's a relief, really, to hear what I have most feared.

I don't deserve Melody's forgiveness.

I don't deserve Zen's help.

I don't deserve Jondoe's love.

This is my punishment.

I take a breath and force a smile to my face. "I have blessed news, Ram."

"What?" His eyes are shiny with tears.

I swallow hard and pat my belly.

"We're having a baby."

He blinks.

"But . . . I didn't . . ."

There had always been rumors about Ram being of an unmentionable kind. That despite his brawn, he was soft. More interested in watching the boys than the girls.

"We didn't . . ."

That's why the Church Council chose him for me. Better to put the two unteachable spirits together than admit defeat and cast us off entirely.

"Did we?"

I hold my hand up to stop his stammering. Ram needs me far more than I need him. He can't go back to Goodside without me. And I can't stay in Otherside with him. It wouldn't be fair, not when I know that Jondoe is out here too. The temptation to be unfaithful—in my heart if not in action—would be too great.

"Do you want to start over?"

As the first tear falls down his face and splashes into his steepled hands, I know his answer.

"Yes."

"Me too."

It's finally time for *me* to assert *my* spiritual leadership. One of us has to.

"Let's go back home and have this baby," I say. "Together."

melody
harmony

WITH ZEN'S KISS STILL FRESH ON MY LIPS, I'M READY TO FACE anything.

"Hello?" I call out as I open the front door.

Before the vowel bounces its echo off the walls, I know my house is empty. I know that Ram has gone. And with a sudden spine-tingling chill, I know something else.

Harmony is gone too.

I walk, zombielike, to the common room, where there's a note lying on top of the ergomatic couch cushions still dented by Ram's bulk. It's written on a page torn out of a Bible. Just the title page, nothing more, no verses offering clues to her state of mind when she wrote two words in a handwriting that I could easily mistake for my own:

Forgive me.

But I *have* forgiven her! Why didn't she believe me?

It's true that Harmony shouldn't have gone off with Jondoe like that. But she's still my sister, maybe the only blood relation I will ever know. She must still think I hate her as deeply as I thought I did, that is, before I realized that spermjacking Jondoe was the best thing that ever could have happened to me.

To us.

Harmony and Ram couldn't have gotten very far on foot, so I immediately take off after her. I fling open the front door, and facesmash right into a perfect set of pectorals.

"It's me!" Jondoe announces unnecessarily.

I must say that crashing into the hottest RePro on the MiNet is not nearly as exciting as I thought it would be. Not now, after everything that has happened. He looks for seriously amped for a second before leaning in to get a good look at my freckleless nose. His whole body sags when he realizes that I'm not the twin he was hoping for.

"You're Melody," he says flatly. "The one who's trying to ruin me."

"I am," I reply. "But I'm not." I try to push past him, but he slings his arm across the door to stop me.

"CONDOMS?!" His eyes bug out. It's quite comical, really. I could make a lot of money selling a foto of him looking goofy like that.

"I was only trying to get you two out of hiding," I reply. "And it worked, didn't it? You're here."

He cranes his neck to stalk over my shoulder. "Where's Harmony?"

"She's not here," I say. "She just took off, and I was on my way after her."

"She ran off on you too?" he says. "She climbed out my window! My *window*!"

He's almost too impressed by her escape act to be upset by it. Almost. I realize I have no idea what really happened between these two. As queasy as I am to hear the details, I have to ask.

"Why did she go out the window?"

"She must have overheard me bullshitting your agent."

Lib found her before I did, as I knew he would. But I can't worry about Lib right now.

"About what?"

"About tricking her into believing that I have God," he says, visibly agitated. "The thing is, I was telling her the truth! Well, at first I was scamming. But then, I don't know, something came over me and I wasn't faking it anymore. It's like I really felt God laying love for her in my heart, but I couldn't let Lib know that!"

As much as I don't want to know, I have to know.

"So you two . . ."

I search for the most tactful way to say what I want to say, and abandoning that, find myself mimicking Zen's finger-in-the-hole gesture.

Jondoe flashes his famous trillion-dollar smile. "Did we *ever*."

Gaaaah.

When I've recovered from gagging, I ask, "Do you think you bumped?"

The smile disappears. A vein pops out of his forehead.

"What's it with everyone questioning my spermhood? I don't turn eighteen for another six months!"

I burst out laughing. I can't believe this icon of maleness is acting so wanky. Shoko would never believe it.

"Lib wants to cut you out of the deal, you know," Jondoe warns. "He thinks he can make a side deal with the Jaydens for Harmony's delivery."

"Yeah, I know," I say. "And I don't care."

"You don't *care*?" Jondoe double-takes.

"There's not enough money in the world for me to bump with you."

I can't believe I've just said this to the world-famous cock jockey. I expect him to be offended. But instead he says, "I know exactly what you mean."

He closes his eyes and rests his head on the doorframe. I seize this opportunity to lean in and take a quick whiff. You know. For Shoko. I can now confirm that Jondoe smells like every other teenage boy who hopes to jack his swagger by dousing themselves in bottle after bottle of Jondoe: the Fragrance.

"When I first got into the business, my agent warned me against falling for a girl who would make me want to

322

give it all up," he says. "A girl who could see the real me, not just what's in my file."

He looks up in agony. An *alluring* agony.

"Your sister is that girl," he says. "And you've got to help me find her."

Is Jondoe really smitten with Harmony? Or is he plotting with Lib? I don't know what to believe.

"Everything changed when I met your sister," Jondoe says. "It's like I didn't even know myself until she came into my life."

I smile, thinking that Harmony did the same thing for me.

"Please help me find her," he says quietly. "Please."

I want to believe that Jondoe's being sincere. But I'm hesitant to buy into his sad-eyed, pouty-lipped sexy act. Did Harmony find him irresistible because she didn't know any better? Or because he really showed her part of himself that he'd never revealed before? I guess there's only one way of finding out.

"Maybe," I suggest, "we can all help each other."

And that's when the hottest RePro on the MiNet pulls me into those perfect pecs of his and squeezes me in gratitude.

I'm sixteen. I'm not pregnant.

But at this very moment, I feel like the most important person on the planet.

Acknowledgements

MANY THANKS GO OUT TO:

Alessandra Balzer, whose no-nonsense editorial wisdom saved me—and this book. Period. And Donna Bray and everyone else at this fantastic imprint and HarperCollins at large for helping me make my debut as an "official" YA author.

Heather Schroder at ICM, whose eye-popping response to my hypothetical ("What if only teenagers could get pregnant?") began what I hope to be a long and rewarding relationship. And Josie Freedman, also at ICM, for trying to introduce my characters to a whole new audience on screen.

Rachel Cohn, for convincing me that I was up to the challenge, especially at the overwhelming start.

CJM, whose early insight inspired me so much more than he will ever give himself credit for.

And CJM, for always asking, "How was your day today?" and reminding me that even a bad day of writing is better than not writing at all.